P9-DWE-703

MOON HANDBOOKS®
SAN JUAN ISLANDS

SECOND EDITION

DON PITCHER

© DON PITCHER

AVALON TRAVEL

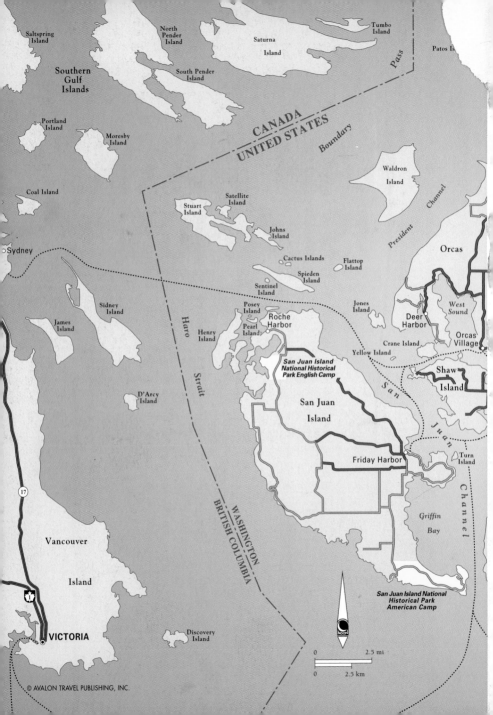

Saltspring
Island

North Pender
Island

Saturna
Island

Tumbo
Island

Patos Is.

Southern
Gulf
Islands

South Pender
Island

CANADA
UNITED STATES

Boundary

Pass

Portland
Island

Moresby
Island

Waldron
Island

Orcas

Coal Island

Stuart
Island

Satellite
Island

Johns
Island

President

Channel

Sydney

Cactus Islands

Flattop
Island

Spieden
Island

Sentinel
Island

Jones
Island

West
Sound

Deer
Harbor

James
Island

Sidney
Island

Posey
Island

Roche
Harbor

Crane Island

Orcas
Village

Henry
Island

Pearl
Island

Yellow Island

Haro

San Juan Island
National Historical
Park English Camp

San

Shaw
Island

D'Arcy
Island

Strait

San Juan
Island

Juan

Vancouver

Friday Harbor

Turn
Island

Channel

Island

WASHINGTON
BRITISH COLUMBIA

Griffin
Bay

17

VICTORIA

Discovery
Island

San Juan Island National
Historical Park
American Camp

MOON

0   2.5 mi

0   2.5 km

© AVALON TRAVEL PUBLISHING, INC.

CONTENTS

Discover the San Juan Islands

Explore the San Juan Islands

Gateways to the Islands 22

Cypress Island · Doe Island Marine State Park · James Island Marine State Park · Jones Island Marine State Park · Matia Island Marine State Park · Patos Island Marine State Park · Posey Island Marine State Park · Saddlebag Island Marine State Park · Stuart Island · Sucia Island Marine State Park · Turn Island Marine State Park

Blakely Island · Canoe Island · Deadman and Goose Islands · Decatur and Center Islands · Johns Island · Obstruction Island · Satellite Island · Sentinel Island · Sinclair Island · Spieden Island · Waldron Island · Yellow Island

Victoria and the Southern Gulf Islands

Inner Harbour · Old Town · South of the Inner Harbour · Rockland · Scenic Route to Oak Bay · The Gorge Waterway · West of Downtown · Saanich Peninsula

Hiking and Biking · Water Sports · Tours

Performing Arts · Drinking and Dancing · Shopping

Downtown · Saanich Peninsula · Sooke · Malahat

Bakeries and Cafés · Quick Bites · Seafood · Pubs · Italian · Other European Restaurants · Carribean · Vegetarian · Chinese · Other Asian Restaurants · Out-of-Town Splurges

Information Centers · Bookstores and Main Library · Emergency Services · Access for Disabled Travelers · Communications · Currency Exchange · Photography

By Air · Bus · Ferry · Getting Around

Salt Spring Island · The Penders · Mayne Island · Galiano Island · Saturna Island · Getting There and Around

Know the San Juan Islands

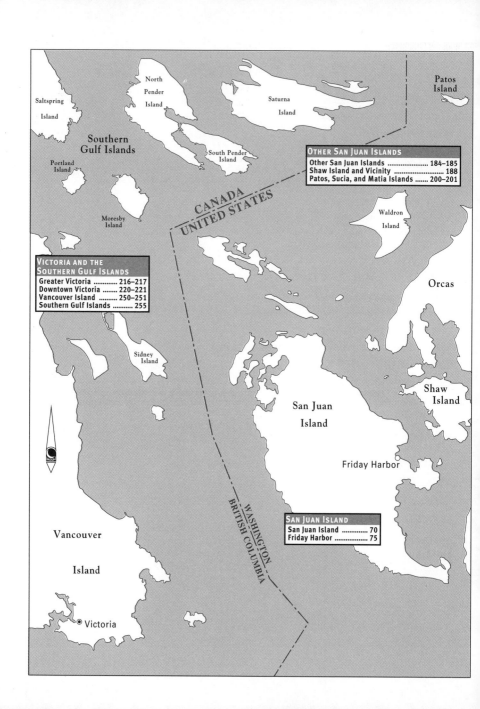

Patos
Island

North
Pender
Island

Saturna
Island

Saltspring
Island

Southern
Gulf Islands

South Pender
Island

Portland
Island

CANADA
UNITED STATES

Moresby
Island

Waldron
Island

Orcas

Sidney
Island

Shaw
Island

San Juan
Island

Friday Harbor

Vancouver

Island

WASHINGTON
BRITISH COLUMBIA

Victoria

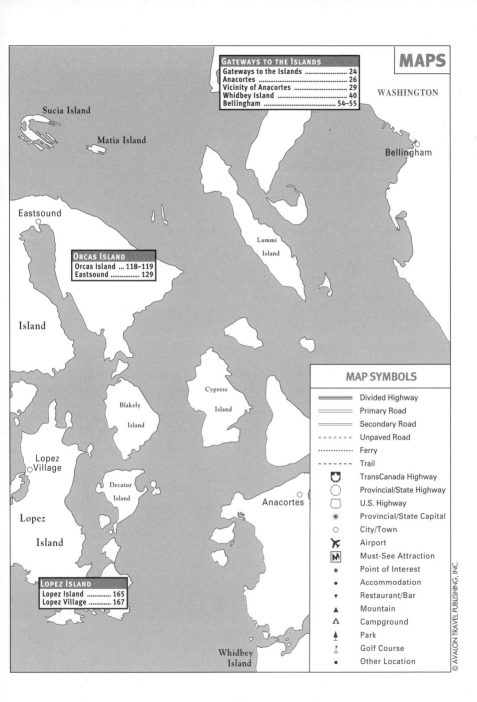

MAPS

WASHINGTON

Sucia Island

Matia Island

Bellingham

Eastsound

Lummi
Island

Island

Cypress

Blakely
Island

Island

Lopez
Village

Decatur
Island

Anacortes

Lopez

Island

Whidbey
Island

MAP SYMBOLS

═══	Divided Highway
═══	Primary Road
───	Secondary Road
= = = =	Unpaved Road
··········	Ferry
- - - - -	Trail
🛡	TransCanada Highway
◯	Provincial/State Highway
⬡	U.S. Highway
◉	Provincial/State Capital
○	City/Town
✈	Airport
Ⓜ	Must-See Attraction
★	Point of Interest
•	Accommodation
▼	Restaurant/Bar
▲	Mountain
Λ	Campground
⚑	Park
⛳	Golf Course
▪	Other Location

© AVALON TRAVEL PUBLISHING, INC.

For Rio Jalen
May you grow to love this earth's wild places
May you never lose that beautiful smile and sharp wit

Discover the San Juan Islands

Nestled between the Washington mainland and Vancouver Island, the San Juan Islands offer a perfect weekend or one-to-two-week getaway. The islands are equidistant—around 80 air miles each—from two major Northwest cities, Seattle to the south, and Vancouver to the north. Despite this proximity, they remain largely rural, with no fast food restaurants or big-box discount stores anywhere. Instead, you'll find a host of small bed-and-breakfasts, distinctive art galleries, specialty farms selling everything from alpaca garments to kiwi fruit, family-run whale-watching and sea-kayaking companies, and fine restaurants where the owner might also be your waiter.

Visiting the San Juans means escaping to a place where the natural world dominates and where folks raise a hand to wave as you pass. When the ferry leaves the dock at Anacortes, a sense of timelessness seems to descend upon all onboard. Children wave excitedly to passing sailboats, clusters of cyclists huddle around maps, locals read books and sip coffee at window tables, and birders gather outside to watch for eagles or murres. The pace of life here is slow and clothing is casual, so leave your ties and fancy dresses at home.

With their dark evergreen forests and rocky shorelines, the islands have become one of Washington's favorite places to get away, and when summer rolls around, they are flooded with tourists, temporarily doubling the population. Particularly popular attractions include whale-watching trips, sea kayaking (guided or on your own), bicycling, boating, sailing, hiking, diving, and even skateboarding. But it isn't just tourists who travel to the San Juans. In recent years they have served as a place to flee the crime, traffic, and crowds of the city and as a haven for retirees. They now attract an increasingly sophisticated and educated population, and the three largest islands all have modern multipurpose theaters that buzz with activity year-round. To house the 40-percent population increase in the 1990s, real estate offices sprang up in every small cluster of businesses throughout the San Juans. The growth rate has slowed a bit in the last few years, but it's still growing at more than two percent per year.

Although the islands see many thousands of visitors each year, they are still largely unknown to people outside the Pacific Northwest. The islands tend to attract an upscale clientele who appreciate luxurious inns and acclaimed restaurants, but families on a budget can also enjoy the islands. Families can opt to rent a vacation home for a week or more, taking the time to explore the San Juans at their own pace or set up camp at one of the many wonderful campsites—particularly within Moran State Park on Orcas Island. Backpacking international travelers and cyclists will also find reasonably priced hostels on San Juan and Orcas Islands.

The islands also attract famous people who own land (or entire islands), including folks from the Microsoft clan—Paul

Allen and Bill Gates (Jr. and Sr.)—along with actor Gene Hackman, musicians Jewel and Steve Miller, filmmaker Warren Miller, director Richard Donner (*Free Willy, Lethal Weapon,* and *Superman*), author Richard Bach (*Jonathan Livingston Seagull*), and cartoonist Gary Larson.

From the air, it's easy to imagine the San Juan archipelago as broken pieces from a shattered plate. They encompass 172 named islands, and a total of 743 islands, islets, and reefs at low tide (or 428 at high tide). Thirty of these are inhabited. Some 14,500 people live on the islands year-round, half of them on San Juan Island, home to Friday Harbor, the islands' only incorporated town. The three largest islands—Orcas, San Juan, and Lopez—form a cluster of oddly shaped puzzle pieces around Shaw Island, with many of the smaller islands strewn outward to the north and east from this hub.

Orcas is the largest of the San Juan Islands, but just barely. It covers 57 square miles and measures roughly a dozen miles across by eight miles north to south. San Juan Island is 55 square miles, while Lopez Island covers 30 square miles. These are followed by several midsize islands: Cypress, Shaw, Blakely, Waldron, and Decatur.

The San Juan Islands include all of San Juan County, along with several islands (Cypress, Guemes, and Sinclair) in Skagit County, plus Lummi Island within Whatcom County. In addition to these islands, this book provides coverage of the beautiful city of Victoria on Vancouver Island and Canada's Southern Gulf Islands: Salt Spring, North and South Pender, Mayne, Galiano, and Saturna. Several important gateways to the San Juans are also highlighted: Anacortes, Whidbey Island, Bellingham, and Seattle.

The San Juan Islands cover a relatively small area—it's less than 30 miles across the archipelago—but there are no bridges to or between the islands, so everyone and everything (from oranges to cement) must get to the islands onboard boats, ferries, or planes. Fortunately, the islands have good transportation, along with excellent lodging, food, and recreational opportunities, making them easy for travelers—especially those arriving from the Pacific Northwest.

Whether you're aboard a state ferry threading its way through the islands or in a small floatplane dipping down to a watery landing, getting to the islands is half the fun. Access is primarily by Washington State Ferry from the town of Anacortes (an 80-mile drive north from Seattle), but quite a few visitors fly in, while others ride private passenger ferries, motorboat, or sail to the islands. The state ferry system links the four main islands—San Juan, Orcas, Lopez, and Shaw—with Anacortes, with some ferries continuing eastward to the town of Sidney on Vancouver Island, British Columbia. Bikes and kayaks are welcome onboard these ferries, making the islands an ideal destination for adventurous travelers. Private ferries run from Seattle, Victoria, Bellingham, Everett, and Port Townsend, and scheduled flights are available out of Seattle, Anacortes, and Bellingham. Many island visitors bring their own vehicles onboard the state ferries, but you can also rent a car or take a local taxi once you arrive. Both San Juan and Orcas Islands have reasonably priced shuttle bus services.

Newcomers to the San Juans often wish they'd planned more time on the islands. If you can take the time and have the money, it's very easy to spend at least a week exploring the islands. There's plenty to do if you want to stay busy the whole time, or you can simply use the chance to relax. Many island resorts have a one-week summertime minimum, allowing guests the time to kick back and get into the rhythms of island living. For the full version, you can rent a house for a month or two and really sink into the spirit of the place.

Short trips to the San Juans are also rewarding, and weekend ferries in the summer are packed with other folks who have the same cram-it-in idea. Many lodging places require at least a two-night stay, but you'll want at least that much time anyway.

WHEN TO GO

The San Juans are primarily a summertime destination, and anyone heading to the islands between mid-June and early September will find throngs of fellow travelers. Many of the best accommodations fill up far in advance, especially on weekends when some places are booked a year or more ahead.

The islands are truly delightful in the summer, with warm and mostly dry weather, lush floral displays, and plenty of chances to view wildlife (most notably killer whales). If you don't mind the wait for a table at the restaurants and lengthy ferry queues—and if you can get lodging or campground reservations—this is a great time to visit.

The shoulder seasons (mid-May to mid-June and mid-September to mid-October) provide ideal times to visit. By May, many plants are already flowering but school is still in session so most folks haven't yet headed out on vacation. Lodging prices aren't at peak summer rates and businesses welcome travelers. Some businesses may not be in full swing, but most places are open. Fall brings a bit of color to the trees, cooler temperatures, and the chance to soak up the beauty in relative peace and quiet.

By mid-November, the queues at the Friday Harbor ferry are pretty much gone, shopkeepers have time to sit and talk, bed-and-breakfasts usually have rooms on short notice, and it's easy to take a romantic walk along an unpopulated beach—at least on weekdays. Holiday weekends around Thanksgiving, Christmas, and New Year's get busy again, but for much of the winter season, particularly weekdays in January or February, you'll pretty much have the place to yourself. Island lodging prices plummet—sometimes by more than 50 percent—in the winter season. Of course, this is also the chilliest and rainiest part of the year, with bare trees and brown grass. Some businesses shutter their doors for a month or two as the owners take their own vacations in Mexico or Costa Rica.

WHAT TO TAKE

As a general rule, keep it casual when it comes to clothing. Be sure to bring a bathing suit even if you don't plan on swimming in local lakes or pools—many hotels and bed-and-breakfasts have hot tubs. Even the most upscale island restaurants don't require a sports jacket or tie, but you may feel like Michael Moore at a Republican fundraiser if you show up wearing shorts and sandals while others are dressed for a night out. For travel at any time of year, pack comfortable walking shoes, sunglasses, and a hat or two.

Summers on the islands are mild and often sunny, so you won't need down jackets or heavy raingear. July and August each average only an inch of rain per month, and May, June, and September are also reasonably dry. Short pants and t-shirts are ubiquitous throughout the summer, though you will want long sleeve shirts and pants for cooler evenings and cloudy or rainy days. Carry a light jacket for rainy days or on-the-water trips.

Boaters and sea kayakers will need something more protective, even in the summer. Avoid cotton since it soaks up water and dries slowly; jeans are an especially poor choice. Synthetic fabrics and layering are the keys to staying comfortable on the water.

For winter travel to the San Juans, plan your packing around dressing in layers (polypropylene works especially well), and be sure to have a sweater or two and Gore-Tex or another breathable rain jacket.

The Regions

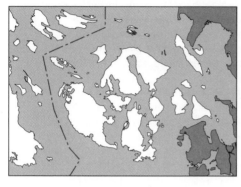

GATEWAYS

Most visitors to the San Juan Islands arrive onboard Washington State Ferries that depart from the town of Anacortes, located 80 miles north of Seattle. Nearby is Deception Pass State Park, the most popular state park in Washington, and farther south is bucolic Whidbey Island, with the artsy towns of Coupeville and Langley. The island provides a scenic access route for people driving up from Seattle.

Another entry point is Bellingham, with its many museums, the historic Fairhaven neighborhood (great for shopping), and a winding, shore-hugging route south called Chuckanut Drive. This book provides a brief overview of Seattle, home to a myriad of attractions. Immediately south is Sea-Tac, the primary airport for the region. Access to the islands from Seattle is by air or private passenger ferry.

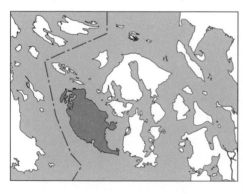

SAN JUAN ISLAND

Located on the western edge of the archipelago, San Juan Island is a favorite island destination. The main town, Friday Harbor, is a picturesque spot, with the excellent Whale Museum, fine dining, lodging of all types (from a hostel to a luxurious inn), and abundant opportunities for recreation, most notably whale-watching and sea kayaking.

Roche Harbor on the northwest end of San Juan Island has a busy marina, gorgeous grounds, historic buildings, and a sculpture garden. San Juan Island National Historical Park reveals the island's vivid history with historic structures and interpretive sites at protected English Camp and at windswept American Camp, located on the southern end of the island. You'll also find great beaches at American Camp. Other island attractions include a much-photographed lighthouse, the only whale-watching park in the nation at Lime Kiln Point State Park, and a number of interesting farms, including one that grows lavender.

ORCAS ISLAND

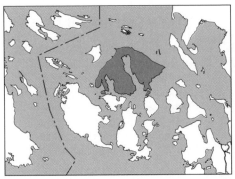

The "Gem of the San Juans," Orcas Island is both the largest and most diverse island in the archipelago. The island is perfect not just for newlyweds and wealthy trust-funders, but also for families who just want a quiet place to camp under tall trees. The main settlement is Eastsound, with its picture-perfect inns, New England–style church, cozy cafés, earthy farmers market, and even a renowned skateboard park.

The west end of Orcas is home to marinas, old-fashioned resorts where families return year after year, farmhouse bed-and-breakfasts, and pottery studios. The east side of the island is dominated by woodsy Moran State Park, with mountaintop vistas, miles of hiking and biking trails, great camping, and a pleasant lake for swimming. Nearby is the century-old mansion at Rosario Resort. Down the road is a cooperative café–art gallery in existence for more than two decades, and a New Age–style resort where the restaurant emphasizes vegetarian meals.

LOPEZ ISLAND

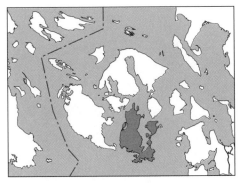

Lopez Island lacks the mountainous terrain of Orcas Island or the rich history, cultural activities, and whale-watching adventures of San Juan Island, but it makes up for that with its slow-down-and-smell-the-horses sort of culture. "The Wave" isn't a surfer's term here, but one applied to the ubiquitous hands that lift off the steering wheel to acknowledge every passing car or bike. There aren't a lot of sights on Lopez, and that just might be the real attraction. The main settlement of Lopez Village has shops, eateries, and a little museum, and up the road at Lopez Island Vineyards, organic grapes grow next to a kiwi fruit farm. Several parks are scattered around Lopez, most notably Spencer Spit State Park, popular for camping, walking on the beach, and kayaking. The island is a destination for bicyclists, and the 30-mile paved loop around Lopez traverses flat or gently rolling farm country.

OTHER SAN JUAN ISLANDS

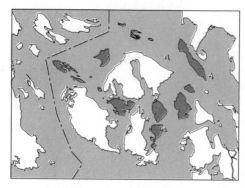

Once you get beyond the three largest of the San Juan Islands, the number of visitors decreases markedly. The state ferry visits Shaw Island, but not the other islands, where access is by water taxi, boat, kayak, or plane. Shaw Island is mostly in private hands, though it does have a little natural area and a county park with tenting spaces. A few miles west of Bellingham, Lummi Island provides comfortable lodging, good food, and a couple of galleries. Quite a few of the smaller islands in the San Juans are maintained as marine state parks or other public areas. Cypress Island has rugged scenery and tall stands of old-growth forests. Jones Island is a short boat ride from Orcas Island, with hiking trails, protected coves, and semi-tame deer. Stuart Island serves up a mix of private and public lands, with a remote and scenic lighthouse on the easternmost end. Sucia Island is one of the most popular marine parks with miles of scenic hiking and biking trails and protected bays that attract sailors, motorboaters, and kayakers.

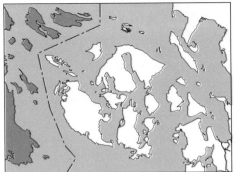

Victoria, the elegant capital of British Columbia, Canada, lies on the southern tip of Vancouver Island, just a short ferry ride from the San Juan Islands. Locals will be quick to tell you that the weather is nicer and the pace is slower than nearby Vancouver. And they are right on both accounts. But the city also projects an intriguing mixture of images, old and new. Well-preserved century-old buildings line inner-city streets; ancient totem poles sprout from shady parks; restored historic areas house trendy shops, offices, and exotic restaurants; double-decker buses and horse-drawn carriages compete for summer trade; and the residents keep alive the original traditions and atmosphere of Merry Olde England. Victoria is also a gateway to the Southern Gulf Islands, which are part of the same archipelago but separated by an international border from the San Juan Islands. Six of the Gulf Islands are served by ferries. Hiking, kayaking, and biking are major draws, but you can also soak in hot springs or tour an island winery.

In 10 days it's possible to get a good taste of the San Juan Islands without having to move every night. The trip below is packed with activities, so many travelers may want to pare things down to provide additional time at selected stops instead of trying to see it all. Another option for more adventurous travelers is to replace two or three days of this itinerary with a guided multi-night sea kayaking trip to the outer islands. Most of these kayak trips start from San Juan Island, where several companies are based. Travelers who don't like to move as often may prefer to drop the overnight on Lopez Island, replacing it with a day trip from Orcas Island.

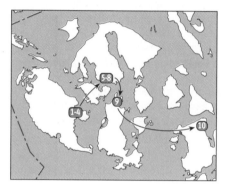

DAY 1

Drive from Seattle or Vancouver to Anacortes, stopping to explore the artsy town of La Conner en route. Pick up a box lunch from La Vie en Rose French Bakery in Anacortes and drive onto the ferry heading toward the town of Friday Harbor on San Juan Island. There are many lodging choices here, including well-maintained budget rooms at Discovery Inn, reasonably priced apartments at Sandpiper Condominiums, and eclectic downtown rooms at Friday's Historic Inn.

DAY 2

In Friday Harbor visit the Whale Museum, and then take a half-day whale-watching trip from Cascade Harbor, or head to Lime Kiln Point State Park to watch from the shore (recommended to re-

duce impacts). Drive south along the coast, stopping at Westside Park to soak up the view before visiting Pelindaba Lavender Farm, Krystal Acres Ranch (alpacas), and the wine-tasting room at San Juan Vineyards.

DAY 3

Time for a history lesson. This is a full day, so get an early start or choose a couple of sights instead of trying to see them all. Drive over to English Camp for a guided walk in this portion of San Juan Island National Historical Park, then on to beautiful Roche Harbor for lunch and a saunter through the Westcott Bay Sculpture Park. Continue south to American Camp for a hike through the flower-filled meadows or a stroll along South Beach — one of the finest beaches in the islands. End the

Whale Museum at Friday Harbor

© DON PITCHER

© DON PITCHER

Outlook Inn

easy destinations from Orcas Island are Jones Island, with its quick access, woodsy hikes, and tame deer, and Sucia Island, with a multitude of sandy bays and excellent hiking and biking trails. If you have camping supplies, both of these are great places to pitch a tent for a night or two. Kayakers love to explore the protected coves of Sucia.

DAY 7

Explore Moran State Park, including the paved road to the stone tower atop Mount Constitution. Hike the trails, try some mountain biking, or play in the waters of Cascade Lake.

day with dinner at The Place Bar & Grill or Friday Harbor House.

DAY 4

This is a good day to hop onboard a water taxi to one of the more remote islands in the archipelago. The Nature Conservancy owns nearby Yellow Island, a delightful spot for florally enhanced hikes in late spring and early summer. Another option is Stuart Island, where a six-mile day hike leads to Turn Point Lighthouse; the panorama encompasses Haro Strait, the Gulf Islands, and Vancouver Island, along with the occasional pod of killer whales.

DAY 5

Next stop is Orcas Island, so catch an early ferry for a timely start on this diverse island. With a central base in the Eastsound area, you can easily get to most of the sights on the island. Families will enjoy the condos at Landmark Inn or the two-bedroom units at Cascade Harbor Inn. Outlook Inn features a great in-town setting and a variety of room choices, including inexpensive ones in the historic main building. On this day you may want to spend time exploring the sights around Eastsound, such as the Orcas Island Historical Museum or rent a kayak from Shearwater Adventures to paddle the bay.

DAY 6

Take a long day trip to one of the neighboring islands managed as marine state parks. Two

DAY 8

Take it easy on your last day on Orcas Island and tour the local galleries and gift shops in Eastsound. Try Trinidadian dishes or Cuban-style steaks on the patio at Callaloo Caribbean Kitchen. End the evening with a movie, or if you have kids—or you're just a kid-at-heart—visit The Funhouse.

DAY 9

The last destination is Lopez Island, but first you should catch an early-morning ferry to Shaw Island. Head to the south side of the island for a hike in Cedar Rock Biological Preserve or take a glance at the historic Little Red Schoolhouse. Board the next ferry heading west toward Lopez Island. Once you've settled into your lodging place, enjoy dinner at The Bay Café and end the day watching the sunset from the beach at Otis Perkins County Park.

DAY 10

Rent a bike from Lopez Islander Resort to see Lopez Island at an appropriately slow pace, or join a half-day sea-kayaking tour with Lopez Kayaks for a "see" level view of nearby waters. Catch an afternoon ferry back to Anacortes and continue home from there. If you have the time, take the scenic route south via Whidbey Island.

The San Juan Islands are an easy half-day drive and ferry ride from Seattle and Vancouver. Because of this, the islands are exceptionally popular destinations, particularly on summer weekends. Avoid the crowds by visiting in the off-season or in the middle of the week if possible. But even at their most crowded, the San Juans are still much more peaceful than city living.

For a weekend trip, it is probably best to leave your vehicle in Anacortes to avoid the lengthy queues. Both Orcas and San Juan Islands have excellent shuttle buses and car rentals, and taxis are available on Lopez Island. Some lodging places also provide limited transportation.

SAN JUAN ISLAND WEEKEND GETAWAY

Always a favorite of visitors, San Juan Island is great for a three-day escape, with plenty to do and a range of lodging and food choices. The ferry docks right at Friday Harbor, making this a good base for your trip.

DAY 1

Take the ferry from Anacortes to Friday Harbor as early in the day as possible, providing time to check into your hotel or bed-and-breakfast before heading out to visit the Whale Museum and downtown shops. Enjoy a fine dinner at the Backdoor Kitchen or spicy Asian fare from Thai Town.

Pelindaba Lavender Farm, San Juan Island

DAY 2

Take a shuttle bus tour of the island, with stops at San Juan Vineyards, Roche Harbor, Lime Kiln Point State Park, and Pelindaba Lavender Farm. The bus returns every hour to take you to your next destination.

DAY 3

Max out your time in Friday Harbor before ferrying back to Anacortes. Do a little shopping, buy an ice cream, browse the galleries, or rent a bike and pedal the loop road around Pear Point, stopping for a picnic lunch at Jacksons Beach.

ORCAS ISLAND WEEKEND GETAWAY

Orcas Island is too big to really take in over a long weekend, but this short trip provides a sampler that will make you wish for more time there.

DAY 1

Leave your car in Anacortes and take the ferry to Orcas Village, where a shuttle bus provides service to Eastsound. Drop luggage at your bed-and-breakfast or hotel and head off to see the local sights and shops. Check out the small Orcas Island Historical Museum and reserve a porch table for dinner at the Sunflower Café. If it is a summer Saturday, be sure to visit the farmers market.

DAY 2

Take the shuttle bus to Moran State Park for a day of hiking the trails or swimming at Cascade Lake. It's a long climb to the scenic summit of 2,409-foot Mount Constitution, but you can call for a taxi ride and walk downhill instead. Before returning to Eastsound, take the shuttle bus to Rosario Resort & Spa for a tour of the historic getaway.

DAY 3

Sleep in a bit before a brunch at Roses Bakery Café. Take the shuttle to the ferry landing, where you can take a short kayak trip through Orcas Outdoors while waiting for your return ferry.

LOPEZ ISLAND WEEKEND GETAWAY

Lopez is all about relaxing, so this weekend adventure is short on activities and long on letting go.

DAY 1

Park your car at the lot next to the Anacortes ferry terminal and get onboard for a truly relaxing weekend. Call for a taxi ride to your hotel or bed-and-breakfast once you reach Lopez Island. If you choose Edenwild Inn, you're right in the heart of Lopez Village. Wander through the handful of shops, the museum, and over to Weeks Wetland Preserve to watch migrating birds. Wind down with a pastry and coffee at Holly B's Bakery.

Lopez Village

DAY 2

Get up late and pick up the *Seattle P-I* on your way to Isabel's Espresso. Settle into the early afternoon on their outdoor deck with a latte and pastry. If you're feeling adventurous after a relaxing morning, rent a bike at Lopez Bicycle Works and pedal all or part of the 30-mile loop around Lopez Island. Reward your efforts with a delicious gourmet dinner at Bay Café.

DAY 3

Sleep in again and miss your ferry back to the mainland. After grabbing a gourmet panini at Vita's Wildly Delicious, call your boss to say you quit, and phone your broker to say you're going to need to cash in your retirement account. Go to the real estate office and buy an old fixer-upper farmhouse. Have the movers pack your belongings and ship them. Grow your hair long, start riding bikes, eat organic veggies, and cover your Subaru's bumper with anti-war stickers. You're home.

The San Juan Islands are a perfect destination for romance, with beautiful scenery, cozy cottages, candlelit restaurants, upscale day-spas, and lots of fun adventures. They're a favorite spot for both weddings and honeymoons, but also appeal to couples looking to relax in a luxurious bed-and-breakfast. Also appealing are a variety of "soft adventures" on the islands, such as short kayak trips, evening sails, gentle bike rides, or beach campfires.

DAY 1

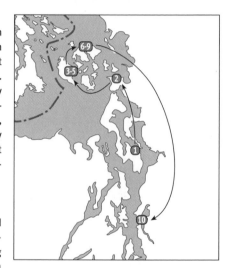

Many romantic getaways on the islands begin with a marriage ceremony in a spectacular setting, such as Roche Harbor Resort or the summit of Mount Constitution, followed by a fabulous honeymoon. Let's assume, though, that you're either already married or you just want some time with that special someone. From Seattle, drive north to Mukilteo, catch the ferry over to Whidbey Island, and stay overnight at the Inn at Langley. Enjoy a gourmet dinner here, followed by a massage and aromatherapy from the spa.

DAY 2

Explore local galleries and shops on Whidbey Island before continuing north up to Meerkerk Rhododendron Gardens and Greenbank Farm, stopping for lunch in quiet Coupeville. Continue to Deception Pass State Park for an evening stroll along the beach. It's another nine miles to Anacortes where you've booked a room at a comfortable hotel (try Ship Harbor Inn) and reservations for two at Bella Isola Ristorante.

Greenbank Farm

DAY 3

After a nice brunch at Café Adrift, take in the sights of Anacortes, sticking around long enough to stock up for your stay on the islands. Drive onto the ferry and head to Friday Harbor on San Juan Island. There are many romantic lodging places from which to choose; try Harrison House or Concord Inn.

DAY 4

Take in the south end of the island today, starting with a visit to Pelindaba Lavender Farm and Lime Kiln Point State Park (whales and a picturesque lighthouse), before ending the afternoon with a hike in American Camp or a walk along South Beach. For dinner, head to Vinny's or Duck Soup Inn.

DAY 5

Drive to Roche Harbor to enjoy the historic buildings and gorgeous gardens. Continue south to English Camp and wander the lush grounds, before continuing to San Juan County Park for a sea-kayak tour that takes you into waters where killer whales are often spotted. Return to Friday Harbor, stopping at San Juan Vineyards to sample their wines.

DAY 6

Moving day, so pack things up and catch the ferry to Orcas Island, where you'll settle into your country room for a couple of nights at Turtleback Farm Inn. Eat dinner at Christina's in Eastsound, watching the sunset from the big deck.

DAY 7

Explore the Eastsound area. Drive to the top of Mount Constitution, eat lunch amid the art at Orcas Island Artworks, and head over to Doe Bay Resort for a soak in a creekside hot tub. Enjoy a sumptuous dinner from The Inn at Ship Bay.

DAY 8

Drive to Deer Harbor for an all-day sailing trip through nearby waters on the 54-foot *Na' walak*. Enjoy a south-of-the-border feast at Bilbo's Festivo.

© DON PITCHER

hikers on Mount Constitution in Moran State Park

DAY 9

Your credit card is smoking from overuse, so choose a light Asian lunch at The Kitchen, and walk out to Madrona Point to take in the view. Visit local galleries today, including the Lambiel Museum with its collection of island artworks, Howe Art Gallery with mobile sculptures, and two fine pottery shops: Crow Valley Pottery and Orcas Island Pottery.

DAY 10

All good things must end. Prolong the fun just a bit more by taking a late ferry back to the mainland, providing time for a lazy brunch at West Sound Café and a bit of bird-watching at Frank Richardson Wildlife Preserve in Deer Harbor.

Family trips don't have to resemble the 1983 film *National Lampoon's Vacation*. On the San Juan Islands it's easy to bring the family, rent a cottage or house (it will probably cost $1,000/week), and launch out on day trips from this base. The itinerary below is a low-rent version to Lopez and Orcas Islands; similar all-week trips are also very popular on San Juan Island.

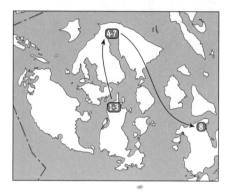

DAY 1

Load up the mini-van and drive to Anacortes, where you have time to stock up on snacks and diapers at Food Pavilion. After an interminable wait, roll onboard a ferry heading toward Lopez Island and set up camp at Spencer Spit State Park.

DAY 2

If you brought bikes along, everyone can hop on for a ride around the island; if not, they're available for rent from Lopez Bicycle Works. Afterwards, return to Spencer Spit, where the kids can roast marshmallows over a campfire.

DAY 3

Enjoy another day of biking around the island that can be broken up with a hike through the forest at Shark Reef Park and the chance to look for colorful stones at Agate Beach County Park. Get burgers and grilled cheese sandwiches from the soda fountain at Lopez Island Pharmacy, and wander the shops and galleries in nearby Lopez Village.

DAY 4

Pack everyone up and take the ferry to Orcas Island. Drive up the west side to Eastsound for lunch

© DON PITCHER

Orcas Island Skateboard Park

© DON PITCHER

entrance to Moran State Park

at Portofino Pizzeria, and continue out the eastern end to Moran State Park with its abundant campsites among the trees.

DAY 5

Drive the twisting road up to Mount Constitution to take in the view, and head back down to Cascade Lake for swimming with other families and a balanced lunch of hot dogs, lemonade, and popcorn.

DAY 6

For a change of pace, take in a horseback ride at Once in a Blue Moon Farm, with trail rides for adults, and arena sessions and a petting zoo for children. Browse pottery galleries on the east side of Orcas before a side trip to the Orcas Island Skateboard Park and an afternoon at The Funhouse (for something more intellectually stimulating).

DAY 7

Put the kids in daycare at Children's House or Kaleidoscope, and take the time to explore the shops of Eastsound, brunching at Roses Bakery Café. If you're feeling ambitious, join a three-hour paddle tour from Shearwater Kayaks or rent a mountain bike from Wildlife Cycles. On your way to pick up the kids, stop by the Homegrown Market to pick up fresh seafood to cook back at the campsite.

DAY 8

It's time to exit the islands, but if you take an afternoon ferry you'll have time for a hike in Obstruction Pass State Park before heading out. Waiting in your car as the ferry approaches the terminal, with the kids sleeping peacefully in the backseat, you may think that family trips aren't so bad after all.

The lovely and civil city of Victoria has enough to keep visitors busy for days, with a mix of picturesque buildings built when England ruled Canada, spectacular floral gardens, fine museums, and upscale lodging and food choices. A short ferry ride away are the Southern Gulf Islands, where nature reigns supreme. The following itinerary includes highlights from Victoria and the Southern Gulf Islands, with time allotted for some interesting sights that many visitors pass by. It combines natural wonders with historic must-sees to create a tour that appeals to all tastes. This trip assumes you will have your own vehicle or will be renting one in Victoria.

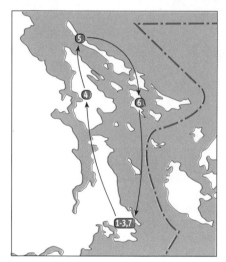

Fisherman's Wharf. If you have children, consider afternoon visits to the Royal London Wax Museum and the Pacific Undersea Gardens, otherwise spend your time wandering around the historic downtown area and Chinatown.

DAY 1

Catch a ferry or flight to Victoria. Check in to the historic Beaconsfield Inn for a three-night stay. Enjoy an afternoon double-decker bus tour of Victoria to help get oriented, then relax over dinner at the Blackfish Café.

DAY 2

Start your day at the Royal British Columbia Museum, then stroll down the harbor to the Parliament Buildings. For lunch, try Barb's Place in

Gatsby Mansion Inn in Victoria

© ANDREW HEMPSTEAD

© JUSTIN MARLER

view from Maple Ridge Cottages on Saltspring Island

DAY 3

Rise early and spend the morning hiking in Goldstream Provincial Park. Return to the city and take the scenic route between downtown and Oak Bay, timing your trip to enjoy afternoon tea at one of the local tearooms.

DAY 4

Beat the crowds to Butchart Gardens by arriving before 10 A.M.; allow two hours at Victoria's premier attraction. Continue up the Saanich Peninsula and catch a ferry to Saltspring Island. Stay overnight in the village Ganges, within walking distance of the many cafés and galleries along the waterfront.

DAY 5

Spend the day at your leisure shopping for arts and crafts, hiking to the summit of Mt. Maxwell, or joining a fishing charter. Catch a late-afternoon ferry to Galiano Island. Stay at the Galiano Inn and dine in-house or up the road at the laidback Grand Central Emporium.

DAY 6

Join an early-morning kayak tour from Montague Harbour. After returning to shore, drive around to the park of the same name and relax on one of Vancouver Island's finest beaches. Catch a ferry to North Pender Island and check into the Oceanside Inn.

DAY 7

Spend the morning exploring North Pender Island on foot, bike, or kayak. Return by ferry to Vancouver Island, where you can catch a ferry or flight back to your starting point. (Travelers starting from Vancouver can take a ferry directly from North Pender Island to Tsawwassen on the mainland.)

Explore the San Juan Islands

Gateways to the Islands

Located 80 miles north of Seattle, the town of Anacortes is Washington's primary gateway to the San Juan Islands, with ferries departing several times a day. Immediately south of Anacortes is Whidbey Island, a scenic access route for people driving up from Seattle. The city of Bellingham is on the mainland northeast of the San Juans, and several local companies there run passenger ferries to the islands. Seattle is another gateway, with a private passenger ferry and several air taxis connecting to the San Juans. All of these places are described in this chapter, with complete coverage for Anacortes and more limited details on Whidbey Island, Seattle, and Bellingham.

PLANNING YOUR TIME

Most visitors en route to the San Juans start from Anacortes on Fidalgo Island. It offers a good mix of restaurants, reasonably priced lodging, and sights to see, including **Washington Park** and the historic sternwheeler *W. T. Preston.* A few miles

Must-Sees

M *W.T. Preston:* Now landlocked along the Anacortes waterfront, this historic sternwheeler operated around Puget Sound from 1914 to the early 1970s. Today, it's open for self-guided tours (page 28).

M **Washington Park:** Covering 200 prime waterfront acres, this Anacortes park has camping, hiking trails, and a very scenic two-mile loop road (page 30).

BRITISH COLUMBIA

CANADA
USA

Strait of Georgia

Whatcom Museum of History and Art

M — Fairhaven

Chuckanut
M Drive

Washington Park

Vancouver
Island

M WT Preston

M Deception Pass
State Park

Meerkerk
Rhododendron
Gardens

Fort Casey
State Park

M

Ebey's Landing National
Historical Reserve

Whidbey Island
Greenbank Farm

WASHINGTON

**GATEWAYS TO
THE ISLANDS**

M **Deception Pass State Park:** Best known for the arching bridge that links Whidbey and Fidalgo Islands, this very popular park has hundreds of campsites, miles of hiking trails, freshwater lakes for swimming, and sandy beaches (page 31).

M **Whidbey Island Greenbank Farm:** Famous for its big red and white barn and loganberry wines, this historic farm is a top attraction on Whidbey Island (page 45).

M **Meerkerk Rhododendron Gardens:** In April and May, more than 1,500 varieties of these fragrant flowers bloom on Meerkerk's 53 acres of gardens (page 45).

M **Fort Casey State Park:** One of a triangle of forts that guarded the entrance to Puget Sound till the 1920s, this one still has two of the ingenious disappearing guns. Also here is pretty Admiralty Head Lighthouse (page 45).

M **Ebey's Landing National Historical Reserve:** Managed by the National Park Service, this reserve is a mix of preserved agricultural lands bordered by an impressive shoreline of cliffs and beaches (page 46).

M **Fairhaven:** Bellingham's famous historic district is a great place to search for that perfect gift or enjoy a fine meal while waiting for your train, bus, boat, or ferry (page 53).

M **Whatcom Museum of History and Art:** The main building is a distinctive red-brick structure from 1892 that served for decades as Bellingham's city hall. Adjacent buildings house additional collections, and nearby are several other interesting museums (page 56).

M **Chuckanut Drive:** This exceptionally scenic road stretches south from Fairhaven, with tall trees, the waters of Samish Bay, and several notable restaurants, before emerging onto the farmland of Skagit Valley (page 57).

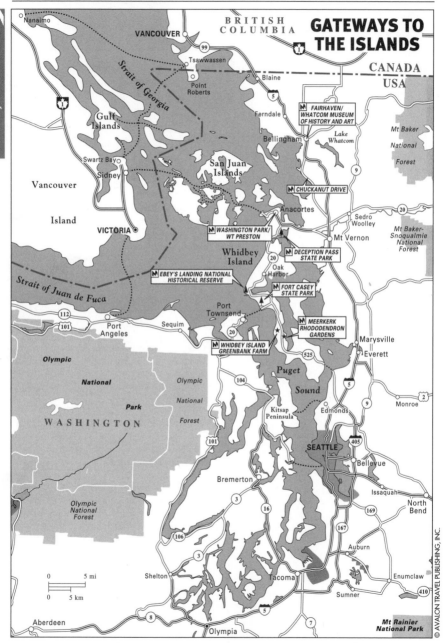

south of town is **Deception Pass State Park,** famous for the high arched bridge that links Fidalgo Island with Whidbey Island to the south.

One of the longest islands in America, Whidbey has one large town (Oak Harbor) and two smaller—and far more interesting—ones: Langley and Coupeville. Colorful **Whidbey Island Greenbank Farm** is a fun stop, with loganberry wines and other treats for sale, and just up the road is **Meerkerk Rhododendron Gardens,** which shows 1,500 varieties in late spring, including Washington's state flower, the coast rhododendron. Visit **Fort Casey State Park** to check out the disappearing guns and Admiralty Head Lighthouse, or nearby **Ebey's Landing National Historical Reserve** for verdant fields and a gorgeous coastline.

The city of Bellingham is a destination in its own right but also provides a jumping off point for private ferries to the San Juan Islands. The historic **Fairhaven** district boasts a collection of nicely restored buildings from the 1880s, many fine shops, and the multi-modal transportation center for trains, buses, boats, and the Alaska State Ferry. Downtown Bellingham is home to the **Whatcom Museum** and a couple of more offbeat collections, including the American Radio Museum and Mindport—filled with amusing and educational junk. South of Bellingham, **Chuckanut Drive** is one of the most scenic roads in the region, hugging the coast through lush forests before opening into the farm country northeast of Anacortes.

Anacortes

Many visitors know Anacortes (anna-KOR-tez) only as the launching point for the San Juan Islands, but this city of 15,000 is far more than a ferry dock. It is also one of the more pleasant cities of that size in the Puget Sound basin and has a casual end-of-the-road atmosphere. The city is 80 miles north of Seattle and 90 miles south of Vancouver.

Although it looks like part of the mainland, Anacortes is legally on **Fidalgo Island;** Swinomish Slough cuts a sluggish, narrow swath from the La Conner area around the hills known as Fidalgo Head. The slough is kept open for boaters, and is spanned by a beautiful curving arc of a bridge.

HISTORY

Anglos first resided on the island in the 1850s, but William Munks, who called himself "The King of Fidalgo Island," claimed to be the first permanent settler and opened a store in 1869. A geologist named Amos Bowman tried to persuade the company he worked for, the Canadian Pacific Railroad, to establish its western terminus at Fidalgo—despite the fact that Bowman had never seen the island. When the railroad refused,

Bowman came down to check out the land himself, bought 168 acres of it, and opened a store, a wharf, and the Anna Curtis Post Office, named after his wife, in 1879. Bowman was so determined to get a railroad—any railroad—into Anacortes that he published a newspaper, *The Northwest Enterprise,* to draw people and businesses to his town.

He was so convincing that the population boomed to more than 3,000 people, even though, by 1890, the town's five railroad depots had yet to see a train pull up. The Burlington Northern Railroad eventually came, and residents found financial success in salmon canneries, shingle factories, and lumber mills. Anacortes grew to prominence as a shipping and fishing port; by its heyday in 1911, it was home to seven canneries and proclaimed itself "salmon canning capital of the world." Workers were needed for all these plants, and Anacortes became a major entry point of illegal laborers from China and Japan; several outlaws made a prosperous living smuggling in both workers and opium. Anacortes's title for salmon canning has long since been lost as salmon stocks dwindled in Puget Sound due to overfishing (and particularly the use of fish traps), but the city still maintains a strong seaward orientation.

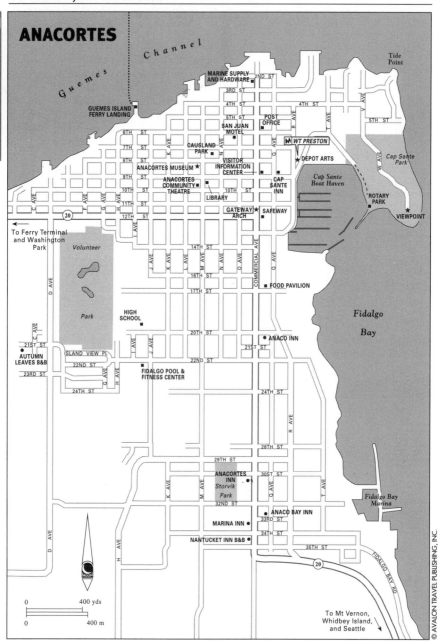

ANACORTES

Guemes Channel

Tide Point

MARINE SUPPLY AND HARDWARE
2ND ST
3RD ST
4TH ST
4TH ST
5TH ST
GUEMES ISLAND FERRY LANDING
POST OFFICE
SAN JUAN MOTEL
6TH ST
7TH ST
CAUSLAND PARK
WT PRESTON
Cap Sante Park
8TH ST
VISITOR INFORMATION CENTER
DEPOT ARTS
ANACORTES MUSEUM ★
9TH ST
ANACORTES COMMUNITY THEATRE
CAP SANTE INN
Cap Sante Boat Haven
10TH ST
10TH ST
LIBRARY
ROTARY PARK
11TH ST
GATEWAY ARCH ★
SAFEWAY
VIEWPOINT ★
12TH ST

20

To Ferry Terminal and Washington Park

Volunteer
14TH ST
16TH ST
17TH ST
Park
FOOD PAVILION

HIGH SCHOOL
Fidalgo Bay
20TH ST
ANACO INN
21ST ST
21ST ST
AUTUMN LEAVES B&B
ISLAND VIEW PL
22ND ST
22ND ST
FIDALGO POOL & FITNESS CENTER
23RD ST
24TH ST
24TH ST

28TH ST

29TH ST
ANACORTES INN
30ST ST
Storvik Park
Fidalgo Bay Marina
32ND ST
ANACO BAY INN
33RD ST
MARINA INN
34TH ST
NANTUCKET INN B&B
35TH ST

20

0   400 yds
0   400 m

To Mt Vernon, Whidbey Island, and Seattle

© AVALON TRAVEL PUBLISHING, INC.

COURTESY OF ANACORTES MUSEUM

In the 1930s and 1940s, Black Ball Line was the primary ferry company serving the San Juan Islands.

Anacortes Today

Anacortes relies on its two oil refineries, the Dakota Creek shipyard, two seafood processing plants (including the Trident Seafoods plant that turns Alaskan pollock into fish burgers for Burger King and Long John Silver's), and tourists en route to the San Juan Islands. A fleet of gillnetters and seiners supplies salmon for local markets, and many of the boats here head north to Alaska each summer. In recent years, the city has grown with the increase in tourism as well as an increase in retirees looking to enjoy the mild and relatively dry weather. A **gateway arch** at the corner of Commercial Avenue and 11th Street welcomes visitors to downtown Anacortes—now a National Historic District—and a number of the historic Victorian buildings have been restored.

SIGHTS

Museum and Historic Sites

The **Anacortes Museum** (1305 8th St., 360/293-1915, www.anacorteshistorymuseum .org, year-round 1–5 P.M. Thurs.–Mon., $2) has local historical photos and exhibits focused on the town's multi-ethnic heritage. Get another taste of the past in a walk around Anacortes to see almost 50 (mostly small) **historic murals** on local buildings. The visitor center has descriptions of each, including the mural of Anna Curtis across the street from the center.

Don't miss **Causland Park,** which covers a city block at 8th Street and N Avenue (right across from the museum). The park's playfully ornate mosaic walls, gazebo, and amphitheater were built in 1920 with colorful stones from area islands. Nearby are a number of 1890s homes and buildings, many restored to their original splendor. The home owned and built by Amos and Anna Curtis Bowman in 1891 stands at 1815 8th Street. At 807 4th Street, an architect's office is now housed in what was probably the finest bordello in the county in the 1890s. The little church at 5th and R was built by its Presbyterian congregation in 1889; still in use is the Episcopal Church at 7th and M, built in 1896.

Founded in 1913, **Marine Supply & Hardware Co.** (2nd and Commercial Ave., 360/293-3014, www.marinesupplyandhardware.com) is the oldest continuously operating marine supply store west of the Mississippi. The original oiled wood floors and oak cabinets are still here, along with a potpourri of supplies. It's a fascinating place to visit, with three generations of the Demopoulos family running things. Nearby is the large shipyard of **Dakota Creek Industries** (820 4th St., www.dakotacreek.com), which builds and repairs boats of all sizes, including the Washington State Ferries. Another company here, Northern Marine (www.northernmarine.com) constructs luxury yachts.

W.T. Preston

Remnants of Anacortes's earlier days are scattered throughout town, including the fascinating historic sternwheeler *W.T. Preston* (7th St. and R Ave., 360/293-1916), now a National Historic Landmark (next to the marina). The *Preston* operated as a snagboat for the U.S. Army Corps of Engineers from 1914 till the 1970s, when she was given to the city of Anacortes. The *Preston* was the last sternwheeler operating on Puget Sound and kept waterways clear of debris by towing off snags, logs, and stumps that piled up against bridge supports. Self-guided tours (pick up the handout and wander to your heart's content) are $2 for adults, $1 for kids and seniors, and free for kids under eight. The *Preston* is open

Memorial Day–Labor Day, 11 A.M.– 5 P.M. daily; April and September, 11 A.M.–5 P.M. Sat.–Sun.; closed the rest of the year.

Right next to the *Preston* is the 1911 Burlington Northern Railroad Depot at 7th and R, now home to the Depot Arts Center, plus the Anacortes Farmers Market on summer Saturdays.

Viewpoints

Five miles south of downtown Anacortes, 1,270-foot **Mount Erie** is the tallest "mountain" on Fidalgo Island. A steep and winding road rises 1.5 miles to a partially wooded summit where four short trails lead to dizzying views of the Olympics, Mount Baker, Mount Rainier, and Puget Sound. Don't miss the two lower overlooks, located a quarter-mile downhill from the summit. Get to Mount Erie by following Heart Lake Road south from town past Heart Lake to the signed turnoff at Mount Erie Road. Trails lead from various points along the Mount Erie Road into other parts of Anacortes Community Forest Lands.

For an impressive low-elevation viewpoint of the Cascades and Skagit Valley, visit **Cap Sante Park** on the city's east side, following 4th

© DON PITCHER

The historic snagboat *W.T. Preston* once cleared logs from local riverways.

Gateways to the Islands

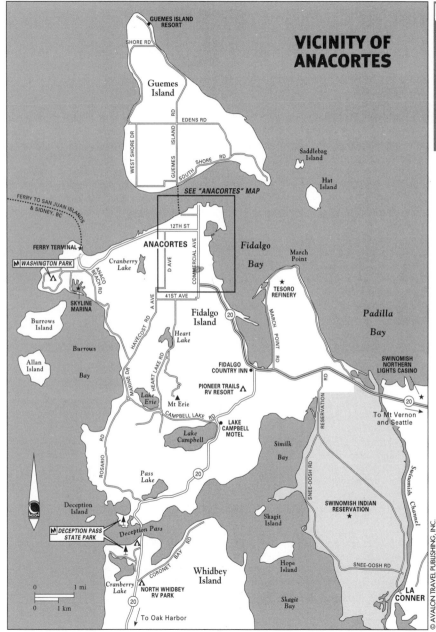

VICINITY OF ANACORTES

Guemes Island Resort

SHORE RD

Guemes Island

EDENS RD

WEST SHORE DR

GUEMES ISLAND RD

SOUTH SHORE RD

Saddlebag Island

Hat Island

SEE "ANACORTES" MAP

FERRY TO SAN JUAN ISLANDS & SIDNEY, BC

12TH ST

ANACORTES

D AVE

COMMERCIAL AVE

Fidalgo Bay

March Point

FERRY TERMINAL ★

WASHINGTON PARK

Cranberry Lake

ANACO BEACH RD

SKYLINE MARINA

41ST AVE

Fidalgo Island

TESORO REFINERY ★

Padilla Bay

Burrows Island

HAVECOST RD

A AVE

HEART LAKE RD

MARINE DR

Heart Lake

FIDALGO COUNTRY INN

MARCH POINT RD

SWINOMISH NORTHERN LIGHTS CASINO

Allan Island

Burrows Bay

PIONEER TRAILS RV RESORT

RESERVATION RD

20

Lake Erie

Mt Erie ▲

CAMPBELL LAKE RD

LAKE CAMPBELL MOTEL

To Mt Vernon and Seattle

ROSARIO RD

Lake Campbell

Similk Bay

SNEE-OOSH RD

Swinomish Channel

Pass Lake

20

SWINOMISH INDIAN RESERVATION ★

Deception Island

Skagit Island

Deception Pass

DECEPTION PASS STATE PARK

CORONET BAY RD

Hope Island

SNEE-OOSH RD

Cranberry Lake

NORTH WHIDBEY RV PARK

20

Whidbey Island

Skagit Bay

LA CONNER

To Oak Harbor

0   1 mi
0   1 km

MOON

Street to West Avenue. Scramble up the boulders for a better look at Mount Baker, the San Juans, and the Anacortes refineries that turn Alaskan oil into gasoline. Not far away, a short trail leads to **Rotary Park** next to Cap Sante Marina, where you'll find picnic tables overlooking the busy harbor.

Washington Park

Three miles west of downtown Anacortes, Washington Park is a strikingly beautiful picnic spot with 200 waterfront acres on Rosario Strait affording views of the San Juans and Olympics. Walk, bike, or drive the two-mile paved scenic loop, and stop off at one of many waterfront picnic areas. Other facilities include a busy boat launch, several miles of hiking trails offering views of the San Juans and the Olympics, a playground, and crowded campsites. The original park acreage was donated by one of Fidalgo Island's earliest pioneers, Tonjes Havekost, who said, "Make my cemetery a park for everybody." His grave stands on the southern edge of the park, overlooking Burrows Channel. The Anacortes Women's Club bought additional acreage in 1922 from the sale of lemon pies—they paid just $2,500 for 75 beachfront acres.

Guemes Island

Skagit County operates ferry service ($7.50 rt for a car and driver) to residential Guemes (GWEE-mes) Island from 6th Street and I Avenue. Take your bicycle along for a scenic tour of this rural island that is home to 500 year-round residents, and more than twice that in the summer. You'll find a mile-long public shoreline on the southwest end, plus two small county parks. **Anderson's General Store,** (7885 Guemes Island Rd., 360/293-4548, www.guemesislandstore.com) next to the ferry landing on Guemes, has limited supplies, and serves tasty breakfasts and lunches. **Guemes Island Resort** (4268 Guemes Island Rd., 360/293-6643 or 800/965-6643, www.guemesislandresort.com) on the north end of the island provides lodging.

THE MAIDEN OF DECEPTION PASS

The Samish Indians told the story of the beautiful Maiden of Deception Pass, Ko-Kwal-Alwoot. She was gathering shellfish along the beach when the sea spirit saw her and was at once enamored; when he took her hand, Ko-Kwal-Alwoot became terrified, but the sea spirit reassured her, saying he only wished to gaze upon her loveliness. She returned often, listening to the sea spirit's declarations of love.

One day a young man came from the sea to ask Ko-Kwal-Alwoot's father for permission to marry her. Her father, suspecting that living underwater would be hazardous to his daughter's health, refused, despite the sea spirit's claim that Ko-Kwal-Alwoot would have eternal life. Miffed, the sea spirit brought drought and famine to the old man's people until he agreed to give his daughter away. There was one condition: that she return once every year so the old man could be sure she was properly cared for. The agreement was made, and the people watched as Ko-Kwal-Alwoot walked into the water until only her hair, floating in the current, was visible. The famine and drought ended at once.

Ko-Kwal-Alwoot kept her promise for the next four years, returning to visit her people, but every time she came she was covered with more and more barnacles and seemed anxious to return to the sea. On her last visit, her people told her she need not return unless she wanted to; and since that time, she's provided abundant shellfish and clean spring water in that area. Legend has it that her hair can be seen floating to and fro with the tide in Deception Pass.

Today this Samish legend is inscribed on a story pole on Fidalgo Island within Deception Pass State Park. To get there, follow Highway 20 to Fidalgo Island; go west at Pass Lake, following the signs for Bowman Bay and Rosario Beach, and hike the trail toward Rosario Head.

Padilla Bay

This shallow bay east of Anacortes is home to the **Breazeale Interpretive Center** (10441 Bayview-Edison Rd., 360/428-1558, www.padillabay.gov, 10 A.M.–5 p.m. Wed.–Sun., free). Stop by to learn more about this important estuary; there's even a hands-on room for kids. Nearby is tiny **Bay View State Park** (360/757-0227, www.parks.wa.gov, $5) with access to the bay, a two-mile shoreline trail, and campsites.

DECEPTION PASS STATE PARK

Washington's most popular state park, Deception Pass (360/675-2417, www.parks.wa.gov, $5) has facilities that rival those of national parks: swimming at two lakes, four miles of shoreline, 28 miles of hiking trails, freshwater and saltwater fishing, boating, picnicking, rowboat rentals, boat launches, viewpoints, an environmental learning center, and several hundred campsites. The park, nine miles south of Anacortes on Highway 20, covers almost 3,600 forested acres on both sides of spectacular **Deception Pass**

Bridge. (The north side is on Fidalgo Island, while the south end is on Whidbey Island.)

When Capt. George Vancouver first sighted this waterway in 1792, he called it Port Gardner. But when he realized the inlet was actually a tidal passage between two islands, he renamed it "Deception Pass." Because of the strong tidal currents that can reach nine knots twice a day, the passage was avoided by sailing ships until 1852, when Capt. Thomas Coupe (for whom nearby Coupeville is named) sailed a fully rigged three-masted vessel through the narrow entrance.

Deception Pass Bridge

Completed in 1935, Deception Pass Bridge, a steel cantilever-truss structure, links Fidalgo, Pass, and Whidbey Islands. Much of the work was done by the Civilian Conservation Corps (CCC), which also built many other park structures. The bridge towers 182 feet above the water. It's estimated that each year more than three million people stop at the bridge to peer over the edge at the turbulent water and whirlpools far below, or to enjoy the sunset vistas. A delightful and very scenic trail leads down from the southwest side of

© DON PITCHER

Deception Pass Bridge

the bridge to a beautiful beach. The beach is also accessible by taking the road to the North Beach picnic area.

Other Sights

Bowman Bay is just north of the bridge on the west side of the highway and has campsites, a boat launch, and a fishing pier, plus a **CCC Interpretive Center** inside one of the attractive structures the corps built. Three rooms contain displays on the CCC and the men who worked for it in the 1930s. You may find one of the original CCC workers on duty, ready to talk about the old times. Open Thurs.–Mon. summers only.

Rosario Beach, just north of Bowman Bay, features a delightful picnic ground with CCC-built stone shelters. A half-mile hiking trail circles Rosario Head, the wooded point of land that juts into Rosario Bay (technically this is part of the 75-acre Sharpe County Park). The shoreline is a fine place to explore tidepools. The **Maiden of Deception Pass** totem pole commemorates the tale of a Samish girl who became the bride of the water spirit. Walla Walla College Marine Station (www.wwc.edu) is adjacent to Rosario Beach, and an underwater park offshore is popular with scuba divers.

A mile south of the Deception Pass bridge is the turnoff to Coronet Bay Road. This road ends three miles out at **Hoypus Point,** a good place to fish for salmon or to ride bikes, with striking views of Mount Baker.

Lakes and Hikes

Only electric motors, canoes, and rowboats are allowed on the park's lakes. You can observe beaver dams, muskrats, and mink in the marshes on the south side of shallow **Cranberry Lake,** which also hosts a seasonal concession stand. Trout fishing is good here, and the warm water makes it a favorite swimming hole. North of the bridge is **Pass Lake,** another place to fish or paddle.

A 15-minute hike to the highest point on the island, 400-foot **Goose Rock,** provides views of the San Juan Islands, Mount Baker, Victoria, and Fidalgo Island. You may possibly see a bald eagle soaring overhead. The trail starts at the south end of the bridge, heading east from either side of the highway; take the wide trail as it follows the pass, and then take one of the unmarked spur trails uphill to the top. Other hiking trails lead throughout the park, ranging from short nature paths to unimproved trails for experienced hikers only.

RECREATION
Hiking

Some of the finest local hiking is at Deception Pass State Park. Stop by the Anacortes visitor center for a guide to trails within the 2,800-acre **Anacortes Community Forest Lands** (360/293-1918, www.cityofanacortes.org) around Mount Erie and Cranberry, Whistle, and Heart Lakes. More than 50 miles of trails are here, and many of them can be linked into loop hikes.

The 3.5-mile **Whistle Lake Shore Loop** circles small Whistle Lake, offering water views, lots of bird life, and old-growth stands of Douglas fir and western red cedar. An easy and almost level path, the **Erie View Trail** departs from Heart Lake Road and follows a seasonal creek to a fine view of Mount Erie a mile out. Return the same way.

From the trailhead at the intersection of Mount Erie and Heart Lake Roads, hike the half-mile **Pine Ridge Loop Trail** for more views of Mount Erie and Sugarloaf. This moderately difficult hike takes from one to two hours. Another short hike is the 1.6-mile **Sugarloaf Trail,** starting on Ray Auld Drive, six miles from its intersection with Heart Lake Road. Follow the trail from the marshy trailhead straight up, ignoring side trails. To the west, enjoy views of Port Townsend, the San Juan Islands, and the Strait of Juan de Fuca; to the north, Bellingham.

The Cranberry Lake area also has a number of hiking paths, including the mile-long **John M. Morrison Loop Trail,** which starts at the end of 29th Street. This easy loop hike provides blufftop views of Cranberry Lake and old-growth Douglas fir forests, where some trees are seven feet in diameter.

Sea Kayaking

Island Outfitters (2403 Commercial Ave.,

360/299-2300 or 866/445-7506, www.seakayak-shop.com) is a full-service kayak shop. It features the latest boats and gear from Eddyline, which owns the shop and manufactures kayaks in nearby Burlington. The shop offers classes for all levels of ability, rents kayaks ($65/day for doubles or $45/day for singles) to experienced paddlers, and guides day tours along the Fidalgo Bay shoreline ($30/person for two hours). All-day trips ($149/person) to the more remote San Juan Islands include a water taxi to the islands and sea kayaking.

Anacortes Kayak Tours (1801 Commercial Ave., 360/588-1117 or 800/992-1801, www.ana-corteskayaktours.com) operates from the Island Adventure Center, which also leads whale-watching trips. Nearby Burrows Island is a popular destination for three-hour paddles ($59) departing from Skyline Marina. For something more adventurous, join a five-hour trip ($89) to Cypress, Sucia, or Lopez Islands. These include roundtrip transportation by water taxi and kayaking in out-of-the-way spots.

Boating and Fishing

Anacortes is home to one of the largest concentrations of bareboat charters in North America, with dozens of power yachts and sailboats heading out from two large marinas. The largest charter companies are **ABC Yacht Charters** (360/293-9533 or 800/426-2313, www.abcyachtcharters.com), **Anacortes Yacht Charters** (360/293-4555 or 800/233-3004, www.ayc.com), **Charters Northwest** (360/378-7196 or 800/258-3119, www.chartersnw.com), and **Ship Harbor Yacht Charters** (360/299-9193 or 877/772-6582, www.shipharboryachts.com).

A number of companies provide fishing charters out of Anacortes, including **Highliner Charters** (360/293-3072) or **Catchmore Charters** (360/293-7093, www.catchmorecharters.com).

Whale-Watching

Two local companies offer whale-watching trips from Anacortes. **Island Adventures** (1801 Commercial Ave., 360/293-2428 or 800/465-4604, www.island-adventures.com, $69 for adults, $59 for seniors, and $45 for kids) boasts a fast boat that can find orcas even when they've moved into Canadian waters around the Southern Gulf Islands.

Mystic Sea Charters (360/466-3042 or 800/308-9387, www.mysticseacharters.com) has a comfortable 100-foot boat with room for 75 folks. Four-and-a-half-hour whale-watching trips cost $68 for adults, $58 for seniors, or $39 for kids.

Other Recreation

Similk Beach Golf Course (12518 Christianson Rd., 360/293-3444) is a nine-hole course with Puget Sound vistas. Swim at the public **Fidalgo Pool and Fitness Center** (1603 22nd St., 360/293-0673, www.pioneernet.net/pooland-fitness). Lap swims are $2.50–4.25, and they provide childcare ($2) while you work out.

Anacortes Diving and Supply (2502 Commercial Ave., 360/293-2070, www.anacortes-diving.com) is a full-service shop that runs a variety of dive trips to the San Juans and surrounding areas.

ACCOMMODATIONS

Anacortes is blessed with an abundance of cozy bed-and-breakfasts and fine hotels. Make reservations far ahead for the summer months; some places fill up by March for the peak season in July and August. The Anacortes Chamber of Commerce website (www.anacortes.org) has links to many local lodging options, including guest houses and cottages.

Hotels and Inns

Centrally located **San Juan Motel** (1103 6th St., 360/293-5105 or 800/533-8009, $49 d) is a clean, quiet place with newly remodeled rooms that include small fridges and microwaves. Suites with two queen beds and kitchenettes are a real bargain at $59 d.

Lake Campbell Motel, four miles south of Anacortes (1377 Hwy. 20, 360/293-5314, $74 d), is a good family place with clean rooms that include fridges and microwaves. Larger units with two bedrooms and kitchenettes are $84–95; the biggest sleeps seven. A continental breakfast is included on summer weekends. Pretty Lake

$179 king suite

Campbell is right across Highway 20 from the motel, but traffic can be heavy at times.

Cap Sante Inn (906 9th St., 360/293-0602 or 800/852-0846, www.capsanteinn.com, $74 s or $78–82 d) is a fine mid-priced motel in the heart of town with comfy beds, plus microwaves and fridges in all rooms. Pets ($10 extra) are allowed in two rooms. Similar rates at **Anacortes Inn** (3006 Commercial Ave., 360/293-3153 or 800/327-7976, www.anacortesinn.com, $78–90 d), where rooms include fridges and microwaves, and guests enjoy a seasonal outdoor pool and continental breakfast.

Marina Inn (3300 Commercial Ave., 360/293-1100 or 800/231-5198, www.marinainnhotel.com, $74–79 s or $79–84 d) is a modern motel with big and immaculate rooms, in-room fridges and microwaves, a continental breakfast, and an indoor Jacuzzi.

Also quite new and a bit more luxurious is **Fidalgo Country Inn** (1250 Hwy. 20, 360/293-3494 or 800/244-4179, www.nwcountryinns.com, $89–109 d), with spacious rooms, a large outdoor pool and Jacuzzi, plus a continental breakfast. Suites run between $149 and $169 d. The inn is located south of town at the junction of Highway 20 and Spur 20.

Islands Inn (3401 Commercial Ave., 360/293-4644 or 866/331-3328, www.islandsinn.com) offers comfortable motel rooms ($79–86 d) with fireplaces, plus suites ($130 d) containing fireplaces, wet bars, and jetted tubs. An outdoor pool and Jacuzzi are on the premises, and guests are treated to a complimentary Dutch breakfast (the owner is from Amsterdam). Downstairs is Sasso's, serving Northwest cuisine with a continental flair.

Anyone heading out to the San Juans by ferry should consider homey **M Ship Harbor Inn,** located near the ferry west of town (5316 Ferry Terminal Rd., 360/293-5177, 800/852-8568 U.S. or 800/235-8568 Canada, www.shipharborinn.com). It is quiet and peaceful, with clean rooms ($80–95 d), cottages with kitchenettes and fireplaces ($95–105 d), and a Jacuzzi suite ($125 d). A continental breakfast is included.

Anaco Bay Inn (916 33rd St., 360/299-3320 or 877/299-3320, www.anacobayinn.com) is Anacortes's newest lodging place. The immaculate rooms ($79–99 d) have gas fireplaces, and larger ones include kitchenettes and jetted tubs; suites ($119 d) and two-bedroom apartments with full kitchens ($119–139 d) are also available. A continental breakfast and large indoor Jacuzzi are included.

The same owners also manage **Anaco Inn** (905 20th St., 360/293-8833 or 888/293-8833, www.anacoinn.com, $74–99 d), another well-kept, newer place. Rooms with jetted tubs and kitchens cost $99–119 d, and apartment units cost $119–139 d. An indoor Jacuzzi is available, and a continental breakfast is included.

Bed-and-Breakfasts

Autumn Leaves B&B (2301 21st St., 360/293-4920 or 866/293-4929, www.autumn-leaves.com, $145 d) is a contemporary home with three romantic guest rooms furnished with French antiques, gas fireplaces, and jetted tubs. Rates include a gourmet breakfast. No kids under 13.

Nantucket Inn B&B (3402 Commercial Ave., 360/293-6007 or 888/293-6007, www.whidbey.com/nantucket, $85–120 d, $145 d suite) is a large 1925 Cape Cod home with five rooms and a suite, all with private baths. A Jacuzzi sits in the garden, and downstairs is Bella Isola, one of the best local restaurants. No children under 12.

Island Breeze Guest House (11110 Marine Dr., 360/293-4477, www.islandbreezegh.com, $155–210) is an elegant waterside home with four guest rooms, all with king beds, plus private entrances and baths. Guests are served a big breakfast and appreciate the big deck that takes in Burrows Bay and the islands beyond. No kids.

Resort

Just a five-minute ferry ride from downtown Anacortes, **Guemes Island Resort** (325 Guemes Island Rd., 360/293-6643 or 800/965-6643, www.guemesislandresort.com) is a pleasant family escape. Six waterfront cabins—each with a kitchen and wood stove—face a grassy lawn on the north side of the island with views of Mt. Baker. Rates are $120 d for a one-bedroom cabin, $130 for up to four guests in units with lofts, and $140 for two-bedroom cabins. Also available are two larger places: a three-bedroom house sleeps up to 10 for $250, and a two-bedroom house with space for six at $165. No TVs, radios, or room phones in any of these, but guests are welcome to use the seasonal rowboats, and sea kayaks. There's a minimum stay of three nights in the summer and holidays, or two nights the rest of the year.

Campgrounds

Three miles west of Anacortes and near the ferry terminal, city-run **Washington Park** (360/293-1918, www.cityofanacortes.org, $12 for tents or $15 for RV hookups) has crowded campsites in the woods, as well as showers, picnic tables, boat launches, and a delightful beach and playground. No reservations (except for Anacortes residents), but the campground is open all year.

Nine miles south of Anacortes, **Deception Pass State Park** (360/675-2417, www.parks .wa.gov, $16 for tents, $22 for RVs, or $10 for bikes) has some of the finest camping in this part of Washington, with tall Douglas firs and a gorgeous lakeside setting. Unfortunately, the park's popularity means that you'll be accompanied by a multitude of fellow visitors. There are 261 tent and RV sites at Deception Pass, with hot showers and dump stations. The primary campground along Cranberry Lake has year-round sites, and a second seasonal campground is just north of the bridge at Bowman Bay. Make reservations ($7 extra) at 888/226-7688, www.parks .wa.gov. Head to the park's outdoor amphitheater on weekend evenings in the summer for natural history lectures and slide shows.

Two private RV parks are across the road from the park: **North Whidbey RV Park** (565 W. Cornet Bay Rd., 360/675-9597 or 888/462-2674, www.northwhidbeyrvpark.com), and **Sunrise Resorts at Deception Pass** (550 W. Cornet Bay Rd., 360/675-6575, www.sunriseresorts.com).

Pioneer Trails Campground (527 Miller Rd., 360/293-5355 or 888/777-5355, www.pioneertrails.com) provides a peaceful in-the-woods setting on 28 acres south of town off Highway 20. Sites cost $25 ($69 for those with a private cabana), and "covered wagons" are $25. They also have a number of cabins for $40–89 d. No tent camping allowed.

Park RVs at **Fidalgo Bay Resort** (1107 Fidalgo Bay Rd., 360/293-5353 or 800/727-5478, www.fidalgobay.com, $25–40 for full hookups). **Lighthouse RV Park** (6060 Sands Way, 360/293-3344) isn't much more than a gravel lot with crammed-together sites near Skyline Marina.

FOOD
Breakfast and Lunch

Start your day at **Calico Cupboard Café & Bakery** (901 Commercial Ave., 360/293-7315) for homemade country breakfasts and healthy lunches. Save room for dessert; the fudge pecan pie and apple dumplings are legendary. Get there early on weekends to avoid a wait.

La Vie en Rose French Bakery (418 Commercial Ave., 360/299-9546, www.laviebakery.com) has wonderful French pastries (including a white chocolate raspberry cake) and breads, plus tasty soups, pot pies, sandwiches, pizza slices, and casseroles. If you're heading out on the ferry, grab a box lunch special. Get filling breakfasts (waffles, smoked salmon scramble, breakfast tacos, and more), along with lunchtime wraps, salads, soups, smoothies, and fresh-squeezed juices next door at **Star Bar Café** (360/299-2120).

Penguin Coffee (2110 Commercial Ave., 360/588-8321) has start-me-up cappuccinos and free wireless Internet access for customers. It's a good spot to hang out if you can resist the delectable confections made on the premises. **Donut House** (2719 Commercial Ave., 360/293-4053, Tues.–Sun. 24 hours) is locally famous for their donuts.

One of the dining highlights in Anacortes, **Café Adrift** (510 Commercial Ave., 360/588-0653) is open three meals a day with a relaxing atmosphere and from-scratch meals. Unusual breakfasts include chai-spiced oats and breakfast curry. Lunch is equally creative, with lamb sausage sandwiches, smoked salmon sandwiches, and chili garlic chicken skewers. Dinner entrées start at $8 for a cinnamon black been quesadilla with mango, up to $23 for organic beef tenderloin medallions.

American and Seafood

Village Pizza (807 Commercial Ave., 360/293-7847) has pizzas and mini-pizzas, subs, grinders, and more for reasonable prices.

On the downtown waterfront, **Randy's Pier 61** (209 T Ave., 360/293-5108, www.randys-pier61.com) is a fine seafood restaurant with vistas of Guemes Channel. Specialties include a tasty clam chowder, seafood gumbo, salmon Wellington, smoked prime rib, and Greek-style prawns. The big menu also includes such all-American favorites as steak, ribs, chicken, and pasta. Open for lunch and dinner, with entrées ranging widely: $15–35. Sunday brunch here (10 A.M.–2 P.M.; $16) is also popular.

Charlie's Restaurant, next to the ferry (5407 Ferry Terminal Rd., 360/293-7377) has a moderately priced steak, prime rib, seafood, and pasta menu, and boasts water and dock views; $14–20 entrées. It's a convenient place to stop for a drink while waiting for your ship to come in.

Billy Ray's (5320 Ferry Terminal Rd., 360/588-0491) is just up from the ferry terminal. The fresh-from-the-sea menu includes mahi mahi, razor clams, Alaskan halibut, and fish and chips, but chef Billy Ray also serves up East Indian chicken curry, BBQ spare ribs, pizzas (try the salmon and pesto version), and a good choice of appetizers. Dinner entrées run $15–26. Watch the ferries come and go from the back deck.

Facing the boats of Skyline Marina, **Flounder Bay Cafe** (2201 Skyline Way, 360/293-3680, www.flounderbaycafe.com) has food to match the scenery. All the usual seafood specials are at this classy eatery, and the outside deck provides an expansive view of the action. The Sunday champagne brunch buffet ($17) is the best in town.

Located inside Swinomish Northern Lights Casino (12885 Casino Dr., 360/293-2691 or 800/877-7529, www.swinomishcasino.com) the **Two Salmon Cafe** has nightly specials, including Saturday-evening steak and Dungeness crab for $16. Lunch and dinner buffets are equally popular and reasonable (if you stay away from the slots).

International

Housed within Nantucket Inn, **Bella Isola Ristorante Italiano** (3402 Commercial Ave., 360/299-8398), serves classic Italian pastas, plus pizzas, steaks, and seafood. Diners enjoy the graceful setting: a 1925 home that is now also a bed-and-breakfast. The restaurant is packed most nights, so reservations are advised. Dinner entrées cost $14–26, and there's live jazz on Wednesday and Sunday nights in the summer.

Tokyo Restaurant (818 Commercial Ave., 360/293-9898) has a sushi bar and also serves teriyaki, sukiyaki, tempura, and other Japanese standards. Lunch specials are a bargain: all under $7.

Two places serve Thai food (including vegetarian specialties) in town: **Bangkok Bistro** (1202 Commercial Ave., 360/588-1536), and **Naung Mai Thai Kitchen** (3015 Commercial Ave., 360/588-1183). **Esteban's** (1506 Commercial Ave., 360/299-1060) is Anacortes's hometown spot for Mexican meals, with all the standards for reasonable prices.

Pubs

Anacortes's two best drinking establishments are both smoke-free. You definitely won't go wrong with a lunch or dinner at **Rockfish Grill & Anacortes Brewery** (320 Commercial Ave., 360/293-3666, www.anacortesrockfish.com), where the menu includes local seafood, small wood-fired pizzas, steaks, and burgers, along with fresh ales from the on-the-premises brewery. Most dinner entrées are $16–18, but you can get a small pizza or great fish and chips for $7–10. Families are welcome. Just down the street is **Brown Lantern Ale House** (412 Commercial Ave., 360/293-2544, www.brownlantern.com), where the burgers and the halibut and chips are noteworthy and the pool table sees plenty of action.

Markets and Wines

Stock up on groceries for the San Juans at two big stores along Commercial Avenue: **Safeway** and **Food Pavilion**. **Seabear Smokehouse** (30th St. and T Ave., 360/293-4661 or 800/645-3474, www.seabear.com) sells smoked salmon and other treats, and has free tours daily in the summer.

The **Anacortes Farmers' Market** (7th St. and R Ave., 360/293-1294, www.anacortesfarmers-market.org) takes place at the Depot Arts Center on Saturdays 9 A.M.–2 P.M. from mid-May to early October. It's a good place to buy fresh produce, baked goods, flowers, handmade crafts, clothing, and jams.

For an impressive selection of wines—including the most extensive selection of Washington wines anywhere—head to **Compass Wines** (1405 Commercial Ave., 360/293-6500, www .compasswines.com).

ARTS AND ENTERTAINMENT

Several downtown galleries line Commercial Avenue, the best of which are **Anne Martin Mc-Cool Gallery** (711 Commercial Ave., 360/293-3577, www.mccoolart.com) which displays her vivid watercolors, **Scott Milo Gallery** (420 Commercial Ave., 360/588-9508, www.scott milo.com), with a variety of artists and changing exhibits, and **Insights Gallery** (516 Commercial Ave., 360/588-8044, www.insightsgallery.com), featuring contemporary artists. **Depot Arts Center** (7th St. at R Ave., 360/293-3663, www.de-potartscenter.com) houses a gallery that showcases local talent. It's next to the historic *W.T. Preston.*

The **Anacortes Community Theatre** (10th and M Sts., 360/293-6829, www.acttheatre.com) stages plays, musicals and annual Christmas performances. The **Vela Luka Croatian Dancers** (www.velaluka.org) is a local group that performs all over the world. This is the most obvious example of Anacortes's strong Croatian community; an estimated 25 percent of the local population is of Croatian descent.

Meet regional authors during book and poetry readings at **Watermark Book Co.** (612 Commercial Ave., 360/293-4277 or 800/291-4277).

The small **Anacortes Cinemas** (4th and O Sts., 360/293-7000), shows first-run films. Find live music on Friday and Saturday nights at three downtown bars, all of which sometimes share a cover charge: **Rockfish Grill & Anacortes Brewery** (320 Commercial Ave., 360/293-3666, www.anacortesrockfish.com), **Brown Lantern Ale House** (412 Commercial Ave., 360/293-2544, www.brownlantern.com), and **Watertown Pub** (314 Commercial Ave., 360/293-3587).

Drop some cash at **Swinomish Northern**

Lights Casino & Bingo (just across the Highway 20 bridge on Fidalgo Island, 360/293-2691 or 800/877-7529, www.swinomishcasino.com), which offers gambling—including bingo, craps, roulette, blackjack, poker, and *sic bo* (Chinese dice game). The gift shop sells Native arts, and the cabaret has live music.

Festivals

Throughout the month of April, the ever-popular **Skagit Valley Tulip Festival** (360/428-5959, www.tulipfestival.org) brings activities to Anacortes, La Conner, and Mount Vernon, including everything from garden tours to a quilt show. The **Anacortes Waterfront Festival,** held at Cap Sante Boat Haven the weekend before Memorial Day each May, celebrates the city's maritime heritage with a food court and beer garden, live music, craft booths, boat show and regatta, and art show.

Anacortes, like every other town in America, has a parade and fireworks on the **4th of July.** During **Shipwreck Days Flea Market** on the third Saturday in July, more than 300 vendors turn downtown Anacortes into a giant garage sale.

The **Anacortes Arts and Crafts Festival** (360/293-6211, www.anacortesartsfestival.com), held the first weekend of August, attracts more than 70,000 people with a juried fine art show, 250 arts and crafts booths, kid events, ethnic foods, classic cars, and plenty of live music and entertainment. Don't miss this one!

Other popular events are the **World's Largest King Salmon Barbecue** the third weekend of August, **Anacortes Jazz Festival** the third weekend of September, and **Oyster Run** (360/757-1515) the last weekend of September. The last of these brings thousands of motorcyclists to Anacortes; it's a great place for leather lovers. You'll also find stunt motorcyclists, a beer garden, and oysters on the half-shell.

INFORMATION AND SERVICES

For maps, brochures, and up-to-date information, drop by the **Anacortes Visitor Information Center** (819 Commercial Ave., 360/293-3832, www.anacortes.org). Across the street is a mural of Anna Curtis, for whom the town was named. The information center is open mid-May to mid-September 9 A.M.–5 p.m. Monday, 10 A.M.–5 P.M. Saturday, and 10 A.M.–3 P.M. Sunday, with reduced weekend hours the rest of the year (closed Sundays November to mid-February). The *Anacortes Newcomers' & Visitors' Guide* is a helpful free publication available at the information center or online at www.plaidnet .com/guides. Also check out the *Anacortes American* newspaper's website, www.goanacortes.com, for local information and links.

Island Hospital (1211 24th St., 360/299-1300, www.islandhospital.org) is the local hospital, with a 24-hour emergency room and 43 beds. There are no hospitals on the San Juan Islands.

Built in 2003, the spacious **Anacortes Library** (1220 10th St., 360/293-1910, www.library.cityofanacortes.org) has a kids' room and a dozen computers with free Internet access.

TRANSPORTATION
Washington State Ferries
To reach the San Juan Islands or Sidney, British Columbia, via state ferry, you have no choice but to leave from Anacortes—and ferry traffic keeps a good portion of local businesses in business. The **Washington State Ferries** (206/464-6400 or 888/808-7977 Washington and British Columbia only, www.wsdot.wa.gov/ferries) website has details on the ferry system, including current wait times in Anacortes. Around town, tune your radio to **AM 1340** for broadcasts of the current ferry status.

If you're bringing your car, be prepared for a lengthy wait on summer weekends. Avoid delays by leaving your car in the lot next to the terminal ($20 for three days); there's always space for walk-on passengers. A free park-and-ride lot is located at March Point eight miles east of here, and a shuttle bus transports you to the ferry terminal. Reservations are recommended for ferry service between Anacortes and Sidney, British Columbia, but reservations are not available for other routes.

The Anacortes ferry terminal is three miles west of downtown on 12th Street, and has a small café with espresso. Two restaurants are just steps away: Billy Rae's and Charlie's. Warning: Anacortes police often stop folks speeding in an attempt to catch the ferry. Keep your speed down or you might get delayed considerably longer, with a fine to boot!

For travel to the San Juan Islands, the state ferries charge higher rates Thursday–Sunday and lower fares Monday–Wednesday; rates are also higher in summer than in the off-season. Peak-season Wednesday–Saturday fares from Anacortes to Friday Harbor, the last American stop, are $11.40 for passengers and walk-ons, or $43.75 for a car and driver. Bikes are $4 extra, and kayaks cost $19.20 more. Car-and-driver fares to the other islands from Anacortes are a few dollars less.

Ferry travelers are only charged in the westbound direction; eastbound travel within the San Juans or from the islands to Anacortes is free. The only exception to this is for travelers leaving from Sidney, British Columbia, for the islands. If you're planning to visit all the islands, save money by heading straight to Friday Harbor, and then work your way back through the others at no additional charge. Credit cards are accepted at the ferry terminal in Anacortes but not on San Juan, Orcas, or Lopez Islands.

Twice a day (once daily in winter), a ferry heads from Anacortes to Sidney, British Columbia (20 miles north of Victoria). One-way peak-season fares to Sidney are $13.80 for passengers and walk-ons or $46.75 for a car and driver. Vehicle reservations are required for this route, and must be made at least 24 hours in advance.

Other Boats
Skagit County operates the small **Guemes Island Ferry** (6th St. and I Ave., 360/293-6356, www.skagitcounty.net) to this nearby residential island. The five-minute crossing costs $7.25 round-trip for a car and driver, and $1.50 ($.75 for kids) round-trip for passengers or walk-ons. The ferry departs daily on the hour (or better) from 6:30 A.M. most days to at least 6 P.M. It doesn't run between 11 A.M. and 1 P.M.

Based at Cap Sante Marina in Anacortes,

Island Express Charters (360/299-2875 or 877/473-9777, www.islandexpresscharters.com) has a high-speed 32-passenger landing craft with plenty of space for kayaks, bikes, and gear. Rates depend upon the number of passengers, and they'll head most anywhere in the San Juans.

In business since 1992, **Paraclete Charters** (Skyline Marina, 360/293-5920 or 800/808-2999, www.paracletecharters.com) runs three boats (the largest can carry 64 folks) from Anacortes. Prices depend on your destination and number of people, but you don't need to charter an entire boat, and they have room for kayaks, bikes, and pets.

By Air

Departing from Anacortes Airport, **San Juan Airlines** (360/293-4691 or 800/874-4434, www.sanjuanairlines.com) offers commuter flights year-round to Lopez, San Juan, and Orcas Islands in the San Juans, along with flightseeing and air charters.

By Bus

Skagit Transit (360/299-2424, www.skat.org) has daily bus connections from Anacortes (including the ferry terminal) to Mount Vernon, La Conner, and other parts of Skagit County. Most buses have bike racks. **Airporter Shuttle** (360/380-8800 or 800/235-5247, www.airporter.com) runs vans between Anacortes and Sea-Tac Airport a dozen times a day year-round. The one-way cost is $31 ($16 for kids) to the Anacortes ferry terminal.

By Taxi and Car

Call **Triangle Taxi** (360/588-8294 or 888/675-1244, www.triangletaxi.com) or **County Taxi** (360/333-1456 or 866/670-2020, www.countytaxi.com) for a rides around town or out to the ferry terminal ($11). Car rentals are available from **U-Save Auto Rental** (360/293-8686 or 877/451-6985, www.usave.net) and **Enterprise Rent a Car** (360/293-4325 or 800/261-7331, www.enterprise.com).

Whidbey Island

One of the longest islands in the lower 48 states, Whidbey Island encompasses 208 square miles in its 45-mile length. No spot on it is more than five miles from the water.

Whidbey is a favorite place for a Sunday-afternoon drive, with Deception Pass State Park the primary "stop and gawk" spot along the way. Also popular are the quaint towns of Coupeville and Langley, the quiet shoreline and picturesque agricultural land of Ebey's Landing National Historical Reserve, and South Whidbey State Park and Fort Casey State Park. The largest metropolitan center, Oak Harbor, is home to Whidbey Naval Air Station.

Exploring the Island

Whidbey is a perfect destination for a day trip or a weekend outing, with lots to explore and a wide variety of places to stay. The island is also great for cyclists, with many miles of quiet back roads. The charm of the picturesque towns of Langley and Coupeville is natural—a result of their history,

not a theme created to attract tourism. Fittingly enough, the official Island County website is www.donothinghere.com; it's filled with details on Whidbey and Camano Islands.

For a fast day tour, ride the Mukilteo-Clinton ferry to the south end of the island and take a leisurely drive up-island, with stops in each town and park. To really see Whidbey right, you'll need more than a day. Take the time to explore the many natural areas and historic sites, camping out in one of the excellent state parks or staying in a local bed-and-breakfast. Reservations are highly recommended for summer weekends.

Contact **Island County Tourism Information** (360/675-3755 or 888/747-7777, www.donothinghere.com) for information on Whidbey. The online **Whidbey Island Visitor's Guide** (www.visitwhidbey.com) is also of interest. For tours of the island, check with **Whidbey Tours** (360/678-5641 or 877/881-1203, www.gardenislecottages.com). The **Whidbey Island B&B**

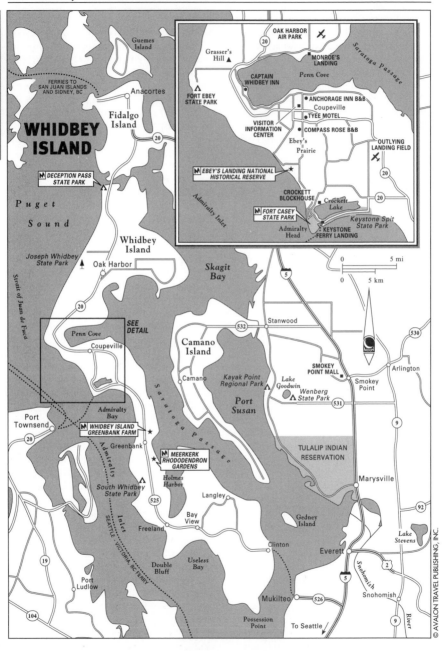

WHIDBEY ISLAND

FERRIES TO
SAN JUAN ISLANDS
AND SIDNEY, BC

Guemes
Island

Anacortes

Fidalgo
Island

DECEPTION PASS
STATE PARK

Puget

Sound

Joseph Whidbey
State Park

Whidbey
Island

Oak Harbor

Strait of Juan de Fuca

Penn Cove

SEE
DETAIL

Coupeville

Skagit
Bay

Camano
Island

Camano

Kayak Point
Regional Park

Lake
Goodwin

Stanwood

SMOKEY
POINT MALL

Smokey
Point

Arlington

Admiralty
Bay

Port
Townsend

WHIDBEY ISLAND
GREENBANK FARM

Greenbank

MEERKERK
RHODODENDRON
GARDENS

Saratoga Passage

Port
Susan

Wenberg
State Park

TULALIP INDIAN
RESERVATION

Marysville

Holmes
Harbor

South Whidbey
State Park

Langley

Bay
View

Gedney
Island

Lake
Stevens

Admiralty Inlet   SEATTLE-VICTORIA, BC FERRY

Port
Ludlow

Freeland

Double
Bluff

Useless
Bay

Clinton

Everett

Snohomish

Snohomish
River

Port
Ludlow

Mukilteo

Possession
Point

To Seattle

Detail inset:

OAK HARBOR
AIR PARK

Grasser's
Hill

MONROE'S
LANDING

Saratoga Passage

CAPTAIN
WHIDBEY INN

Penn Cove

FORT EBEY
STATE PARK

ANCHORAGE INN B&B

Coupeville

TYEE MOTEL

VISITOR
INFORMATION
CENTER

COMPASS ROSE B&B

Ebey's
Prairie

OUTLYING
LANDING FIELD

EBEY'S LANDING NATIONAL
HISTORICAL RESERVE

Admiralty Inlet

CROCKETT
BLOCKHOUSE

Crockett
Lake

FORT CASEY
STATE PARK

Keystone Spit
State Park

Admiralty
Head

KEYSTONE
FERRY LANDING

0   5 mi

0   5 km

Association (800/399-5587, www.whidbeyislandbandb.com) has details on local bed-and-breakfasts and last-minute reservations.

Getting There

To drive onto Whidbey Island, you've got only one option: the Deception Pass Bridge at the island's north end. To get there, go west on Highway 20 from I-5. Access to the south end of Whidbey is a relaxing **Washington State Ferry** (206/464-6400 for general info or 888/808-7977 in Washington and British Columbia only) ride from Mukilteo or Port Townsend. Find all the details—including current ferry wait times—at www.wsdot.wa.gov/ferries.

The Mukilteo ferry leaves for Clinton about every half-hour 5 A.M.–1 A.M., and the 20-minute crossing costs $3.40 round-trip for passengers or walk-ons, $1 extra for bikes, and $7.50 one-way for a car and driver. (No charge for eastbound passengers and bikes.) Busiest times are during the weekday commute, Saturday mornings (after 9 A.M. en route to the island), and late in the afternoon on Sundays. Sunday evenings after 7 P.M. are quieter, so just enjoy the island and let folks in a hurry wait in the traffic jams while you sit on a beach or in a café.

From the Olympic Peninsula, board the ferry in Port Townsend to arrive at the Keystone landing next to Fort Casey State Park a half-hour later. These ferries operate about every 45 minutes between 7 A.M. and 9 P.M. in the summer, and one-way fares are $2.20 for passengers ($.50 extra one-way for bikes), or $9.75 for a car and driver. Be ready for a two-hour wait during peak times on summer weekends.

Getting Around

Whidbey Island seems like it was designed for biking. The rolling hills, clean air, and beautiful weather are inspiring enough; occasional whale and eagle sightings add to the pleasure. **Island Transit** (360/678-7771 or 800/240-8747, www.islandtransit.org) is a free bus system that offers Monday–Saturday service all across Whidbey Island, from Clinton on the south to Deception Pass on the north. All buses have bike racks. **Backroads** (510/527-1555 or 800/462-

2848, www.backroads.com) runs cycling tours of Whidbey Island during the summer, either as camping trips or rides where you stay at local inns and bed-and-breakfasts. A sag wagon carries your gear.

LANGLEY

This tiny waterfront artists' community (pop. 1,200) is a great browsing stop, and several of its lodging establishments have views across Saratoga Passage to Camano Island and beyond. You'll find an abundance of gourmet restaurants, boutiques, bed-and-breakfasts, bookstores, and art galleries.

History

Langley is probably the only Washington town founded by a teenager. In 1880, an ambitious 15-year-old German immigrant, Jacob Anthes, settled here. Because he was too young to file for a homestead, Anthes spent $100 to buy 120 acres of land, adding to his holdings with a 160-acre homestead claim when he reached 21. He later built a store and post office and teamed up with Judge J.W. Langley to plat the new town.

Sights

The main attraction in Langley is simply the town itself, situated right along Puget Sound. A favorite downtown spot for photos is the life-size bronze *Boy and Dog,* by local sculptor Georgia Gerber. The 160-foot fishing pier offers great views and a chance to pull out your fishing pole, and the beach is a popular place for picnicking and swimming. **South Whidbey Historical Museum** (312 2nd St., 360/730-3367, 1–4 P.M. Sat.–Sun.) has local memorabilia in a century-old building. Just up the way at the corner of 2nd and Anthes is a cozy little town park with a colorful shelter and tables. Children love the wooden castle in the community park a mile west of town on Maxwelton Road.

Galleries

Tiny Langley is home to eight art galleries. The two best, **Museo Piccolo Gallery** (215 1st St., 360/221-7737) and **Gaskill/Olson Gallery** (302

1st St., 360/221-2978, www.gaskillolson.com) have unusual and highly creative works. Also of note are **Lowry-James Rare Prints & Books** (101 Anthes, 360/221-0477, www.lowryjames .com), with natural history engravings and lithographs, **Artists Cooperative Gallery** (314 1st St., 360/221-7675), and **Isle of Art Gallery** (138 2nd St., 360/221-8499, www.whidbey art.com). The last of these galleries features Dan O'Halloran's amazing works, which blend Chinese and Native American themes.

Langley's galleries open for evening **Art Walks** on the first Saturday of each month.

Accommodations

The Langley Chamber of Commerce (208 Anthes, 360/221-5676, www.whidbey.com/langley) has details on local bed-and-breakfasts and inns and keeps track of vacancies. Stop by the visitors center to see photos of each place. The day's vacancies are posted in the front window each night after 5 P.M. Its website has links to more than 50 local lodging places.

Hotels and Inns

Langley's largest lodging option is the modern **Saratoga Inn** (201 Cascade Ave., 360/221-5801 or 800/698-2910, www.foursisters.com, $165–200 d, or $275 d for the honeymoon suite). This 16-room place combines the privacy of a hotel with a hot buffet breakfast and wine and hors d'oeuvres each afternoon. Spacious rooms are attractively appointed, and all include gas fireplaces.

Langley Motel (526 B Camano Ave., 360/221-6070, www.langleymotel.com, $85–105 d) has four units with '50s retro-style rooms (but king-sized beds) designed by the architect-owner.

The luxurious **M Inn at Langley** (400 1st St., 360/221-3033, www.innatlangley.com, $235 d, $395 d suite, $575 d cottage) has 26 rooms, suites, and a cottage, each with its own private patio overlooking Saratoga Passage, a jetted tub, fireplace, and continental breakfast. Two-night minimum on weekends, and no kids under age 12. Also on premises is a renowned restaurant, along with Spa Essencia, providing massage, aromatherapy, body masks, and more.

Located right along the beach and just up

from the marina, **Boatyard Inn** (200 Wharf St., 360/221-5120, www.boatyardinn.com, $175 d, $230 suites) has spacious and modern studio units and loft suites for up to four guests. Each of these features a waterfront deck and mini-kitchen.

Six miles west of Langley is **Primrose Path Properties** (3191 E. Harbor Rd., 360/730-3722 or 800/333-4724, www.primrosepath.net) with four lodging options, ranging from a small cottage ($139 d) to a luxurious two-bedroom cottage with a path to its private beach ($189 for up to six guests). A two-night minimum stay is required.

Bed-and-Breakfasts

Find links to local bed-and-breakfasts at www .langleylodging.com or www.whidbeyisland-bandb.com. Unless otherwise noted, all serve full breakfasts and do not allow young children. Most of these also require a two-night minimum stay on summer weekends.

The rambling **Ashingdon Manor B&B Inn** (5023 Langley Rd., 360/221-2334 or 800/442-4942, www.ashingdonmanor.com, $95–135 d) is one of the more distinctive local places, with a 14-acre country location, six guest rooms with private baths (three with fireplaces), a grand piano, and a lovely pond and patio. A gourmet breakfast is included and evening drinks are served in the English-style pub. Co-owner Jennifer Johnson is a chef and will prepare dinners ($25–45 per person) upon request. A separate three-bedroom, two-bath (with Jacuzzi tubs) house is available for $185 d or $295 for six guests.

Country Cottage of Langley B&B (215 6th St., 360/221-8709 or 800/713-3860, www .acountrycottage.com, $149–189 d) is a 1920s home with five cottages, all with water views, private entrances, and decks. Breakfast is served in the main house or brought to your cottage. Three of these cottages also feature in-room Jacuzzis, king beds, and fireplaces; all have private decks.

Island Tyme B&B Inn (4940 S. Bayview, 360/221-5078 or 800/898-8963, www.island-tymebb.com, $99–155 d) is a modern Victorian-style home set on 10 wooded acres. Inside, you'll find five guest rooms with private baths (some with jetted tubs and fireplaces), and outside

decks. Kids over eight are accepted, and pets are allowed in one room.

Lone Lake Cottage B&B (5206 S. Bayview Rd., 360/321-5325, www.lonelake.com, $140 d) has two cottages and a suite along Lone Lake. Guests can use the canoes, bikes, tennis court, and rowboat. A continental breakfast is provided.

Victoria's B&B (117 6th St., 360/221-3898, www.victoriasbandb.com, $99–125 d) is a comfortable Victorian-style home with three guest rooms just a short distance from downtown.

Villa Isola B&B Inn (5489 S. Coles Rd., 360/221-5052 or 800/246-7323, www.villa-isola.com, $105–170 d) sits in the country two miles from Langley and features lovely grounds (including a lawn-bowling court), a Jacuzzi, and six suites with private baths—most with Jacuzzi tubs. A full breakfast is served, along with evening espresso.

Just a short walk from the center of Langley, **Cat & Fiddle B&B** (430 4th St., 360/221-5460 or 888/535-6222, www.catandfiddlebb.com, $115 d) has a quiet two-room suite with private bath, plus ingredients for a self-serve breakfast. Guests can relax in the beautiful front garden, with no TV or phone to disturb your reverie.

Housed within Langley's oldest Victorian house, **The Maine Stay B&B** (619 1st St., 360/221-8173, $90 d, $125 d suite) has two guest rooms that share a bath, plus a suite with private bath and French doors that open to a large viewing deck. Guests are served a full breakfast, and kids over 10 are welcome.

Campgrounds

Camp at nearby **South Whidbey State Park**; $16 for tents or $22 for RVs. **Island County Fairgrounds** (819 Camano Ave., 360/221-4677, www.islandweb.org/fair, $10 tents, $15 RVs) has year-round tent sites and RV hookups with showers. Coin-operated showers are located at the marina at the foot of Wharf Street.

Food

Langley is blessed with fine and surprisingly reasonable restaurants. **Langley Village Bakery** (360/221-3525) bakes out-of-this-world breads and sweets. A personal favorite, **Star Bistro** (up-stairs at 201 1st St., 360/221-2627, www.star-bistro.com, $10–29), serves pasta, fresh seafood, salads, lamb, and more. They feature live entertainment most Friday and Saturday nights, and the deck is great for summertime alfresco dining with a water view. Downstairs, the **Star Store** is a fun place to explore, with gourmet groceries and imported items.

Up the street a bit, **Café Langley** (113 1st St., 360/221-3090, $14–26) has a huge local following for its artful presentation of great Greek and Middle Eastern dishes. Right across the street is tiny **Village Pizzeria,** (360/221-3363) where the New York–style thin-crust pizza packs folks in on weekends. Get a slice to go if you're in a hurry. No credit cards.

Located atop a hill a five-minute walk from downtown, **Edgecliff Bar & Grill** (510 Cascade Ave., 360/221-8899, $13–26) has a diverse menu of steak, seafood, and Italian dishes. Prices are surprisingly reasonable given the upscale setting. Big windows offer striking 180-degree views of Saratoga Passage and the Cascades.

On the hill next to Langley's pocket park, **The Fish Bowl** (317 2nd St., 360/221-6511) is locally famous for fish (especially the seafood paella and clam chowder), but the duck breast and rack of lamb are equally delicious. No children.

For more proletarian fare, **Braeburn Restaurant** (197 2nd St., 360/221-3211, under $14) serves stuffed apple French toast or corned beef mash for breakfast, curry chicken salad (and lots more) for lunch, and country-style dinners of chicken and dumplings, meatloaf, and liver and onions.

Near the intersection of Highway 525 and Langley Road turnoff is **Trattoria Giuseppe** (360/341-3454, www.trattoriagiuseppe.com, $14–23) open for lunch and dinner with delicious Italian food and seafood in a romantic, white-linen setting. There's classical piano music Friday and Saturday evenings.

Dog House Tavern and Backdoor Restaurant (1st and Anthes, 360/221-9996) is a fun and funky place to have burgers, chili (don't ask for the recipe), fish and chips, or perhaps just a drink while enjoying the bay vistas. Built in 1908, this classic eatery keeps most of the menu items under $10. A pool table provides entertainment in the front room.

The **South Whidbey Tilth Farmers' Market** (Hwy. 525 at Thompson Rd., 360/579-1871, May–October 10 A.M.– 2 P.M. Sat.) offers all-organic fruits and vegetables, plus flowers, baked goods, and seafood. Held at the same time, the **Bayview Farmers Market** (Bayview Rd. at Hwy. 525, 360/221-6903) is located at the beautifully remodeled Cash Store.

The **M Inn at Langley** (400 1st St., 360/221-3033, www.innatlangley.com, year-round Fri.–Sun., $80/person, wine extra) features Whidbey's four-star restaurant, with six-course Northwest cuisine dinners. Celebrity chef Matt Costello puts on quite a performance in the open kitchen, explaining the meal as he prepares it. Highly recommended, but you may need to reserve space two weeks in advance.

Located at the Holmes Harbor Golf and Beach Club in Greenbank, **Beachfire Grill** (5023 Harbor Hills Dr., 360/331-2363, www.holmesharbor.com, $10–27) serves delicious steaks, grilled seafood, and regional specialties. On summer days, take in the water view from the deck, or relax in front of the fire when the weather isn't as agreeable.

Winery
Whidbey Island Winery (5237 S. Langley Rd., 360/221-2040, www.whidbeyislandwinery.com, tastings noon–5 P.M. daily, except Tues.) is a family operation that produces wines from estate-grown vinifera grapes, along with surprisingly good rhubarb wines. Stop for a picnic overlooking the adjacent vineyard and apple orchard.

Events
In late February, the **Langley Mystery Weekend** attracts sleuths in search of a make-believe murderer. Clues are planted all over town, and actors serve up information to help (or confuse) hundreds of amateur detectives. It's been going on for more than two decades. **Island County Fair,** (360/221-4677, www.islandweb.org/fair) is a four-day event in late August that includes a carnival, parade, music, and 4-H exhibits. For something a bit less countrified, return to Lang-

ley for **DjangoFest Northwest** (www.djangofest.com) on the first weekend of October, with Gypsy jazz celebrating the life and music of Django Reinhardt.

Shopping and Recreation
Moonraker Books (209 1st St., 360/221-6962) carries a fine selection of regional titles. **North Star Trading Co.** (101 1st St., 360/221-1202 or 800/446-9276, www.sheepskingoods.com) produces ultra-soft sheepskin slippers and hats.

Half Link Bicycle Shop (5603 Bayview Rd, 360/321-5275) rents bikes and provides free Whidbey Island road and trail maps. **Whidbey Island Kayaking Company** (360/321-4683, www.whidbeyislandkayaking.com) leads two-hour kayak trips from the southern end of the island.

Information and Services
Drop by the **Langley South Whidbey Chamber of Commerce** (208 Anthes St., 360/221-6765, www.whidbey.com/langley, 10 A.M.–5 P.M. daily) for the full scoop on Langley and vicinity. In the summer, hour-long **historical walking tours** of Langley depart from the visitor center; $5/person or $10/family.

The **Whidbey Island Center for the Arts** (565 Camano Ave., 360/221-8268 or 800/638-7631, www.whidbey.net/wica) features concerts and plays throughout the year. **Clyde Theatre** (217 1st St., 360/221-5525, www.theclyde.net) is the only place to watch first-run movies on the south end of Whidbey.

SOUTH WHIDBEY STATE PARK
Easily the island's most underrated park, South Whidbey State Park (360/331-4559) has outstanding hiking and picnicking, plus clamming and crabbing on a narrow sandy beach, campsites, and striking Olympic views. The 85 acres of old-growth Douglas fir and western red cedar protect resident black-tailed deer, foxes, raccoons, rabbits, bald eagles, ospreys, and pileated woodpeckers. Be sure to hike **Wilbert Trail,** a 1.5-mile path that circles through these ancient forests; it starts directly across from the park entrance. State park campsites are $16 for tents,

© DON PITCHER

Whidbey Island Greenbank Farm

or $22 for RVs with hookups. Make reservations ($7 extra) at 888/226-7688, www.parks.wa.gov. The park is open year-round, and a $5 day use fee is charged. Get to the park by heading east from Freeland on Bush Point Road; it becomes Smugglers Cove Road and continues past the park, a distance of seven miles.

WHIDBEY ISLAND GREENBANK FARM

The large red barn at Whidbey Island Greenbank Farm (14 miles north of the ferry dock at Clinton, 360/678-7700, www.greenbankfarm.com) is a well-known sight to anyone driving across Whidbey Island. Once the largest loganberry farm in the world, it is now owned by the county. New loganberry vines have been planted, and the farm's wine shop sells loganberry wine (produced elsewhere), along with grape and fruit wines from small local wineries. Besides wines, the shop also sells preserves, jellies, and loganberry wine–filled chocolates. In the summer, the farm is open 10 A.M.–5 P.M. daily; the rest of the year, 11 A.M.–4 P.M. Mon.–Fri. and 10 A.M.–5 P.M.

Sat.–Sun. Alpacas graze in the pasture out front, and the café serves delicious pies. A **Farmer's Market** takes place May–September 11 A.M.–3 P.M. Sundays.

MEERKERK RHODODENDRON GARDENS

This delightful garden (360/678-1912, www.meerkerkgardens.org, 9 A.M.–4 P.M daily, $5, free for children) boasts more than 1,500 varieties of rhododendron species and hybrids on a 53-acre site just south of Greenbank off Resort Road. Begun by Max and Anne Meerkerk in the 1960s, the gardens are now maintained by the Seattle Rhododendron Society. Peak season for "rhodies" is in late April and early May. By the way, the coast rhododendron is Washington's state flower.

FORT CASEY STATE PARK

Fort Casey State Park (360/678-4519, www.parks.wa.gov, $5) is a historic Army post three miles south of Coupeville next to the Keystone ferry dock. It has two miles of beach, an underwater park, a boat ramp, hiking trails, picnic areas, spectacular Olympic views, and campsites, plus good fishing in remarkably clear water.

History

Fort Casey was one of the "Iron Triangle" of forts that guarded the entrance to Puget Sound and the Bremerton Naval Shipyard at the turn of the century. This deadly crossfire consisted of Fort Casey, Fort Worden at Port Townsend, and Fort Flagler on Marrowstone Island; fortunately, the guns were never fired at an enemy vessel. Fort Casey's big weapons were the ingenious 10-inch disappearing carriage guns; the recoil sent them swinging back down out of sight for reloading, giving the sighter a terrific ride. By 1920, advances in naval warfare made them obsolete, so they were melted down. During World War II, Fort Casey was primarily a training site, although anti-aircraft guns were mounted on the fortifications. The fort was closed after the war and purchased by Washington in 1956 for a state park.

Sights

If you're arriving on Whidbey Island by ferry from Port Townsend, get to Fort Casey by taking an immediate left onto Engle Road as soon as you exit the ferry terminal. Much of the fort is open for public viewing, including ammunition bunkers, observation towers, underground storage facilities (bring your flashlight), gun catwalks, and the main attraction: two disappearing guns. Because the originals are long gone, these were brought here in 1968 from an old American fort in the Philippines.

Be sure to visit the **Admiralty Head Lighthouse Interpretive Center** (360/679-7391, June–Sept. 11 A.M.–5 P.M. Wed.–Sun.; reduced hours the rest of the year) where you can learn about coast artillery and the 1890 defense post. The lighthouse itself has not been used since 1927, but you can climb to the top for a wonderful view of Puget Sound and the Olympic Mountains. The hilltop location is a great place to watch ferries crossing from Port Townsend, and kids will have fun on the beach.

The fort's historic buildings are now used as a conference center and the Fort Casey Inn, both run by Seattle Pacific University (www.spu.edu/

depts/casey). Also nearby is shallow **Crockett Lake,** a good place to look for migratory and resident birds. The **Crockett Blockhouse,** one of four remaining fortifications built in the 1850s to defend against Native American attacks, stands on the north shore of the lake. An offshore underwater park is popular with divers. Northeast of Crockett Lake is Outlying Landing Field, used by Navy pilots to simulate aircraft-carrier landings.

Campgrounds

The small and crowded campground ($16 for tents, $22 for RVs hookups) at Fort Casey is open year-round and has showers. These exposed sites are right on the water next to the busy ferry terminal. Pleasant hiking trails lead through the wooded grounds and uphill to the fort's canons. No reservations, so get here early on summer weekends.

◪ EBEY'S LANDING NATIONAL HISTORICAL RESERVE

Ebey's Landing (360/678-6084, www.nps.gov/ebla), two miles southwest of Coupeville center, has easily the most striking coastal view on the island; no wonder portions of *Snow Falling on Cedars* were filmed here. As the roads wind through acres of rich farmland, the glimpses of water and cliff might remind you of the northern California or Oregon coastline; the majestic Olympics add to the drama.

Managed by the National Park Service and covering 17,400 acres, Ebey's Landing National Historical Reserve helps keep this land rural and agricultural through scenic easements, land donations, tax incentives, and zoning. Approximately 90 percent of the land remains in private hands. Created in 1978, this was America's first national historical reserve.

History

The native Skagit people were generally friendly toward the white settlers, but their northern neighbors were considerably less forgiving of the invaders. Alaska's Kake tribe of the Tlingit people had a fierce reputation, as exemplified

© DON PITCHER

Ebey's Landing National Historical Reserve

by the following incident recorded by Richard Meade (1871):

> *In 1855 a party of Kakes, on a visit south to Puget Sound, became involved in some trouble there, which caused a United States vessel to open fire on them, and during the affair one of the Kake chiefs was killed. This took place over 800 miles from the Kake settlements on Kupreanof Island. The very next year the tribe sent a canoe-load of fighting men all the way from Clarence Straits in Russian America to Whidby's Island in Washington Territory, and attacked and beheaded an ex-collector—not of internal revenue, for that might have been pardonable—but of customs, and returned safely with his skull and scalp to their villages. Such people are, therefore, not to be despised, and are quite capable of giving much trouble in the future unless wisely and firmly governed.*

The beheaded man was Col. Isaac Ebey, the first settler on Whidbey Island; his head was eventually recovered and reunited with his body before being buried at Sunnyside Cemetery. To fend off further attacks (which never came), the pioneers built seven blockhouses in the 1850s, four of which still stand.

The Anglo settlers were attracted to this part of Whidbey Island by the expansive prairies and fertile black soil. These prairies occupy the sites of shallow Ice Age lakes; when the water dried up, the rich, deep soil remained. The indigenous practice of burning helped keep them open over the centuries that followed, and the white settlers simply took up residence on this prime land.

Sights

The main attraction at Ebey's Landing National Historical Reserve is simply the country itself: bucolic farmland, densely wooded ridges, and steep coastal bluffs. Pick up an informative tour brochure, which describes a detailed tour of Ebey's Landing, at the Coupeville museum.

For a scenic bike ride or drive, turn onto Hill Road (two miles south of Coupeville) and follow it through the second-growth stand of Douglas fir trees. It emerges on a high bluff overlooking Admiralty Inlet before dropping to the shoreline at tiny **Ebey's Landing State Park.** From the small parking area at the water's edge, hike the 1.5-mile trail along the bluff above **Parego Lagoon** for a view of the coastline, Olympics, and the Strait of Juan de Fuca that shouldn't be missed. The lagoon is a fine place to look for migratory birds. Return along the beach, or continue northward to Fort Ebey State Park (three miles from Ebey's Landing). Along the way, keep your eyes open for gem-quality stones, such as agate, jasper, and black and green jade, plus quartz and petrified wood.

Another trail leads 1.4 miles from Ebey's Landing to **Sunnyside Cemetery,** where you can look north to snowcapped Mount Baker and south to Mount Rainier on a clear day. The cemetery is also accessible from Cook Road. The **Davis Blockhouse,** another of the blockhouses used to defend against Tlingit and Haida attacks, stands at the edge of the cemetery; it was moved here in 1915. Colonel Isaac Ebey is buried here.

COUPEVILLE

The second oldest town in Washington, the "Port of Sea Captains" was founded and laid out in 1852 by Capt. Thomas Coupe, the first man to sail through Deception Pass. The protected harbor at Penn Cove was a perfect site for the village that became Coupeville (pop. 1,700). Timber from Whidbey was shipped to San Francisco to feed the building boom created by the gold rush. Today, modern businesses operate from Victorian-era buildings amid the nation's largest historical preservation district. Coupeville is the county seat for Island County, and has the only public hospital on Whidbey. Downtown has an immaculate cluster of false-fronted shops and restaurants right on the harbor and a long wharf that was once used to ship local produce and logs to the mainland. This is a cat-friendly town; perhaps half the downtown businesses have one inside. Summer weekends are busy times in Coupeville, but in the winter months, life in Coupeville slows to a crawl and downtown is a very quiet place.

Sights

Island County Historical Society Museum (Alexander and Front Sts., 360/678-3310) has pioneer relics, including a shadowbox with flowers made from human hair, interesting newsreels from the 1930s on the Indian Water Festival, a 1902 Holsman car (first car on Whidbey), woolly mammoth bones, and changing exhibits. Out front is a garden with drought-tolerant native plants and herbs. The museum is open May–Sept. 10 A.M.–5 P.M. Wed.–Mon.; the rest of the year 11 A.M.– 4 P.M. Fri.–Mon. Entrance is $3 for adults, $2.50 for seniors, students, and military personnel, $6 for families, and free for kids under five.

Another of the original Whidbey Island fortifications, the **Alexander Blockhouse,** built in 1855, stands outside the museum, along with a shelter housing two turn-of-the-century Native American racing canoes.

Penn Cove

For a scenic drive, head northwest from Coupeville along Madrona Way, named for the Pacific madrone or madronatrees whose distinctive red bark and leathery green leaves line the roadway. Quite a few summer cottages and cozy homes can be found here, along with the one-of-a-kind Captain Whidbey Inn. Offshore are dozens of floating pens where mussels grow on lines hanging in Penn Cove. On the northwest corner of Penn Cove, Highway 20 passes scenic **Grasser's Hill,** where hedgerows alternate with open farmland. Development restrictions prevent this open country from becoming a mass of condos. Just north of here are the historic **San de Fuca schoolhouse** and Whidbey Inn.

Fort Ebey State Park

Located southwest of Coupeville on Admiralty Inlet, Fort Ebey State Park (360/678-4636, www.parks.wa.gov, $5) has campsites, a large picnic area, three miles of beach, and two miles of hiking trails within its 644 acres. The fort was constructed during World War II, though its gun batteries were never needed. The concrete platforms remain, along with cavernous bunkers, but the big guns have long since been removed. Thanks to its location in the Olympic rain shadow, the park is one of the few places in western Washington where cactus grows, but it also has stands of second-growth forest and great views across the Strait of Juan de Fuca.

Although not as well known as other parks on Whidbey, Fort Ebey is still a favorite summertime spot. Much of its popularity stems from tiny **Lake Pondilla,** a glacial sinkhole—and a bass fisher's and swimmer's delight. Follow the signs from the north parking lot for a two-block hike to the lake; half a dozen picnic tables and a camping area are reserved for hikers and bicyclists. Other trails lead along the bluffs south from here, and down to the beach. Adventurous folks (after consulting a tide chart and with a bit of care) can walk all the way to Fort Casey State Park, eight miles away.

Accommodations

Coupeville is blessed with many historic buildings, several of which have been turned into bed-and-breakfasts and inns. Be sure to make advance reservations, especially on summer weekends. Useful websites with links to local lodging places are www.coupevillelodging.com and www.come-tocoupeville.com.

Hotels and Inns

Tyee Motel (405 S. Main St., 360/678-6616, www.tyeehotel.com, $65 d) provides simple accommodations at an affordable price. A restaurant and lounge are on the premises. Right in town, **Coupeville Inn** (200 N.W. Coveland St., 360/678-6668 or 800/247-6162, www.coupeville inn.com, $83–127 d) has standard motel rooms with waterside views of Penn Cove.

Captain Whidbey Inn (2072 W. Captain Whidbey Inn Rd., 360/678-4097 or 800/366-4097, www.captainwhidbey.com, $85–95 d, $155 d suites) is a classic two-story inn built in 1907 from madrone logs. It also features modern cabins and cottages ($175–185 d). Add $15 to these prices for a big breakfast for two. The expansive grounds, studded with Pacific madrone trees, face Penn Cove. Even if you aren't staying here, be sure to stop and take in the scenery or sip a drink in the bar. The lodge also operates a 52-foot wooden ketch, the *Cutty Sark,* with sailing trips on Saturdays in the summer; $33/person for a two-hour cruise.

Right next to Fort Casey State Park, **Fort Casey Inn** (360/678-5050 or 866/661-6604,

© DON PITCHER

Captain Whidbey Inn is a historic and picturesque Coupeville lodging.

www.fortcaseyinn.com) consists of 10 restored Georgian Revival homes that served as officers' quarters during World War I. These large two-story homes are divided into two units each, with complete kitchens and private baths. Basements were built to be used as bomb shelters in case of attack and some still have the original steel-shuttered windows. These duplexes sleep four or five, and rent for $145 d, plus $20/person for additional adults. One motel-style unit is also available for $75 d. Fort Casey Inn is owned by Seattle Pacific University.

A mile and a half south of town and right on the highway is **Countryside Inn** (360/678-5610, $68–135 d), with remodeled rooms, some of which include full kitchens. The courtyard out back is great for relaxing in the evening.

Cottage on the Cove (6 Front St., 360/678-0600 or 800/720-5019, www.cottageonthe-cove.com, $135 for up to four) is a homey little place close to downtown, with a full kitchen, loft, and private deck. There's a two-night minimum on weekends.

Bed-and-Breakfasts

Anchorage Inn B&B (807 N. Main St., 360/678-5581 or 877/230-1313, www.anchorage-inn.com, $85–140 d) has seven guest rooms (all with private baths) in a large and luxurious Victorian-style inn. They also have an historic two-bedroom cottage that's perfect for families; $150 for up to six.

One of the most striking local places is **Compass Rose B&B** (508 S. Main St., 360/678-5318 or 800/237-3881, www.compassroseband b.com, $95 d), a Queen Anne Victorian home built in 1890 and packed with antiques. The two guest rooms have private baths. Well-behaved kids are welcome. Friendly owners, too.

The Inn at Penn Cove B&B (702 N. Main, 360/678-8000 or 800/688-2683, www .whidbey.net/penncove, $60–125 d) spreads across two lovingly restored Victorian homes built in 1887 and 1891. Inside each are three guest rooms, some of which have fireplaces. The less expensive rooms are on the small side and share a bath, but all guests have access to common areas in both buildings and enjoy a hearty breakfast. Kids are accepted with advance notice.

Old Morris Farmhouse B&B (south of Coupeville at 105 W. Morris Rd., 360/678-6586 or 866/440-1555, www.morrisfarm-house.com, $85–110 d) is a comfortable 1908 home on 10 acres of forests and verdant gardens. Six guest rooms have shared or private baths. A filling breakfast is served, and the owners welcome both kids and pets. The farm is a popular wedding spot.

The Victorian B&B (602 N. Main St., 360/678-5305, www.whidbeyvictorianbandb.com) is a beautiful two-story home built in 1889. Stay in a separate cottage ($125 d) or one of the two guest rooms in the house ($90 d) with a full breakfast. Kids are welcome. The first-floor restaurant (Rosi's) is popular for lunch and dinner.

Campgrounds

Find year-round camping at **Fort Casey State Park** (three miles south of Coupeville, 360/678-4519, $16 tents or $22 RVs) or **Fort Ebey State Park** (five miles west of Coupeville, 360/678-4636 or 888/226-7688 for reservations, www .parks.wa.gov). Both are open year-round. No advance reservations for Fort Casey, but campsites at Fort Ebey can be reserved ($7 extra).

Rhododendron Park, a Department of Natural Resources park, is two miles east of Coupeville on Highway 20. It's easy to miss; look for the small blue camping sign on the highway. Here you'll find six free in-the-woods campsites (with water) in a second-growth stand of Douglas firs. The understory blooms with rhododendrons in April and May.

Food

Great Times Waterfront Coffee House (12 N.W. Front St., 360/678-5860) has a patio right on the water, plus espresso and sweets. Get good homemade soups, fresh-baked breads, and enormous cinnamon rolls at the unpretentious **Knead & Feed Bakery Restaurant** (downstairs at 4 N.W. Front St., 360/678-5431), with full breakfasts on weekends.

Find dependably good pub grub, including fish and chips, Reubens, and mussel chowder, at **Toby's Tavern** (8 N.W. Front St., 360/678-4222, www.tobysuds.com). The 1884 red building *is* a bar, so no kids allowed. Across the street is **Christopher's** (23 N.W. Front St., 360/678-5480, $13–20), which lacks the view, but its menu is less greasy. Featured are seafood, chicken, steaks, soups, and sandwiches.

The Oystercatcher (901 Grace St., 360/678-0683, $18–25), is a delightful little out-of-the-way place where the limited menu changes frequently, but always includes oyster and mussel hors d'oeuvres.

Housed within Captain Whidbey Inn, **The Cove Restaurant** (2072 W. Captain Whidbey Inn Rd., 360/678-9325, www.captainwhidbey.com, $30–33) serves some of the finest seafood on Whidbey—including fresh Penn Cove mussels—in a pleasantly nautical setting. Chef James Roberts has gained a regional reputation for his creative dishes. Open three meals a day; reservations recommended for dinner.

The **Coupeville Farmers Market** (8th and Main Sts., 360/678-6757) is held April to mid-October 10 A.M.–2 P.M. Saturdays.

Housed in a grand Victorian home that doubles as a bed-and-breakfast, **Rosi's Garden Restaurant** (602 N. Main St., 360/678-5305, www.whidbeyvictorianbandb.com, $16–32) serves Northwest lunches and dinners that include fresh seafood, pasta, pizzas, salads, and creative desserts.

The Arts

A couple of local galleries are well worth a look: the cooperatively run **Penn Cove Gallery** (9 N.W. Front St., 360/678-1176, www.penncovegallery.com) and **Blue Heron Studio** (98 Front St., 360/678-9052, www.barbaramarks.com).

Coupeville Arts Center (15 N.W. Birch St., 360/678-3396, www.coupevillearts.org) teaches a wide range of first-rate workshops throughout the year, from photography to watercolor to fiber arts.

Information and Services

The Central Whidbey Chamber of Commerce's **Visitor & Information Center** (107 S. Main St., 360/678-5434, www.centralwhidbeycham-

ber.com, 10:30 A.M.–4:30 P.M. Mon. and Thurs.-Sat., 1–4:30 P.M. Sun.) is on the south side of town. Another helpful website is www.cometocoupeville.com.

Whidbey General Hospital (101 N. Main St., 360/678-5151, www.whidbeygen.org) is the only public hospital on the island.

OAK HARBOR

Settled first by sea captains, then the Irish, and at the turn of the 20th century by immigrants from Holland, Oak Harbor (pop. 20,000) takes its name from the many ancient Garry oak trees that grew here; those remaining are protected by law. The city was founded by three men in the early 1850s: a Swiss named Ulrich Freund, a Norwegian named Martin Tafton, and a New Englander named C.W. Sumner. The military arrived during World War II and transformed this town into a busy place.

The city's historic waterside downtown retains considerable character and is worth a detour, but the main drag—State Route 20—is yet another sad example of the malling of America. This is the only place on the island where you'll find burger joints, shopping malls, traffic jams, and noise. It's on a far smaller scale than many Puget Sound cities, but comes as a shock if you've just driven in from genteel Coupeville and Langley.

Whidbey Island Naval Air Station

Oak Harbor's main employer is the largest naval air base in the Northwest, Whidbey Island Naval Air Station (360/257-2211, www.naswi.navy.mil). It is home to electronic warfare squadrons of EA-6B carrier-based jets, EA-6B Prowlers, and EP-3E surveillance planes, and employs 9,000 military and civilian personnel.

Recreation

City Beach Park, on Beeksma Drive, has a sandy beach with piles of driftwood, sheltered picnic tables, swimming and wading pools, a gazebo, tennis courts and baseball diamonds, campsites, and a Dutch-style windmill. There's a nice view of the peaceful and protected harbor from here, and a great kiddie playground. Look for ducks along the shore. **Smith Park** at Midway Boulevard has a fine collection of old Garry oak trees and a large boulder left behind by the last Ice Age.

Joseph Whidbey State Park (www.parks .wa.gov, $5), just south of the Naval Air Station on Swantown Road, is largely undeveloped, with picnic tables and a few trails. The real attraction here is a long and scenic beach, one of the finest on the island.

The hip-roofed **Neil Barn** (100 E. Whidbey Ave.) was once the largest barn on the West Coast. Today it is owned by the city parks department and used as a roller-skating rink. The distinctive water tower out front now houses a small historical museum that's open occasionally. **Hummingbird Farm Nursery** (2319 Zylstra Rd., 360/679-5044, www.hummingbirdfarmnursery.com) has extensive display gardens, a nursery, and garden shop.

For something completely different, **Blue Fox Drive-In Theatre** (two miles south of town at 1403 Monroe Landing Rd., 360/675-5667, www.bluefoxdrivein.com) is one of only five surviving outdoor movie theaters in Washington.

Swim at **City Beach Park** in the summer or the year-round indoor pool (85 S.E. Jerome St., 360/675-7667), which also includes a sauna, two Jacuzzis, and a wading pool. The city is home to the 18-hole **Gallery Golf Course** (Crosby Rd., 360/257-2295). Rent kayaks at the marina from **Adventure Marine** (360/675-9395).

Accommodations

Oak Harbor has some of the least expensive lodging on Whidbey Island. **Auld Holland Inn** (33575 State Rt. 20, 360/675-2288 or 800/228-0148, www.auldhollandinn.com) is a Dutch-style motel with an outdoor pool, Jacuzzi, sauna, tennis court, exercise room, and lawn games. Rates start at $59 d for a standard room, up to $149 d for the windmill suite.

Best Western Harbor Plaza (33175 State Rt. 20, 360/679-4567 or 800/927-5478, www.best-western.com/harborplaza, $109 s or $119 d) is another fine place, with an outdoor pool, Jacuzzi, fitness center, microwaves, fridges, and continental breakfast.

Coachman Inn (35959 State Rt. 20, 360/

675-0727 or 800/635-0043, www.thecoachman inn.com) has an outdoor pool, exercise room, fridges, and continental breakfast. Rooms range from simple units ($75 d) to Jacuzzi suites ($110–199 d) and even a two-bedroom townhouse apartment ($150 for up to six).

Camping

City Beach Park (at the end of Beeksma Dr., 360/679-5551, $12 tents, $20 RVs with full hookups) has campsites along the lagoon. No reservations, but the park does have hot showers. Beautiful **Deception Pass State Park** (360/675-2417, www.parks.wa.gov, $16 tents, $22 RVs) is located nine miles north. In addition, the local Wal-Mart parking lot (1250 S.W. Erie St., 360/279-0665) becomes an unofficial RV park each summer.

Food

As might be expected given the strong military presence in Oak Harbor, most eating places serve up the traditional American food groups: McDonald's, pizza, and steak. A better bet is **Kasteel Franssen** at the Auld Holland Inn (33575 State Rt. 20, 360/675-2288 or 800/228-0148, www .kasteelfranssen.com), specializing in seafood, European cuisine, and excellent desserts. Good service, but try to ignore the faux-Dutch trappings.

Get authentic Mexican fare at **Esteban's Mexican Restaurant** (31359 State Rt. 20, 360/675-4800).

Oak Harbor's historic downtown is home to several of the best local restaurants, including **Zorba's** (841 S.E. Pioneer Way, 360/279-8322, closed Sundays), a delightful Greek restaurant that gets very busy (and loud) most evenings. **Erawan Thai Cuisine** (885 S.E. Pioneer Way, 360/679-8268, www.eatspicythai.com) serves Thai meals and sushi. A few doors away, switch continents for **P.W. Murphy's** (930 S.E. Pioneer Way, 360/279-2528), with hearty Irish pub grub. **Big Cup Coffee** (670 S.E. Pioneer Way, 360/675-4053) is the local latte joint.

Just a mile south of Deception Pass Bridge, **Seabolt's Smokehouse** (360/675-6485 or 800/574-1120, www.seabolts.com) produces tasty smoked salmon, beef jerky, and tuna.

The **Oak Harbor Public Market** (next to the visitor center, 360/675-0472) takes place June–September 3–7 P.M. Thursdays.

Information and Arts

The **Oak Harbor Visitor Center** (32630 Hwy. 20, 360/675-3535, www.oakharborchamber.org) is open year-round 9 A.M.–5 P.M. Monday–Friday; in the summer 10 A.M.–4 P.M. Saturdays.

Get books downtown at **Wind & Tide Bookshop** (790 S.E. Pioneer Way, 360/675-1342).

Whidbey Playhouse (730 S.E. Midway Blvd., 360/679-2237 or 800/606-7529, www.whidbeyplayhouse.com) puts on plays throughout the year.

Events

Holland Happening on the last weekend of April includes a street fair, parade, and international dance festival. The **4th of July** festivities include a parade and fireworks, followed in mid-July by **Whidbey Island Race Week** (206/286-1004, www.whidbey.com/raceweek), one of the top-20 yachting regattas in the world.

Bellingham

With a population of more than 70,000, Bellingham is no longer a town, though it still maintains a friendly small-town feel. The city is an almost perfect blend of the old and the new, with stately homes, extraordinary museums, and an abundance of cultural events, plus many fine shops and restaurants. Bellingham has managed to hold onto both its blue-collar paper-mill jobs and white-collar positions at Western Washington University, while attracting increasing numbers of tourists.

The city is a jumping-off point for private ferries and whale-watching trips to the San Juan Islands, and is also the base for northbound travelers taking Alaska Marine Highway ferries. The terminal for all of these boats is in Bellingham's historic Fairhaven district. In addition, it is only 43 miles to the ferry terminal at Anacortes, and the route takes you along beautiful Chuckanut Drive. Because of this, Bellingham is a popular stopping point for people driving down from Vancouver en route to the San Juans.

SIGHTS

Fairhaven

This historic section of Bellingham has quite a few buildings constructed in the late 1880s. At the time, rumors were circulating that Fairhaven would be the western terminus for the Great Northern Railroad. The railroad chose Tacoma instead, and the buildings are now part of the Fairhaven Historic District. Walking-tour maps of the area are available from the visitors bureau. A wonderful two-mile paved walkway connects Fairhaven with downtown Bellingham, including a portion that extends into the bay.

© DON PITCHER

Fairhaven Historic District

BELLINGHAM

To Mt Baker
542
BARKLEY VILLAGE

To Big Rock
Garden Park

ALABAMA ST
IOWA ST
EXIT 254
5

JAMES ST

BAKERVIEW RD

EXIT 255

ST JOSEPH'S
HOSPITAL
ELLIS ST

BEST WESTERN HERITAGE INN
RODEWAY INN

Cornwall
Park

D ST
F ST

BROADWAY
GIRARD ST

ILLINOIS ST

MERIDIAN ST

MARITIME
HERITAGE
CENTER

539
EXIT 256

ELM AVE

DUPONT ST

BELLIS
FAIR MALL

KELLOGG AVE

SQUALICUM WAY
Squalicum Creek

WALNUT ST

JEFFERSON ST

MONROE ST
DECANN HOUSE B&B

ELDRIDGE AVE

EXIT 257

NORTHWEST AVE

MAPLEWOOD AVE

MCLEOD RD

5

MARINE DR

Squalicum
Harbor

To Vancouver, BC

EXIT 258

BENNETT RD

Gateways to the Islands

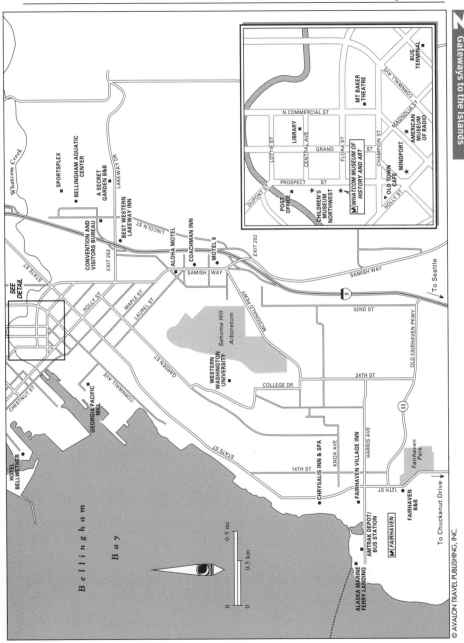

SEE DETAIL

Inset map labels:

- BUS TERMINAL
- CORNWALL AVE
- MAGNOLIA ST
- AMERICAN MUSEUM OF RADIO
- MT BAKER THEATRE
- N COMMERCIAL ST
- LIBRARY
- LOTTIE ST
- CENTRAL AVE
- GRAND
- FLORA ST
- CHAMPION ST
- MINDPORT
- OLD TOWN CAFÉ
- HOLLY ST
- PROSPECT ST
- DUPONT ST
- POST OFFICE
- CHILDREN'S MUSEUM NORTHWEST
- WHATCOM MUSEUM OF HISTORY AND ART
- EXIT 252

Main map labels:

- Whatcom Creek
- SPORTSPLEX
- BELLINGHAM AQUATIC CENTER
- A SECRET GARDEN B&B
- LAKEWAY DR
- CONVENTION AND VISITORS BUREAU
- EXIT 253
- BEST WESTERN LAKEWAY INN
- LINCOLN ST
- STATE ST
- HOLLY ST
- MAPLE ST
- LAUREL ST
- ALOHA MOTEL
- COACHMAN INN
- MOTEL 6
- SAMISH WAY
- MCDONALD PKWY
- Sehome Hill Arboretum
- GARDEN ST
- WESTERN WASHINGTON UNIVERSITY
- COLLEGE DR
- 32ND ST
- OLD FAIRHAVEN PKWY
- SAMISH WAY
- To Seattle
- CHESTNUT ST
- CORNWALL AVE
- GEORGIA PACIFIC MILL
- STATE ST
- 24TH ST
- HOTEL BELLWETHER
- CHRYSALIS INN & SPA
- FAIRHAVEN VILLAGE INN
- 14TH ST
- KNOX AVE
- HARRIS AVE
- Fairhaven Park
- 12TH ST
- FAIRHAVEN B&B
- To Chuckanut Drive
- Bellingham Bay
- AMTRAK DEPOT/BUS STATION
- FAIRHAVEN
- ALASKA MARINE FERRY LANDING
- 0   0.5 mi
- 0   0.5 km

Several interesting shops and galleries can be found in the district. **Good Earth Pottery** (1000 Harris Ave., 360/671-3998) has fine ceramics. In the same building, the cooperatively owned **Artwood** (360/647-1628, www.pacificws.com/artwood) sells handcrafted woodworking. **Gallery West** (1300 12th St., 360/734-8414) has paintings, sculptures, pottery, weavings, and jewelry.

One of the most popular places in Fairhaven—or in all of Bellingham for that matter—is **Village Books** (1200 11th St., 360/671-2626 or 800/392-2665, www.villagebooks.com) and its companion, **Colophon Café,** downstairs. Village Books has frequent book readings, workshops, and signings. A fine shop with used titles is **Eclipse Bookstore** (1104 11th Ave., 360/647-8165).

Whatcom Museum of History and Art

Located on a high bluff overlooking Bellingham Bay, the **Whatcom Museum of History and Art** (121 Prospect St., 360/676-6981, www.whatcommuseum.org, free) is housed in the old city

© DON PITCHER

The Whatcom Museum of History and Art is located in the old City Hall building.

hall, an ornate red-brick building capped by a four-corner cupola and a tall clock tower. The old city hall building was built in 1892, and remained in use until 1939. Today, the museum has expanded to include three nearby collections. Hours for all but the Children's Museum are year-round noon–5 P.M. Tuesday–Sunday.

The main building contains historical displays, changing exhibits, and a small gift shop with unusual items from around the globe. Next door is the **Syre Education Center,** featuring beautiful Native American baskets, bentwood boxes, reed mats, and even a Chilkoot blanket, plus a large number of stuffed birds. Also here are displays on the early days of Northwest logging—including the famous Darius Kinsey collection of images. These and thousands of other historical photographs make the archives one of the most complete in Washington.

Two nearby structures house separate collections that are also part of the Whatcom Museum "campus." The **Arco Exhibits Building** (across the street at 206 Prospect), houses changing fine-art and historical exhibits. The **Children's Museum** (227 Prospect St., 360/733-8769, $2.50), has many participatory exhibits for kids of all ages, including an infant/toddler exploration center and puppet theater. Open noon–5 P.M. Sunday, Tuesday, and Wednesday; 10 A.M.– 5 P.M. Thursday–Saturday.

Other Museums

Make it a point to visit **Mindport** (210 W. Holly St., 360/647-5614, www.mindport.org, noon–6 P.M. Wed.–Fri., 10 A.M.–5 P.M. Sat., and noon–4 P.M. Sun., $2), a creative center that will amuse, fascinate, and educate both kids and adults. The exhibits are mostly made from reused old junk, with a touch of whimsy thrown in. Great fun.

For something completely different, check out the unique **American Museum of Radio** (1312 Bay St., 360/738-3886, www.americanradiomuseum.org, 11 A.M.–4 P.M Wed.–Sat., $4), with more than a thousand radios, some dating from the early 1900s.

The **Bellingham Railway Museum** (1320 Commercial St., 360/393-7540, www.bellinghamrailwaymuseum.org, noon–5 P.M. Thurs.–Sat.,

$3, $1 for kids) features exhibits on historic railroads and has model-railroad displays.

Something Fishy

Bellingham's **Maritime Life Center** (1600 C St., 360/676-6806, 9 A.M.–dusk daily, free) is an urban park where you can fish for salmon and steelhead on Whatcom Creek, watch salmon spawning in mid-October, and learn about hatchery operation. Kids will enjoy the marine life touch tank, where they can pet intertidal creatures. It's located inside the Harbor Center Mall at Squalicum Harbor off Roeder Avenue.

CHUCKANUT DRIVE

One of the most scenic stretches of highway in the state, Chuckanut Drive (Hwy. 11, www .chuckanutdrive.com) stretches south from Fairhaven and then across Skagit Valley. The road doesn't have a straight stretch for seven miles as it swoops and swerves along the face of a cliff.

Chuckanut Drive, south of Bellingham

Grand views span across to Anacortes, Guemes Island, and, farther north, the San Juan Islands. With no shoulder, a narrow strip of pavement, and tight corners, it's a bit dicey for bikes (especially on weekends when traffic is heaviest), but the views are stunning. Several restaurants dot Chuckanut Drive. You will also pass the road to **Taylor Shellfish Farm** (360/766-6002, www.tay-lorshellfish.com), which has fresh oysters, clams (including geoduck), scallops, and mussels; they're the largest producers of Manila clams in the United States.

Larrabee State Park

Established in 1923, this was the first Washington state park. Larrabee State Park (360/676-2093, www.parks.wa.gov, $5) occupies one of the most beautiful stretches of mountainous country along Chuckanut Drive, and has a popular campground. Covering more than 2,500 acres, the park borders Samish Bay and boasts a boat launch, a sandy beach for sunning, and tidepools for marine explorations. Nine miles of hiking trails include the southern end of the **Interurban Trail,** connecting the park with Bellingham. Other trails lead to scenic Fragrance and Lost Lakes for trout fishing and to dramatic vistas from the 1,941-foot summit of **Chuckanut Mountain** (also accessible via a gravel road).

CITY AND COUNTY PARKS

Whatcom County (360/676-6985, www.co.what com.wa.us/parks) has one of the best collections of city- and county-owned parks in the state. In Bellingham alone, there are more than 35 places that qualify as parks, including greenbelts, fitness areas, and trails. These parks range from less than half an acre to more than a thousand acres.

Beautiful **Samish Park** (at I-5 Exit 246 south of Bellingham, 360/733-2362), is a 39-acre county park along Lake Samish with swimming, fishing, boating, picnicking, hiking, boat rentals, and a playground.

Whatcom Falls Park (near Lake Whatcom at 1401 Electric Ave.) has hiking trails, tennis courts, a playground, a picnic area, and a state fish

© DON PITCHER

hatchery on 241 acres. With 12 acres on the lake itself, **Bloedel Donovan Park** (2214 Electric Ave.) includes a swimming beach, boat launch, playground, and picnic area.

Lake Padden Park (4882 Samish Way) has more than 1,000 acres of hiking and horse trails, a golf course, picnic areas, and a playground, plus swimming, fishing, and non-motorized boating on the lake.

RECREATION

Hiking

Stop by the visitors bureau for descriptions and maps of more than 20 hiking trails in and around Bellingham, including trails in Whatcom Falls Park and Sehome Hill Arboretum. Another 2.6 miles of paths circle Lake Padden Park.

The **Interurban Trail** is a six-mile path that follows a former railroad bed from Old Fairhaven Parkway south to Larrabee State Park. It's a great place for a jog or bike ride.

Equipping for the Outdoors

Rent sea kayaks, rowboats, and sailboats in summer from **Fairhaven Boatworks** (501 Harris Ave., 360/714-8891). **Bellingham Boat Rentals** (3034 Silvern Lane, 360/676-1363) has canoes and pedal boats for rent on Lake Whatcom; open May–August.

Brenthaven (200 W. Holly St., 360/752-5537 or 888/212-5301, www.brenthaven.com), sews and sells high-quality day packs, shoulder bags, and soft luggage. Rent bikes from **Fairhaven Bike & Mountain Sport** (1103 11th St., 360/733-4433, www.fairhavenbike.com).

Swimming and Skating

Bellingham's **Arnie Hanna Aquatic Center** (1114 Potter St., 360/657-7665) has an indoor pool, wading pool, diving tank, and waterslide. A second pool is available at **Whatcom Family YMCA** (1256 N. State St., 360/763-8630). In the summer, you can also swim at **Lake Padden Park** (4882 Samish Way, 360/676-6985), **Lake Samish** (673 N. Lake Samish Dr., 360/733-2362), and **Bloedel Donovan Park** (2214 Electric Ave., 360/676-6985).

Sportsplex (1225 Civic Field Way, 360/733-9999) has indoor ice skating year-round.

Sailing

The visitors bureau has a complete listing of sailing and fishing charter operators and cruises. **Gato Verde Adventure Sailing** (360/220-3215, www.gatoverde.com) sails a 42-foot catamaran on day trips from Bellingham. Prices start at $30/person for a 1.5-hour sunset cruise (minimum of four). All-day and multi-day trips are also available.

Sail the San Juans (360/671-5852 or 800/729-3207, www.sailthesanjuans.com) offers six-day fully crewed charters around the islands, departing from Bellingham. The 50-foot *Northwind* comfortably accommodates six guests.

Kayaking and Whale-Watching

Moondance Sea Kayaking Adventures (360/738-7664, www.moondancekayak.com) leads sea kayak tours in the area, from half-day paddles to seven-day adventures.

Island Mariner Cruises (5 Harbor Loop, 360/734-8866 or 877/734-8866, www.orcawatch.com) operates the largest whale-watching boat in the area, the 110-foot *Island Caper,* with space for 100 passengers. Seven-hour trips are $55/person (same rate for children). Also popular are two-and-a-half-hour narrated historical harbor cruises for $20/person. These are offered Thursday evenings mid-June to mid-August.

Based at the ferry terminal in Fairhaven, **Great Orca Adventures** (360/734-3431 or 800/480-4390, www.orcawhales.com) provides four-hour whale-watching trips aboard a high-speed catamaran. They operate late May–September, with twice-daily trips in the peak season. Trips cost $65 adults, $60 seniors, or $55 for children and students.

ACCOMMODATIONS

The **Bellingham and Whatcom County Convention and Visitors Bureau** (904 Potter St., 360/671-3990 or 800/487-2032, www.bellingham.org) keeps track of local lodging availability on weekends during the summer months. Stop here for brochures, discount coupons, or to check out photographs of local bed-and-breakfasts. An abundance of weekend soccer tournaments makes for crowded conditions in summer. The CVB has a Bellingham Best Buys (888/261-7795, www.bellingham.org) program with substantial discounts—up to 50 percent in the off-season—for selected local hotels.

Surprisingly, there are no hostels in Bellingham. The closest one is the seasonal **Birch Bay Hostel** (360/371-2180, www.biz.birchbay.net/hostel) 15 miles north of Bellingham.

Hotels and Inns Under $100

Shangri-La Downtown Motel (611 E. Holly St., 360/733-7050) is a good in-town lodging choice. Weekend summertime rates are $49 s or $51–55 d; subtract $10 if you visit on a weekday. Kitchenettes are available. Those on a budget should also consider **Aloha Motel** (315 N. Samish Way, 360/733-4900, $45 d), where all rooms include microwaves and fridges.

Motel 6 (3701 Byron St., I-5 Exit 252, 360/671-4494 or 800/466-8356, www.motel6.com, $64 s or $70 d) has an outdoor pool. Avoid rooms on the noisy freeway side if you're a light sleeper.

Coachman Inn (120 N. Samish Way, 360/671-9000 or 800/962-6641, www.coachman innmotel.com, $45 s or $50–55 d) has an outdoor pool.

Travel House Inn (3570 Meridian St., 360/671-4600 or 800/633-8300, $44 s or $49–54 d) is a large in-town motel with an outdoor pool, Jacuzzi, and continental breakfast.

Rodeway Inn (across from Bellis Fair Mall at 3710 Meridian St., 360/738-6000, 800/476-5413 U.S., or 800/543-5478 Canada, www.rodeway.com), is a deal at $70–90 d on weekends or $50–60 d on weekdays, including continental breakfast and a Jacuzzi.

Best Western Heritage Inn (151 E. McLeod Rd., 360/647-1912 or 800/528-1234, www.bestwestern.com/heritageinnbellingham, $89 d), has the look of a New England Colonial building and features attractive grounds, fashionable rooms, an outdoor pool, Jacuzzi, fitness center pass, airport shuttle service, and a continental breakfast. Ask for a room facing away from noisy I-5.

Hampton Inn (3985 Bennett, 360/676-7700 or 800/426-7866, www.hamptoninn-bellingham.com, $89–109 d), offers comfortable accommodations that are popular with business travelers. It offers a heated seasonal outdoor pool, buffet breakfast, and airport and ferry shuttle. Some rooms have jetted tubs.

Hotels and Inns Over $100

Best Western Lakeway Inn (714 Lakeway Dr., I-5 Exit 256, 360/671-1011 or 888/671-1011, www.bellingham-hotel.com, $119–149 d), is one of Bellingham's better hotels, with an indoor pool, exercise room, Jacuzzi, sauna, Internet access, and airport shuttle. It's a favorite of business travelers, who appreciate the comfortable rooms and large conference center.

Fairhaven Village Inn (1200 10th St., 360/733-1311 or 877/733-1100, www.fairhavenvillageinn.com, $139–159 d rooms, $279 d suites) is a 22-room boutique hotel that blends well with its historic Fairhaven neighbors. Rooms are large and include gas fireplaces, king beds, continental breakfast, high-speed Internet, and other amenities.

One of Bellingham's most indulgent lodging choices, **Hotel Bellwether** (1 Bellwether Way, 360/392-3100 or 877/411-1200, www.hotelbellwether.com) offers a waterfront location, large rooms (many with king beds), balconies, Italian furnishings, gas fireplaces, large TVs, marble baths with jetted tubs, and a lavish breakfast buffet. Weekend rates start at $209 d for the smaller rooms facing the plaza, $305 d for more spacious ones, all the way up to $800 d for the distinctive three-level lighthouse suite. Downstairs is the classy Harborside Bistro, and golfers will appreciate the small putting green.

The acclaimed **Chrysalis Inn & Spa** (804 10th St, 360/756-0005 or 888/808-0005, www.thechrysalisinn.com, $179–265 d) is another gorgeous waterside option with luxurious rooms and a decadent spa (extra charge). Unfortunately, the hotel's trackside location brings train noise throughout the night.

Bed-and-Breakfasts

Quite a few of Bellingham's historic homes have been transformed into attractive bed-and-breakfasts.

A Secret Garden International B&B (1807 Lakeway Dr., 360/650-9473 or 800/671-5327, www.secretgardenbb.com, $85–95 d rooms, $100 d suites), is a graceful Craftsman home that Tana Chung has transformed with a multicultural blend of Asian and Western sensibilities. There's a grand piano, a relaxing massage chair, and wireless Internet, but the main emphasis is on Asian artistry, including a tea and meditation room. The two suites and two guest rooms feature quality furnishings, private baths, and a gourmet breakfast. A small gallery downstairs displays alternative-process photography. Ms. Chung also owns **Lake Whatcom Vacation Rental** (2536 Lake Whatcom Blvd., 360/650-9473 or 800/671-5327, $179 d, plus $25 each for additional guests, 12 maximum) a grand and kid-friendly five-bedroom home with a large lakeside deck, fireplace, Jacuzzi, and private beach.

Above Lake Whatcom and surrounded by tall evergreens is the **Schnauzer Crossing** (three miles east of Bellingham at 4421 Lakeway Dr.,

360/734-2808 or 800/562-2808, www.schnauzercrossing.com). You'll find two luxurious and spacious rooms ($140–190 d) in the house and a separate one-room cottage ($225 d) facing the lake. Enjoy a gourmet breakfast, Jacuzzi, and 1.5 acres of gardens. Two-night minimum on weekends and holidays, and kids are welcome ($30/person for additional guests). Friendly owners, too.

The Castle Gate House B&B (1103 15th St., 866/756-2224, www.castlegatehouse.com, $109–159 d) was built in 1889 by Kirtland Cutter, one of the top architects of his era. This Fairhaven District house is decorated with antique furniture, including a 10-foot-tall Renaissance Revival bed. Stroll the grounds to take in the hilltop vista or enjoy the gardens. The house is adjacent to a far more impressive mansion, Wardner's Castle, built at the same time for its millionaire owner, Jim Wardner. The 22-room masterpiece could pass for the Addams Family home.

DeCann House B&B (2610 Eldridge Ave., 360/734-9172, www.decannhouse.com, $75–85 d) is a 1902 home accentuated with stained glass, an antique pool table, and fine views of the San Juan Islands. The two reasonably priced

A Secret Garden International B&B

guest rooms include private baths and a full breakfast, and they'll pick up guests from the airport or train station.

Fairhaven B&B (1714 12th St., 360/734-7243 or 888/734-7243, www.fairhavenbandb .com, $125 d, plus $10 each for extra guests) began as a 1908 bungalow and was transformed in 1970 into a striking Victorian-style home filled with European antiques. A single guest suite spreads across an entire floor, encompassing two bedrooms, two baths, a dining room, and full kitchen. Guests are served a light breakfast and have access to a hot tub on the deck.

Located along scenic Chuckanut Drive south of Bellingham, **Chuckanut Manor B&B** (3056 Chuckanut Dr., 360/766-6191, www.chuckanutmanor.com, $145 d or $170 for four) is a two-bedroom suite with a large deck facing Samish Bay, plus a full kitchen and private bath with jetted tub. A continental breakfast is served, and Chuckanut Manor Restaurant is right downstairs. Railroad tracks are just down the hill, so trains may wake you in the night.

Campgrounds

The closest public campsites are seven miles south of Bellingham at **Larrabee State Park** (360/676-2093, $16 tent or $22 RV). Year-round tent and RV sites are available, along with showers. Make reservations ($7 extra) at 888/226-7688, www.parks.wa.gov.

Bellingham RV Park (3939 Bennett Dr., 360/752-1224 or 888/372-1224, www.bellinghamrvpark.com) has RV hookups for $26.

FOOD

Bellingham has an amazing variety of creative eating establishments. Head to Fairhaven and just walk around to see what looks interesting.

Breakfast

Enjoy great breakfasts and lunches at ℕ **Old Town Café** (316 W. Holly St., 360/671-4431), an earthy place where the queue of customers stretches out the door on a weekend morning. The atmosphere is laid-back and noisy, and it's open till 3 P.M. Another popular downtown place

is **Café Toulouse** (114 W. Magnolia St., 360/733-8996), with a diverse breakfast menu. It's a favorite of the suit-and-tie crowd.

A completely different dining experience can be found at **The Little Cheerful Café** (113 E. Holly, 360/738-8824). The setting is casual and the breakfasts are always great (especially the hash browns), with ample portions. Be prepared to wait if you get here after 10 A.M. on weekends.

Cafés

Many Bellingham places make espresso, but one stands out: **Tony's Coffee & Teas** (1101 Harris Ave. in Fairhaven, 360/733-6319, www.tonys coffee.com), where the smell of roasting coffee wafts through the air. There's another location downtown, but Fairhaven is the hangout for the long-hair-and-leather-jacket crowd. Read the newspaper, sample the carrot cake, play a chess game, or just lean back and take in the scene. This is as close to Berkeley as you'll get this far north. The owners also run **Harris Ave. Café** next door, with good brunches and a shady patio.

A popular downtown coffeehouse with a hip feeling, along with music and poetry some nights, is **Stuart's Coffee House** (1302 Bay St., 360/752-2024, www.barstop.com/stuarts).

Quick Bites

Get healthy, quick eats at reasonable prices from **Casa Qué Pasa** (1415 Railroad Ave., 360/738-8226), where the burritos are the best in town. There's also a great tequila bar. **Swan Café** inside the Community Food Co-Op (1059 N. State, 360/734-8158, www.communityfoodcoop.com) serves hearty soups, salads, and sandwiches. This is a fine place for an inexpensive ($4 for soup and salad) downtown lunch.

If you're in Fairhaven and want great sandwiches, bagels, quiche, or just a scoop of ice cream, drop by **Colophon Café** inside Village Books (1210 11th St., 360/671-2626). It's also great for Paul Bunyan–size slices of carrot cake.

D'Anna's Deli Café (1307 11th St. in Fairhaven, 360/752-3390) is a bright little bistro with panini, lattes, and a couple of outside tables.

Located across the street from the museum, **Wild Garlic** (114 Prospect St., 360/671-1955,

$14–26), is an intimate and romantic place for lunch or a date. The food ranges from burgers and salads to filet mignon and gourmet pizzas, all well prepared.

Italian and Pizza

Giuseppe's Italian Restaurant (1309 Commercial St., 360/714-8412, www.giuseppes.biz) is a classy downtown café that's popular for business lunches and evenings on the town. The menu features well-prepared pastas and the wine bar has a big selection. You can choose a simple spaghetti dish for $11, all the way up to a $26 rack of lamb.

For pizzas, **Stanello's Italian Restaurant** (1514 12th St. in Fairhaven, 360/676-1304) has been around for more than 30 years. **La Fiamma** (200 E. Chestnut, 360/647-0060, www.lafiamma.com) is a stylish but family-friendly spot with crunchy wood-fired pizzas (even a moo shu pork version), panini sandwiches, and salads. Locals say it's the best in town.

Other International

Fairhaven's **Dos Padres Restaurante** (1111 Harris Ave., 360/733-9900, www.dospadres.com) has an extensive selection of Mexican dishes with a Southwest twist, along with locally famous margaritas and nachos. Another very good Mexican restaurant, with more traditional fare, is **El Gitano's** (1125 Sunset Dr., 360/714-1065, www.elgitano.com). Some of the area's best Southwestern-style meals can be found at **Pepper Sisters** (1055 N. State St., 360/671-3414).

India Grill (1215 Cornwall Ave., 360/714-0314), is *the* place for Indian lunches and dinners, including tandoori and vegetarian specials. The lunch buffet is just $6. Several local places have flavorful Thai food; two of the best are **Busara Siamese Cuisine** (324 36th St., Sehome Village Mall, 360/734-8088), and **Thai House Restaurant** (187 Telegraph Rd., 360/734-5111).

Oriento Restaurant (2500 Meridian, 360/733-3322) has a big Chinese menu that includes Mandarin, Sichuan, and Cantonese favorites along with vegetarian specials. **Little Tokyo** (in Barkley Village, 360/752-2222) is a casual sushi bar and Japanese restaurant open for lunch and dinner.

American and Eclectic

Fairhaven's **Dirty Dan Harris'** (1211 11th St., 360/676-1011), serves prime rib, steaks, and fresh seafood dinners in an 1800s-style saloon. It's named for Daniel Jefferson Harris, a feisty eccentric best known for his bathing habits—or lack thereof—who platted the town's streets, built a dock, and sold lots to the thousands of folks who rolled into Fairhaven in 1883. He made a small fortune in the process. If you aren't looking for the gourmet-variety burger, **Boomer's Drive In** (310 N. Samish Way, 360/647-2666) has the best anywhere around.

Pacific Café (downtown at 100 N. Commercial, 360/647-0800), serves moderately priced East-meets-West/Northwest cuisine, including steak, seafood, pasta, and teriyaki dishes in a warm atmosphere. Very good.

Calumet Restaurant (113 E. Magnolia, 360/733-3331) has a trendy menu that successfully blends Southwest flavors with Northwest favorites in a romantic setting. The main draws here, however, are mixed drinks and live jazz on weekends.

It isn't in Bellingham, but **Rhododendron Café** (360/766-4031, www.rhodycafe.com, $13–17) is certainly worth the drive. This little country café is a centerpiece for the town of Bow near the south end of Chuckanut Drive. Weekend breakfast is always a draw, and lunches include pan-fried oysters, grilled Portobello sandwiches, and chicken paninis. Check the blackboard for dinner specials, including various ethnic specialties and Northwest cuisine.

Seafood

Cliff House Restaurant (331 N. State St., 360/734-8660, $16–39), is famous for its whiskey crab soup, oyster bar, fresh seafood, and Angus beef. This is an old favorite with a big deck facing Bellingham Bay for alfresco dining.

Right next to the Hotel Bellwether, **Marina Restaurant** (360/733-8292, $17–22) has a terrific harbor view with a menu of seafood (best local fish and chips) and pasta.

A trio of seafood places hug Chuckanut Drive south of Bellingham; all are closed Mondays. **Chuckanut Manor Restaurant** (360/766-6191, www.chuckanutmanor.com), at the southernmost end of the drive, specializes in fresh seafood and continental dishes, Friday night seafood smorgasbord ($25), and Sunday champagne brunch ($19).

The Oyster Bar (240 Chuckanut Dr., 360/766-6185, www.theoysterbaronchuckanutdrive.com, $19–28), is a cozy place clinging to the side of the hill; it serves oysters (of course) but fresh fish and other seafood are the real stars, and the wine list is equally notable. Tables line two levels of windows that face the San Juan Islands. Reservations are essential, especially on weekends.

Specializing in Northwest food and wine in a romantic setting, **M Oyster Creek Inn** (190 Chuckanut Dr., 360/766-6179, www.oyster-creekinn.com, $18–30) serves seafood (including fresh oysters from Taylor Shellfish Farm, just down the hill), chicken, lamb, and other dishes. This "treehouse" of a place is perched along a cascading creek; outside diners are surrounded by ferns and tall trees.

Microbreweries and Pubs

The perpetually crowded and smoke-free **Orchard St. Brewery** (709 W. Orchard Dr., 360/647-1614) has great fresh brews and a surprisingly sophisticated restaurant fare that goes far beyond pub grub; filet mignon, king salmon, spot prawns, stone-oven pizzas, and other superb dishes fill the menu. Reasonable prices, too. Find award-winning brews in a no-smoking atmosphere at **Boundary Bay Brewery & Bistro** (1107 Railroad Ave., 360/647-5593, www.bbaybrewery.com), with seven beers on tap and a pub menu of steak, fish, pizzas, wraps, sandwiches, and pasta. The big doors open onto a flower-filled deck and beer garden.

Markets and Bakeries

Bellingham's **Community Food Co-Op** (1059 N. State, 360/734-8158, www.communityfoodcoop.com) is a spacious natural foods market and home to the Swan Café. **Haggen Foods** (www.haggen.com) has three large gourmet markets at 210 36th, 2814 Meridian St., and Barkley Village, with fine delis offering Chinese food, pizza by the slice, sandwiches, and a salad bar. They're a good deal for fast meals.

Find European-style breads, plus sandwiches and soups, at **Avenue Bread Co.** (1313 Rail-

road Ave., 360/676-9274). A few doors away is **The Bagelry** (360/676-5288), a popular place, with New York–style bagels. For French pastries, try **La Vie en Rose French Bakery** (111 W. Holly St., 360/715-1839, www.laviebakery.com).

The **Bellingham Farmers Market** (parking lot at Chestnut St. and Railroad Ave., 360/647-2060, www.bellinghamfarmers.org) is held April–October 10 A.M.–3 P.M. Saturdays and Sundays. They're also open at Barkley Village July–September 3–7 P.M. Tuesdays. Across town, the **Fairhaven Farmers Market** (11th and McKenzie, 360/647-2060) takes place June–September 3–7 P.M. Wednesdays.

ARTS AND ENTERTAINMENT

The historic **Mt. Baker Theatre** (106 N. Commercial St., 360/733-5793, www.mtbakertheatre.com), opened in 1927 as a vaudeville and movie palace, hosts the **Whatcom Symphony Orchestra** (360/734-6080, www.whatcomsymphony.com), plus many other musical and theatrical performances. The two-week-long **Bellingham Festival of Music** (360/676-5997, www.bellinghamfestival.org) each August brings world-class classical and jazz musicians to town, and the **Brown Bag Music Series** (360/676-6985) features concerts on the public library lawn each Friday mid-June through August.

For the latest on the local music scene, pick up a copy of the *Bellingham Weekly* (www.bellinghamweekly.com) or Bellingham Herald's *Take Five* (www.bellinghamherald.com). Two smoke-free places to start are Boundary Bay Brewing Company and **Wild Buffalo** (208 W. Holly St., 360/752-0848, www.wildbuffalo.net).

Galleries

Bellingham has a diverse arts community, with a number of fine galleries. **Gallery Walks** bring out art enthusiasts on the first or second Friday of the month, and each October, the **Whatcom Artist Studio Tour** (360/734-9472, www.studiotour.net) provides an open house for local studios.

Allied Arts of Whatcom County (1418 Cornwall Ave., 360/676-8548, www.alliedarts.org) has a large downtown gallery. **Hamann's**

Gallery (2940 New Market, in Barkley Village, 360/733-8898) displays original artwork, etchings, and limited-edition prints, and the **Blue Horse Gallery** (301 W. Holly St., 360/671-2305) shows works from 20 regional artists. Located in the Bellwether complex, **Mark Bergsma Gallery** (11 Bellwether Way, 360/671-6818, www.markbergsma.com) exhibits this artist's unique photographic triptychs.

INFORMATION AND SERVICES

For maps, brochures, and general information, contact the **Bellingham and Whatcom County Convention and Visitors Bureau** (904 Potter St., Exit 253 off I-5, 360/671-3990 or 800/487-2032, www.bellingham.org, open 8:30 A.M.–5:30 P.M. daily). An information booth at the Bellingham Cruise Terminal (where the Alaska ferry docks) is staffed Tuesdays and Fridays in the summer, and a second information kiosk is located inside Bellis Fair Mall.

TRANSPORTATION

The **Bellingham Cruise Terminal,** (www.portofbellingham.com/transportation), three blocks downhill from Fairhaven, is where you can catch passenger ferries to the San Juans and Victoria, and the larger **Alaska Marine Highway** (360/676-8445 or 800/642-0066, www.ferryalaska.com) ferry to Southeast Alaska.

Ferries to the San Juans and Victoria

Based at the Bellingham ferry terminal, **Victoria-San Juan Cruises** (355 Harris Ave., 360/738-8099 or 800/443-4552, www.whales.com, mid-May to early October) has all-day cruises from Bellingham to Victoria and back, with time around (but not on) the San Juan Islands. You'll sail aboard the *Victoria Star II,* a 150-passenger boat. The cost is $89 for adults, $84 for seniors, $45 for ages 6–17, free for younger kids; add $10 for a seafood dinner.

The same folks also run **San Juan Island Commuter** (360/734-8180 or 888/734-8180, www.islandcommuter.com, mid-May to early September daily, $39 for adults, $20 for kids, bikes for $5, and kayaks for $20), a 50-foot, 42-passenger boat with service to Friday Harbor on San Juan Island. A combination day trip to Friday Harbor and three-hour whale-watching voyage is $69 for adults or $39 for kids.

By Train

Amtrak (800/872-7245, www.amtrak.com) provides daily train connections on its Cascades train north to Vancouver, British Columbia, and south to Mount Vernon, Everett, Edmonds, and Seattle. It stops at the Fairhaven depot, just a short walk from the ferry terminal.

By Air

Horizon Air (800/547-9308, www.horizonair.com) has frequent service from Bellingham International Airport (www.portofbellingham.com/airport) to Sea-Tac. Many Canadians use this airport because they can get more convenient flights to some U.S. destinations and cheaper tickets, and the parking—$6/day—is a big savings, too.

San Juan Airlines (360/293-4691 or 800/874-4434, www.sanjuanairlines.com) has scheduled daily service to San Juan, Orcas, and Lopez in the San Juan Islands, plus charter flights and flightseeing.

Allegiant Air (702/851-7300 or 800/432-3810, www.allegiantair.com) provides nonstop flights between Bellingham and Las Vegas several times a week.

If you're flying into Sea-Tac Airport, **Airporter Shuttle** (360/380-8800 or 866/235-5247, www.airporter.com), offers daily van service to Bellingham for $32 ($17 kids) one-way. **Quick Shuttle** (604/940-4428 or 800/665-2122, www.quickcoach.com), has service to Vancouver; $24 ($15 kids) one-way.

By Bus

Locally, **Whatcom Transit** (360/676-7433, www.ridewta.com), provides bus service Monday–Saturday to Bellingham, Ferndale, Lynden, Blaine, and the Lummi Indian Reservation. **Greyhound** (401 Harris Ave., 360/733-5251 or 800/231-2222, www.greyhound.com) has nationwide bus connections from the Amtrak depot in Fairhaven.

Seattle

Seattle is not only the largest city in the Pacific Northwest, but also a delightful place to spend several days—or years—of adventurous, 16-oz. whipped-cream-on-top mocha sightseeing. Below is a skim-the-surface version of the city; see *Moon Handbooks Washington* for detailed coverage.

SIGHTS

If you only have a day in the city, be sure to take in **Pike Place Market** (85 Pike St., 206/682-7453, www.pikeplacemarket.org) for a wonderful introduction to Seattle at its best. The market is downtown at the waterfront end of Stewart Street, and is open daily. The true heart and soul of Seattle, Pike Place is where visitors and locals buy the freshest fish, most colorful flowers, and most squeezable produce in town. Listen to the street musicians, enjoy the parade of humanity, and explore a myriad of shops and eateries, and look out for flying fish.

Other not-to-be-missed downtown sights include the **Seattle Art Museum** (100 University St., 206/654-3100, www.seattleartmuseum.org), **Pioneer Square**, with its juxtaposition of fine art galleries, hip nightclubs, and down-in-the-dumps alcoholics, and the **Seattle Aquarium** (Pier 59, 206/386-4320, www.seattleaquarium.org). A short distance north of downtown is **Seattle Center,** where you'll find the city's landmark **Space Needle** (206/443-2111 or 800/937-9582, www.space-needle.com), the kid-friendly **Pacific Science Center** (206/443-2001 or 866/414-1912, www.pacsci.org), **Experience Music Project** (206/367-5483 or 877/367-5483, www.emplive.com)—where everyone gets to be 17 again—and the out-of-this-world **Science Fiction Museum** (206/724-3428, www.sfhomeworld.org). Just south of downtown are the striking baseball and football stadiums, and farther to the south is the **Museum of Flight** (9404 E. Marginal Way, 206/764-5720, www.museumofflight.org), with a world-class collection of aircraft.

Check out **Lake Union** with its quaint houseboats, sailboats, kayaks, and maritime exhibits. If

the Space Needle and Seattle skyline

© DON PITCHER

you're flying to the San Juans on Kenmore Air, you'll probably depart from here. **Recreation Equipment Inc.** (222 Yale Ave. N., 206/223-1944, www.rei.com), known to most folks as REI, is a must-stop for anyone interested in the outdoors, and a great place to get ready for a trip to the San Juans. Its enormous flagship store is located up the hill from Lake Union.

The **University District** is home to—you guessed it—the University of Washington, and has all the usual student-oriented shops, including a plethora of great little ethnic eateries. Be sure to visit the **Burke Museum** (206/543-5590, www.washington.edu/burkemuseum) and **Henry Art Gallery** (www.henryart.org).

Other neighborhoods well worth exploring include **Capitol Hill** with its fun shops, great food, and strong gay presence, **Fremont,** where funky is in vogue, and **International District,** with a wide diversity of Asian shops and restaurants.

Gateways to the Islands

© PHIL SHIPMAN

Seattle Harbor

ACCOMMODATIONS

Seattle's lodging choices cover the spectrum from basic hostels all the way up to five-star hotels. The Convention and Visitors Bureau's **Seattle Hotel Hotline** (206/461-5882 or 800/535-7071) is a one-stop place to find a room in your price range. Their online lodging guide at www.seeseattle.org is categorized by location and price, with direct links to hundreds of local options; it's an excellent starting place.

Backpacking travelers willing to sleep in a bunk bed should check out two downtown hostels: **Hostelling International** (84 Union St., 206/622-5443 or 888/622-5443, www.hiseattle.org) or **Seattle Green Tortoise Hostel** (1525 2nd Ave., 206/282-1222 or 888/424-6873, www.greentortoise.com).

If you have a car, a couple of decent and inexpensive options are **Park Plaza Motel** (4401 Aurora Ave. N, 206/632-2101, $45–60 d); and **College Inn** (4000 University Way NE, 206/633-4441, www.collegeinnseattle.com, $60–80 d). For well-maintained airport lodging that won't break the bank, try **Jet Motel** (17300 International Blvd., SeaTac, 206/244-6255 or

800/233-1501, $55 d). Looking for something more upscale? Try a couple of downtown places: **Inn at Queen Anne** (505 First Ave. N, 206/282-7357 or 800/952-5043, www.innatqueenanne.com, $120 d) or **Pensione Nichols B&B** (1923 1st Ave., 206/441-7125 or 800/440-7125, www.seattle-bed-breakfast.com, $110 d).

At the $220-and-up end of the price spectrum you won't go wrong at **The Edgewater** (2411 Alaskan Way, 206/728-7000 or 800/624-0670, www.edgewaterhotel.com) or the elegant **Inn at the Market** (86 Pine St., 206/443-3600 or 800/446-4484, www.innatthemarket.com). For homier lodging choices, contact the **Seattle B&B Association** (206/547-1020 or 800/348-5630, www.lodginginseattle.com).

INFORMATION AND SERVICES

Seattle's Convention and Visitors Bureau (800 Convention Place, 206/461-5840, www.seeseattle.org) stocks the *Seattle Visitors Guide,* a fat compendium of local entertainment, restaurants, shopping, and sights. Also check out the CVB's useful *Lodging Guide.* Sea-Tac Airport has a little information center with the usual blizzard of brochures and freebie papers.

Located inside the REI store, the **Outdoor Recreation Information Center** (206/470-4060, www.nps.gov/ccso), has complete details on natural areas around the state, including National Park Service, Washington State Parks, and Department of Natural Resources lands.

Useful websites for Seattle information include the **City of Seattle's** official website (www.ci.seattle.wa.us), Microsoft's **Citysearch** site (www.seattle.citysearch.com), and those of local newspapers: **Seattle Times** (www.seattletimes.com), **Seattle Post-Intelligencer** (www.seattlep-i.com), and **Seattle Weekly** (www.seattleweekly.com).

TRANSPORTATION

Seattle's airport is 12 miles south of the city and midway between Seattle and Tacoma, hence the name, **Sea-Tac International Airport.** It is the primary entry point for flights into Washington state, and has the expected array of bus, shuttle van, and taxi transit choices.

The San Juan Islands are 65 air miles northeast of Seattle, with access by air, boat, shuttle van and ferry, or car and ferry. (See the *Know San Juan Islands* chapter for complete details on transportation into Seattle and onward to the islands.)

San Juan Island

The second largest island in the archipelago (Orcas is slightly bigger), San Juan Island is about 20 miles long and seven miles wide, covering a total of 55 square miles. Picturesque and tidy **Friday Harbor** sits along the west side, its marina protected by Brown Island. It has all the charm of a coastal Maine town, with white clapboard buildings, busy shops, art galleries, and fine restaurants tucked into hills surrounding the harbor. Friday Harbor is the only incorporated town in the chain, and is also the county seat, the commercial center of the San Juans, and home to half of San Juan Island's 7,000 residents. It is a U.S. Customs port of entry, as is **Roche Harbor** on the other side of the island. Roche Harbor is regionally famous for its wonderful deep-water marina and historic buildings that are now part of a popular resort.

Once you leave Friday Harbor the country quickly opens into expansive farms and fields, forests, hills, and rocky shorelines. It is a wonderfully diverse island with something to please almost any traveler. On the south end of San Juan the land is grassy and open, with a couple of long beaches. The western shore is relatively undeveloped and rugged, with the only whale-watching park in the nation at **Lime Kiln Point State Park.** Two historic and especially scenic areas at English Camp on the west side and American Camp on the southeast end of the

© DON PITCHER

Must-Sees

M Whale Museum: Learn about orca whales and other marine mammals at this very informative museum in Friday Harbor. Kids love to try on the whale costumes (page 77).

M San Juan Island National Historical Park: This twofold park commemorates the conflict

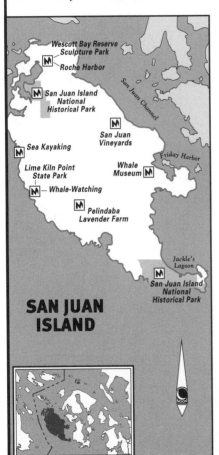

between the United States and Britain for control of the San Juan Islands. English Camp has historic buildings and a formal garden along a protected cove, while American Camp is a windswept, open spot with grand scenery and the best beaches anywhere on the San Juans (page 80).

M Roche Harbor: Beautifully maintained, this marina and resort has a historic hotel, flower-packed gardens, and abundant recreation options (page 83).

M Westcott Bay Reserve Sculpture Park: More than 100 sculptures dot this 19-acre nature and art preserve located near the entrance to Roche Harbor Resort (page 84).

M Lime Kiln Point State Park: Often called Whale Watch Park, this Westside natural area has a photogenic lighthouse and underwater hydrophones to listen for the orca (killer) whales that often pass just offshore (page 85).

M San Juan Vineyards: A boutique winery here produces wines from 10 acres of madeleine angevine and siegerrebe grapes (page 87).

M Pelindaba Lavender Farm: The fragrance often reaches you before you ever see the 20 acres of organic lavender used for a wide range of culinary and other products. The owners also have a shop featuring their wares in the heart of Friday Harbor (page 87).

M Sea Kayaking: A favorite of adventurous visitors, kayaking is the perfect way to explore waters around San Juan Island. A number of companies lead short day trips or multi-night paddles to surrounding marine state parks (page 89).

M Whale-Watching: Each year, more than 500,000 people board whale-watching boats in the San Juans, many of which depart from Friday Harbor, Roche Harbor, or Snug Harbor (page 90).

San Juan Island

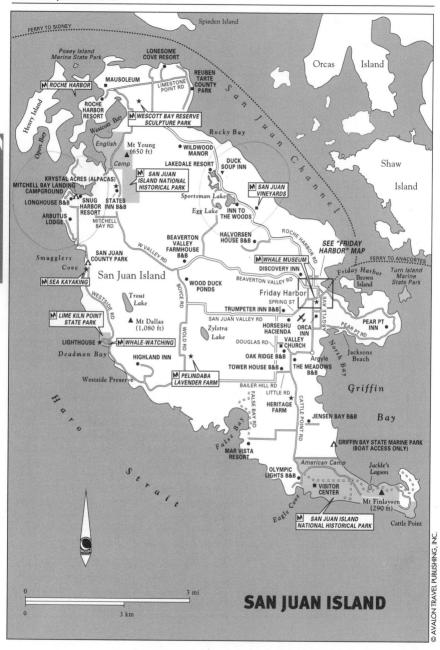

FERRY TO SIDNEY

Spieden Island

Orcas   Island

Posey Island
Marine State Park

LONESOME
COVE RESORT

REUBEN
TARTE
COUNTY
PARK

Ⓜ ROCHE HARBOR

MAUSOLEUM

LIMESTONE
POINT RD

ROCHE
HARBOR
RESORT

Ⓜ WESCOTT BAY RESERVE
SCULPTURE PARK

Rocky Bay

Shaw

Henry Island

Open Bay

Westcott Bay

English
Camp

Mt Young
(650 ft)

WILDWOOD
MANOR

DUCK
SOUP INN

Island

KRYSTAL ACRES (ALPACAS)

LAKEDALE RESORT

MITCHELL BAY LANDING
CAMPGROUND

Ⓜ SAN JUAN
ISLAND NATIONAL
HISTORICAL PARK

Ⓜ SAN JUAN
VINEYARDS

San Juan Channel

LONGHOUSE B&B

SNUG
HARBOR
RESORT

STATES
INN B&B

Sportsman Lake

INN TO
THE WOODS

ARBUTUS
LODGE

MITCHELL
BAY RD

Egg Lake

HALVORSEN
HOUSE B&B

ROCHE HARBOR RD

SEE "FRIDAY
HARBOR" MAP

FERRY TO ANACORTES

Smugglers
Cove

SAN JUAN
COUNTY PARK

BEAVERTON
VALLEY
FARMHOUSE
B&B

W VALLEY RD

Ⓜ WHALE MUSEUM

DISCOVERY INN

Friday Harbor
Brown
Island

Turn Island
Marine
State Park

Ⓜ SEA KAYAKING

San Juan Island

Trout
Lake

WOOD DUCK
PONDS

BOYCE RD

BEAVERTON VALLEY RD

Friday Harbor

SPRING ST

PEAR PT
INN

WESTSIDE RD

TRUMPETER INN B&B

SAN JUAN VALLEY RD

ARGYLE AVE

PEAR PT RD

Ⓜ LIME KILN POINT
STATE PARK

Mt Dallas
(1,080 ft)

Zylstra
Lake

HORSESHU
HACIENDA

ORCA
INN

North Bay

LIGHTHOUSE

Ⓜ WHALE-WATCHING

WOLD RD

Douglas Rd

VALLEY
CHURCH

Argyle

Jacksons
Beach

HIGHLAND INN

OAK RIDGE B&B

THE MEADOWS
B&B

Griffin

Deadman Bay

Westside Preserve

Ⓜ PELINDABA
LAVENDER FARM

TOWER HOUSE B&B

BAILER HILL RD

LITTLE RD

CATTLE POINT RD

Bay

Haro

FALSE BAY RD

HERITAGE
FARM

JENSEN BAY B&B

GRIFFIN BAY STATE MARINE PARK
(BOAT ACCESS ONLY)

Strait

False Bay

MAR VISTA
RESORT

American Camp

Jackle's
Lagoon

OLYMPIC
LIGHTS B&B

Eagle Cove

VISITOR
CENTER

Mt Finlayson
(290 ft)

Ⓜ SAN JUAN ISLAND
NATIONAL HISTORICAL PARK

Cattle Point

0   3 mi

0   3 km

SAN JUAN ISLAND

© AVALON TRAVEL PUBLISHING, INC.

San Juan Island

island are within **San Juan Island National Historical Park.**

A handful of celebrity types have homes on San Juan, including the '70s rocker Steve Miller and Richard Nixon's one-time head of the EPA, William Ruckelshaus. Heading farther back in time, the late John Wayne often stayed on the island, particularly at Roche Harbor. And presidents Theodore Roosevelt and Howard Taft overnighted here while in office.

PLANNING YOUR TIME

San Juan Island is popular both for weekend vacationers and those with more time on their hands. It's possible to fly directly to the island, but most folks arrive by state ferry. A ferry trip requires getting to Anacortes (or Sidney if you're visiting from Vancouver Island), waiting in line for an hour or more, and then sailing to Friday Harbor. Unless you get a very early start and leave late the evening of your return, you can lose big chunks of your weekend to travel. Take as much time as you can afford, but even a short trip can be fun.

Friday Harbor is the center of action on San Juan Island, and a good base from which to explore surrounding areas. It's also home to the fun and educational **Whale Museum,** several fine restaurants, and a multitude of gift shops and galleries. After visiting the museum, many visitors climb onboard one of the many **whale-watching** boats that converge on killer whales feeding in nearby waters. There is considerable controversy over the impacts of whale-watching boats, and the museum recommends instead that people stay onshore to view whales. The best place for that is **Lime Kiln Point State Park** on the undeveloped west side of the island. Just north of here is a small county park that serves as a popular put-in point for guided and private groups of **sea kayakers.**

San Juan Island National Historical Park and **Roche Harbor** mix history with grand scenery. San Juan Island National Historical Park commemorates the Pig War and Roche Harbor features gracious gardens, an old clapboard hotel, a busy harbor, and an intriguing mix of nature and art at **Westcott Bay Reserve Sculpture Park.**

On the south end of the island, **Pelindaba Lavender Farm** grows fragrant lavender flowers for a variety of uses, and has a big shop in the heart of Friday Harbor. These attractions are just

herding sheep down Spring Street, circa 1905

COURTESY OF SAN JUAN HISTORICAL MUSEUM

San Juan Island

a starting point, and inveterate travelers will discover all sorts of other delights on San Juan Island.

HISTORY

The Pig War, a turf battle between the United States and Britain, threatened to escalate into violent conflict in 1859. Once tensions eased, both sides stationed troops on San Juan Island to pro-

tect their interests until a settlement could be reached. (See the sidebar, *The Pig War,* for background on the most unusual part of San Juan Island's history.)

The Americans stayed on the south end of the island at "Fort Pickett," as American Camp came to be called, building a small cluster of structures on this lonely and windswept spot. Crushing boredom, bad food, and dreadful quar-

THE PIG WAR

Because of vague wording in the Oregon Treaty of 1846—the document that established the boundary between the United States and Canada—the San Juan Islands were not only the subject of a territorial dispute, but also the stage for an international incident commonly referred to as the Pig War. The treaty noted that the boundary would extend "to the middle of the channel which separates the continent from Vancouver's Island and thence southerly through the middle of the said channel, and of Fuca's Straits, to the Pacific Ocean." Unfortunately, there are actually two main channels. Britain said the boundary was Rosario Strait, the channel between the mainland and the San Juans, while the United States claimed Haro Strait—which separated the San Juans from Vancouver Island — as the border. In between were the San Juan Islands, claimed by both England and America.

Collision Course

Britain lacked a strong military or political presence in the Pacific Northwest, so the powerful Hudson's Bay Company was given free rein on Vancouver Island, with the head of the company also serving as governor of British Columbia. In the 1850s and '60s, western Canada was under the control of a man with fierce loyalties to both the company and England, James Douglas.

Worried that the Americans might next lay claim to Vancouver Island, Douglas pushed England to throw down the gauntlet over the San Juan Islands. In 1851 he set up a fishing operation on San Juan Island to brine and barrel salmon caught by Native American fishermen. Two years later he sent John Charles Griffin (for whom Griffin Bay is named) to establish a sheep ranch called Belle Vue

Farm on the southern end of the island. Hawaiian shepherds tended the 1,400 sheep, crops were planted, and a few pigs rounded out the farm.

The United States also showed a keen interest in the San Juans, with the Washington Territorial legislature declaring them a part of Whatcom County in 1853. By 1859, around 18 American settlers had moved onto San Juan Island. The relationship between the two sides grew strained, and neither nation recognized the other's authority. Several tit-for-tat incidents raised the level of tension, but a dead pig brought everything to a boil.

Pig Trouble

Lyman A. Cutlar arrived on San Juan Island in April 1859, took a Native American wife, and soon began clearing land for a home and a potato patch. Unfortunately, the place he had chosen was smack in the midst of land grazed by Hudson's Bay Company sheep. One of the boars from Belle Vue Farm kept wandering into Cutlar's potatoes, and each time he'd have to chase it out. Complaints to Charles Griffin got him nowhere; he suggested the problem was Cutlar's weak fence. On June 15, 1859, Cutlar awoke to see Griffin's Hawaiian herdsman laughing as the pig rooted in the potatoes once again. This was just before the Civil War, and Cutlar's temper flared at the "independence of the Negro, knowing as he did my previous loss." With a shot from his rifle, the offending pig was dead.

Cutlar decided honesty was now the best course, and walked over to Belle Vue to pay Griffin for the pig. Griffin's response: "You Americans are nothing but a nuisance on the island and you have no business here." He then claimed the

ters made this a hardship post, augmented only by surreptitious visits to nearby San Juan Town for whiskey and women. On March 21, 1860, a contingent of British Royal Marines landed at beautiful Garrison Bay on the west side of the island. The site had been an important winter village for Coast Salish peoples for a thousand years. The British built a comfortable camp with prim white buildings and a formal garden, but the men here were no less unhappy and bored than those at American Camp. Desertions and even suicides took place. In the years that followed, the two camps gradually developed a camaraderie that led to joint celebrations of the 4th of July and Queen Victoria's birthday by both nationalities.

The sudden flare-up on San Juan died down almost as quickly, perhaps in large part because attentions turned elsewhere. A much bigger event

boar was worth $100 (it was probably closer to $10 at best), and Cutlar stormed out. Later that day, a Hudson's Bay ship arrived and another heated discussion ensued, with the British threatening to haul Cutlar off to Victoria for trial and Cutlar threatening to shoot anyone who attempted to do so. By the time the 4th of July arrived two weeks later, American settlers on San Juan were agitating for U.S. sovereignty.

Into this fracas stepped William Harney, a brash U.S. Army brigadier general known for his dislike of the British and his penchant for recklessness. Within days, an American steamer arrived, carrying a company of soldiers under another arrogant man, Captain George E. Pickett. He was already known for his Mexican War exploits and would later gain fame as the Confederate general who led his men up Cemetery Ridge during the Battle of Gettysburg.

The troops landed and quickly set up a camp near the Hudson's Bay Company wharf. It was an odd choice. Instead of putting his men out of range of British naval guns (which could not elevate to reach him higher up the slopes), Pickett chose a totally exposed beach. When the number of warships grew, he moved to the opposite beach. This really puzzled the British officers. Of course, they didn't know he had graduated last in his class at West Point: 59th out of 59.

An Escalating Crisis

Over in Victoria, the *Colonist* newspaper featured an incendiary story headlined "San Juan Island Invaded by American Troops." Governor James Douglas didn't take kindly to the sudden American military presence. He ordered three British warships under Captain Geoffrey Hornby to occupy the island but to avoid a military collision. That confrontation nearly came on August 3, when Hornby told Pickett that his British troops would be landing that day. Pickett's forces were vastly outnumbered, but he said they would fight to the last man. Fortunately, Captain Hornby had the presence of mind to avoid bloodshed, though his warships did stay threateningly close to shore.

Instead of landing his men, Hornby decided to wait for word from Douglas's superior, Rear Admiral Robert L. Baynes, who was expected back soon from Chile. When he arrived two days later, Baynes was appalled. He told Douglas that he would not "involve two great nations in a war over a squabble about a pig," and ordered his men to "not on any account whatever take the initiative in commencing hostilities." Still, five of Her Majesty's ships stood ready to land Royal Marines and to open fire on the Americans.

In the meantime, General Harney continued to build up his forces on San Juan, and by the end of August, 461 American soldiers—protected by an earthen redoubt, 14 field pieces, and eight naval guns — faced off against the British ships. All this military buildup and bluster had taken place without any instructions from Washington, D.C., and when President James Buchanan heard the news, he was horrified. He sent Lt. General Winfred Scott, commanding general of the Army, to seek a peaceful settlement. After much bickering, both sides agreed to leave a token force of men until a final settlement could be brokered. That settlement did not come until 1872, when the United States was awarded the islands by an arbitrator, Kaiser Wilhelm I of Germany.

was steaming over the horizon, a conflict that would not end so peaceably: the Civil War. By 1861, nearly everyone had forgotten about the silly argument over an island in Puget Sound. Interestingly, a number of the participants in the San Juan brouhaha—including Pickett and Harney—were Southerners. A few conspiracy theorists even suggest (without any real evidence) that the Pig War was an effort by southerners to have the Union fighting both the Confederacy and Britain at once.

America Takes Over

The Civil War and other matters kept the issue of boundary claims on a back burner for a dozen years, and settlers from both sides occupied the land. Finally, in 1871, a deal was struck to let an arbitrator make the final boundary decision. The man they chose was Kaiser Wilhelm I of Germany, and on October 21, 1872, he pronounced the Haro Strait the dividing channel, awarding the islands to the United States. On November 25, 1872, the Royal Marines withdrew from English Camp, but before they did, they cut down the camp flagpole and used it to replace a spar on one of the British ships. Americans had intended to immediately run the Stars and Stripes up the flagstaff, and were nonplussed at not getting the chance. Within days, nearly all of the British settlers in the islands had rushed to change their citizenship, allowing them to keep their land as American homesteaders.

The Pig War is barely a footnote to history today, but it marked a turning point in relations between Britain and America. No more would the two countries view each other as enemies. Their last conflict had just one casualty, the pig. See Michael Vouri's *The Pig War* (Griffin Bay Bookstore) for the complete machinations of this strange episode. The National Park Service took over the sites of American Camp and English Camp in 1966 and now maintains them as San Juan Islands National Historic Park.

San Juan Town and Friday Harbor

Shortly after American soldiers landed on the southern end of San Juan Island in 1859, a settlement sprang up along nearby Griffin Bay.

Originally called San Juan Town, it would later be known as Old Town. The turmoil over ownership of the islands made them ripe for all sorts of illicit activities, the primary one being the uncontrolled selling of alcohol. Within a year, the entire area was verging on anarchy, with robberies, attacks on women at any time of the day or night, rampant drunkenness by both Native Americans and whites, saloon brawls, prostitution, and even murder. The American military stepped in to restore order, but San Juan Town's reputation was already ruined.

One of the few reputable civilians on San Juan in the early years was **Edward Warbass,** who came to the island to run the Army's post store and stayed around to become justice of the peace, a state legislator, and the crafter of a bill that created San Juan County. Warbass is best known today as the father of Friday Harbor. Fed up with the boozing reputation of San Juan Town, he resolved to create a grand metropolis at a protected harbor on the west side of the island. He claimed that it would rival Seattle. An old Hawaiian herder named Joe Friday grazed his sheep at this scenic spot; hence the name.

In 1873, Warbass staked 160 acres for the new San Juan County seat on the shores of Friday's Harbor, erected a shack for the courthouse, and waited in vain for the hordes to arrive. It was three years before the first settler, other than Warbass, finally moved in to open a store, and almost a decade before the town contained more than a handful of homes and residents. In 1882, a second store opened at Friday Harbor, creating competition that led the owners to add a backroom bar. This was what folks really needed: cheap beer. Within a few months, the island's economic focus shifted to Friday Harbor, and over the next few years, San Juan Town became a ghost town. A fire in 1890 destroyed all that remained of Old Town, and nobody shed any tears. Friday Harbor was now clearly the chief—and only—town on the islands, and it remains so today, with some 2,000 permanent residents.

The Lime King

Today, Roche Harbor is famous for its beautiful protected harbor, large marina, and immaculately

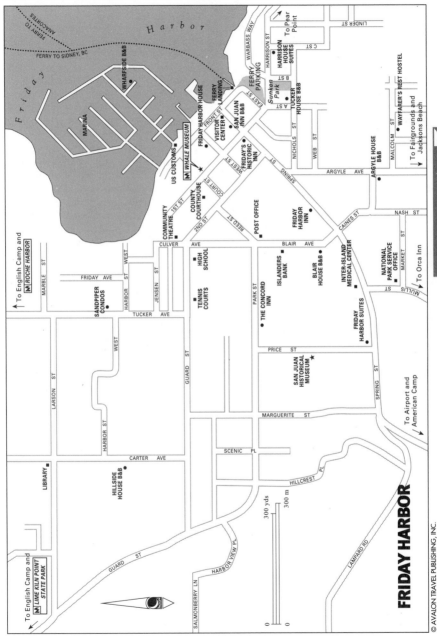

San Juan Island

Harbor

FERRY TO ANACORTES

FERRY TO SIDNEY, BC

Friday Harbor

WHARFSIDE B&B

MARINA

To Pear Point

LINDER ST

WARBASS WAY

HARRISON ST

C ST

HARRISON HOUSE SUITES

B ST

FERRY LANDING

FERRY PARKING

Sunken Park

EAST ST

A ST

TUCKER HOUSE B&B

WAYFARER'S REST HOSTEL

MALCOLM ST

FRIDAY HARBOR HOUSE

FRONT ST

VISITOR CENTER

SAN JUAN INN B&B

NICHOLS ST

WEB ST

To Fairgrounds and Jacksons Beach

US CUSTOMS

WHALE MUSEUM

WEST ST

FRIDAY'S HISTORIC INN

SPRING ST

ARGYLE HOUSE B&B

ARGYLE AVE

COUNTY COURTHOUSE

1ST ST

COURT ST

2ND ST

REED ST

POST OFFICE

FRIDAY HARBOR INN

CAINES ST

NASH ST

To English Camp and ROCHE HARBOR

COMMUNITY THEATRE

CULVER AVE

BLAIR AVE

INTER-ISLAND MEDICAL CENTER

NATIONAL PARK SERVICE OFFICE

MARKET ST

MARBLE ST

WEST ST

FRIDAY AVE

HARBOR ST

HIGH SCHOOL

PARK ST

ISLANDERS BANK

BLAIR HOUSE B&B

MULLIS ST

To Orca Inn

SANDPIPER CONDOS

JENSEN ST

TENNIS COURTS

THE CONCORD INN

FRIDAY HARBOR SUITES

TUCKER AVE

WEST ST

GUARD ST

PRICE ST

SPRING ST

LARSON ST

HARBOR ST

SAN JUAN HISTORICAL MUSEUM

MARGUERITE ST

To Airport and American Camp

LIBRARY

HILLSIDE HOUSE B&B

CARTER AVE

SCENIC PL

HILLCREST PL

To English Camp and LIME KILN POINT STATE PARK

GUARD ST

HARBOR VIEW PL

300 yds

300 m

0

SALMONBERRY LN

LAMPARD RD

FRIDAY HARBOR

© AVALON TRAVEL PUBLISHING, INC.

maintained historic buildings, which operate as the largest resort on San Juan Island. The harbor was discovered early, and by 1850 the Hudson's Bay Company had built a log trading post along the shore. In 1881, the brothers Robert and Richard Scurr bought the harbor and began mining an incredibly rich deposit of lime.

In 1884, **John S. McMillin,** a Tacoma lawyer, learned of the limestone and bought the land for $40,000. By 1886, McMillin's Tacoma and Roche Harbor Lime Company had begun operation. The old Hudson's Bay cabin became the basis for his Hotel de Haro, a still-standing structure that has hosted presidents and paupers over the decades. Business boomed, and by the 1890s, Roche Harbor had become not only the primary employer in the San Juans, but also the largest producer of lime west of the Mississippi. The lime was mined from 13 hillside quarries. Workers drilled holes for dynamite and then used sledgehammers to crush the rock once it had been blasted loose. The rock was hauled to kilns by horse-drawn wagon. In later years, a steam locomotive carried the ore, and this in turn was replaced by trucks.

The limestone was processed in brick-lined kilns along the shore of Roche Harbor. The rock was dumped into steel receptacles lined with fire-brick and then heated with wood fires. The intense heat eventually changed the rock into lime. It took 4,000 acres of forest just to keep the kilns running; each kiln burned 10 cords of wood every six hours! The company had its own small fleet of ships to transport the lime to markets as far away as San Francisco and Hawaii.

The company continued to grow, adding a modern lime factory and a barrel works, along with docks and warehouses that extended hun-

dreds of feet into the bay. McMillin built a company town that included segregated housing for nearly 800 Asian and white employees. Single men were barracked in large bunkhouses, and families were housed in rows of trim and well-kept cottages. Payment was in scrip, useable only at the company store on the wharf, alcohol was banned, and the company even owned a school and church.

McMillin prospered immensely from all this development, buying out his partners and running his various businesses in ways that would lead to fraud charges (they were later dismissed). For half a century, John McMillin was the undisputed king of San Juan Island. When union organizers demanded a wage increase at the quarries, he summarily fired 50 men associated with the union. McMillin also used his money, power, and influence to dictate local politics for years, handpicking candidates for office who toed the pro-business Republican line. On the plus side, McMillin did continue to provide jobs when hard times came in the Depression of the 1930s. He died in 1936, and is buried in the Masonic symbol–covered family mausoleum just above Roche Harbor; it is, of course, built of cement from the local limeworks.

The quarries at Roche Harbor finally closed in 1956, and a Seattle businessman and physician, Dr. Reuben J. Tarte, purchased all 4,000 acres and 12 miles of coastline. Over the next three decades, he and his family restored the old hotel and other buildings. The complex was sold in 1988 to Verne Howard and Rich Komen, who have continued the process of transforming this old lime operation into one of the finest resorts on the San Juans.

Sights

It's easy to see Friday Harbor sights on foot, but for many of the most interesting spots, you'll need transport. **San Juan Transit** (360/378-8887 or 800/887-8387, www.sanjuantransit.com) provides an inexpensive way to see the sights in the summer, with stops at many destinations, including Roche Harbor, Pelindaba Lavender Farm, Lime Kiln Point State Park, San Juan County Park, and English Camp. Fares are $5 one-way or $10 for an all-day pass.

WHALE MUSEUM

One of the must-see stops on San Juan Island, the Whale Museum (62 1st St. N. in Friday Harbor, 360/378-4710 or 800/946-7227, www.whalemuseum.org, March–Oct. 10 A.M.– 5 P.M. daily; call for off-season hours) opened its doors in 1979 as the first museum in America dedicated to the interpretation of living whales in the wild. Exhibits focus on whale biology and human-whale interactions, with a particular spotlight on the famous killer whale (orca) populations of Puget Sound.

Downstairs are several free exhibits that introduce you to these incredible animals, including details on recent sightings. The main collection is up a narrow staircase bordered by a colorful whale mural. You are introduced to these creatures through the legends of the Salish people who first lived here. One room in the museum shows a video about orca whales in Puget Sound; sit in for an excellent overview. Another small room has exhibits especially for children, and they'll love the chance to dress up with orca fins and tails for photos to send to the grandparents. The large exhibit hall upstairs contains life-size models and the full skeletons of a baby gray whale, plus adult killer and minke whales. Step into a phone booth to hear the songs of various whales and other marine mammals; learn about hydrophones and how the depth sounders from whale-watching boats can be a problem for whales; examine whale fetuses; and compare the pickled brains of a spotted dolphin, a fin whale, and a human. The museum operates a network of hydrophones to help pinpoint the locations of the three pods of Puget Sound orcas, and a wall chart shows their genealogy.

San Juan Island

© DON PITCHER

Whale Museum

KILLER WHALES

Killer whales (also called orcas) are a major attraction for visitors to the San Juan Islands. Each year more than 500,000 people board commercial whale-watching trips in the waters off Washington and British Columbia, pumping $10 million into the economy. In addition, several thousand other boaters head out to watch whales on private vessels each year.

Why all this attention? Perhaps it is just a simple human interest in the natural world—and large mammals in particular. But anyone who has seen these magnificent creatures in the wild will tell you that it is something more significant, for here are intelligent and beautifully patterned animals who share close family bonds, communicate long distances underwater, enjoy play, and share our taste for salmon (though theirs is in the raw, sashimi form).

Natural History

With a range from tropical seas south to the edge of Antarctica and north into the Bering Sea, killer whales are the second most widely distributed mammals on the planet; only humans range farther. And like humans, some individuals may live up to 90 years, with sexual maturity around age 15. At birth, the calves are eight feet long and weigh more than 400 pounds. By adulthood, females are around 23 feet long, while males can reach 30 feet. A member of the order of cetaceans—whales, dolphins, and porpoises—the killer whale might best be viewed as a large dolphin that happens to have *whale* in its name.

Killer whales, *Orcinus orca,* have long had a reputation befitting their murderous name. Historically they were regarded as bloodthirsty predators and a threat to humans on or in the water. More recently, the "Save the Whales" crowd has promoted them as lovable creatures that should instead be called the more lyrical orcas. (Ironically, the word "orca" comes from a Latin word meaning "kingdom of the dead.") The orca frenzy was fueled in part by the three sappy *Free Willy* movies that played fast and loose with the facts. (Portions of *Free Willy I* and *II* were shot on the San Juans.) The truth is actually much more complex; some killer whales known as residents hunt only fish. Others, called transient killer whales, kill marine mammals, including sea lions, porpoises, other whales, and even sea otters.

Orcas travel in matrilineal groups called pods. These consist of extended families that follow the eldest female, though they mate with whales from other pods. Even the males may remain for life within these extended families. Intensive research has revealed that orcas have a highly complex social structure and diverse patterns of behavior, including a vocal dialect for each pod that is distinctive from one population to the next.

Killer whales can be surprisingly kind to members of their own pod. In 1973, a British Columbia ferry collided with a young killer whale, seriously injuring it with the propeller. Other members of the pod rushed to the calf's aid, physically supporting it for two weeks to help it breathe. Unfortunately, the animal later died of its wounds.

Resident Killer Whales

The whales most commonly seen around the San Juans are considered residents, though some of the pods migrate out of the area seasonally. Ninety percent of their diet is salmon, particularly the fatty chinook (king) salmon.

Nearly 300 resident killer whales swim in the waters along Washington and British Columbia. They are divided into two groups: a large northern community of approximately 215 whales in 16 pods found mainly in British Columbia's Johnstone Strait area, and a smaller southern community of whales who spend much of their time in the Salish Sea around the San Juan Islands. These southern residents are subdivided into family groups known as the J, K, and L pods. Each pod contains closely related whales around an older female; she is often the mother or grandmother of others in the pod. Both the J and K pods have matriarchs that were born around 1910, and both have four generations of descendents.

With a few more than 40 members, the L pod is the largest, followed by the J pod and K pod with around 20 members each. The J pod is the one most often seen by whale watchers because it stays in local waters year-round. The K and L pods head to the outer coast of Washington and Vancouver Island, and even as far south as Monterey Bay, California during the winter and spring.

Saving the Whales

When intensive research on the orcas began in 1976, the southern community (J, K, and L pods) consisted of 71 individuals. It gradually increased to a peak of 98 in 1995, but declined to 78 whales in 2001, prompting scientists to request protection under the Endangered Species Act. As of this writing, that status was still under consideration, but in Canada they are already listed as endangered.

Several factors certainly play a role in this decline. Because they are long-lived top-level predators, killer whales tend to concentrate environmental contaminants in their fatty tissue. The whales have frighteningly high levels of polychlorinated biphenyls (PCBs), dioxins, and other chemicals; PCB levels in these orcas are among the highest ever found in whales.

Another problem is that their primary food source, salmon, has been on the decline, and half of the local salmon runs appear threatened with extinction. When the whales lack food, they consume stored blubber that contains PCBs, and these can cause reproductive and other problems.

During the 1960s and '70s some 48 young killer whales from this population were captured in Puget Sound for aquariums around the world; only one of these is still alive, an L-pod female known as Lolita, living in the Miami Seaquarium in Florida. This was a significant part of the population, and the loss of this 10-year age cohort of females is still being felt.

What role does whale-watching have in the whales' decline? This question comes immediately to mind if you've ever been on a whale-watching trip and discovered a flotilla of dozens of boats tailing the whales for hours at a stretch. Current research appears to show that the dramatic increase in the number of whale-watching boats in recent years may be causing the whales to compensate for boat noise in the way they communicate, adding stress to animals that have been weakened by other factors.

The Whale Museum in Friday Harbor recommends watching from shore if possible, buying organic foods, fertilizers, and pest control products to help keep chemicals out of the food chain, working to protect habitat for salmon, and pressing Congress to support an international ban on persistent organic pollutants such as PCBs.

San Juan Island

There's also an art gallery, plus a gift shop with books on whales, educational toys, games, videos, T-shirts, and jewelry. If you spot a whale anywhere around the San Juans, swimming or stranded, call the museum's 24-hour **Whale Hotline:** 800/562-8832. The museum posts hotline reports on its website.

Admission is $6 adults, $5 seniors, $3 ages 5–18 and college students, and free for kids under five. Group tours and educational programs are available year-round. You can "adopt" one of the more than 80 local orcas for $35.

SAN JUAN HISTORICAL MUSEUM

Housed in a two-story 1890s farmhouse in Friday Harbor, this museum (405 Price St., 360/378-3949, www.sjmuseum.org) includes fascinating antiques, old photos, and historical artifacts. Outside you will find a variety of old farm equipment, the first county jail, a log cabin, barn, milk house, and carriage house. Those interested in a more in-depth look at local history will want to check out the resource center here, with its extensive collection of historic photos, oral histories, and genealogical information. A small gift shop sells books, cards, and toys.

The San Juan Historical Museum is open May–September 10 A.M.–3 P.M. Tuesday, Wednesday, and Thursday and 1–4 P.M. Saturday–Sunday; plus October, March, and April 1–4 P.M. Saturdays; and by appointment the rest of the year. Entrance is $2 adults, $1 ages 6–18, and free for younger kids. A variety of museum activities take place throughout the year, including outdoor concerts (Wednesday evenings mid-July to mid-Aug.) and the 4th of July Pig War picnic.

A number of other historic structures dot the island. One of the nicest is **Valley Church,** on Madden Lane two miles south of Friday Harbor. The church was built in 1892, and two cemeteries are nearby.

OTHER FRIDAY HARBOR SIGHTS

Head up Front Street from the ferry landing for a couple of hidden attractions. Next to the ferry is the **Spring Street Landing** building, with an interesting saltwater aquarium containing sea stars, anemones, sea urchins, shrimp, and other creatures from nearby waters.

A short distance farther at Waterfront Park is **Interaction,** a large and striking wood sculpture by Native Canadian artist Susan Point. The piece is inspired by traditional Coast Salish house posts, but uses contemporary techniques to represent the interface between people and their environment on San Juan Island.

SAN JUAN ISLAND NATIONAL HISTORICAL PARK

In one of the stranger pieces of Northwest history, the killing of a pig by an American settler nearly set off a war between the United States and Britain. Conflict was averted when saner heads prevailed, and the San Juan Islands were eventu-

© DON PITCHER

San Juan Historical Museum, Friday Harbor

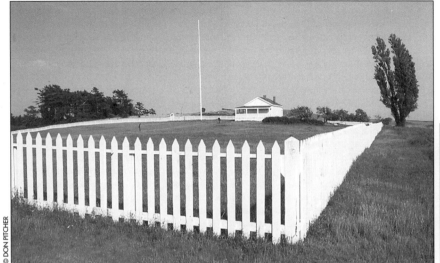

© DON PITCHER

San Juan Island

American Camp, San Juan Island National Historical Park

ally declared American territory. The sites where the American and British forces were based are now part of San Juan Island National Historical Park, with headquarters in Friday Harbor (640 Mullis St., 360/378-2240, www.nps.gov/sajh). The park itself is in two sections on different sides of the island: American Camp on the south end and English Camp on the western shore. Both sites have small visitor centers, along with picnic areas and beach access for day use. The grounds of both are open year-round, but they do not have campgrounds.

Summertime activities include guided historical walks at both American Camp and English Camp at 11:30 A.M. Friday–Saturday, living history exhibitions 12:30–3:30 P.M. Saturdays, plus historical songs and blacksmithing demonstrations on Sundays. Get the park's summer schedule for many other program offerings, including the popular Encampment in late August at English Camp.

American Camp

On the southeast corner of San Juan Island, American Camp sits on a windswept grassy peninsula six miles from Friday Harbor. This is a wonderful

place on a sunny summer afternoon, with both the Cascades and Olympics in view. It's also a deliciously lonely place to explore on a rainy winter day. American Camp covers 1,220 acres.

The **American Camp Visitor Center** (360/378-2902, 8:30 A.M.–4:30 P.M. daily except holidays) houses a few historical exhibits, along with bottles, pipes, marbles, a comb, and other small items found in archaeological excavations of the military encampments. Be sure to pick up the park brochure for a self-guided mile-long walking tour.

Two original buildings remain at American Camp from the occupation in the 1860s—an officer's quarters and a laundress's quarters—along with an earthen gun fortification (redoubt) that was constructed by an army engineer named Henry M. Roberts. You probably know him from a still-in-print book he wrote in 1876: *Roberts' Rules of Order,* the internationally used manual of parliamentary procedure. A long white picket fence circles the grounds, and a trail leads downhill past the site of **Belle Vue Farm** near Grandma's Cove. Belle Vue was the old Hudson's Bay Company Farm and the home of the British-owned pig that American Lyman Cutlar shot.

American Camp is a good place to watch for bald eagles and other birds of prey. Ask at the visitor center for directions to an eagle nest in use during the summer; you can watch the adults coming and going from the edge of the parking lot.

The park (especially near South Beach) is home to thousands of European rabbits whose ancestors were brought to the islands as a food source. The inevitable happened and they kept multiplying like rabbits. Red foxes were later brought to the island to help control the rabbit population; the foxes did fine but didn't seem to dent the rabbit population. Watch out for rabbit holes while walking!

American Camp is a fun place for a hike at any time of the year, with all-encompassing vistas, a long sandy beach, three bird-filled lagoons, and a protected cove with tall trees. If the weather is sunny and the wind isn't too strong, you certainly won't go wrong with a trek up the towering summit of **Mount Finlayson.** Okay, it's hardly a mountain at just 290 feet, so leave your climbing ropes and carabiners at home, but you're bound to be pleased at the panorama on top. On a clear day, you should be able to pick out Mount Baker, Mount Rainier, the Olympic Mountains, and Vancouver Island. There are several routes up the hill; a good one starts at the Jakle's Lagoon Trailhead, where parking is available. The path climbs grassy and flower-filled slopes (with scattered boulders for variety) and for the next mile you can just take a deep breath of fresh air, practice a little tai chi, pull out the binoculars to check for whales, eat a peanut butter sandwich, or kiss your sweetie. Once you reach the end near Third Lagoon, you can return on a separate path above Griffin Bay. Follow an old roadbed through a canopy of Douglas firs, western red cedar, and Western hemlock along **Jakle's Lagoon** to reach your original starting point. The total loop is around 3.5 miles, but you can come up with shorter versions if you just want a quick view from the hill or a one-mile round-trip saunter to the lagoon.

A maze of short trails covers the open country around the American Camp Visitor Center, taking you to the historical locations (marked by signs) of the Hudson's Bay Company Farm, the officers' quarters, laundress's quarters, redoubt, and then downhill to the shore along pretty **Grandma's Cove.** This cove is less than a mile round-trip from the visitor center.

If beaches are your thing, don't miss driftwood-jammed **South Beach,** a truly wonderful place for a sunset walk (or run). A parking lot is right next to South Beach, and you can hike a mile or so in either direction from here on this, San Juan Island's longest public beach. It's also one of the best beaches anywhere in the archipelago. It can become a log-walk at the highest tides, so check a tide chart before heading out. This is also a good place to watch for birds, including terns, gulls, plovers, ruddy turnstones, greater and lesser yellowlegs, and bald eagles. Tidepools on the western end of the beach have a multitude of marine life. Restrooms and picnic tables are available.

On the north side of the peninsula along Griffin Bay, **Fourth of July Beach** is another easy walk. It's a short hike from the parking area to the beach, and from here you can walk to Old Town Lagoon, the site of the rough-around-the-edges town when American Camp was occupied.

Near the tip of the peninsula is tiny **Cattle Point Interpretive Area,** where you'll find a picnic shelter housed in an old powerhouse. You can walk to **Cattle Point Lighthouse** via a trail that starts 150 yards down the road to the south. Two pretty pocket-size beaches are just down from the lighthouse parking area. A number of private residences are located on the eastern end of the peninsula, as this area lies outside the boundaries of San Juan Island National Historical Park.

English Camp

Nine miles from Friday Harbor on the northwest side of the island, English Camp (360/378-4409) covers 530 acres and includes four buildings from the 1860s that have been restored: a small white barracks, hospital, commissary, and a picturesque blockhouse. The last of these sits right at the water's edge and has a peculiar design. The second story is rotated 45 degrees from the bottom level, allowing troops to repel attacks from any side. Fortunately, the attack never came.

Befitting the civilized British modus operandi, the camp had a small **formal garden,** an impressive replica of which has been reestablished.

The blockhouse and barracks at English Camp are open 8:30 A.M.–4:30 P.M. daily in the summer, but closed the rest of the year. Park volunteers staff the buildings during the summer and show a video that explains the "Pig War." Be sure to pick up the park brochure for a self-guided walking tour of historical sites. It's day-use only here, with no camping allowed.

English Camp is a quiet and peaceful spot with protected waters on both sides of Bell Point. It contrasts sharply with American Camp's exposed and windswept location. The grounds include several old pear trees from a homestead family who lived here after the British military departed in 1872. Enormous bigleaf maples are also here, one of which was once proclaimed the world's largest. The loss of two major limbs reduced its spread, so the tree is now simply a very big and beautiful maple.

A 650-foot hill, **Mount Young,** rises directly behind Garrison Bay, with open meadows atop its forested slopes. The three-quarter-mile Mount Young Trail starts at English Camp, crosses the road, and climbs to the old **British cemetery,** where six Royal Marines are buried—though none of them died in a battle over the islands. Beyond this, the trail continues up through second-growth forests to the open summit of Mount Young, where you are treated to outstanding vistas across the archipelago. Old Garry oak trees grow up here as well.

An easy alternative walk departs from the blockhouse and leads along an almost-level path to the tip of **Bell Point** and then back along Westcott Bay. This wooded little peninsula is a good place for a picnic lunch. Keep your eyes open for Canada geese and wild turkeys below, and bald eagles and turkey vultures overhead.

Ⓜ ROCHE HARBOR

On the north end of San Juan Island, 10 miles from Friday Harbor, Roche Harbor (360/378-2155 or 800/451-8910, www.rocheharbor.com) is a delightful step into the past.

John McMillin's **Hotel de Haro** began as a log cabin built by the Hudson's Bay Company, but later grew into the distinctive three-story mansion of today. President Theodore Roosevelt

© DON PITCHER

Hotel de Haro at Roche Harbor Resort

visited it twice, in 1906 and 1907, and it later hosted President William Howard Taft. The quarries operated till 1956, when they were essentially mined out. Pick up the walking tour brochure at the hotel and start your exploration of this picturesque harbor.

Roche Harbor is named for Richard Roche, a British surveyor and midshipman during two 19th-century expeditions of the area. Hotel de Haro is named for nearby Haro Strait, which in turn got its name from Lopez Gonzales de Haro, a Spanish sailor and the first European to discover the San Juan Islands.

Resort and Marina

The white-clapboard Hotel de Haro, now on the National Register of Historic Places, has been lovingly restored. If it isn't occupied, you can peek in the presidential suite (room 2A) upstairs where Roosevelt stayed, or see his 1907 signature in the guest book below his portrait. The hotel's sloping floors, creaking steps, and crooked windows add charm, and provide a gracious setting for the antique furnishings.

Take some time to explore the area around the hotel. Out front is a wonderful **formal garden** with rose trellises and brilliant swaths of various flowers throughout the summer. The yellow brick road between the garden and the hotel was built from firebricks that once lined the lime kilns. McMillin's home is now a waterside restaurant, facing the protected and busy harbor filled with sailboats, motorboats, and kayaks. Roche Harbor is still the primary U.S. Customs port of entry for boaters heading to the San Juans from Canadian waters. The old general store is still in use, and well worth a visit. Behind it, warehouses once stretched hundreds of feet into the bay, holding up to 20,000 barrels of lime. Across the parking lot are the two original **stone kilns** built by the Scurr brothers in 1881. The 13 old lime quarries are uphill behind the resort, but you need to exercise caution since the slopes are unstable.

Just up from the hotel is the quaint little New England–style **Our Lady of Good Voyage Chapel,** built in 1892. John McMillin was a devout Methodist, but when Reuben Tarte bought Roche Harbor in 1956, he turned it into the only privately owned Catholic church in America. Mass is held on Easter Sunday and periodically throughout the summer. Other denominations also use the chapel, and it's a favorite spot for a wedding-with-a-view. A carillon was added in 1972, followed a few years later by a stained-glass window that depicts two of the late Dr. Tarte's devotions: medicine and tennis.

A short walk north of the church are nine simple cottages once used by McMillin's employees; they're now rented out to guests. Ten larger cottages were torn down, along with the old Japanese settlement on the south side of the harbor. The Japanese buildings were replaced by ugly condos in the 1970s, a glaring affront to this historic site.

A surprisingly moving **Colors Ceremony** takes place each evening at sunset from mid-May to late September, as the U.S., Canadian, and British flags are lowered to the national anthems, followed by taps and a shot from the cannon. This event always attracts a big crowd. You can surprise your friends by having a message read to them during the ceremony; just leave the message at the front desk of Hotel de Haro in advance.

Death Do Us Part

The exuberant **McMillin family mausoleum** ("Afterglow Vista," no less) is about a mile north of Hotel de Haro. Located north of the cottages and a quarter-mile hike up a dirt side road, the mausoleum's centerpiece is a stone temple packed with Masonic symbols and containing the family's ashes in chair-shaped crypts around a limestone (of course) table. There's even a broken column symbolizing the "unfinished state" of life, but the planned bronze dome was never added to this once-grandiose mausoleum. Step out of the past at the fly-in aviation community nearby, where planes taxi down Cessna Avenue and park in hangars next to nearly every house.

M Wescott Bay Reserve Sculpture Park

Covering 19 acres near the entrance to Roche Harbor, **Westcott Bay Reserve Sculpture Park** (360/370-5050, www.wbay.org, open daily dawn to dusk; donation requested) is home to more than 100 stone, wood, and metal sculptures. Trails lead through a diverse habitat of forest, meadow, pond, wetland, and shoreline. The sculptures change each year at this kid-friendly sculpture park, so there's always something new to see (and touch).

Family Art Days take place every Saturday Memorial Day to Labor Day, with lots of hands-on activities for kids. In addition, demonstrations on stone carving, bronze casting, wood-carving, and blacksmithing fill several summer weekends. Many classes and workshops take place under pavilion tents here and cover such diverse topics as casting metal sculpture, documentary filmmaking, fused glass production, edible seaweeds, and handmade felt. Other events include a dedication of new sculptures on Memorial Day weekend, and a Best of the San Juans Festival in early September, which showcases art, food, and music.

LIME KILN POINT STATE PARK

Locally known as **Whale Watch Park** (360/378-2044, www.parks.wa.gov), this is a premier spot to look for killer whales as they pass along Haro Strait on the island's west side. It's the only park in the nation dedicated primarily to whale-watching. Sit here long enough on a summer day (it may be quite a while) and you're likely to see killer whales, and possibly minke whales, Dall's porpoises, or harbor porpoises.

Picturesque **Lime Kiln Point Lighthouse** was built in 1914 and has a foghorn that announces its presence frequently in inclement weather. Researchers use the lighthouse as a base to watch for whales visually and by using an offshore hydrophone. They also use it to determine if boats are affecting whale behavior. If there aren't any whales to watch, you can just take in the vistas that stretch to Victoria.

The park has plenty of parking and a wheelchair-accessible trail to the whale-viewing area. No camping, but there are picnic tables, drinking water, and privies. Tune your radio to 89.1 FM when you approach the park to hear a broadcast

of underwater sounds—including whales if they happen to be in the area.

In the summer months, park staff lead lighthouse tours (7 P.M.–sunset Thursday and Saturday), interpretive orca whale talks (at 3 P.M. Friday and Saturday), and walks to the limestone kilns (four times a day on Friday and Sunday). At other times, you can watch a video on whales, listen to underwater sounds from the hydrophone, take in the view, or pull out the binoculars to scan for orcas.

A loop hike leads past one of the restored lime kilns and several in disrepair and then heads south to the old quarry and Deadman Bay. The trail continues out of the park and onto adjacent land within the **Limekiln Preserve,** owned by the San Juan County Land Bank. South of Lime Kiln, West Side Road hugs the steep shoreline of San Juan Island. This stretch of road is part of the Land Bank's **West Side Preserve,** where three

San Juan Island

© DON PITCHER

Lime Kiln Point Lighthouse at Lime Kiln Point State Park

pullouts provide additional chances to watch for whales and to take in panoramic views of Vancouver Island and the Olympic Mountains.

SAN JUAN COUNTY PARK

On the west side of the island at Smallpox Bay, San Juan County Park (360-378-8420, www.co .san-juan.wa.us/parks) is the only public camping spot on San Juan. In addition to camping, the 12-acre park has a pebble beach, pretty forests, picnic tables, restrooms, drinking water, and a boat launch. The waters here are popular with kayakers and divers, and this is a good place to watch for wild turkeys on land and killer whales offshore. Portions of the 1998 film *Practical Magic* were filmed here.

San Juan County Park is located along **Smallpox Bay.** In the 1860s two sick sailors from an unknown boat were put ashore to prevent them from contaminating the rest of the crew with smallpox. Local Coast Salish people, who had no immunity to the disease, helped the men, and smallpox quickly spread across San Juan Island. The feverish victims jumped into the bay to cool off and died of pneumonia. The few survivors burned their possessions and fled the island.

REUBEN TARTE COUNTY PARK

This tiny day-use-only area (360/378-8420, www.co.san-juan.wa.us/parks) is a secluded and delightful place to escape the Friday Harbor crowds. Located on the north end of the island near Limestone Point, it consists of a rocky point with two minor coves facing Haro Strait. The ferry connecting the islands with Sidney, British Columbia, goes right past the park. This is one of the few pieces of public land on the north end of San Juan Island; everything else around here is posted No Trespassing.

Get to Reuben Tarte by following Roche Harbor Road eight miles from Friday Harbor, and turning right onto Rouleau Road. Follow it a mile, then turn right onto Limestone Point Road. After another mile, turn right again onto San Juan Drive and continue a quarter-mile to the park, located on the left. You should proba-

bly park at the top and hike down the steep dirt road to Reuben Tarte, as only a couple of parking spaces are available at the bottom. No facilities (other than an outhouse) here, but bring your picnic lunch for a delightful afternoon along the shore.

FALSE BAY BIOLOGICAL RESERVE

Owned by the University of Washington, False Bay is a half-mile-wide undeveloped bay on the south end of San Juan Island. This large and shallow bay becomes a mudflat when the tide is out, though there are some sandy stretches along the shore. It's an easy stroll, and a good place to look for shorebirds. Access is from a pullout off False Bay Road; Mar Vista Resort is a short distance southeast of here.

ADDITIONAL AREAS

A number of other day-use-only spots are scattered around San Juan Island. **Jacksons Beach** is a small public beach a mile south of Friday Harbor off Argyle Avenue. It has a sandy shore littered with driftwood, a boat ramp, picnic tables, sand volleyball courts, and restrooms.

Eagle Cove sits on the south end of the island just west of American Camp, and is a favorite of sports fishers who enjoy the delightful pocket beach. Two north-end bodies of water, **Egg Lake** and **Sportsmans Lake,** are also popular with anglers in search of trout.

Sunken Park in Friday Harbor is a little pocket park with a gazebo, basketball court, and picnic area.

The **San Juan County Land Bank** (360/378-4402, www.co.san-juan.wa.us/land_bank) maintains several hundred acres of protected lands on San Juan Island that are open to the public, including Westside Preserve and Limekiln Preserve.

Other areas open to hiking include forested lands near **Roche Harbor Resort.** Although these are privately owned, the public is welcome on the trails, some of which connect with Park Service trails at English Camp. A 320-acre parcel of DNR land at **Mitchell Hill** is nearby and offers three miles of trails. The **San Juan Island Trails Committee** (www.sanjuanislandtrails.org) has a very helpful website with downloadable maps for these and other public areas.

FARMS

Several dozen small farms dot the San Juan Island landscape, producing such specialty products as cider apples, wines, miniature horses, medicinal herbs, strawberries, goat cheese, organic vegetables, and rabbits (do they really need more of these?). At **Heritage Farm** along Cattle Point Road, you're likely to see draft horses at work in the fields. For a complete list of local agriculture, pick up the *San Juan Island Farm Products Guide* (360/378-4414, http://sanjuan.wsu.edu) at the visitor center. Many local farm products are sold at the San Juan Farmers Market in Friday Harbor, held on summer Saturdays.

Pelindaba Lavender Farm

San Juan Vineyards

San Juan Vineyards (3136 Roche Harbor Rd., 360/378-9463 or 888/983-9463, www.sanjuanvineyards.com) is housed inside a restored one-room schoolhouse built in 1896 and was originally located along nearby Sportsmans Lake. The little 10-acre vineyard grows madeleine angevine and siegerrebe grapes. Winemaker Kurt Niznik produces a limited bottling of these—and they sell out quickly—but most of what he crafts comes from eastern Washington grapes, including gewürtztraminer, semillon-chardonnay, reserve chardonnay, and syrah. Stop by for wine tasting in the summer 11 A.M.–5 P.M. daily, with reduced hours in the spring and fall. Call for an appointment at other times. Grapes are harvested in early October by local volunteers.

Pelindaba Lavender Farm

Pelindaba Lavender Farm (off Wold Rd. at 33 Hawthorne Ln., 360/378-4248 or 866/819-1911, www.pelindaba.com) grows these pungent flowers on 20 acres on the south side of the island. Owners Susan and Stephen Robins have 12,000 plants in production on their organic farm, plus a distillery to extract the oil. Organic lavender flowers and essential oils are used in a wide range of products, all of which are made here: body oil, eye pillows, sachets, lavender pepper, pet shampoo, and even a lavender-based product that kills pond algae. A lavender cookbook is available, and local restaurants use their lavender in special dishes. There's a cutting field if you're just looking for a fresh bouquet during the flowering season in July and August. Pick up a brochure for a self-guided tour, or call ahead to set up a 45-minute tour ($3.50/person) that includes time in the fields, drying racks, and distillery.

The gift shop is open April–September 10 A.M.–5 P.M. daily; head to their Friday Harbor shop at other times of the year. The farm hosts a **Lavender Harvest Festival** the third weekend of July with tours, distillation demonstrations, craft workshops, lavender-accented foods, and music. Also on the property is **Lavender Fields Day Spa** (360/378-3637) with a full menu of day spa services: massage, reflexology, facials, body wraps, and more.

San Juan Island

LAVENDER LEMONADE

2 cups water
6 sprigs fresh lavender spikes, or 2 teaspoons dried Pelindaba Lavender
Juice of 3 lemons (about ½ cup)
1 quart water
½ cup sugar, or to taste, or ½ cup Pelindaba Lavender Syrup, or to taste
Additional lavender for garnish

Bring the 2 cups of water to a boil. Add lavender, cover the pan, and let it steep over very low heat for 30 minutes. Strain and reserve the liquid, which is the lavender tea you will use later.

Roll the lemons on a hard surface to help release the juices. Cut and squeeze them, straining out the seeds. To the quart of water, add ⅛ cup of the lavender tea, ½ cup of lemon juice, and ½ cup of sugar or Lavender Syrup (or to taste). Stir well to dissolve. Chill and serve over ice. Garnish with a fresh lavender spike. Makes 1 quart of lemonade.

Recipe courtesy of Pelindaba Lavender Farm

Alpacas

Fans of these friendly animals will certainly want to visit **Krystal Acres Ranch** (on West Valley Rd. south of English Camp, 360/378-6125, www.krystalacres.com) a picturesque 70-acre farm bordered by white picket fences. The multicolored herd is a favorite of photographers who happen by, and the teddy bear–faced alpacas are bound to elicit "I want one" from any child. A walking path leads between pastures containing more than 40 grazing alpacas, and the gift shop sells alpaca yarn, stuffed animals, home furnishings, and Peruvian sweaters made from alpaca wool.

Recreation

BICYCLING

San Juan Island is very popular with cyclists, but it isn't as bike-friendly as slower-paced Lopez Island. The terrain is varied, with quiet lanes through rolling farm country, wide-open grasslands and gorgeous beaches at American Camp, densely forested areas, and stunning shorelines fronting Haro Strait. The hilly western shore of San Juan (rising to 400 feet) is especially inviting, and is highlighted by a whale-watching stop at Lime Kiln Point State Park. Friday Harbor has a good bike shop and all the other travel amenities, but traffic can get congested and drivers distracted, so use caution, particularly around the ferry loading area. The San Juan Island Trails Committee website (www.sanjuanislandtrails .org) provides bike route information showing roads with wide shoulders. If you need a lift, **San Juan Transit** (360/378-8887 or 800/887-8387, www.sanjuantransit.com) will haul your bike along.

Bike Rentals

Rent bikes to cruise around San Juan Island from **Island Bicycles** (380 Argyle Ave., 360/378-4941, www.islandbicycles.com), a full-service shop just a few blocks from the ferry dock. Knowledgeable owner Paul Ahart has well-maintained, high-quality bikes, including mountain, cross, racing, tandem, and kid's bicycles. Mountain or cross bikes rent for $7/hour, $35/day, or $75 for three days; helmets and other essentials are included. The shop also rents bike trailers, trail-a-bikes, car racks, and baby strollers, and is open year-round (daily in the summer). Reservations are strongly recommended in the summer months.

Seasonal bike rentals are also available from **Susie's Mopeds** (Roche Harbor Village, 360/378-5244 or 800/532-0087, www.susiesmopeds.com, $10/hour or $35/day).

⬛ SEA KAYAKING

Sea kayaking is very popular in the waters around San Juan Island, with local companies offering day trips or extended tours. Each company has its own specialties, so ask around before deciding, particularly on a multi-day kayaking trip. Reservations are recommended for summer weekends. Most companies operate late April–September.

Day Trips

A number of companies lead short sea-kayaking paddles from San Juan Island in the summer months. No experience is needed, but you should be in decent physical condition, and young children are not allowed. You aren't likely to get too far in such a short time, but this will at least provide a guided introduction to saltwater paddling under protected conditions. If you're looking for killer whales, go with a company whose trips begin from San Juan County Park; Friday Harbor and Roche Harbor are fun but busy places to paddle. All companies provide free transportation from Friday Harbor.

In business since 1987, **Outdoor Odysseys** (360/378-3533 or 800/647-4621, www.outdoorodysseys.com) has day trips ($69) departing from San Juan County Park. Kayakers spend four hours on the water and are served a gourmet lunch, something not typically included by other operators. The guides are some of the most experienced around.

The non-profit **Sea Quest Expeditions** (360/378-5767 or 888/589-4253, www.seaquest-kayak.com) leads day trips that depart from San Juan County Park. Guides all have scientific backgrounds and emphasize natural history during their three-hour ($45) and six-hour ($65) trips. In addition to San Juan trips, Sea Quest sponsors environmental education and scientific

research, and guides lead kayak trips to Baha and Southeast Alaska.

Discovery Sea Kayaks (440 Spring St., 360/378-2559, www.discoveryseakayaks.com) is one of the newer companies on the island, but the two guides are extremely experienced, and the emphasis is on small groups—generally less than six. Discovery has the only kayak shop on San Juan Island, and also offers kayaking lessons. Day trips cover the west side of the island, departing from San Juan County Park; a six-hour trip is $69, and four-hour sunset paddles are $55. Also available is a six-hour mothership adventure based on the 30-foot *Bon Accord* for $180/person including lunch.

San Juan Safaris (360/378-1323 or 800/450-6858, www.sanjuansafaris.com) heads out at least twice daily from both Friday Harbor and Roche Harbor in the summer. In addition to standard three-hour trips and sunset tours ($55) from both ports, San Juan Safaris also has five-hour paddles ($75) out of Roche Harbor that stand a better chance of seeing orcas.

The largest kayaking company in the islands, **Crystal Seas Kayaking** (360/378-4223 or 877/732-7877, www.crystalseas.com) operates from Snug Harbor Marina on the west side of the island. They offer three-hour paddles ($49) for a quick sample, along with five-hour day trips ($65) that cover more coastline and increase your likelihood of viewing whales. Group sizes never exceed eight clients. In addition, the company leads kayak trips out of Edmonds, and in Maine, Florida, and Costa Rica.

Leisure Kayak Adventures (360/378-5992 or 800/836-1402, www.leisurekayak.com) is two miles south of Friday Harbor along quiet Griffin Bay, with free transportation provided. Two-hour kayak tours cost $39.

Multi-Day Kayak Tours

It takes time to really get a taste of the islands, and multi-day kayaking treks provide a fun way to explore places most visitors will never see. Three-day trips typically cost $360–450/person, with five-day trips at $600–700/person.

At **San Juan Kayak Expeditions** (360/378-4436, www.sanjuankayak.com), owner-operator

Tim Thomsen personally leads all trips—as he has for more than a quarter century. You won't find his brochures since he doesn't really need to advertise; word of mouth brings in the customers. He's even invented a unique sail that allows kayakers to take advantage of the winds when conditions are right. Three-day trips are $380/person, and four-day trips cost $480.

Another long-established company with a well-deserved reputation, **Sea Quest Expeditions** (360/378-5767 or 888/589-4253, www.sea-quest-kayak.com) has multi-day trips to Stuart, Jones, Posey, Turn, and other islands. Their five-day trips even cross over into Canada's southern Gulf Islands when weather permits.

A respected kayak company with experienced guides, **Outdoor Odysseys** (360/378-3533 or 800/647-4621, www.outdoorodysseys.com) has three-day tours that depart San Juan Island for remote Stuart Island, and more leisurely five-day trips that include Stuart, Jones, Turn, and other islands. The company also offers a soft-adventure three-night tour with two days of paddling and one day of hiking and exploring, plus lodging at States Inn B&B, wine tasting, and meals at Friday Harbor restaurants. The cost is $725/person.

Crystal Seas Kayaking (360/378-4223 or 877/732-7877, www.crystalseas.com) offers a wide variety of two- to six-day trips, including kayak-and-camping trips, inn-to-inn soft adventures, and multi-sport trips that combine kayaking, biking, and lodging at inns. Groups are kept small—not more than eight people.

In business for more than 25 years, the Seattle-based **Northwest Outdoor Center** (206/281-9694 or 800/683-0637, www.nwoc.com) leads three-day "whale search" trips a couple of times in the summer, using San Juan County Park as their camping base.

Discovery Sea Kayaks (440 Spring St., 360/378-2559, www.discoveryseakayaks.com) guides all-inclusive three- to five-day adventures to the more remote parts of the archipelago, including Sucia, Patos, Matia, and Jones Islands. They'll drop the price substantially if you provide food and camping equipment. Overnight trips have a maximum of just six clients.

Kayak Rentals

Discovery Sea Kayaks (440 Spring St., 360/378-2559, www.discoveryseakayaks.com) operates the only full-service kayak shop on San Juan Island (Kings Market also sells kayaks and supplies). The small shop has sea kayaks and camping gear for sale, and rents kayaks: plastic doubles are $65 ($75/day for fiberglass), and singles run $50/day. These are only rented to experienced paddlers, and come complete with paddles, spray skirts, and even wet suits. Lessons are available to get you up to speed. **San Juan Kayak Expeditions** (360/378-4436, www.sanjuankayak.com) rents double kayaks with gear for $60/day.

Located along Griffin Bay—two miles from Friday Harbor—**Leisure Kayak Adventures** (360/378-5992 or 800/836-1402, www.leisurekayak.com) rents two-person kayaks at $45 for two hours or $60/day, and singles at $30 for two hours or $45/day. No experience required. A free shuttle is available from Friday Harbor.

San Juan Safaris (360/378-1323 or 800/450-6858, www.sanjuansafaris.com) rents sit-on-top kayaks in Roche Harbor for playing around the harbor; hourly rates are $15/single or $18/double.

Lakedale Resort (360/378-2350 or 800/617-2267, www.lakedale.com) rents canoes, paddleboats, and sit-on-top kayaks for use on Neva Lake, four miles from Friday Harbor on Roche Harbor Road.

Kayaks can be launched from the public dock just north of the Friday Harbor ferry landing (fee charged), but parking can be a challenge. Other options include Shipyard Cove (half a mile from Friday Harbor), Pinedrona Cove (near Turn Island), Jacksons Beach, San Juan County Park, Roche Harbor, American Camp, and English Camp. Anyone planning their own kayak trip to the islands should get a copy of Randel Washburne's *Kayaking Puget Sound, the San Juans, and Gulf Islands* (The Mountaineers, www.mountaineers.org). It contains information on routes, safety issues, and much more.

WHALE-WATCHING

For thousands of visitors, seeing a killer whale is *the* highlight of a trip to San Juan Island.

Whale-watching has become a big business, particularly during June and July when a flotilla of boats and kayaks hovers around pods of orcas, trailing them as they move. Boat operators insist that they are not negatively impacting the whales and all local companies are members of the **Northwest Whalewatch Operators Association** (www.nwwhalewatchers.org), which has a code of conduct to minimize disturbances to the whales. The Whale Museum encourages folks to watch from shore, especially from such places as Lime Kiln Point Lighthouse (a.k.a. Whale Watch Park) and American Camp. Drop by the museum to ask where whales have been reported today and then take a bike, car, or shuttle bus over for the day. It's cheaper than a boat and you won't need to worry about impacting the whales.

Some companies promise "guaranteed whales" in their brochures. In reality, the entire fleet knows where the whales are, so you're probably as likely to see them on one boat as another. The only difference may come when the orcas are too far away for the slower boats to reach in three hours.

Expect to pay $55 adults or $39 kids for a three-hour (sometimes longer) trip, with half that time around the whales and the remainder in transit. Killer whales are most often seen on the west side, so companies operating out of Roche Harbor typically spend an hour less time en route. (On the other hand, a fast boat can quickly get around the island from Friday Harbor, and the whales move around quite a bit.)

You should bring a warm jacket, snacks, drinks, camera, and binoculars. Ask if the boat has a hydrophone onboard—most do. In the peak season, be sure to make reservations for these very popular trips.

In addition to killer whales, keep your eyes open for Dall's porpoises, harbor porpoises, harbor seals, Steller sea lions, bald eagles, and many species of seabirds. You might also spot an occasional minke or gray whale.

The Operators

Quite a few companies run scheduled whale-watching trips from Friday Harbor, and each has its advantages and disadvantages. Some of the bigger outfits have flashy brochures and larger boats that pack folks on, while the small operators offer more intimate trips, though their boats may be slower and bounce around a lot (not good if you get seasick easily). Operators based on the west side of San Juan Island at Snug Harbor or Roche Harbor are often closer to the whales, but fast boats can get there from Friday Harbor and the whales aren't always in that area.

A very good west-side operation is **Salish Sea Charters** (360/378-8555 or 877/560-5711, www.salishsea.com) based at Snug Harbor Marina Resort along Mitchell Bay. Three-hour trips on their 18-passenger boat are $55 ($45 for kids). Guests always enjoy Elmer the whale watch dog.

Another good company operating out of Snug Harbor, **Maya's Whale Watch Charters** (360/378-7996, www.mayaswhalewatch.biz) has a speedy little six-passenger boat for personalized trips at the same price as the bigger operators. Maya's heads out three times a day in the summer.

Bon Accord Charters, (360/378-5921 or 800/677-0751, www.bonaccord.com) has a beautiful 30-foot wooden trawler with space for six people. These slow-paced trips ($74 adults, $59 kids) last five hours and are offered once a day from Friday Harbor.

Friday Harbor–based **Western Prince Cruises** (360/378-5315 or 800/757-6722, www.westernprince.com) has a 46-foot boat with a maximum of 30 guests. Their longer four-hour trips and fast boat are advantages.

San Juan Excursions (360/378-6636 or 800/809-4253, www.watchwhales.com) operates the largest boat you're likely to see around the whales, the 65-foot *Odyssey*, a wooden boat with space for 97 passengers. Three-hour tours depart from Friday Harbor.

One of the biggest local operators, **San Juan Safaris** (360/378-1323 or 800/450-6858, www.sanjuansafaris.com) has 3.5-hour trips out of both Friday Harbor and Roche Harbor. One boat carries 16 and the other up to 24 passengers. Trips depart twice daily from each location in mid-summer.

Salish Sea Charters, Bon Accord Charters, Western Prince, and Maya's Whale Watch Charters all head out year-round; the other companies

San Juan Island

San Juan Island

WHALE-WATCHING TRIPS

Guided whale-watching trips began in the early 1980s around the San Juan Islands and have exploded into a major business. Dozens of commercial operators run some 85 boats today. Some of these are based on San Juan and Orcas Islands, while many others make day trips from Victoria, Seattle, and other cities. The best viewing is usually in Haro Strait on the west side of San Juan Island from the shores of Lime Kiln State Park, but killer whales move almost constantly and may be seen elsewhere around the San Juans, particularly near Stuart and Waldron Islands northwest of Orcas Island.

Operated by the Whale Museum, the **Soundwatch Boater Education Program** works to protect the orcas from vessel impacts through education, along with a bit of verbal arm-twisting and "report cards" to commercial whale-watching companies. Flagrant violations are reported to the National Marine Fisheries Service, which may impose stiff fines. Boaters heading out on their own should pick up a copy of the Soundwatch whale-viewing guidelines from the Whale Museum in Friday Harbor or download them from its website: www.whalemuseum.com.

Where Are the Whales?

The best time to see killer whales is May and June, when salmon are moving into Puget Sound and killer whales are seen 90 percent of the time. The J pod is typically present year-round, while the K and L pods often head farther out to sea to hunt December through April, when most of the salmon are elsewhere. The Whale Museum's website has a monthly chart showing which pods have historically been seen in waters around the San Juans, plus webcams showing the current view from Lime Kiln Point State Park, along with live audio from underwater hydrophones just offshore.

Choosing a Trip

The least intrusive way to watch killer whales is from land at scenic **Lime Kiln Point State Park** (a.k.a. Whale Watch Park) on the west side of San Juan Island along Haro Strait. Other good spots to look for orcas are San Juan County Park and South Beach. The whales come in close to shore at times, though their arrival can't be predicted with certainty.

Many boat companies compete for your whale-viewing business, and their snazzy brochures

typically operate April–September when whales are more plentiful. Wintertime trips tend to focus on viewing eagles and other wildlife.

A number of companies lead **sea kayak trips** along the west coast of San Juan Island—through prime orca waters. Kayaks are quiet and don't leave behind the odor from exhaust fumes, but kayakers should raft up to minimize their impacts on the whales. Look for kayak companies that depart from San Juan County Park or Snug Harbor.

BOATING

Sailing and powerboating are very big on San Juan Island, and the surrounding waters fill with

a flotilla of watercraft on summer weekends. Two large marinas at Roche Harbor and Friday Harbor offer guest moorage, sailboat and motorboat charters, fishing charters, and showers, with lodging, restaurants, and other amenities close by. Public boat launch ramps are located at San Juan County Park, Friday Harbor, and Jacksons Beach. A fee is charged to launch at Roche Harbor and Shipyard Cove Marina.

Founded in 1964, the **San Juan Island Yacht Club** (237 Front St., 360/378-3434, www .sjiyc.com) is a private club that sponsors a dozen or so local cruises for powerboats and sailboats each year, along with two major sailing events, the Shaw Island Classic and the Round the Island Race.

fill the racks on ferries and tourist venues. Not all of these tours are created equally. Some brag about their personalized trips aboard boats that hold just six passengers; some claim to be "closest to the whales"; others talk up their speedy boats, colorful captains, stable larger vessels, or hydrophones to listen underwater. From an environmental standpoint, larger boats may be better since this means fewer vessels bobbing around the whales, but you'll also hear complaints about the jam-'em-on whale-watching boats and the small inflatable Zodiac-type boats that come across from Victoria and buzz around the whales like angry bees. The latter have a bad reputation for "leapfrogging": intentionally positioning the boats where the whales are expected to surface. This makes for good photos and gives tourists a thrill but is frowned upon by whale researchers and more reputable operators.

When choosing a whale-watching trip, take the time to learn more about the companies and how they operate. Be sure to ask about onboard naturalists' training and affiliated organizations. Companies listed in this book are all members of the **Northwest Whalewatch Operators Association** (www.nwwhalewatchers.org), which has a code of conduct that tries to minimize disturbances to the whales. Let the company know it is important to you that it follow the guidelines; it shows you expect high standards. The Whale Museum does not lead trips—and in fact, encourages shore-based viewing instead—but the best companies are affiliated with it.

Learning More

Killer Whales, by John K. B. Ford, Graeme M. Ellis, and Kenneth C. Balcomb (UBC Press, www.ubcpress.ca), is the definitive volume on these whales, with a detailed natural history and a genealogy of the British Columbia and Washington orcas. One of the authors, Dr. Kenneth Balcomb, heads the nonprofit **Center for Whale Research** (360/378-5835, www.whaleresearch.com) in Friday Harbor on San Juan Island. The center doesn't have facilities for visitors, but it does take volunteers for seasonal research projects in which the whales are photographed and identified.

For a hands-on chance to learn about killer whales and other marine mammals, be sure to visit another nonprofit, the excellent **Whale Museum** (360/378-4710 or 800/946-7227, www.whalemuseum.com) in Friday Harbor.

Sailing Charters

Several companies offer sailing charters out of Friday Harbor or Roche Harbor for the day or longer. The best local winds are generally found in San Juan Channel and Haro Strait. With offices and boats in both Friday Harbor (next to the ferry) and Roche Harbor, **Charters Northwest** (360/378-7196 or 800/258-3119, www.charters northwest), prides itself as "the only full-service bareboat charter company in the San Juan Islands." Experienced sailors can charter from them, starting around $1,400/week. Those who lack the skills or want someone with local knowledge can hire a skipper for an extra $225/day (plus meals).

With more than two decades of experience on these waters, Howard Crowell of **Cap'n** **Howard's Sailing Charters** (360/378-3958 or 877/346-7245, www.capnhoward.com) offers custom cruises of all lengths out of Friday Harbor. You'll sail on the *Capricious Desires,* a luxurious 35-foot Columbia sloop. He can carry up to six people for $70/hour. In the off-season, Captain Howard is most likely sailing in the Caribbean.

Powerboat Charters and Cruises

Charters Northwest (360/378-7196 or 800/258-3119, www.chartersnw.com) has 15 or so powerboats available, ranging from a 34-foot boat ($2,000/week) to a luxurious 56-foot power yacht that costs nearly $8,000/week. For something really special, charter the *Arequipa* through them. This elegant 65-foot wooden motor yacht was built in 1927 and has three staterooms, a vintage wheelhouse, and an enclosed aft deck.

The *Scamper* (360/370-5133 or 877/314-3532, www.scampercharters.com) is a classic motor yacht built in 1920 and painstakingly restored to her original glory. This beautiful wooden boat—it once graced the cover of *Woodenboat Magazine*—departs Friday Harbor on daily trips in the summer. Three-hour sunset cruises start at $55/person (minimum two, max six people).

Marinas and Boat Rentals

Friday Harbor Marina (360/378-2688, www .portfridayharbor.org) is at the center of the Friday Harbor action. This 500-slip marina has space for 150 visiting boats, plus a chandlery. Just about anything else you might need can be found within a few blocks, from whale-watching to gallery snooping. Charter boats and fishing trips are available, along with showers, laundry, pump-out service, and a launch ramp. It is also a U.S. Customs port of entry and seaplane base.

Roche Harbor (360/378-2155 or 800/451-8910, www.rocheharbor.com) is the largest marina in the San Juans and a U.S. Customs port of entry for boaters coming in from Canada. Facilities here include permanent and guest moorage for 350 boats, fuel, a free pump-out service (called, naturally, the "Phecal Phreak"), showers, laundry, and a launch ramp. Boat charters are through Charters Northwest. This full-service resort includes a grocery store, post office, restaurants, bar, hotel, cabins, and swimming pool. Whale-watching tours and guided kayak trips are popular summertime diversions, and sit-on-top kayaks are available for rent through San Juan Safaris (360/378-1323 or 800/450-6858, www.sanjuansafaris.com). Roche Harbor Village is one of the biggest attractions on San Juan Island.

Snug Harbor Marina Resort, on the west side of the island (1997 Mitchell Bay Rd., 360/378-4762, www.snugresort.com) rents a variety of powerboats, from a 14-foot aluminum skiff ($75/day) to a 22-foot Marlin with a 200-horsepower engine ($375/day). Moorage is available for those with their own boats, and a small general store offers a limited selection of groceries, fishing tackle, and dive tank refills.

Leisure Kayak Adventures (360/378-5992 or 800/836-1402, www.leisurekayak.com) rents 14- and 16-foot Hobie Cat catamarans ($40/hour) for folks who want to try a bit of sailing on their own. The shop is two miles south of Friday Harbor along Griffin Bay, with free transportation provided.

FISHING CHARTERS

Fishing for salmon (kings, silvers, and sockeye) is best in August and September, with bottomfish available year-round. You can also fish for trout at Egg Lake and Sportsmans Lake. For fishing and other boat charters ($85–95/person for a half-day), contact **Trophy Charters** (360/378-2110, www.sanjuanislandfishingcharters.com), or **Buffalo Works** (360/378-4612, www.sanjuan salmon.com). Both operate out of Snug Harbor Marina on the west side of the island.

Haro Strait near Lime Kiln Point State Park

DIVING

Scuba diving is popular in the cold but amazingly productive waters off San Juan Island. **Island Dive and Water Sports** (2A Spring Street Landing in Friday Harbor, 360/378-2772 or 800/303-8386, www.divesanjuan.com) is a full-service operation. The shop sells and rents diving and snorkeling equipment, and offers chartered dives from its boats, complete instruction and certification, and air fills. Two-tank boat dives cost $75 if you provide the gear, or $125 if they provide everything. The owners put together dive packages for all budgets, starting at just $100/day, including lodging.

SWIMMING AND FITNESS

Roche Harbor Resort (360/378-2155 or 800/451-8910, www.rocheharbor.com) has a large outdoor pool and children's wading pool that is open to the general public mid-May through September from sunrise to sunset, and costs $6 adults or $3 kids. Lap swim is 8–9 A.M.

Fitness fanatics may want to take advantage of one-day memberships ($15 with pool access) to **San Juan Fitness and Athletic Club** (435 Argyle Ave., 360/378-4449, www.interisland.net/sjfit). Although privately owned, the fitness center is viewed by most locals as a community resource akin to a YMCA. The facilities include an indoor 25-yard swimming pool and wading pool, kids' gym with climbing wall, racquetball courts, coed sauna, steam room, and Jacuzzi, plus a cramped weight room. A variety of classes—from yoga to swimming lessons—are included at no extra charge.

Lakedale Resort (4313 Roche Harbor Rd., 360/378-2350 or 800/617-2267, www.lakedale.com) allows swimming and rents canoes and other water toys at its mid-island private lakes.

GOLF AND TENNIS

The longest nine-hole course in the Northwest at 3,194 yards, the **San Juan Golf & Country Club** (2261 Golf Course Rd., 360/378-2254, www.sanjuangolf.com) overlooks beautiful Griffin Bay on the east side of San Juan Island. The course is open to the public and nine holes of golf costs $23; golf carts are an extra $15–25. It is open year-round, with tennis courts available at $10 for 1.5 hours. Tennis courts are also available at Roche Harbor Resort, and public ones are at the high school at 45 Blair Avenue.

TRAIL RIDES

Based at States Inn on the west side of the island, **Saddle Up Trailriding** (26887 West Valley Rd., 360/378-4243, www.saddleuptrailriding.com) has seasonal guided horseback rides. These last an hour, and cost $42/person. In the off-season you'll pay a bit less and get the chance to learn more about handling horses in the arena.

Covering 16 acres off San Juan Valley Road, **Horseshu Ranch** (131 Gilbert Ln., 360/378-2298, www.horseshu.com) has 20 or more horses and ponies. Even young children are welcome on the ponies (with parental help, of course). Short, half-hour rides provide an introduction for $20/person, while hour-long rides cost $30. More experienced riders can join a three-hour trip ($78) that starts in Roche Harbor before entering Park Service and DNR lands. There's a two-person minimum on these fun rides. Horseshu Ranch has an arena and provides riding lessons and horse boarding.

Accommodations

During the summer it's a good idea to make reservations several months ahead of time to be assured of a bed on San Juan Island, particularly on weekends.

VACATION RENTALS

For weekly vacation rentals, **Windermere Real Estate** (360/378-3601 or 800/391-8190, www .windermerevacationrentals.com) has a big selection, with more than 45 places on San Juan, plus additional rentals on Orcas and Lopez. These range from bungalows that sleep two for $950/week all the way up to $3,800/week for a luxurious waterfront mansion. There's a one-week minimum mid-June to mid-September, or three nights at other times.

San Juan Central (360/378-8775 or 800/722-2939, www.sanjuanisland.com) is a booking agency for 50 vacation rentals on San Juan Island, including simple cabins, homes of all sizes, cottages on the beach, and more. Most require at least a two-night minimum stay. Prices are lower by the week or in the off-season.

Other places to check are **San Juan Island Vacation Rentals** (360/378-3190 or 888/367-5211, www.sanjuanislandvacationrentals.com), and **Re/Max San Juan Island** (360/378-5858 or 877/757-3629, www.sanjuanrealestate.com). Many of San Juan Island's resorts, inns, and cottages also offer weekly rates.

APARTMENTS

Conveniently located just a few blocks from downtown Friday Harbor, **Sandpiper Condominiums** (570 Jenson Alley, 360/378-5610, www.sandpiper-condos.com) has six studio units and a pair of one-bedroom apartments, all with fully equipped kitchens, plus access to an outdoor pool, Jacuzzi, and exercise room, but no phones. Rates are $85–95/night for a studio ($450/week), or $115/night for a one-bedroom unit ($625/week). Borrow an air bed to put extra folks on the living room floor. This may be the best bargain on the island for couples and small families.

HOSTEL

The only hostel on San Juan Island, **Wayfarers Rest** (35 Malcolm St., 360/378 6428, www.rock-island.com/~wayfarersrest) is located within a comfortable ranch-style home just four blocks from the ferry terminal in Friday Harbor. The hostel has a coed dorm room that sleeps six in bunk beds ($25/person), and two options for couples: a separate private room in the house, and two little cabins out back with room for two ($60) or three ($70). Children are welcome, but pay the same rates (toddlers under three are charged half-price). Linens are included, and travelers share a bath, full kitchen, living room, dining room, and phone. Bike rentals are also available for guests. The hostel is open year-round, but is often booked by groups in the summer. Make reservations as far ahead as you can (at least two weeks if possible).

HOTELS AND INNS
Discovery Inn
The 20-room Discovery Inn (1016 Guard St., 360/378-2000 or 800/822-4753, www.discovery-inn.com, $115–140 d) is three-quarters of a mile from the ferry landing. It's a casual place with attractive gardens, a cedar sauna, a huge outdoor Jacuzzi, sun decks, barbecue area, porch swings, and a small pond. Rooms include one or two queen beds, private baths, and TV; some also contain kitchenettes, and the largest rooms sleep five. The town library is just up the block.

Friday Harbor House
Located right along the harbor, Friday Harbor House (130 West St., 360/378-8455, www.friday-harborhouse.com, $195–325 d; $35/person for extra guests) is one of the nicest and most romantic choices in town. The 20 rooms are stylish and modern, with gas fireplaces, large jetted

tubs, queen beds, fridges, and ceiling-to-floor windows facing the harbor. A homemade continental breakfast is served in the dining room. The inn is popular for meetings, retreats, and wedding parties. A two-night minimum is required for summer at this AAA-approved hotel.

Friday's Historic Inn

Just a block from the water, Friday's Historic Inn (35 First St., 360/378-5848 or 800/352-2632, www.friday-harbor.com) is close to restaurants and shops. This lovingly remodeled inn is one of downtown's oldest buildings, dating from 1891. The 15-room hotel has a wide range of classy accommodations, including rooms with shared baths ($99–129 d) or private baths ($149–269 d). Additional guests (maximum of six in the largest suite) are $20 each. Each room is different. The pricier rooms have king beds, private baths with Jacuzzi tubs and double-headed showers, balconies, and wet bars; one even has its own outdoor hot tub. Guests are served a light breakfast each morning in the lobby, along with afternoon tea and cookies. One wheelchair-accessible room is available, and you can check your email on the computer. On-street parking only, but there is space for bicycles in the courtyard. Friday's Historic Inn is AAA-approved. They also rent three apartments in other parts of town for $169–299 d; the largest has two bedrooms, a full kitchen, and private deck.

Friday Harbor Inn

The 72-room Friday Harbor Inn (410 Spring St. in Friday Harbor, 360/378-4000 or 800/793-4756, www.fridayharborinn.com, $139–175 d) has fridges and microwaves in the rooms, plus a small indoor pool, Jacuzzi, sauna, and exercise bikes. Lodging ranges from older no-frills rooms to spacious studios with full kitchens and a dining area. Add $10 per extra person; one unit sleeps five. The motel is AAA-approved.

Friday Harbor Suites

The largest employer on the island, the sprawling Friday Harbor Suites (680 Spring St., 360/378-3031 or 800/752-5752, www.friday-harborsuites.com) is six blocks from downtown.

The building was originally an assisted living center, and is a bit sterile compared to other local offerings. Fortunately, the 63 units are large, with well-maintained furnishings. This all-suites facility includes kitchenettes (full fridges, microwaves, and sinks), ceiling fans, and sitting rooms with large TVs; many also have gas fireplaces. Studio units are $140–160 d, one-bedroom suites cost $225 d, while two-bedroom suites are $265 d. Add $15/extra person; the two-bedroom units can sleep six. All units have sliding glass doors leading to tiny patios or balconies. A couple of the rooms are wheelchair-accessible.

In addition, three places are available behind the hotel. Two nicely renovated bungalows sleep four each for $180–200. A three-bedroom, two-bath home has a gas fireplace and full kitchen, along with four televisions and three phones. It sleeps up to 10 people for $450.

Guests staying at the Suites are welcome to use the indoor pool, Jacuzzi, and sauna two blocks away at Friday Harbor Inn. Friday Harbor Suites is AAA-approved, and is now part of the Best Western chain.

Orca Inn

Located in Friday Harbor, the 65-room Orca Inn (770 Mullis St., 360/378-2724 or 877/541-6722, www.theorcainn.org, $59–89 s or $64–89 d; additional guests are $5 each) has some of the cheapest rooms around. Rooms are small and not at all fancy, but they're clean and comfortable.

GUEST HOUSES
Wood Duck Ponds

Located four miles northwest of Friday Harbor, Wood Duck Ponds (242 Wood Duck Lane, 360/378-2356, www.woodduckponds.com) is a favorite in-the-country wedding place, with two ponds, an arching footbridge, white swans, and a gazebo, all on a 25-acre estate. You don't, however, have to get married to stay in the two pond-side homes. The larger option is a fully furnished five-bedroom home with two large living rooms (one with a fireplace) and decks to take in the ponds and gardens. Other amenities include two baths, washer/dryer, TV/VCR, and rowboat. All this for $350 for up to eight people.

A smaller house has a king and queen beds, a full kitchen, bath, washer/dryer, TV/VCR, wood-burning fireplace, private greenhouse, and Jacuzzi on the deck. This one rents for $200 d. There is a two-night minimum stay for both houses, and kids are welcome.

Horseshu Hacienda

This beautiful modern home (131 Gilbert Ln., 360/378-2298, www.horseshu.com) is less than two miles from town off San Juan Valley Road. It's part of a 16-acre spread where pastures are filled with horses and ponies. The home contains a full kitchen, washer/dryer, jetted tub in the master bath, and a deck overlooking the pasture. It comfortably sleeps six for $225, with a three-night minimum. Call well ahead for summer bookings. Horse boarding is available.

RESORTS

Lonesome Cove Resort

This is what getting away from it all means. Lonesome Cove (416 Lonesome Cove Rd., 360/378-4477, www.lonesomecove.com) sits on the quiet north end of San Juan Island facing Spieden Channel, the passageway for ferries connecting Friday Harbor with Vancouver Island. To get there you drive a half-mile down a narrow dirt road through tall trees before emerging onto the lovely grounds bordering Lonesome Cove and Spieden Channel. The resort centers on an old apple orchard, a small pond, and creek. Semi-tame deer wander through.

Lonesome Cove Resort is a favorite of the just-married crowd, but also remains popular with families. Guests stay in six charming waterfront log cabins, each with a double bed and futon, full kitchen with dishes, private bath, stone fireplace and wood, and large decks just 40 feet from the beach. No phones or TVs to disturb your time here. Nightly rates are $115 d or $140 for four people; kids are welcome but are charged the same as adults. A separate two-bedroom apartment suite is also available with its own gazebo; it sleeps six for $170.

Lonesome Cove is a delightful spot, but it was long ago discovered. You'll need to make reservations a year in advance to be assured of space in the peak season; all the cabins are booked by the previous November! A five-night minimum is required June–August, with a two-night minimum at other times. During the summer, a 100-foot dock is available here, making this a fine base for boaters.

Lakedale Resort

A modern and upscale place, Lakedale Resort (four miles from Friday Harbor at 4313 Roche Harbor Rd., 360/378-2350 or 800/617-2267, www.lakedale.com) on an 80-acre spread in the heart of San Juan Island. The rustically modern, 9,000-square-foot log lodge faces Neva Lake and features a great room with stone fireplace. Inside are 10 immaculate guest rooms, each with a fireplace, jetted tub, and private deck. Most rooms face the lake, and one is wheelchair-accessible, while a second is set up specifically for the hearing-impaired. Lodge rooms rent for $195 d, with additional guests at $20/person. The lodge isn't for kids.

Six log cabins, also recently built, are situated along a lake or set beneath tall second-growth Douglas firs. Each includes two bedrooms, two baths, a full kitchen with dishes, a loft (great for kids), fireplace, and covered back porch, but no televisions or phones. The cabins sleep up to six, and guests can use the central hot tub, or head to the lake to swim or fish for trout and bass. Cabins rent for $265 d, plus $20/person for additional guests ($10 each for kids). No maid service at the housekeeping cabins, but guests get free use of rowboats, and can rent canoes, paddleboats, and sit-on-top kayaks. The most spacious lodging choice is a three-bedroom house with loft, kitchen, fireplace, and deck overlooking the lake; it rents for $425 d. A breakfast of fresh fruit, muffins, cereal, yogurt, and more is served each morning for all Lakedale guests. The resort is AAA-approved.

Mar Vista Resort

Anyone with even rudimentary Spanish knows that Mar Vista (2005 False Bay Dr., 360/378-

© DON PITCHER

Lakedale Resort offers six modern log cabins.

4448, www.marvistaresort.com) means Sea View. The name fits. Located on a remote corner of southern San Juan Island, this small resort occupies 40 acres of land along the Strait of Juan de Fuca. It has beachfront one-, two- and three-bedroom cabins, all with kitchens and access to the private beach and tidepools. Orca whales, bald eagles, deer, and otters are all commonly seen. Nightly rates start at $110 d in one-bedroom units, up to $180 for a cabin that sleeps eight. Mar Vista is open mid-April to mid-October, with a two-night minimum stay. Kids are welcome.

Roche Harbor Village Not avail.
On the National Register of Historic Places, Roche Harbor Village (360/378-2155 or 800/451-8910, www.rocheharbor.com) features impressive 19th-century buildings and a wide range of lodging options. Facilities include a restaurant and café, general store, tennis and volleyball courts, a heated Olympic-size outdoor pool and wading pool, and a kids' playground (the best on San Juan Island), plus rentals of motorboats, mopeds, and sit-on-top kayaks. Whale-watching and sea-kayak tours depart from the

harbor, a fascinating sculpture garden is just up the hill, and the lounge has live music and dancing on summer weekends. (By the way, the official name is Roche Harbor Village, but almost everyone refers to it as Roche Harbor Resort.)

Built in 1886, the classic **Hotel de Haro** fronts a gracious formal garden and marina. The hotel's downstairs lobby is worth a look even if you aren't staying here, with historic photos and a big fireplace. Rates at the hotel start at $85–92 d for an old-fashioned room (bath down the hall and no TV) with a double bed, up to the presidential suite ($182 d) with its own fireplace, private bath, and veranda facing the harbor. This one really is a presidential suite; Theodore Roosevelt slept here in 1906 and 1907. The hotel is not for everyone. If you're accustomed to modern hotels with all the accompanying luxuries, this will definitely not be to your taste, but those who enjoy slipping into the past will love it.

Employees of the Roche Harbor Lime Company once occupied the resort's rustic cottages, which are now rented out for $179–229. All of these have two bedrooms and full kitchens, and the more expensive ones face the water. Same price for up to six guests here. Also available are a number of **condos,** starting at $199 for one-bedroom units up to three-bedroom condos for $360. These '70s-era condos are glaring eyesores in this historic and scenic place. One consolation: From their windows, you can't see them. A two-night minimum stay is required for the cottages and condos in the summer.

For the most luxurious Roche Harbor accommodations, book one of the four **McMillin Suites,** in an old harborside home. Each of these has a wrap-around covered deck, king bed, gas fireplace, ceiling fans, clawfoot tubs and radiant-heated floors in the bath, and tasteful furnishings. These cost $299 d and are a great splurge. One of the suites is wheelchair-accessible.

Snug Harbor Marina Resort

Cozy Snug Harbor Marina Resort (1997 Mitchell Bay Rd., 360/378-4762, www.snugresort.com, $159–209 d) snuggles along Mitchell Bay on the west side of the island, eight miles from Friday Harbor and just south of English Camp. A variety of well-maintained accommodations are here, from simple Panabode studio cabins (gas stove, mini-fridge, and microwave, but no television) to modern prefab log units with a bedroom and loft, small deck, kitchenette, miniature gas fireplace, and pint-size TV. Most of these are right on the water facing the marina, and guests can borrow the canoe to paddle around. The marina has kayak trips (through Crystal Seas Kayaking), whale-watching voyages (through Maya's Whale Watch Charters or Salish Sea Charters), and salmon-fishing (through Buffalo Works Fishing Charters). Snug Harbor is open year-round, and also has a small store and campground.

BED-AND-BREAKFASTS

The **Bed & Breakfast Association of San Juan Island** produces an excellent lodging brochure with brief listings and a map showing bed-and-breakfast locations. Pick one up onboard the ferry or in regional visitor centers. Call their hotline (360/378-3030 or 866/645-3030) for availability at more than 20 of the finest local bed-and-breakfasts, or head to www.san-juan-island.net for direct links to bed-and-breakfast

homepages. Several of the places listed under *Hotels and Inns* also provide a light breakfast for their guests.

Argyle House B&B

A comfortable Craftsman-style home, Argyle House (685 Argyle Ave., 360/378-4084 or 800/624-3459, www.argylehouse.net) was built in 1910 and sits on an acre of land in Friday Harbor. Upstairs are three guest rooms ($135 d) with small private baths. Two downstairs rooms usually rent as a suite ($235 for up to four), and out back is an attractive and private little cottage—it was once a downtown shop—for $145 d. All guests have access to the backyard Jacuzzi and patio and are served a filling breakfast. This bed-and-breakfast is AAA-approved. No kids under eight. Owners Carlos and Tammra Bea also operate Inn to the Woods B&B.

Beaverton Valley Farmhouse B&B

Situated on three tranquil acres near the center of San Juan Island, Beaverton Valley Farmhouse B&B (4144 Beaverton Valley Rd., 360/378-3276 or 877/378-3276, www.beavertonvalley.com, $100–145 d) is a charming 1907 home. Each of the four guest rooms has a private bath, and the rate includes an earthy breakfast featuring local produce and meats, along with homemade jams and hot entrées. For something more rustic, book the log cabin built in the early 1900s. It includes a kitchenette and gas fireplace, and goes for $165 d or $195 for four guests. A light breakfast is brought to cabin guests each morning. Pets are welcome in the cabin, and cat lovers will appreciate the farm's nine felines. Friendly owners Richard Foote and Angel Michaels welcome children to Beaverton Valley Farmhouse, and the cabin works well for families (no charge for kids under 16).

Blair House B&B

Built in 1909, Blair House (345 Blair Ave. in Friday Harbor, 360/378-5907 or 800/899-3030, www.slowseason.com) contains a variety of lodging options, including a room with private patio ($165 d), two suites ($195 for four people), and a studio ($175 d) with a Jacuzzi tub and gas fireplace. A separate two-bedroom cottage with full kitchen costs $265 for four; kids and pets are welcome here. All guests are served full breakfasts, and an outdoor Jacuzzi is available. Owner Patrick Rothlisberger also manages Wharfside B&B.

Concord Inn

A lovely and romantic Craftsman home, Concord Inn (595 Park St. in Friday Harbor, 360/378-3757 or 800/639-2762, www.theconcordinn.com, $150–180 d) was built in 1907 as a summer retreat for industrialist Peter Kirk, the namesake of Kirkland, Washington. Four inviting guest rooms have private entrances and baths. Two rooms contain king beds and Jacuzzi tubs, and one room has a wood-burning fireplace. The multi-course gourmet breakfast might feature strawberry salsa or peach pancakes. No children under 15. This bed-and-breakfast is AAA-approved.

Halvorsen House B&B

Built as a B&B, Halvorsen House (1165 Halvorsen Rd., 360/378-2707 or 888/238-4187, www.halvorsenhousebb.com, $120–145 d rooms, $175 d suite) is an elegant contemporary home on five country acres two miles from Friday Harbor. Three guest rooms have private baths and phones, and a luxury suite includes a king bed and sofa bed, full kitchen, and private entrance and bath. Additional guests are $25 each. The living room contains a fireplace and TV, plus games and videos. A big gourmet breakfast is served each morning—you probably won't need lunch—and kids over four are welcome in the apartment. A two-night minimum stay is required in the summer. This bed-and-breakfast is AAA-approved.

Harrison House Suites B&B

One of the nicest Friday Harbor lodging choices, Harrison House (235 C St., 360/378-3587 or 800/407-7933, www.san-juan-lodging.com) offers the perfect blend of privacy and comfort, and it's just two blocks from the ferry landing. The main house was built in 1905, with a cottage added in the 1930s. Today, they have been lovingly transformed into five spacious apartment suites, each with a private entrance, full kitchen, and bath. The largest—1,600 square feet—encom-

passes two bedrooms, one-and-a-half baths with a Jacuzzi tub, hardwood floors, a piano and woodstove, plus a large private deck and sunroom. It can sleep 12 and goes for $300 d. The other suites (one has its own Jacuzzi) sleep 2–8, and rent for $140–240 d. Additional guests are $20/person in any of the rooms. Owners Anna Maria DeFreitas and David Pass are scuba instructors, and specialize in all-inclusive packages for divers and other adventurous types. Guests will appreciate the three-course breakfasts, game room, outdoor Jacuzzi, flower-filled grounds, plus mountain bikes and sea kayaks for no extra charge. Children are welcome and cribs are available for those traveling with children, making this a fine (albeit pricey) option for families and gatherings. Pets are accepted for an additional $15–25 fee. A three-night minimum stay is required in the summer.

Highland Inn

Set on a wooded hillside on the west side of San Juan with spectacular view of Mt. Baker, Highland Inn (360/378-9450 or 888/400-9850, www.highlandinn.com) offers some of the finest and most private lodging on the island. The two elegantly appointed suites ($275 d) each have a king bed, down comforter, steam shower, jetted tub, wood-burning fireplace, and small fridge. Sliding-glass doors open onto a covered deck that runs the length of the house, providing knock-your-socks-off views across Haro Strait. It's a killer place to watch for killer whales on a summer day, or to hear them at night as they blow and splash.

A fine breakfast is served each morning, along with afternoon tea and fresh cookies. Guests are also welcome to use the outdoor Jacuzzi. Owner Helen King has a reputation for graciousness, and she really goes all out to make your visit a pleasure. Be sure to ask about her 270-pound Pacific tuna mounted in the foyer. A two-night minimum stay is required on weekends. This bed-and-breakfast is not for children, due to the high decks.

Hillside House B&B

A 4,000-square-foot contemporary dwelling, Hillside House (365 Carter Ave., 360/378-4730

San Juan Island

MRS. KING'S COOKIES

2 cups butter
2 cups brown sugar
2 cups white sugar

Blend the above until creamy and add:

4 eggs
2 teaspoons vanilla
grated rind and juice of one orange

Beat until well mixed.

Sift together:

4 cups flour
2 teaspoons baking powder
2 teaspoons salt
2 teaspoons baking soda

Stir into the egg and butter mixture and mix until just blended, and then add:

2 cups white chocolate chips
2 cups semisweet chocolate chips
3 cups raisins
3 cups chopped nuts
2 cups old-fashioned rolled oats
3 cups orange-almond granola, or any good granola

When well mixed, shape into Ping Pong–size balls and bake on an ungreased cookie sheet at 350°F for 8–10 minutes or until just turning brown around the edges. The cookies are best when warm from the oven. This recipe makes 12-dozen cookies. Dough keeps refrigerated or frozen. Bake them fresh as needed.

Recipe courtesy of Highland Inn on San Juan Island

or 800/232-4730, www.hillsidehouse.com) sits on an acre of wooded land less than a mile from the ferry. There are magnificent views of Friday Harbor, the islands, and Mount Baker from the deck, and the grounds feature an ornamental pond and atrium. This is one of the larger bed-and-breakfasts on San Juan, with six guest rooms ($135–175 d), all with private baths, plus a large room ($275 d) that takes up the entire third floor with a king bed, jetted tub, fireplace, and private balcony. A big buffet breakfast is offered each morning. No children under age 10, and a two-night minimum is required on holiday weekends. This bed-and-breakfast is AAA-approved.

Inn to the Woods B&B

A luxurious hillside bed-and-breakfast, Inn to the Woods (46 Elena Drive, 360/378-3367 or 888/522-9626, www.inntothewoods.com) is set amid serene Douglas firs four miles northwest of Friday Harbor. Guests will appreciate the deck overlooking Sportsmans Lake. Four guest rooms and suites cost $125–225 d. One suite includes a king bed and private outdoor Jacuzzi, and the largest unit has a loft, king bed, private entry, kitchenette, and space for four ($249). The latter is popular with families or two couples traveling together. A filling breakfast is served each morning, with coffee and pastries each evening. Check you email on the computer in the living room. Owners Carlos and Tammra Bea also run Argyle House B&B.

Jensen Bay B&B

A 1920s one-bedroom home, Jensen Bay B&B (363 Jensen Bay Rd., 360/378-5318, www .jensenbay.com, $175 d, plus $15/person for additional guests) sits on five peaceful acres on the south end of the island. The entire house is rented to a maximum of five guests. Fresh baked goods arrive each morning, and the fridge is stocked with all ingredients for a big make-it-yourself breakfast. Kids are welcome, and there is a two-night minimum. Open April–September.

Longhouse B&B

Located on the west side of the island, Longhouse B&B (2387 Mitchell Bay Rd., 360/378-2568, www.rockisland.com/~longhouse) is an eclectic and modern waterfront home with a fine view from the great room. Two spacious bedrooms ($110–120 d) are available, both with private baths. Owner Patty Rasmussen once owned a restaurant, and her kitchen skills come to the fore each morning with gourmet breakfasts. Four-course dinners are also available upon request ($30/person). A quaint and rustic cottage ($125 d or $155 for four) has a kitchen (no breakfast here) with a wrap-around deck along Mitchell Bay. Kids are okay in the small cottage, which dates back more than 125 years. Guests can rent kayaks or take whale-watching trips from the adjacent Snug Harbor Marina Resort. A two-night minimum stay is usually required in the summer at Longhouse B&B.

Oak Ridge B&B

At Oakridge B&B (360/378-6184 or 800/687-3558, www.oak-ridge.net, $95–105 d), the four upstairs guest rooms share two baths, and a light breakfast is included. This 1921 Craftsman farmhouse occupies a six-acre ridgetop spread two miles south of Friday Harbor; stroll the grounds for a great view of Griffin Bay. Open May–October. Kids over age 10 are welcome. No TVs or phones in the rooms, but this Christian bed-and-breakfast has a wireless Internet connection.

Olympic Lights B&B

Olympic Lights (146 Starlight Way, 360/378-3186 or 888/211-6195, www.olympiclights.com, $130–140 d) is one of the more remote bed-and-breakfasts on the island. Located out in the open meadows on the south end of the island near American Camp, it boasts spectacular Olympic Mountains views. Hosts Christian and Lea Andrale discovered the old Johnson farmhouse when they were on vacation in 1985 and opened it as a bed-and-breakfast the following year. This beautifully maintained Victorian farmhouse was built in 1895, and has four guest rooms with down comforters and private baths. The front garden becomes a riot of flowers in the summer, and the big lawn is a good place for a game of croquet.

Guests are served a full vegetarian breakfast that typically includes fresh eggs from resident hens, along with scones or biscuits, fruit juice smoothies, and more. The grassy parklands of American Camp are an easy after-breakfast walk, or you can saunter down to the shore at nearby Eagle Cove. A two-night minimum is required in the summer and on holiday weekends, and children are not allowed.

Pear Point Inn

An elegantly furnished modern home, Pear Point Inn (2858 Pear Point Rd., 360/378-6655, www.pearpointinn.com) occupies seven acres of land, but is less than three miles from Friday Harbor along Pear Point. A large deck and outdoor Jacuzzi both deliver fine views across San Juan Channel, and bald eagles are common sights. Guests can choose either the master bedroom with big windows, king bed, walk-in closet, and private bath for $175 d, or an upstairs suite with queen and twin beds plus a full kitchen for $200 d. A light breakfast is served, and older children are accepted. Friendly owners, too.

San Juan Inn B&B

Just half a block from the ferry, San Juan Inn B&B (50 Spring St., 360/378-2070 or 800/742-8210, www.sanjuaninn.com) has been used as a lodging place since its construction in 1873.

Remodeled rooms and suites evoke a charming Victorian mood, with brass beds, patterned wallpaper, and old-fashioned lamps. The inn's nine guest rooms are on the cramped side, and the least expensive rooms ($89 d) share a bath down the hall, while others ($109–129 d) contain minuscule baths with showers; no televisions or phones. Two suites ($189–229 d; plus $15/person up to four) are available on the lower level, each with a private entrance, full kitchen with dishes, large Jacuzzi tub, double-headed shower, plus a small TV and VCR. Kids are welcome in the suites, but must be over 12 for the guest rooms. The shady backyard garden and Jacuzzi are open to all guests. Guests are served a continental breakfast buffet each morning in the sitting room, a fine place to chat with fellow travelers or your genial host, Steve Judson. On-street parking only.

States Inn B&B

States Inn (2687 West Valley Rd., 360/378-6240 or 866/602-2737, www.statesinn.com, $85–120 d rooms, $195 d suite) began life as a school in 1910, but has since been moved across the island and substantially changed. The bed-and-breakfast, located seven miles northwest of Friday Harbor, is on a working 60-acre ranch with horses (trail rides available seasonally), sheep, chickens, and alpacas. All eight guest rooms have private baths, and a three-room suite works well for families and couples traveling together. Guests share the large sunroom and are served a filling country breakfast. This bed-and-breakfast is AAA-approved, and kids are accepted in the suite.

Tower House B&B

Built in 1930s, Tower House B&B (1230 Little Rd., 360/378-5464 or 800/858-4276, www.san-juan-island.com, $150–165 d) is a beautiful Queen Anne home on 10 acres overlooking San Juan Valley. Two large suites are available, each with a private bath, king bed, and sitting room. A delicious and very filling vegetarian breakfast is served, and guests luxuriate in the hot tub on the front porch. Children are not allowed, but there is no minimum stay.

Trumpeter Inn B&B

A contemporary two-story home, Trumpeter Inn B&B (318 Trumpeter Way, 360/378-3884 or 800/826-7926, www.trumpeterinn.com, $130–190 d) overlooks five pastoral acres a mile and a half southwest of Friday Harbor. Horses and cattle graze in the adjoining fields; the pond is perfect for bird watching; a small orchard has plum, apple, and pear trees; and the gardens are filled with flowers all summer. Six guest room are available, all with private baths and access to the garden hot tub; the two nicest include fireplaces and private decks. Owners Aylene Geringer and Mark Zipkin create a gourmet breakfast each morning and will arrange professional massage upon request. A two-night minimum is required in summer and on holidays, and no children under 12. Trumpeter Inn is AAA-approved.

Tucker House B&B

Just a couple of blocks from the ferry, Tucker House B&B (260 B St., 360/378-2783 or 800/965-0123, www.tuckerhouse.com) offers a variety of lodging options. A total of 10 units are spread across two adjacent homes: a simple Victorian home built in 1898, and a second home that dates from 1910. Rooms rent for $165–185 d, and two suites (one sleeps five) are $225–300 d. Most units have jetted tubs, and two cottages ($150–300 d) also contain kitchenettes and woodstoves. One of these is rather plain, but the other is a modern and attractive log cabin that's perfect for families. Add $20/person for extra guests. All guests can use the central hot tub, and children and pets are welcome in the cottages. A full breakfast is delivered to your room each morning.

Wharfside B&B

One lodging place on San Juan Island isn't really on the island—it's in the water. Wharfside B&B (360/378-5661 or 800/899-3030, www.slowseason.com) is a gracious 60-foot sailing vessel, *Slow Season,* docked at the Friday Harbor Marina, Slip K-13. Two diminutive staterooms rent for $265–295 d. All guests receive a two-hour sailing trip each morning to Seal Rock. A continental breakfast is served along the way, and kids are welcome on-board. The owner also runs Blair House B&B.

Wildwood Manor

A large Queen Anne–style home, Wildwood Manor (5335 Roche Harbor Rd., 360/378-3447 or 877/298-1144, www.wildwoodmanor.com) sits atop a knoll above Roche Harbor. It is a lavish and modern place surrounded by 11 acres of forest, with manicured grounds and a gorgeous view across San Juan Channel to Vancouver Island. Three guest rooms follow the Victorian theme and include queen beds, private baths, and TV/VCRs for $180–195 d. Families or couples traveling together can also rent a suite ($325 for four people) that combines two of these rooms. A full breakfast is served each morning. The home isn't appropriate for toddlers, but children over 10 are accepted. A two-night minimum stay is required on summer weekends.

CAMPGROUNDS

Camping options on San Juan Island are limited and fill fast, so make reservations as far in advance as you can. Coin-operated showers are available at the Friday Harbor Marina and Roche Harbor Marina. **Trailers to Go** (360/376-3033 or 888/317-6516, www.trailerstogo.com) is a unique service that delivers vacation trailers anyplace on San Juan Island. It's a good deal if you have a camping spot and want to stay in pseudo-luxury without bringing along your own RV or travel trailer.

San Juan County Park

Pitch a tent at the 12-acre San Juan County Park (360/378-8420, www.co.san-juan.wa.us/parks), a mile north of Lime Kiln Point State Park along West Side Road. The 21 campsites are $23 (one site goes for $32); open year-round. Cyclist or kayaker sites are $6/person, and mooring is $8. Because this is essentially the only public campground on the island, you'll need to reserve months ahead for the summer. Call 360/378-1842 for reservations ($6 fee) between five days and three months ahead of time. You may find last-minute space on a summer weekday, but weekends are almost always fully reserved, especially in August. The park has a boat ramp, drinking water, picnic tables, and shelters, plus flush toilets, but no RV hookups.

Griffin Bay Marine State Park

This small boat-in-only campsite is on the southeast end of the island just north of American Camp. The 15-acre state park has four campsites ($10), along with picnic tables and pit toilets. You'll need to bring your own water. Griffin Bay is a popular destination for quick overnight kayak trips out of Friday Harbor, and has a pleasant gravely beach, but you're limited to the immediate area by fences that protect adjacent private property. The park is a fine stopping point for kayakers circumnavigating San Juan or Lopez islands, but nearby Cattle Pass can be extremely treacherous under certain tide and wind conditions.

Lakedale Resort

Located in the trees, Lakedale Resort (4313 Roche Harbor Rd., 360/378-2350 or 800/617-2267, www.lakedale.com) has dozens of campsites along two small lakes near the center of San Juan Island. It is four miles from Friday Harbor, and is open March–October. Tents and RVs are the same rate: $26; add an extra $4 for power and water hookups. Sites for hikers, bicyclists, and motorcyclists are a reasonable $9–11 d, and a couple of simple canvas-walled tent cabins with cots cost $45 for four people. All campers share a central bathhouse, and the little store sells basic supplies. Reservations are advised, but they almost always have space for tents. The resort rents out rowboats, canoes, kayaks, paddleboats, fishing poles, and camping gear.

Mitchell Bay Landing

Located on the northwest end of the island near Snug Harbor, Mitchell Bay Landing (2101 Mitchell Bay Rd., 360/378-9296, www.mitchell-baylanding.com) is a small campground with tent sites on the lawn for $25 and RV sites with hookups for $45. Trailer rentals are also available, ranging from 10-foot tent trailers ($60/day) to 31-foot family trailers ($149/day) that sleep four and include a full galley, bath, and covered deck.

Snug Harbor Marina Resort

On the west side of the island, nine miles from Friday Harbor, Snug Harbor Marina Resort (1997 Mitchell Bay Rd., 360/378-4762, www.snug-resort.com) faces Mitchell Bay. Sunsets can be

San Juan Island

Studio — tree house —Tues. Wed.

awesome from this protected bay. Camping is available year-round, with nine wooded tent-camping sites ($25 for four people) and one group site ($45). Reserve campsites six weeks in advance for the summer. Note: After 2005, the campground may be closed and replaced with cabins.

Campers can rent skiffs or mountain bikes at the resort, and local companies offer sea kayaking, whale-watching, and charter fishing. Kayakers can paddle in and camp, or launch from the marina. Moorage is also available. A small general store here sells a few supplies.

Food

San Juan Island has a wide range of restaurants and eateries, including some real gems. Unless otherwise noted, all of these restaurants are in the town of Friday Harbor. *San Juan Islands Dining and Accommodations* is a free little publication from Pixel Publications (www.athome1.com) that includes menus from many local restaurants. You'll find it on ferries and at visitors centers.

BREAKFAST AND LUNCH

An old breakfast standby, **Blue Dolphin Café** (185 1st St., 360/378-6116) opens daily at 5 A.M. and is just a block from the ferry lanes. All the breakfast standards are reasonably priced, including omelets, waffles, eggs Benedict, and hash browns. Try to ignore the rather bizarre and fishy wall mural and the bare-bones dining decor. Breakfast is served all day, but the Blue Dolphin also has a lunch menu. It closes at 2 P.M.

Off the main drag, **Garden Path Café** (135 2nd St., 360/378-6255) is a cozy historic home where you'll find homemade soups, salads, crepes, burgers (served on focacia bread with a side of baked-potato salad and soup), vegetarian dishes, and other nicely prepared lunch favorites. It's also open for breakfast daily and dinner Wednesday–Saturday.

Backdoor Kitchen (400-B A St., 360/378-9540) is a hidden gem known to locals and wandering tourists who happen upon it; find it behind a nondescript warehouse near Mi Casita Restaurant. Step through the gate to a wonderful little garden area with a handful of teak tables for alfresco dining. There's additional seating inside the restaurant, and the lunch menu stars a daily curry, tuna melts, fresh-baked breads, Caesar salads, and chalupas. Dinner is a bit more formal, with in-spired ethnic fare—most notably the Vietnamese rice noodle bowl—along with such treats as sea scallops over homemade pasta, lamb sirloin, or salmon *donbury* (Japanese seasoned-rice dish). Daily specials are often your best bet. Backdoor Kitchen is open Monday–Friday for lunch and Thursday–Sunday for dinner. Dinner reservations are advised. Winter hours are reduced, and the Backdoor's front door is closed for January.

Front Street Café (101 Spring St., 360/378-2245) is a popular hangout, with a convivial atmosphere and a location that's hard to beat: High windows face the always-busy ferry dock. The café serves breakfast and lunch in the week, with dinners (often accompanied by folksy bands) added for weekends. Lunchtime choices include sandwiches, chowder, salads, quiche, and more. Try the candy apple pie for dessert.

Fat Cat Café (1 Nichols St. Walk, 360/378-8646) is a breakfast and lunch stop with a feline decor. Nothing special about the food, but there's an abundance of patio tables for summertime dining. The ferry is just a block away.

Tiny **Market Chef** (225 A St., 360/378-4546) is a great deli/market next to the ferry lanes in Friday Harbor. Owner/chef Laurie Paul creates mouth-watering sandwiches and salads, with a limited selection of gourmet groceries. Call a day ahead to get a boxed picnic lunch to go. Closed Sundays.

Other notable lunch spots (described elsewhere) are Thai Kitchen, Golden Triangle, Vinny's, Front St. Alehouse, and Friday's Crabhouse.

Cafés

San Juan Coffee Roasting Company (360/378-4443 or 800/624-4119, www.rockisland.com/~sjcoffee) specializes in full- and dark-roasted coffees, and sells them from its shop at 18 Cannery Landing. You can get espresso drinks there, but I prefer **The Doctor's Office** (85 Front St., 360/378-8865), inside the green Victorian-style building adjacent to the ferry lines. This place also uses San Juan Coffee Roasting beans, and has a walk-up window so you don't miss the boat, along with a juice bar, sandwiches, soups, sweets, and homemade ice cream. Over in one corner is a computer where you can check email or surf the Web (for a donation). Many, if not most, of the other Friday Harbor cafés also serve mochas, lattes, and the other de rigueur Washington coffee drinks.

Pelindaba Downtown (150 1st St. in Friday Harbor, 360/378-4248, www.pelindaba.com) is home to the world's only lavender café, serving lavender-infused pastries, tea, hot chocolate (with lavender whipped cream), and even ice cream. This bright and artsy café has tall windows, a crackling fire on winter days, classical music in the background, a free wireless Internet connection for laptop users, and occasional poetry readings. The gift shop sells lavender products—from scented bath salts to lavender honey. Pelindaba Lavender Farm (see *Sights*) is on the south side of the island.

Quick Bites

One of the most popular eating establishments on San Juan Island is **Friday's Crabhouse** (360/378-8801) directly across from the ferry. Open seasonally, this is *the* place for finger-lickin' fish and chips, shrimp cocktails, scallops, or grilled crabcakes, along with fajitas, burgers, and veggie burgers—most for under $10. Service is fast, making this a great last-minute stop while waiting for your ship to come in. The dining is alfresco, with picnic tables topped by big umbrellas. It's open daily June–September, and weekends only in April and May.

Another simple family place is **Hungry Clam** (130 1st St., 360/378-3474), where you will find cheap, greasy, and quite good fish and chips served in a basket. The fries are fresh and crunchy. Also on the menu are such staples as clam chowder, burgers, and grilled chicken sandwiches.

If you're in search of a great all-American burger, fries, and shake, head up the hill to **Vic's**

Drive-In (25 2nd St., 360/378-2120). It's open all day Monday–Friday, but closes at 2 P.M. on Saturdays and doesn't open at all on Sundays. Locals also wax enthusiastic about **Herb's Tavern** (80 1st St., 360/378-7076), an old-timey downtown spot where the one-pound monster burger will sate even the most ardent carnivore. Fish and chips, hot dogs, sandwiches, and pizzas round out the menu.

Front St. Ale House (1 Front St., 360/378-2337, www.sanjuanbrewing.com) is a noisy and family-friendly eatery right next door to San Juan Brewing Company. All 10 or so SJBC beers are on tap here, and the wide-ranging menu includes burgers, nachos, fish and chips, shepherd's pie, pasta, steak, and more for reasonable prices: $7–14. It's very popular for lunch and dinner and servings are large, but the food is rather pedestrian. Fortunately, the brews make up for this. Just get a window seat (if you're lucky), some finger food and a pitcher of beer, saving room for dinner elsewhere. Upstairs you'll find live music on occasional weekends, along with a dart board and winter trivia games. Front St. Ale House is entirely smoke-free.

FINE DINING

Dinner reservations are strongly suggested for any of San Juan Island's better restaurants, particularly on weekends and in the summer. Backdoor Kitchen (in the *Breakfast and Lunch* section) is another good dining choice.

Friday Harbor

The Place Bar & Grill (1 Spring St., 360/378-8707, $19–29) gets rave reviews from locals who come here for the friendly service, from-scratch gourmet fare and sophisticated atmosphere. The name should give you a clue to its location: on pilings over the water, with big windows fronting the ferry and marina. It's perfect for a warmly romantic evening. The menu changes seasonally, but typically features a mushroom sauté appetizer with shiitake mushrooms and herbed goat cheese, along with fresh Alaskan king salmon, New Zealand lamb chops, and Angus filet mignon. Be sure to save room for the warm chocolate pudding cake with toffee sauce. The Place is open for dinners only.

Friday Harbor House (130 West St. in downtown Friday Harbor, 360/378-8455, www.fridayharborhouse.com, $16–30) is another culinary star on San Juan Island. The menu changes weekly and emphasizes ultra-fresh local produce and seafood, along with thin-crust pizzas, beef tenderloin, and vegetarian dishes. There's an extensive wine selection and full bar, too. The food is exquisite, and the setting is upscale and fashionable, with a central fireplace and tall windows looking across the harbor. Call ahead to request a window table. Patio dining is available in the summer, and kids are welcome.

M Vinny's (165 West St., 360/378-1934, www.vinnys-restaurant.com) is a casually elegant Italian restaurant under the stewardship of chef Roberto Carrieri. Redolent aromas fill the air, big windows front the harbor, and the tables are draped in white linen at this favorite dinner-out destination for locals. The menu encompasses all the standard favorites, including veal piccata, shrimp scampi, and lasagna, along with "pasta from hell" for those who like it hot: pasta with grilled prawns, garlic, pine nuts, raisins, and vegetables in a very spicy cream sauce. Vinny's is open for lunch and dinner in the summer, and dinners only the rest of the year. Dinners start at $15 for a simple spaghetti with meat sauce, up to $38 for rack of lamb.

Out of Town

Five miles north of Friday Harbor on Roche Harbor Rd., **M Duck Soup Inn,** (360/378-4878, www.ducksoupinn.com, $20–29) specializes in superbly prepared local seafood, along with a changing and eclectic menu with an international bent. The country setting and woodsy interior add to the relaxed and romantic atmosphere. This is where locals go for a celebration night. Duck Soup is closed Mondays and November–March. Reservations recommended.

Three places serve meals out at **Roche Harbor Village** (360/378-2155 or 800/451-8910, www.rocheharbor.com): Lime Kiln Café for forgettable and overpriced quick meals, Madrona

Bar & Grill for waterside patio dining, and McMillin's Dining Room for prime rib, seafood, steaks, and chicken ($22–30 dinner entrées).

INTERNATIONAL
Asian

Friday Harbor has one real standout spot for Asian meals: **M Thai Town** (42 1st St., 360/378-1917). Lunch specials, such as satay chicken or beef broccoli, come with rice, egg roll, and soup for just $8, and flavorful Thai dinner entrées run $10–17. Main dishes come with rice and a choice of meat, seafood, or vegetable; add a Thai iced tea for the full Bangkok effect. The garden patio tables out front are delightful on a warm summer afternoon, and the interior is homey but not ostentatious. Thai Town is a favorite of locals who are looking for a meal out without breaking the bank. You definitely won't go wrong here!

Golden Triangle (Spring at 1st St. in Friday Harbor, 360/378-3560) serves Vietnamese pho, Japanese sushi and terriyaki, Thai noodles, and other fast Asian treats in an eat-in or take-away setting. Laotian owner Avon Mangala also runs Thai Town, so you know the food is good.

Italian and Middle Eastern

Maloula's (1 Front St., 360/378-8485, $14–24) serves Syrian food on a rooftop and flower-filled patio facing the waterfront. Find it upstairs and behind Front St. Ale House; just follow the wonderful smells. Maloula's is open May–October, with a menu that features grilled lamb, beef, poultry, and vegetarian specialties. You'll find kibbeh, kabobs, gyros, and other Mediterranean cuisine using hormone-free beef and organic vegetables.

Bella Luna (175 1st St., 360/378-4118) serves basic pasta and pizzas, along with veal parmesan, prime rib, and other specialties. At least the prices are reasonable and it's open for breakfast and lunch. For a more memorable Italian meal, head to Vinny's.

Mexican

Reasonably priced **Mi Casita** (95 Nichols St., 360/378-6103), occupies a yellow Victorian-style house behind Sunken Park in Friday Harbor. The interior is festive and inviting, and the menu encompasses all the standards, including tacos, fajitas, burritos, enchiladas, and tostadas, along with homemade salsa. House specialties include relleno del mar (chile relleno filled with crab, shrimp, scallops, and vegetables), and carnitas (roast pork with onions, cilantro, tomatoes, and guacamole). Good margaritas, too. Full combination plates are $12–15, but you can get a filling tostada or burrito for $8–10.

If you have wheels, or don't mind a bit of a walk, head to **The Flying Burrito** (near the airport at 701 Spring St., 360/378-1077) for fat burritos ($6), enchilada plates, huevos rancheros, taco salads, and other quick and filling Mexican food. Order at the counter and eat inside or on the little deck with trees and a fenced-in spot for kids. Tasty and good, but closed Sundays.

SEAFOOD

Friday Harbor Seafood (360/378-5779, www.interisland.net/fishcreek) is a tiny floating shop surrounded by the cruise and fishing fleet at the Friday Harbor marina. You'll find fresh salmon, halibut, and snapper, along with live mussels, clams, Dungeness crab, scallops, and prawns. The big 500-gallon aquarium here always has something interesting to see from local waters.

Westcott Bay Seafood Farm (4071 Westcott Dr., 360/378-2489, www.westcottbay.com) supplies gourmet seafood restaurants all over America with European flat (Belon) and petite oysters, plus Manila clams and Mediterranean mussels. Locally, the oysters are served at Friday Harbor House, Duck Soup Inn, Vinny's, and other restaurants. The aquaculture farm cultivates shellfish in lantern nets suspended in deep water at Westcott Bay, a mile east of Roche Harbor. Visit the farm to get fresh shellfish, or have some shipped via FedEx. You can pick your own oysters for just $.25 per oyster on several days each summer when the tides are lowest.

MARKETS, BAKERIES, AND MORE

For a real taste of the islands, head to the **San Juan Farmers Market** (Court and First Sts., 360/378-6301), held in the summer 10 A.M.–1 P.M. Saturdays at the county courthouse parking lot from late April to mid-October. The market features organic fruits, vegetables, berries, flowers, and more.

Kings Market (160 Spring St., 360/378-4505, www.kings-market.com) is the primary grocer on San Juan. You'll find fresh meats and fish, gourmet foods and wines, plus a fine deli with tasty sandwiches. Also here is a gift shop and marine supply center.

A little specialty shop on the edge of town near the airport, **M Kneadful Things** (895 Spring St., 360/378-7089) bakes the finest artisan breads on the island. In addition to breads, the shop has a selection of imported cheeses, pasta, tapenades, sauces, and surprisingly reasonable but distinctive wines. Kneadful Things is out of the way, but definitely worth the side trip! Closed Sundays and Mondays.

Decorated in pink trim and flower boxes, **The Sweet Retreat & Espresso** (264 Spring St., 360/378-1957) is a busy takeaway spot for ice cream cones (20 or so flavors), sundaes, lemonade, Hawaiian shave ice, malts, and frappacinos. Breakfast sandwiches here consist of a biscuit with egg, cheese, and bacon; surprisingly good lunches include deli sandwiches, chili, jumbo hot dogs, and homemade soups with cornbread.

Island Wine Company (360/378-3229 or 800/248-9463, www.sanjuancellars.com) is a cozy wine shop in Cannery Landing, adjacent to the Friday Harbor ferry dock. Owners Dave Baughn and Kathryn Kerr have their own **San Juan Cellars** label, produced from eastern Washington grapes and bottled under contract. You're welcome to sample any of their eight wines, which are only available here. In addition to these, the shop also has a range of upper-end Northwestern wines. Island Wine often stocks wines you won't find in Seattle wine shops.

Entertainment and Events

NIGHTLIFE

Friday Harbor's oldest bar—opened in 1938—is **Herb's Tavern** (80 1st St., 360/378-7076). Inside are a couple of pool tables, a big selection of brews on draught, and decent bar food. Live rock or blues bands often roll in when the weekend rolls around.

China Pearl (51 Spring St., 360/378-5551) has open mike on Thursday nights, and live bands Friday and Saturday nights, plus pool tables, foosball, and pinball.

Front St. Ale House (1 Front St., 360/378-2337, www.sanjuanbrewing.com) has occasional live music on weekends in a no-smoking setting and hosts a lively trivia tournament Monday and Tuesday nights in the winter. The latter is mainly for locals, but they may make room for you on one of the teams. The prizes for winners are, well, trivial.

Bella Luna (175 1st St., 360/378-4118), serves up jazz or blues dinner tunes on Sunday and Wednesday evenings, but the music can be a bit loud if you come here primarily to dine. In addition, the lounge at **Roche Harbor Village** (360/378-2155 or 800/451-8910, www.roche harbor.com) on the northwest side of the island, has live music and dancing on Friday and Saturday nights in the summer.

Watch first-run films at the two-screen **Palace Theatre** (209 Spring St., 360/378-5666).

COMMUNITY THEATER

The impressive **San Juan Community Theatre** (100 2nd St., 360/378-3210, www.sanjuancommunitytheatre.org) is a vital center for local performing arts, with year-round musical programs, plays (including the acclaimed *Life and Times of George Pickett* in July and August), dance performances, chamber music, art shows, and more. Get your tickets early, as some events sell out.

FESTIVALS

Orca Fest provides a celebration of wildlife with different activities each weekend in May, including a street dance, educational presentations, whale-watching, and children's activities. **Memorial Day weekend** in late May is the time for a downtown parade, political speeches, the **Round the Island** sailing race (sponsored by the San Juan Island Yacht Club), and an **Artists' Studios Open House.** It's followed by the **Celebrity Golf Classic** in early June at San Juan Island Golf & Country Club (360/378-2254, www.sanjuangolf.com). This the county's biggest annual fundraising event.

The **4th of July** brings a variety of fun events, including a parade, Pig War picnic, 10k race, music, and dancing, plus evening fireworks above Friday Harbor. Over in Roche Harbor, the 4th of July is the biggest event of the year, with a logrolling contest, blind dinghy race, and other events, topped off with an impressive fireworks display.

Pelindaba Lavender Farm (33 Hawthorne Ln., 360/378-4248 or 866/819-1911, www.pelindaba.com) hosts a **Lavender Festival** on the second weekend of July, with tours, lavender-accented foods, and music.

Summer events at **San Juan Community Theatre** (100 2nd St., 360/378-3210, www.sanjuancommunitytheatre.org) include an **Island Music Series** throughout the summer, and a **Playwrights Festival** in early September. Don't miss *The Life and Times of Gen. George Pickett,* a memorable play by historian Mike Vouri. The play takes place once each month in July and August and always sells out, so call ahead for tickets. Free **Music on the Lawn** concerts take place at the San Juan Historical Museum weekly in July and early August.

Over in Roche Harbor, several summer events attract crowds to the Westcott Bay Reserve Sculpture Park, including two that bookend the summer: the **Art and Nature Festival** during Memorial Day weekend and the **Best of the San Juans** party during Labor Day weekend.

San Juan Island National Historical Park puts on a **Lantern Tour** (360/378-2240) at American Camp in late June, followed by an **Encampment** at English Camp in late August. During the encampment, you'll meet 60 or so British and American "soldiers" and others in mid-19th-century period costume. Old-fashioned canvas tents are set up, and you can watch demonstrations on blacksmithing, woodworking, marching, and cookery. The highlight is a candlelight ball in the barracks building.

A very popular **Summer Arts Fair** (360/378-5240) on the third weekend of July includes art exhibits, food booths, and live music.

The four-day **San Juan County Fair** (360/378-4310, www.sanjuancountyfair.org) on the third week of August features a sheep-to-shawl race, chicken and rabbit races, music, livestock judging, and, of course, carnival rides. Get ready for Christmas with an **Artisan's Holiday Marketplace** around Thanksgiving. The **Northern Lights Fest** throughout December includes a tree lighting, caroling, and lighted boat parade.

Shopping

Downtown Friday Harbor is filled with interesting shops selling everything from Washington wines to bonsai trees. Browse the photos of homes for sale adorning the real estate offices, check out the toy shops for grandchild gifts, or sip a lavender tea while surfing the Web on your laptop.

In business since 1929, **Kings Market** (160 Spring St., 360/378-4505, www.kings-market.com) is Friday Harbor's version of Wal-Mart. Besides being the only real grocery store on the island, Kings has a big gift and clothing shop, plus an upstairs marine center stocked with fishing tackle, boating supplies, charts, outdoor gear, and sea kayaks.

The Garuda & I (60 1st St., 360/378-3733) is a unique space with ethnic home accessories, Asian antiques, beautiful jewelry, and a large cage filled with chirping zebra finches.

GALLERIES AND STUDIOS

Friday Harbor is home to several excellent art galleries, most of which are within a few blocks of the ferry landing. Just walk the streets to see what appeals to your taste. In addition to the galleries, you may want to drop by the library at 1010 Guard St. to see changing exhibits by local artists. During the **San Juan Island Artists' Studio Tour** (360/378-5594, www.sanjuanislandartists.com) in early June, more than a dozen local studios are opened to the public; it's a great way to meet the folks behind the art.

Friday Harbor's don't-miss place is **Waterworks Gallery** (315 Argyle Ave., 360/378-3060, www.waterworksgallery.com) a fine-arts gallery with contemporary paintings, prints, watercolors, and sculpture by island and international artists. A new exhibit is unveiled each month.

Island Studios (270 Spring St., 360/378-6550, www.islandstudios.com) is one of the largest galleries in the San Juans, with works from more than 90 local artists. You'll find paintings, photography, stained glass, jewelry, pottery, and lots more jammed into every square inch of space here. It's a fun place to spend time, with a mix of notable art and pieces that cross the line into kitsch.

Arctic Raven Gallery (130 S. 1st St., 360/378-3433, www.arcticravengallery.com) features quality art by Northwest Coast and Alaska Native Americans, including woodcarvings, bentwood boxes, baskets, soapstone carvings, masks, art prints, and more.

Gallery San Juan (210 Nichols St., 360/378-1376, www.gallerysanjuan.com) is a small gallery with paintings by Barbara and Matt Dollahite, along with changing monthly exhibits from regional artists.

Not my style, but fans of shiny bronze and metal will appreciate **Napier Sculpture Gallery** (232 A St., 360/378-2221 or 888/378-2221, www.napiergallery.com), just above the ferry lanes. Also check out **Egg Lake Studio** (2011 Egg Lake Rd., 360/370-5456, www.egglake.com) with collages and nature photography.

San Juan Island

BOOKSTORES

Friday Harbor has several good places to purchase books. **Griffin Bay Bookstore** (40 1st St., 360/378-5511) is a book-lovers' shop with both new and used books. **Boardwalk Books** (upstairs from Front St. Café, 360/378-2787) houses a small collection of local titles.

The islands' largest bookstore is **Harbor Bookstore** (upstairs in Cannery Landing, 360/378-7222), with a nice selection of regional volumes, plus a comfortable corner where overstuffed chairs offer a bird's-eye view of the ferry action.

Find an abundance of used titles (more than 37,000 books at last count) at the well-organized **Serendipity Books** (360/378-2665), at the top of the ferry lanes.

Information and Services

The **San Juan Island Chamber of Commerce Visitor Center** (1 Front St., 360/378-5240, www.sanjuanisland.org), is upstairs behind Front St. Ale House. Hours are year-round 9:30 A.M.–4:30 P.M. Monday–Friday and 10 A.M.–2 P.M. Saturday, plus June–August 10 A.M.–2 P.M. Sundays. Two useful private websites for San Juan Island are the **Friday Harbor & San Juan Island Web Directory** (www.friday-harbor.net) and **San Juan Sites** (www.sanjuansites.com).

The town of Friday Harbor has its office at 60 2nd St. S (360/378-2810, www.fridayharbor.org).

LAUNDRY, SHOWERS, AND STORAGE

Store bags in the coin-operated **lockers** (\$.75) opposite the ferry terminal and adjacent to Friday's Crab House. **Sail-In Laundromat** is directly behind here, or you can do your laundry at **Sunshine Coin-Op Laundry** (210 Nichols St., 360/378-9755). Showers can be found at the Friday Harbor Marina and Roche Harbor Marina.

KIDS STUFF

Forgot your stroller for that out-of-control three-year-old? **Island Bicycles** (380 Argyle Ave. in Friday Harbor, 360/378-4941, www.islandbicycles.com) rents strollers for \$5 a day, and also has children's bikes and other cycling gear.

The **San Juan Fitness and Athletic Club** (435 Argyle Ave., 360/378-4449, www.interisland.net/sjfit) has a range of kid activities, including a climbing wall, kids' gym, and indoor pools. Day use costs \$10 for kids under 18, or \$15 for adults.

Head out Argyle to the San Juan County Fairgrounds, where you'll find a **skateboard park** that's popular with insane BMX bikers and an adjacent playground for younger kids. Much more impressive is the **playground** at Roche Harbor Resort, and adjacent is a very popular **outdoor pool** and wading pool (\$6 adults, \$3 kids). Both are open to the public.

Weekday childcare is available on a drop-in basis at two places in Friday Harbor: **Childcare University** (445 Spruce St., 360/378-4139) and **Stepping Stones Learning Center** (54 Marguerite Place, 360/378-4455). Call ahead for age requirements and to make sure they have space.

LIBRARY AND INTERNET ACCESS

The spacious and modern **San Juan Island Library** (1010 Guard St., 360/378-2798, www.sanjuan.lib.wa.us) is a nice rainy-day spot and a good place to check your email on the free computers. Library hours are 10 A.M.–6 P.M. Monday, Wednesday, and Friday; 10 A.M.–8 P.M. Tuesday and Thursday; 10 A.M.– 5 P.M. Saturday; and 1–5 P.M. Sunday.

The Computer Place (435 Argyle Ave., 360/378-8488, www.compplace.com) has computer rentals and wireless Internet access if you can bring your own laptop; both are \$8/hour. Closed Sundays. If you need temporary Internet access during your time on the island, they can provide it for \$22/month. Folks with a laptop will appreciate the free wireless

Internet service at **Pelindaba Downtown** (150 1st St. in Friday Harbor, 360/378-4248, www.pelindaba.com).

BANKING AND MAIL

Friday Harbor's four banks all have ATMs: **Wells Fargo** (305 Argyle Ave., 360/378-2128, www.wellsfargo.com), **Islanders Bank,** (225 Blair Ave., 360/378-2265 or 800/843-5441, www.islandersbank.com), **Key Bank** (95 2nd St. S, 360/378-2111, www.keybank.com), and **Whidbey Island Bank** (535 Market St., 800/290-6508, www.wibank.com). You can also ask for cash back from an ATM purchase at Kings Market. Find other ATMs at Roche Harbor Grocery and Hotel de Haro at Roche Harbor, along with Entertainment Tonite and the Little Store in Friday Harbor.

Post offices are located at 220 Blair Ave. in Fri-

MEDICAL AND VETERINARY CARE

Call 911 on a regular phone for medical emergencies or fires; on a cell phone, dial 360/378-4141. There is no hospital on the island, but **Inter-Island Medical Center** (550 Spring St., 360/378-2141) has four physicians on staff, with on-call service at any time. The clinic is open Monday–Saturday, and has x-ray facilities. **San Juan Healthcare Associates** (689 Airport Center, 360/378-1338) has two doctors on staff, and is open Monday–Friday. The nearest hospitals are in Anacortes or Victoria. Fill prescriptions at **Friday Harbor Drug** (210 Spring St. W, 360/378-4421).

Take sick or injured pets to **Islands Veterinary Clinic** (700 Mullis St., 360/378-2333).

day Harbor, 360/378-4511; and at Roche Harbor, 360/378-2155.

San Juan Island

Transportation

Warning: Friday Harbor has a serious parking problem in the summer, and the city *strictly* enforces a two-hour downtown parking limit. Get back to your car three minutes late and you'll probably have a $20 ticket pasted on the windshield. Meters are checked 8 A.M.–5 P.M. Monday–Saturday, and they stop marking cars after 3 p.m., so you can safely park anytime after that.

Eight-hour on-street parking is available at the north end of 1st Street near San Juan Community Theatre, and along Web Street (off Argyle Avenue). Seventy-two-hour parking spaces are up Spring Street beyond the junction with Argyle Avenue (a five-minute walk from the center of town).

WASHINGTON STATE FERRIES

The Washington State Ferries (360/378-8665 for the Friday-Harbor terminal; 206/464-6400 for general info, or 888/808-7977 in Washington and British Columbia only) stop right in Friday Harbor. Find all the details—including current ferry wait times—on their website: www.wsdot .wa.gov/ferries.

ferry at Friday Harbor

© DON PITCHER

SAN JUAN ISLAND MILEAGE

	Friday Harbor	American Camp	English Camp	Roche Harbor	San Juan County Park	Lime Kiln Point State Park
American Camp	6					
English Camp	9	13				
Roche Harbor	10	16	4			
San Juan County Park	10	12	5	9		
Lime Kiln Point State Park	9	9	7	12	3	
Cattle Point	9	4	20	24	15	13

Peak season weekend fares from Anacortes to Friday Harbor are $11.40 for passengers and walk-ons, or $43.75 for a car and driver. Bikes are $4 extra, and kayaks cost $19.20 more. There is no charge for eastbound travel by vehicles or passengers from Friday Harbor to Orcas, Shaw, Lopez, or Anacortes. Reservations are not available for these runs. Vehicle reservations *are,* however, required at least 24 hours in advance if you're heading west on the runs from San Juan Island to Sidney, British Columbia. These tickets to Vancouver Island cost $23.75 for a car and driver or $5 for passengers or walk-ons.

PRIVATE FERRIES

The passenger-only *Victoria Clipper* (206/448-5000 or 800/888-2535, www.victoriaclipper.com) runs high-speed catamaran day trips between Seattle and San Juan Island ($63 adults rt, $32 kids). Adults are $45 and kids under 12 are free if you book at least one day ahead. Cruises operate late May to early September, with daily service after mid-May. The company has a multitude of other travel options in the Northwest, including packages that add whale-watching, sea kayaking, or lodging on San Juan Island. *Victoria Clipper* also has direct year-round service between Seattle and Victoria.

Victoria Express (360/452-8088 or 800/633-1589, www.victoriaexpress.com) operates a 149-passenger ferry connecting Victoria and Friday Harbor, with daily service late May to early Sep-tember. Round-trip fare is $52 for adults and kids (free for babies under age one), and there's no charge for bikes or kayaks. You'll need to clear customs on either end. The boat stops to watch orcas or other marine life along the way, and also has daily runs between Victoria and Port Angeles.

The **Mosquito Fleet** (425/252-6800 or 800/325-6722, www.whalewatching.com) runs summertime boat tours from Everett to San Juan Island. These all-day trips ($79 adults, $74 seniors, or $40 kids) take travelers to Friday Harbor, with the chance to watch whales as the boat circumnavigates San Juan Island. Passengers get off in Friday Harbor for a brief one-hour stop before returning to Everett. A better option is to spend a night or more on the island. The cost is lower ($59 adults, $54 seniors, or $29 kids), and you get the same tour.

San Juan Island Commuter (360/734-8180 or 888/734-8180, www.islandcommuter.com) has daily passenger ferry service between Bellingham and Friday Harbor in the summer. Round-trip fares are $39 adults and $20 ages 6–12; younger children ride free. Add on a three-hour whale-watching trip for an additional $30 ($20 kids).

AIR SERVICE
Floatplanes

Taking off from Lake Union in Seattle, **Kenmore Air** (425/486-1257 or 800/543-9595, www.kenmoreair.com) has daily scheduled floatplane flights to Friday Harbor and Roche Harbor. A 24-pound baggage weight limit is in effect on these flights.

Wheeled-Plane Flights

Port of Friday Harbor Airport (360/378-4724, www.portfridayharbor.org) is immediately south of town. **San Juan Airlines** (360/293-4691 or 800/874-4434, www.sanjuanairlines.com) has scheduled daily wheeled-plane service to San Juan Island from Seattle's Boeing Field and airports in Anacortes or Bellingham, plus connecting service to Orcas and Lopez Islands from Friday Harbor. Flightseeing and air charters are available to the outer islands.

Island Air (360/378-2376 or 888/378-2376, www.sanjuan-islandair.com) runs charter flights and flightseeing out of San Juan Island Airport, and is the only company actually based in the San Juans. The experienced local pilots can take you virtually anywhere in the region, including north to British Columbia or south to Sea-Tac. During the busy summer season, individual seat fares may be available.

BUSES AND TOURS

Island Airporter (360/378-7438, www.islandairporter.com) offers direct van service daily from Friday Harbor ($40) or Roche Harbor ($50), with ferry fare included in the prices.

San Juan Transit

You really don't need a car to get around San Juan Island. San Juan Transit (360/378-8887 or 800/887-8387, www.sanjuantransit.com) operates shuttle buses between the ferry landing in Friday Harbor and Roche Harbor, with stops at San Juan Vineyards, Lakedale Resort, Pelindaba Lavender Farm, Lime Kiln Point State Park, San Juan County Park, Snug Harbor Marina Resort, and English Camp. Unfortunately, the buses do not run to American Camp on the south end of the island, though

you can schedule a drop off or pick up on a charter basis.

Buses operate May–mid-September, with hourly service (9 A.M.–5 P.M.) every midsummer day, and on weekends only for the first half of May. It's $5 one-way ($2 ages 5–12), $8 round-trip ($3 kids), or $10 for an all-day pass ($9 seniors, $5 kids). The passes are a great deal, letting you get off and on anywhere along the way. Just flag down the next bus that comes by.

The buses can carry bikes and luggage. You can take an excellent narrated two-hour bus tour of the island twice a day in the summer; $17 adults, $15 seniors, and $10 kids. The office is in the Cannery Landing building next to the ferry dock.

CAR AND MOPED RENTALS

Rent cars (starting at $50/day for a compact) from **M&W Auto Rentals** (360/378-2886 or 800/323-6037 or 800/323-6037, www.sanjuanauto.com) or **San Juan Airlines** (360/293-4691 or 800/874-4434, www.sanjuanairlines.com) at the airport.

Susie's Mopeds (360/378-5244 or 800/532-0087, www.susiesmopeds.com) rents all sorts of unusual vehicles, including mopeds (starting at $20/hour or $60/day), three-wheel scootcars (straight out of the Jetsons), and tiny Geo Trackers from their shop at the top of the ferry lanes in Friday Harbor. These toys are shockingly expensive: tiny two-person scootcars cost $40/hour or $120/day! The shop is open March–late September. Susie's also rents mopeds and scootcars next to the Roche Harbor airport mid-June to Labor Day.

TAXIS

Call **San Juan Taxi** (360/378-3550, www.sanjuantransit.com) or **Bob's Taxi & Tours** (360/378-6777, www.bobstaxiandtours.com) for local rides and island tours year-round. Friday Harbor to Roche Harbor costs around $17 for two people.

Orcas Island

Known as "The Gem of the San Juans," Orcas Island is considered by many the most beautiful island in the archipelago. It is definitely the hilliest—drive, hike, or bike to the top of 2,409-foot Mount Constitution for a panoramic view from Vancouver, British Columbia, to Mount Rainier. Orcas's most prominent mansion, Rosario Resort, regularly graces the pages of national travel magazines and employs almost 200 people, making it San Juan County's largest private employer. The island is home to around 4,500 people, half of whom seem to now operate real estate offices. It also has one of the only real towns in the archipelago, Eastsound.

Orcas is the largest island in the San Juans, covering 57 square miles. Locals jokingly refer to it as Orcapulco in the hectic summer season, or Orcatraz when winter doldrums make it an isolated rock.

PLANNING YOUR TIME

Because of its size, unusual shape, and rugged topography, Orcas Island takes longer to get around than other islands in the San Juans. It's approximately 25 miles by road from the easternmost end of the island to the western end at Deer Harbor, and that takes an hour or more to drive (if

ust-Sees

ⓜ **Moran State Park:** Acclaimed as one of the best state parks in Washington, this one has it all: more than 5,200 acres of wild country, a road-accessible lookout tower atop 2,409-foot Mount Constitution, many miles of hiking trails, abundant campsites, and a great swimming lake (page 121).

ⓜ **Rosario Resort:** This well-known resort centers around the mansion built for industrialist Robert Moran a century ago (page 126).

ⓜ **Eastsound:** The largest settlement on Orcas, Eastsound has the look and feel of a town along the coast of Maine. Its central location, good shopping, delectable meals, and up-market lodging choices add to the appeal (page 128).

ⓜ **Orcas Island Skateboard Park:** Most visitors to Orcas are unaware that the island has one of the finest skateboard parks in the Pacific Northwest. (page 134).

ⓜ **The Funhouse:** Although ostensibly for kids, this hands-on science discovery center is a blast for all ages, with musical instruments, arts and crafts, a climbing wall, games, and all sorts of other fun activities (page 136).

Orcas Island Skateboard Park

© DON PITCHER

ⓜ **Orcas Island Artworks:** Out of the way, but worth the drive, this cooperative art gallery is one of the oldest in the region. The café serves delicious lunches (page 157).

ⓜ **Orcas Island Pottery:** Step through the gate to discover hundreds of pieces of pottery strewn across a large lawn. Enjoy a million-dollar view across President Channel from one of the benches out back (page 157).

ⓜ **Howe Art Gallery:** Welded-metal mobiles and other kinetic art pieces by artist Tony Howe dot this big field of a gallery. Guaranteed to bring a smile to your child's face (page 157).

Orcas Island

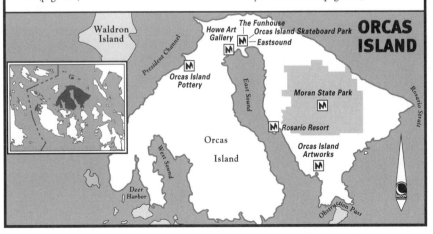

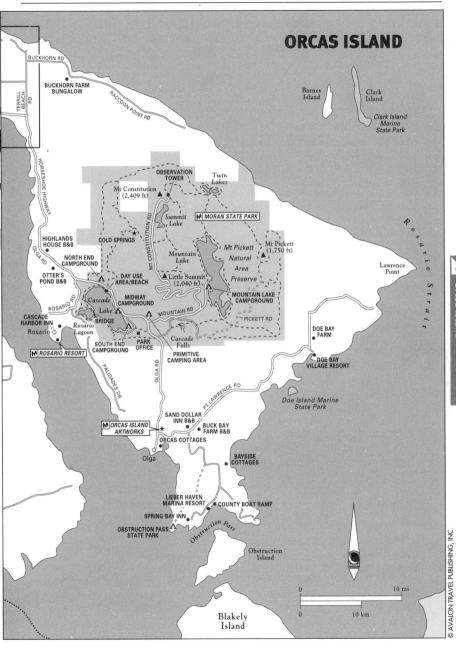

ORCAS ISLAND

Barnes Island

Clark Island

Clark Island Marine State Park

BUCKHORN RD

BUCKHORN FARM BUNGALOW

TERRILL BEACH RD

RACCOON POINT RD

HORSESHOE HIGHWAY

OBSERVATION TOWER

Twin Lakes

Mt Constitution (2,409 ft)

Summit Lake

MORAN STATE PARK

Rosario Strait

COLD SPRINGS

MT CONSTITUTION RD

Mt Pickett Natural Area Preserve

Mt Pickett (1,750 ft)

Lawrence Point

HIGHLANDS HOUSE B&B

OLGA RD

NORTH END CAMPGROUND

Mountain Lake

Little Summit (2,040 ft)

OTTER'S POND B&B

DAY USE AREA/BEACH

ROSARIO RD

Cascade Lake

MIDWAY CAMPGROUND

MOUNTAIN LAKE CAMPGROUND

CASCADE HARBOR INN

BRIDGE

Rosario Lagoon

MOUNTAIN RD

PICKETT RD

DOE BAY FARM

Rosario

SOUTH END CAMPGROUND

PARK OFFICE

Cascade Falls

DOE BAY VILLAGE RESORT

ROSARIO RESORT

PALISADES DR

OLGA RD

PRIMITIVE CAMPING AREA

PT LAWRENCE RD

Doe Island Marine State Park

ORCAS ISLAND ARTWORKS

SAND DOLLAR INN B&B

BUCK BAY FARM B&B

ORCAS COTTAGES

Olga

BAYSIDE COTTAGES

LIEBER HAVEN MARINA RESORT

COUNTY BOAT RAMP

SPRING BAY INN

OBSTRUCTION PASS STATE PARK

Obstruction Pass

Obstruction Island

0   10 mi

0   10 km

Blakely Island

Orcas Island

you don't speed). Yes, you can "see" the main sights in a single day, but why bother? If you can, plan to spend at least three or four days on Orcas.

Because of its central location and abundant amenities, many travelers choose to base their travels in the Eastsound area. Even those staying at Doe Bay Resort or Deer Harbor, however, can easily get to the main island attractions if they set aside a bit of time.

A pair of don't-miss sights are the legacy of Robert Moran: ostentatious **Rosario Resort** and nearby **Moran State Park,** with its winding road up Mount Constitution.

The beauty of Orcas Island has provided an inspiration for countless artists, and their works are displayed in shops and galleries throughout the island. A few miles south of the park is a low building that houses one of the oldest artist-owned cooperatives in the Northwest, **Orcas Island Artworks.** North of the park and just before you reach Eastsound is **Lambiel Museum,** with hundreds of locally produced pieces on display. Just west of Eastsound, a dirt road leads to **Howe Art Gallery,** where Tony Howe's delightful kinetic sculptures fill a big field, bringing smiles to all who discover them.

Orcas Island Pottery—famous for its pottery-filled yard—hugs the western shore of the island, while historic **Crow Valley Pottery** lies right on the main road southwest of Eastsound.

The town of Eastsound is home to not just shops, restaurants, and lodging places, but also to two kid-friendly places: **The Funhouse,** with its mix of science and play, and the extraordinary **Skateboard Park** along Mount Baker Road.

HISTORY

Orcas Island is apparently named for a viceroy of Mexico, Don Juan Vicente de Guemes Pacheco Pedilla Horcasitas y Aguayo, Conde de Revilla Gigedo. Fortunately, his name was shortened rather substantially, with "Horacasitas" becoming "Orcas." (Variations on his name also ended up on nearby Guemes Island and Padilla Bay, along with Southeast Alaska's Revillagigedo Island.) Orcas Island was named by the Spanish explorer Francisco Eliza during his 1791 visit, and some

scholars believe he actually named the island after his schooner of the same name. More imaginative folks claim the name came from the word *orca,* a Spanish term for a mammal still often seen here, killer whales or orcas.

Place names within West Sound highlight the area's sometimes violent history: Haida Point, Indian Point, Massacre Bay, Skull Island, and Victim Island. All of these names originated from Haida raids on the peaceful Coast Salish people who lived here for centuries. Many Salish men were murdered during these attacks, and surviving women and children were typically hauled away as slaves. Both Skull and Victim Island are marine state parks.

Fruitful Times

Early white settlers on Orcas Island hunted deer, logged, farmed, and fished. Louis Cayou came to the island in 1859 as a market hunter for the Hudson's Bay Company, but settled down with a Salish woman and raised a family. He is regarded as the first white settler. Other folks trickled in over the next 15 years, and by 1873 the island was home to 40 or so white settlers. Within a few years, the population grew rapidly as farmers discovered that Orcas was perfect for growing apples, pears, and Italian plums. In the 1880s and onward, thousands of fruit trees were planted across the island for the Orcas Island Fruit Company. A major recession in 1890 forced the company into bankruptcy, but the trees kept producing and growers found other outlets. Competition from farmers in eastern Washington spelled the end to commercial fruit growing by the 1930s, but many of these small orchards still produce fruit a century or more after they were planted.

GEOGRAPHY

From the air, Orcas Island looks like either a giant horseshoe or a misshapen M, with two long inlets cutting in from the south. Washington State Ferries dock on the south end of the island at **Orcas Village** (also called Orcas Landing or simply Orcas), where you'll find a cluster of cafés and gift shops centering on a Victorian gem, the Orcas Hotel.

East Sound is the longest channel, nearly splitting the island into two pieces. The village of **Eastsound** (note the difference in spelling from the body of water) occupies the head of this sound, and is 10 miles from the ferry. Although unincorporated, this is the primary village on the island, and *the* place to go for groceries, gas, and a wide choice of gift shops, cafés, and galleries. It also probably has more lounging cats per shop than any other town in the Pacific Northwest!

The easternmost lobe of Orcas Island offers the most rugged terrain anywhere in the San Juans, including the half-mile-high summit of Mount Constitution within famous **Moran State Park.**

Not far away is **Rosario Resort,** an equally famous historic mansion and resort.

Smaller than East Sound, **West Sound** is home to the predictably named little settlement of West Sound. It is eight miles northwest of the ferry landing, and has a marina, a homey little café, and a couple of lodging places. Approximately four miles west of here is another gathering place for boaters and others, **Deer Harbor,** with its substantial marina and resort, plus bed-and-breakfasts, a couple of restaurants, charter sailboats, and kayak rentals. It's appropriately named for the many black-tailed deer in the area and throughout the San Juans.

Sights

It isn't necessary to have a car on Orcas Island, unless you are lodging well off the main routes. The **Orcas Island Shuttle** (360/376-3414 or 800/516-9010, www.orcasislandshuttle.com, $10 day pass, $5 kids) provides scheduled service connecting the Orcas ferry landing with West Sound, Deer Harbor, Eastsound, Moran State Park, Rosario Resort, Olga, and Obstruction Pass. Buses run four times a day in each direction throughout the summer, and can carry bikes for $1 extra. Get off the bus anywhere along the route, and flag it down on a later run.

M MORAN STATE PARK

Near Eastsound, 5,252-acre Moran State Park (360/376-2326, www.parks.wa.gov) is best-known for its steep paved road to the 2,409-foot summit of **Mount Constitution.** The mountain is crowned by a 52-foot stone observation tower constructed by the Civilian Conservation Corps (CCC) in 1936, and patterned after the 12th-century watchtowers of Russia's Caucasus Mountains. This is the highest point anywhere in the San Juans and offers a commanding view, from Mount Rainier to British Columbia. The park is 14 miles by car from the Orcas ferry landing, and occupies much of Orcas Island's eastern appendage.

The park is open year-round for both day use and camping. A $5 day-use fee is charged, but this permit can be used at various places in Moran or at other state parks that same day, so keep it on your windshield.

History

Moran State Park was the creation of Robert Moran—a shipbuilder, former mayor of Seattle, and builder of the mansion that is now Rosario Resort. (See the sidebar *Robert Moran and Rosario Resort* for more on this fascinating individual.) Moran was working as chief engineer on an Alaskan steamer, the *Cassiar,* when he met famed naturalist John Muir. The two became close friends, and that friendship opened Moran's eyes to the natural world. In later years, Moran prospered, but this appreciation for nature inspired him to do something beneficial with his wealth.

In 1911, he tried to donate 2,700 acres on Orcas Island to establish a state park just uphill from his mansion at Rosario. The offer was turned down, and it wasn't until 1921 that the state finally accepted the land and created Moran State Park. Eventually, Moran would donate nearly 4,000 acres for the park. He later constructed the distinctive concrete entrance arch and the road up Mount Constitution. During the 1930s, the CCC

© DON PITCHER

entrance to Moran State Park

built most of the park's trails, bridges, shelters, and other structures, using sandstone from a local quarry and wood from area forests.

Plants and Animals

Moran State Park is a heavily wooded area, with old-growth forests of Douglas fir (some six feet in diameter), Western hemlock, western red cedar, and Pacific yew in the lower elevations, and hardy stands of shore pine (a subspecies of lodgepole) higher up the slopes. The windswept summit of Mount Constitution has grassy openings accented by lilies, asters, stonecrop, and other flowers in the summer. Columbian black-tailed deer are relatively common, along with river otters, muskrats, raccoons, bald eagles, and many other species.

Information

A **Visitor Information Kiosk** (360/376-2273, www.orcasisland.org) across the road from Cascade Lake is open Memorial Day–Labor Day 9:30 A.M.–1:30 P.M. Monday–Saturday. You will find park maps and other information here, or stop by the park office on the south end of Cascade Lake. Get additional park information at 360/376-2326, www.parks.wa.gov. Interested in

helping the park in its preservation efforts? Join the nonprofit Friends of Moran State Park; call the park for details.

Hiking Trails

Moran State Park has 38 miles of hiking trails, from short nature loops to remote and rugged out-of-the-way hikes. The CCC constructed most of these trails during the 1930s. Get a park map for details on the various routes, or see Ken Wilcox's *Hiking the San Juan Islands* (Northwest Wild Books).

The easiest path is a 0.3-mile **Moran State Park Nature Trail** that takes off from the day-use area along Cascade Lake, with signs identifying plants along the way. Only slightly more challenging is the quarter-mile trail to **Cascade Falls,** where Cascade Creek plummets into a deep pool 75 feet below. The path begins from a parking area a quarter mile up the Mount Constitution Road, and drops downhill to the falls, a 10-minute walk. Come here in spring for the most dramatic show. You can also continue upstream to two less impressive waterfalls.

A longer version, the **Cascade Creek Trail,** begins near the park office on Cascade Lake and follows the creek uphill (with a detour to Cascade Falls) to the picnic area at Mountain Lake, a distance of three miles with a gain of 700 feet. You'll encounter enormous old-growth Douglas firs along the way. From the lake, you can hike back or catch a ride downhill along the Mount Constitution Road.

Cascade Lake is a busy place in midsummer, with three oft-full campgrounds, a popular picnic area, canoe rentals, and a swimming beach. The Orcas Road parallels its northeast shore. For a nearly level walk, follow the **Cascade Lake Loop Trail** for 2.7 miles around the lake, past tall trees drooping over the water and across a picturesque arched wooden bridge at Rosario Lagoon, known for good fishing. Several side trails offer tantalizing options, including one that switchbacks 300 feet uphill over three-quarters of a mile to **Sunrise Rock.** The vistas encompass Cascade Lake below, with the Cascades themselves in the distance on a clear day.

Another relatively easy round-the-lake hike is the **Mountain Lake Loop Trail,** a four-mile path that offers a chance to see Columbian black-tailed deer, particularly in the morning and early evening, and passes enormous old Douglas firs. Circle the lake counterclockwise for the best vistas.

The summit of **Mount Constitution** is readily accessible by car via a paved road, but to really appreciate the views, there's nothing like climbing it yourself. A number of trails ascend the mountain from various sides, but one of the best begins from Mountain Lake Landing (accessible by car). From here, you follow the lakeshore to the north end and continue uphill to **Twin Lakes.** Then ascend sharply up a series of switchbacks to the summit, where you'll suddenly be surrounded by the hoi polloi who drove here. Finally, climb the old CCC viewing tower for a panoramic of northern Puget Sound and the San Juans. It's 3.7 miles to the top of Mount Constitution from Mountain Lake. For variety on the way back, take the trail to **Little Summit,** which leads through stands of shore pine before dropping into dense forests of Western hemlock and Douglas fir. The return is 3.3 miles long, for a round-trip hike of seven miles, with a 1,500-foot elevation gain (and loss) en route. You can, of course, save your legs by catching a ride to the top and hiking downhill instead.

Orcas Island

© DON PITCHER

swimmers at Cascade Lake

ROBERT MORAN AND ROSARIO RESORT

Two of Orcas Island's most famous destinations—Moran State Park and Rosario Resort—were the creations of Robert Moran, a self-made millionaire who turned his back on success in the business world. Born in 1857 to a New York family of 10 children, Robert Moran left home at age 14 to become an apprentice machinist. Three years later, in 1875, he decided that his future lay westward. After walking all the way to Cincinnati, he got a summer job at an iron mill and made enough money to return to New York and book passage on a ship for San Francisco. He arrived in the midst of an economic depression, and after failing to find a job, spent his last $15 on a steerage ticket to Seattle.

Moran stepped onto Yesler's Wharf in the Seattle rain with just $.10 left in his pocket. A hungry belly led him to the aroma of pork sausage and flapjacks at a little eatery called Our House, run by Big Bill Gross, an enormous black man. Gross took pity on Moran and offered him breakfast on credit and later helped him get a job as a cook at a logging camp. Moran's cooking was so bad that the men threatened revolt and he had to hightail it back to Seattle, where Gross found him yet another job, this time as a deckhand on a steamer running between Seattle and Bellingham. Finally, Moran was in his element. Over the next few years he studied mathematics, drafting, and engineering under the tutelage of an experienced ship captain, gradually moving up the ranks to become chief engineer on the steamer *Cassiar*, sailing in southeast Alaska.

Boom Times

In 1881 Moran married Melissa Paul, and together they raised five children. He paid $500 for his mother, five younger brothers, and two sisters to sail from New York to Seattle. Shortly after their arrival, the brothers set up a marine repair shop and Robert also took over management of the adjacent Seattle Drydock and Shipbuilding Company. Within a few years Moran was on the city council, and in 1888 was elected the Republican mayor of Seattle. Within a year of taking office a huge fire swept through downtown, leaving 30 city blocks in ruins—including the Moran brothers' machine shop. Moran moved quickly to rebuild the city after the fire, and within six months, Seattle's population had actually doubled.

The Moran Brothers Co. wasted no time in rebuilding; their new shop was open 10 days after the old one had burned to the ground! The company established an international reputation, and within a few years began getting contracts to build ships for the U.S. Navy.

The 1897 discovery of gold in the Klondike transformed Seattle. Thousands of gold-crazed men flooded the town, intent on getting north as quickly as possible. Ships were needed to haul them there (and the gold out), and Moran Brothers began building stern-wheelers at a furious pace. Eighteen of these—each 175 feet long—were completed in 1898, and Robert Moran himself led the flotilla, starting at Roche Harbor on San Juan Island and sailing all the way to St. Michael at the mouth of the Yukon River, a distance of 4,000 treacherous miles. Only one of the 18 steamers was lost along the way, and it was insured. The Morans were on a roll.

During Robert Moran's two terms as Seattle mayor he made business contacts in Washington, D.C., and impressed the U.S. Navy with his design expertise. In 1900 the shipyard—then the Northwest's largest—landed a contract to build the U.S.S. *Nebraska*, one of a new class of battleships. It was a huge event for Seattle, and more than 55,000 people watched the launching ceremony. The ship became a favorite of naval officers and remained in service through World War I.

Showpiece of the San Juans

The mental and physical stresses of business took a severe toll on Robert Moran, making him, in his own words, "a nervous wreck." Specialists from Europe told him that he was destined to soon gain "permanent residence in Lakeview Cemetery, Seattle, for the reason that they predicted that I had organic heart disease." He retired in 1905 at the age of 49, turning the shipyard over to his brothers. In 32 years he had gone from a boy with $.10 in his pocket to one of the wealthiest men in the Pacific Northwest. The Moran Brothers Company was sold in 1906 to and later became part of Todd Shipyards, a large Seattle operation that survives today.

Shortly after retiring, Robert Moran took a pleasure cruise in the San Juan Islands and fell in love with Orcas Island. It was his paradise:

In the lower reaches of Puget Sound and the Gulf of Georgia, looking out through the Strait of Juan de Fuca, toward the indles and lands of romance on the chief trade routes of the world's future commerce, lies a land unique and apart from anything else in the Western Hemisphere—the San Juan Islands. . . . It is a wonderful place in which to forget one's troubles and worries and get back to Nature in her happiest moods; a delightful place in which to regain health—physical, mental, and spiritual.

He purchased 7,800 acres on Orcas Island and began work on a retirement home he called Rosario after nearby Rosario Strait. But this was no simple waterfront cottage. He hired the finest shipwrights of the day (many of them former employees of Moran Brothers Co.) to create a 54-room mansion covering 35,000 square feet. It cost $1.5 million in 1905 dollars, and took four years to complete. Much of the ironwork—including butterfly hinges, nautical-style lamps, and door fasteners—was wrought at an on-site machine shop. Other touches included an indoor pool (with Italian marble) and bowling alley, a large veranda, beautifully landscaped grounds with a figure-eight-shaped lagoon, and a small hydroelectric plant to supply electricity; it still operates. The home was furnished in custom-made Mission-style pieces of teak and leather.

Moran Departs

In 1932—at the height of the Great Depression—Moran put his estate up for sale. His wife had died two years earlier, his brothers and sisters had also passed away, and his children had other interests. Despite ads in prominent national magazines, there were no takers. The mansion was finally sold in 1938 to a wealthy Californian, Donald Rheem, who paid just $50,000 for the mansion and 1,339 acres of surrounding land. Moran moved to much simpler quarters near the Orcas ferry landing. He died on his beloved Orcas Island on March 27, 1943 at the age of 86 and is buried in the same Lake View Cemetery in Seattle that the doctors had warned him about 37 years earlier. He probably outlived most of those doctors by many years.

For the complete story of Robert Moran and Rosario, read *Rosario Yesterdays* by Christopher Peacock.

Orcas Island

The western portion of Moran State Park encompasses **Mount Pickett Natural Area Preserve,** the largest contiguous tract of unlogged forest remaining in Puget Sound. It is closed to all off-trail hiking or other uses, but trails circle its margins, providing a woodsy 6.5-mile loop hike if you start at Mountain Lake Landing. Mount Pickett itself is a 1,750-foot summit with limited views from the trail.

Water Fun

During the summer, the beach at Cascade Lake is an exceptionally popular family destination, with a roped-off swimming area (no lifeguard), which has a shallow sandy bottom and relatively warm water June–August. There's a fun woodsy playground, and a snack bar selling hot dogs, sodas, microwave pizzas, and other fast food. The boathouse rents rowboats and paddleboats Memorial Day–Labor Day, and has a few fishing supplies. Rowboats are also available at Mountain Lake. Both of these lakes have boat ramps, but motorboats are prohibited. Anglers have fun casting about for rainbow, cutthroat, and kokanee trout; Cascade Lake is stocked annually by the Washington Department of Fish and Wildlife.

Cycling in the Park

Moran is the most challenging cycling destination in the San Juans, with trails (and a paved road) leading from Cascade Lake to the summit of Mount Constitution, a gain of 2,100 feet in elevation. It's a fast and exhilarating ride back down! Eleven miles of park trails are open year-round to cyclists, and from September 15 to May 15, there are 25 miles open to mountain-bike use. Before heading out, purchase a *Local Knowledge Trail Map* for Mount Constitution at Wildlife Cycles in Eastsound. This helpful map includes tips for the various trails and roads, along with difficulty ratings and seasonal closings. Cyclists must yield to hikers and horses. Never ride off-trail within the park.

Other Park Activities

The park has five kitchen shelters—most available on a first-come, first-served basis—plus a multitude of picnic tables. A spacious log kitchen shelter next to the Cascade Lake swim area can

be reserved by calling 888/226-7688. It holds up to 100 people, and includes a stone fireplace, wood grill, sink, electrical outlets, and lights.

Equestrians will appreciate the six miles of trails open to horse use within the park; see the park's official map for details.

Located on the south end of Cascade Lake, the rustic **Camp Moran Environmental Learning Center** (360/376-6173, www.orcasisle.com/~elc/outdoorschool) houses an environmental education program in which several hundred students participate every year. It is also available for group and family rentals.

Guided Hikes

Natalie (Nat) Herner of **Gnat's Nature Hikes** (360/376-6629, www.orcasislandhikes.com) guides nature walks every day in the summer and on weekends at other times. These hikes emphasize both human and natural history, along with wild edible and medicinal plants. The cost is $30/person, including pickup and return to your hotel or bed-and-breakfast, plus three hours on Moran State Park trails. She also offers half-day boat-and-hike trips to the marine state parks on Jones or other islands for $65/person, with a six-person maximum. There's a two-person minimum for the Moran hikes and a three-person minimum for the boat trips. Natalie has a background in environmental studies along with more than a decade of experience as a naturalist and as a guide on whale-watching boats.

ROSARIO RESORT

The largest resort in the San Juans, Rosario Resort & Spa (1400 Rosario Rd., 360/376-2222 or 800/562-8820, www.rosarioresort.com) is five miles south of Eastsound along the protected Cascade Harbor. This famous and historic getaway is well worth a look even if you can't afford to stay here, with a picture-perfect setting that is exceptionally popular for outdoor (and indoor) weddings.

History

Now on the National Register of Historic Places, the ostentatious mansion at Rosario Resort was

© DON PITCHER

Rosario Resort sits on the shore of Casade Harbor.

built almost a century ago by Robert Moran, a shipbuilder and two-term Seattle mayor who—on doctors' orders—came here to retire.

Moran sold his mansion in 1938 to Donald Rheem, the son of Standard Oil Company founder William S. Rheem and a major shareholder in Paramount Studios. Donald Rheem spent $400,000 improving the mansion, but it was his wife who is best remembered today. Some say he bought Rosario to keep her out of sight. Alice Goodfellow Rheem cut a wild swath, drinking and playing cards with the locals, zooming around the island on a motorcycle in a bright red nightgown, and playing host to military personnel while her husband was in California. She died in 1956 after falling from the library balcony into the Rosario music room below. Ghost aficionados report all sorts of haunting experiences here, and some say her presence is particularly strong around Christmas, when she died.

After Alice's death, the mansion was sold a couple of times, and in 1960 it was opened to the public as Rosario Resort. Today, it is owned by RockResorts, founded by the Rockefeller family, but now part of Vail Resorts, Inc.

Rosario Today

The historic mansion at Rosario Resort is open to the public. Visitors are welcome to tour the grounds and check out the antique-filled rooms, distinctive furnishings, parquet floors crafted from Indian teak, and walls paneled in Honduran mahogany.

Head upstairs to the vaulted ballroom with its heavy doors, stained-glass window, Tiffany chandelier, and ornate 1909 Steinway grand piano that is dwarfed by the 1,972-pipe Aeolian organ. A horseshoe-shaped balcony hides the organ itself, which plays from musical rolls, much like a player piano. Moran had absolutely no musical talent, but he often pretended to play the organ and none of his guests were the wiser. The organ was later modified, adding a keyboard to allow it to be played. Today, the gifted musician Christopher Peacock puts on one-hour performances that include music on the organ and piano, along with a video about Moran. Shows take place at 6 P.M. Monday, Wednesday, and Saturday and are free to resort guests and the public. Winter performances typically take place Saturdays and holidays at 5 P.M.

Also upstairs is a small free museum with

original furnishings and Moran's impressive library just as he left it. Historic photos line the walls, and there's even a model of the U.S.S. *Washington,* one of the ships built by Moran's company. An upscale restaurant and lounge are downstairs, and the basement houses a gift shop, pool, and spa. Outside are manicured grounds and a veranda overlooking Cascade Harbor's bobbing boats. The anchor chain from the U.S.S. *Nebraska* and a beautifully carved figurehead from the clipper ship *America* are in front of the mansion. Lodging is available in newer buildings surrounding Moran's historic home, but not in the mansion itself.

For more about the life of Robert Moran, see *Rosario Yesterdays* by Christopher Peacock, who also happens to be the resort's organist. The book is sold at Rosario and in local bookstores.

⚑ EASTSOUND

Located at the north end of Orcas Island near its narrowest point, the settlement of Eastsound is the primary village on the island. Here you'll discover a mix of gift shops, top-end restaurants, comfortable inns, grocery stores, kayak outfitters, and Internet cafés, not to mention the kid's science center, skateboard park, and historical museum.

Orcas Island Historical Museum

The Orcas Island Historical Society began in the 1940s as a small group of individuals dedicated to protecting and preserving the island's history. The organization's first museum consisted of artifacts displayed on the front porch of a pioneer family's home. In the 1950s and 1960s, island families donated six original homestead cabins that were built on Orcas between the 1870s and 1890s. Volunteers reconstructed and linked the structures to create the main museum building. These cedar cabins not only house the collections, but are considered important historical artifacts in themselves.

The collection at the Orcas Island Historical Museum (181 North Beach Rd. in Eastsound, 360/376-4849, www.orcasisland.org/~history, $2 adults, $1 seniors and students, $.50 for kids under 13) has displays covering relics, life stories, and historical photos from 1880s farms and

homesteads, early stores and post offices, fruit farming, and the Coast Salish people. The museum is open late May–September 10 A.M.–3 P.M. Tuesday–Thursday and Saturday–Sunday, 1–6 P.M. Friday; open by appointment the rest of the year.

OTHER SIGHTS
Crow Valley School Museum

This small museum, three miles southwest of Eastsound (2274 Crow Valley Rd., 360/376-4260) is open by appointment only; call a day ahead. It is a quiet spot surrounded by tall trees and makes a pleasant stop during a cycling tour of the island. Built in 1888, the classic one-room school houses old desks and a collection of memorabilia that includes school photos, report cards, school clothes, toys, and other items from a bygone era.

More Historic Buildings

Both Deer Harbor and Olga contain a number of buildings dating from the late 1800s, including the Olga Store, the Deer Harbor Store (1893), and the Deer Harbor Post Office (1893). The last of these is worth a visit, if only for its blue and yellow stained-glass windows. The quaint and beautifully situated **Emmanuel Episcopal Church** faces the water in downtown Eastsound. Built in 1886 and modeled after an English country church, it is also the site for Thursday brown-bag concerts all summer. The church was built on land that was originally intended for a saloon. The owner started clearing land here, but was so harassed by temperance movement women that he finally gave up and left town. The land was later donated to the church.

Victorian Valley Chapel (360/376-5157 or 866/424-2735, www.victorianvalleychapel.com) is one of the hidden gems on Orcas. Located along Victorian Valley Road, this little white chapel was built in the 1950s for the wedding of Lucy Bang's daughter. With its quaint setting, stained glass windows, and a lovely wood interior, the non-denominational building is popular for weddings and other gatherings throughout the year. The road to the chapel is signed Private, but it is open to the general public.

Orcas Island

EASTSOUND

North Beach

SUNSET AVE

SMUGGLER'S VILLA RESORT

ROSE ARBOR COTTAGE

ALDER ST

SPRUCE ST

HEMLOCK ST

BRANDT'S LANDING RD

BARTEL RD

BARTWOOD LODGE

MATIA VIEW DR

AERIE ON ORCAS GUEST HOUSE

KANGAROO HOUSE B&B

SWANNIE'S INN

SHADY LN

EASTSOUND AIRPORT

COMMERCIAL PARK RD

NORTH BEACH RD

BUCKHORN RD

TERRILL BEACH RD

WEBER LN

AIRPORT CENTER LAUNDRY

ORCAS FAMILY PHYSICIANS

MT BAKER RD

ORCAS THEATRE AND COMMUNITY CENTER

ORCAS ISLAND MEDICAL CENTER

BUCK PARK

ORCAS ISLAND SKATEBOARD PARK

THE FUNHOUSE

ENCHANTED FOREST RD

LOVER'S LN

HIGH SCHOOL

SCHOOL RD

CHAMBER OF COMMERCE VISITOR CENTER

POST OFFICE

A ST

BEACH RD

ALLEY

PINE ST

ROSE ST

MADRONA ST

SEA VIEW THEATRE

LIBRARY

FARMERS MARKET

ORCAS SPA AND ATHLETIC CENTER

ORCAS ISLAND HISTORICAL MUSEUM

FERN ST

PRUNE

ISLAND MARKET

NORTH ST

MARKET ST

CRESCENT BEACH DR

LANDMARK INN

OUTLOOK INN

MAIN ST

Crescent Beach

EMMANUEL EPISCOPAL CHURCH

HAVEN

MONTGOMERY LN

ODDFELLOWS HALL

COUNTY DOCK

POINT LN

Ship Bay

HARRISON RD

Indian Island

To Orcas Ferry and Deer Harbor

Fishing Bay

Madrona Point

SHIP BAY INN

MORAN STATE PARK AND ROSARIO RESORT

0   200 yds

0   200 m

Orcas Island

© AVALON TRAVEL PUBLISHING, INC.

© DON PITCHER

Victorian Valley Chapel

Located between Orcas Village and Eastsound, **Crow Valley Pottery** (2274 Orcas Rd., 360/376-4260, www.crowvalley.com) is housed in the oldest building on Orcas Island, an 1866 log cabin. It's well worth a stop.

Lambiel Museum

A true patron of the arts, Leo Lambiel (360/376-4544, www.lambielmuseum.com) has spent more than a quarter-century collecting hundreds of the finest works by 180 San Juan County artists. The pieces cover a wide array of media: paintings, drawings, sculpture, murals, glasswork, photography, and ceramics, with some dating back to the 1920s. This private collection is housed in Lambiel's gracious home/museum, located a mile and a half from Eastsound on Olga Road. The walls are lined with art, and Leo is constantly collecting more; he plans to add three stories to his home to provide more display space. On the grounds, you'll find various sculptures, along with a three-room grotto (with humorous and grotesque pieces), and a "ruined" Greek temple. Exceptionally detailed two-hour tours of the museum are given year-round for $10/person; call for an appointment (required). Anyone with an appreciation for the arts will certainly enjoy a visit to this fascinating private museum. This is not a gallery, and the works are not for sale.

Orcas Island

Recreation

HIKING AND BIRDING

The best hiking on Orcas is found within Moran State Park, but a handful of other trail options exist. Get a copy of *Hiking the San Juan Islands* by Ken Wilcox for detailed descriptions of Orcas trails.

Madrona Point

For ease of access, it's hard to beat Madrona Point, just a few blocks from downtown Eastsound. This small peninsula of land now belongs to the Lummi Indian Nation (the federal government bought it from developers in the 1980s and gave it to the Lummi), but is open to the public. Get here by following Haven Road south from Eastsound to the park, where you will also find a county dock for launching boats and kayaks. Madrona Point is aptly named, with tall and colorful Pacific madrone (a.k.a. madrona) trees, along with graceful Douglas firs framing the view across the water to Eastsound and the rest of Orcas Island. A meadow on the point contains camas plants; the bulbs of the purple great camas were a prized food source for the Coast Salish.

Not far from Madrona Point is **Eastsound Waterfront Park,** a little grassy picnic area across from the intersection of Lovers Lane and Horseshoe Highway. When the tide is low, you can walk out from here to **Indian Island,** just offshore.

Obstruction Pass State Park

Obstruction Pass (360/376-2326, www.parks .wa.gov, $5 day use) is an 80-acre park at the end of a one-mile dirt road off Obstruction Pass Road. It is approximately 2.5 miles southeast of Olga and 17 road miles from the ferry dock. A woodsy (and sometimes muddy) trail leads a half mile from the parking lot to a beach that faces nearby Obstruction and Blakely Islands. Nine campsites are just back from the beach, and a side trail leads to a second beach looking west to Olga and the setting sun. Obstruction Pass is a favorite destination for sea kayakers, who can put in for free at the nearby county boat ramp and dock. No bikes allowed in the park.

Point Doughty Marine State Park

This small peninsula extends from the northwestern edge of Orcas close to the YMCA's Camp Orkila, and is popular with kayakers. Access by larger boats is very difficult, and kayakers may contend with wind and waves at this exposed site. The point contains tall cliffs and a forest of Douglas fir and madrone. Nearby waters are a favorite of scuba divers, and harbor porpoises are common sights in rips just off the point.

Only the four acres at the very tip of Point Doughty are open to the public; the rest is a natural area preserve where trespassing is prohibited. No trails in this little park, and there are no easements to allow access from nearby roads, so you'll need a kayak to visit. Point Doughty's four primitive campsites are part of the Cascadia Marine Trail. No drinking water, but vault toilets are provided.

Frank Richardson Wildlife Preserve

Located close to Deer Harbor, this 20-acre freshwater marsh is a premier birding area, with red-winged blackbirds, wood ducks, hooded mergansers, Canada geese, mallards, widgeons, scaups, buffleheads, teal, rails, marsh wrens, and many other species. It is named for a University of Washington professor of zoology (and birder) who lived nearby. After his death in 1985, the land was saved through the efforts of the San Juan Preservation Trust. Get here by driving or cycling to Deer Harbor, turning right on an unmarked road just before you reach the harbor itself. Cross the bridge and then bear left, heading uphill for three-quarters of a mile. The marsh is on the right.

BICYCLING

Orcas has a great diversity of cycling conditions, all the way up to a difficult five-mile climb (and worth it!) to the summit of Mount Constitution within Moran State Park. The island's 82 miles of county roads tend to be narrow, hilly, and winding, making this the most challenging of the islands for cyclists. Always travel in single file. Be sure to pull well off the road when you stop, and watch out for long lines of traffic heading up the road when a ferry has just docked at Orcas Village. Get a helpful cycling map of Orcas from Wildlife Cycles.

Rentals

Bike rentals are available at Orcas Village, Eastsound, and Deer Harbor; $30–40 for a one-day mountain-bike rental with helmet. Tandems, road bikes, cross bikes, kids' bikes, child and cargo trailers, car racks, joggers, and touring equipment are also available for rent.

The island's only year-round bike shop, **Wildlife Cycles** (350 North Beach Rd. in Eastsound, 360/376-4708, www.wildlifecycles.com) rents high-quality mountain bikes, road bikes, hybrids, and other biking gear. Guided tours are available for groups heading to Moran State Park. This is where you'll meet the hardcore local cyclists. Rides to the summit of Mount Constitution depart on Sunday mornings at 8 A.M. year-round and are open to riders of all levels; stop by Wildlife Cycles for details and a map of park trails open to cyclists.

Head right as you exit the ferry at Orcas Village for **Dolphin Bay Bicycles** (360/376-4157, www.rockisland.com/~dolphin) a small shop run by local schoolteacher Paul Evans.

You can also rent basic mountain bikes at **Deer Harbor Marina** (360/376-3037, www.deerharbormarina.com).

SEA KAYAKING

Orcas Island is an excellent launching point for day trips and multi-day paddles. Several of the most popular kayaking destinations, including Jones, Sucia, Patos, and Matia Islands are within a few miles of Orcas.

Tours

A number of companies lead sea-kayaking trips on Orcas Island during the summer, but one stands out: **Shearwater Adventures** (in Eastsound on Prune Alley across from Island Market, 360/376-4699, www.shearwaterkayaks.com). Established in 1982, the company offers three-hour paddles ($49/person) led by experienced guides. Shearwater tours depart daily from Rosario Resort, Deer Harbor Resort, and Doe

kayakers at Deer Harbor

© DON PITCHER

Bay Resort & Retreat on Orcas Island. All-day trips ($85) provide a chance to explore the islets off Orcas at a leisurely pace. Most trips start at one point and take out at another so you don't retrace your route. Tours generally operate April–September. In addition, Shearwater staff teach sea-kayaking classes for all levels of ability, set up custom tours, and rent kayaks to experienced paddlers with advance notice. The shop in Eastsound sells new and used kayaks, along with quality paddling and camping gear, books, videos, and more.

Osprey Tours (in Eastsound, 360/376-3677 or 800/529-2567, www.ospreytours.com) is certainly the most distinctive kayak company in the San Juans. Owner and guide Randy Monge builds his kayaks with a traditional Aleutian-style wooden frame but covers them with high-tech coated nylon fabric. Add in a hand-painted visor for the full effect. Randy says that his handcrafted kayaks offer better handling in rough conditions and a smoother ride in the water. Half-day tours are $50/person. More fun are the three-hour sunset paddles ($60/person) to Point Doughty; there's often brilliant bioluminescence in the water as you paddle back after dark. Full-day trips cost $120 (including lunch), and overnight trips to Patos or Sucia Islands run $200. In addition, Osprey Tours offers one-hour evening paddles from Eastsound in a unique umiak-style boat based on Native Alaskan designs. These trips take place several times a month and cost $20/person. There's a two-person minimum on all of these trips, with a maximum of six.

Orcas Outdoors Sea Kayaks (360/376-4611, www.orcasoutdoors.com) operates from Orcas Village. A variety of tours are offered, including a don't-blink one-hour paddle ($25) that's popular with folks waiting in line for their ferry. Two-hour paddles cost $35, three-hour trips are $45, and all-day tours cost $95. Multi-day excursions are also available.

West Beach Kayaks (at West Beach Resort, 360/376-2240 or 877/937-8224, www.westbeachresort.com) offers half-day paddles all summer long.

Teenagers may be interested in the 13- to 22-day sea-kayaking trips offered by the YMCA's Camp Orkila (360/376-2678 or 206/382-5009, www.seattleymca.org). In addition, Spring Bay Inn (360/376-5531, www.springbayinn.com) has free two-hour kayak tours for its guests.

Kayak Rentals

Do-it-yourselfers can rent sea kayaks from several places on Orcas, but most of these require that you have considerable experience on the water. Shearwater Adventures (in Eastsound on Prune Alley across from Island Market, 360/376-4699, www.shearwaterkayaks.com) has a limited number of rental kayaks at its Eastsound office; you'll need to know rescue skills and have a familiarity with handling strong currents. It's wise to call them at least a week in advance to set up a rental. West Beach Kayaks (at West Beach Resort, 360/376-2240 or 877/937-8224, www.westbeachresort.com) rents single kayaks year-round.

Other places with rental kayaks include Lieber Haven Marina Resort (360/376-2472, www .lieberhavenresort.com) and funky Crescent Beach Kayaks (at Crescent Beach in Eastsound, 360/376-2464). The latter has all sorts of kayaks—including sit-on-top versions and kid boats. Kayaks are $50/person for a half-day, including a short lesson. The usually placid bay out front has an oyster farm and enormous numbers of sand dollars. No experience necessary.

If you're planning on launching your own kayak, be forewarned that you may be subject to a launching fee ($5 at Deer Harbor) if you aren't on public lands and may be charged for overnight parking. North Beach (near Eastsound) is the primary launching point for kayakers heading to the very popular trio of Sucia, Matia, and Patos Islands. Unfortunately, parking is limited and the spaces are quickly filled on summer weekends. Bartwood Lodge (360/376-2242 or 866/666-2242, www.bartwoodlodge.com), also on the north shore, allows the public to launch kayaks for $6. You can also launch kayaks for free at the county dock near Madrona Point in Eastsound. On the southern edge of the island, kayakers put in at Obstruction Pass, where the county maintains the only public boat ramp. Across the road is Lieber Haven Resort, with a beach that's open to the public and no charge for launching kayaks.

Orcas Island

© DON PITCHER

Orcas Island Skateboard Park

ORCAS ISLAND SKATEBOARD PARK

Head out Mt. Baker Road just past the medical clinic and just before the cemetery to **Orcas Island Skateboard Park** (www.skateorcas.org), recognized as one of the finest skate parks in the Northwest. The park was funded in part by Warren Miller, the guru of extreme skiing, and contains 15,000 square feet of bumps and curving concrete that attract both locals and off-island boarders. No bikes allowed, and helmets are required. The skateboard park is a part of **Buck Park,** which also contains tennis courts and baseball fields. **Orcas Island Board Shop** (365 North Beach Rd., 360/376-7233, www.orcasislandboardshop.com) rents boards, pads, and helmets for $20/day.

WHALE-WATCHING

Two respected companies provide whale-watching trips from Orcas Island. Note, however, that killer whales are most often found in Haro Strait west of San Juan Island, so trips starting from Orcas Island require more time en route than those out of Roche Harbor on San Juan Island. Reservations are advised.

Established in 1990, **Deer Harbor Charters** (360/376-5989 or 800/544-5758, www.deer-harborcharters.com) is the longest-running whale-watching business on Orcas. Owner Tom Averna has a background in marine science and keeps a professional naturalist aboard his two 20-passenger boats. Four-hour trips depart from Deer Harbor Resort and Rosario Resort daily May–October in search of orcas and minke whales; $51 ($35 kids). Wildlife cruises ($40 adults, $25 kids) are available in the off-season.

Orcas Island Eclipse Charters (360/376-4663 or 800/376-6566, www.orcasislandwhales.com), has a spacious 50-passenger boat that heads out from Orcas Village (next to the ferry). Trips last 3.5 hours and cost $52 ($32 kids).

BOATING

Marinas

Located on the southwest end of Orcas Island, picturesque **Deer Harbor Marina** (360/376-3037, www.deerharbormarina.com) is a busy place in the summer. Flowers drape the docks, and you'll find boat rentals, sailing charters, water taxis (North Shore Charters), sea-kayak tours (Shearwater Adventures), whale-watching trips

(Deer Harbor Charters), mountain bike rentals, showers, moorage, boat gas (also for cars in an emergency), showers, and a tiny year-round market. The little sandy beach here is a great diversion for kids. Lodging and food are across the road.

Historic Rosario Resort is the base for **Rosario Resort Marina** (360/376-2222 or 800/562-8820, www.rosarioresort.com) with moorage, fuel, and supplies on Cascade Bay near Moran State Park. There's direct Kenmore Air floatplane service to the marina from Seattle, and you can take sea-kayaking and whale-watching trips, go sailing or fishing with a pro, or rent a motorboat. The resort itself houses a full-service spa.

Located three miles west of Eastsound off Enchanted Forest Road, **West Beach Resort** (360/376-2240 or 877/937-8224, www.westbeachresort.com) has a pier and floating summer-only marina. You can rent motorboats, canoes, rowboats, and sea kayaks. Guided kayak tours are also available. Only cabin guests and campers staying at the resort are allowed to launch boats or kayaks at the resort's private beach.

Orcas Island's largest marina is **West Sound Marina** (360/376-2314, www.boattravel.com/westsound) on the northeast side of West Sound. Here you will find guest moorage, showers, a waste pump-out, fuel dock, marine repair facility, and chandlery. It's open year-round.

Lieber Haven Marina (360/376-2472, www.lieberhavenresort.com) is a small marina where you can rent kayaks, sailboats, and motorboats, or go along on whale-watching and sailing trips, sea-kayak tours, or fishing charters. They even have loaner fishing poles. A little store sells snacks, and public moorage is available. It is located along Obstruction Pass on the southeast end of the island. Across the road is the **Obstruction Pass Boat Ramp,** the only public ramp on Orcas.

Sailing Away

Deer Harbor (www.deerharbor.org) is the primary center for sailboat charters on Orcas Island. Skipper Ward Fay of **Northwest Classic Day Sails** (360/376-5581, www.classicdaysails.com) sails a meticulously maintained cedar sloop, the 33-foot *Aura*. Three-hour trips depart

Deer Harbor Wednesday–Sunday, and cost $50/person, with a two-person minimum and a max of six. Special trips and sailing instruction are also available on this beautiful sailboat built in the 1940s.

Also based at Deer Harbor, **Emerald Isle Sailing Charters** (360/376-3472, www.emeraldislesailing.com) has both six-hour day trips ($115/person with a two-person minimum), and multi-day San Juan Islands skippered charter trips, starting at $800/person for a three-day voyage; longer ones head into Alaska's Inside Passage. The boat is a beautiful 54-foot pilothouse ketch.

Captain Miles McCoy of **Sharon L. Charters** (360/376-4305) has 50 years of experience in these waters and will be glad to impart a bit of that knowledge on his three-hour afternoon sailing trips out of West Sound. The *Sharon L* is a classic 28-foot wooden Cape Cod catboat, and can hold up to six guests. The cost is $60/person with a two-person minimum.

Based at Rosario Resort, **Orcas Island Sailing** (360/376-2113, www.orcassailing.com) has skippered charters ($220–260/half day), sailing instruction, and bareboat charters on board 19- and 26-foot sloops.

Skipper Bill Glass takes guests aboard *Showtime*, a 35-foot performance sailboat; $225/half-day for up to six people or $350/day. The boat is based at Orcas Village; details at **Orcas Sailing Charters** (360/376-3080, www.orcasisland.com/charter).

Lieber Haven Marina Resort (at Obstruction Pass, 360/376-2472, www.lieberhavenresort.com) also has sailing charters in the summer.

Motorboats

Located at Deer Harbor Marina, **Orcas Boat Rentals** (360/376-7616, www.orcasboats.com) rents a variety of boats, from 14-foot skiffs with 15-horsepower engines ($175/day) up to a 17-foot Whaler ($225/day). Boat charters to nearby Jones Island and Yellow Island are popular in the summer.

West Beach Resort (three miles west of Eastsound, 360/376-2240 or 877/937-8224, www.westbeachresort.com) rents motorboats

($129/day), canoes and rowboats ($25/day), and single sea kayaks ($69/day).

Lieber Haven Marina Resort at Obstruction Pass (360/376-2472, www.lieberhavenresort.com) also has sea kayaks and motorboats for rent by the hour or day.

For something different, **Bigwave Sea Adventures** (360/376-7078 or 800/732-4095, www.bigwaveonline.com) offers three-hour trips that circumnavigate Orcas Island (with a stop on Patos Island) in an open and exposed high-speed Zodiac. These 3.5-hour trips are offered twice daily in the summer, and cost $100/person. Charters—such as lighthouse tours—are also popular. The boat departs from either Rosario Resort or Deer Harbor Marina.

DIVING

Based at Rosario Resort on the east side of Orcas, **Island Dive and Water Sports** (360/378-2772 or 800/303-8386, www.divesanjuan.com) is a full-service dive operation with dive boats, chartered dives, instruction, certification, and air fills. A wide variety of dive packages are also available that include lodging on Orcas or on San Juan Island, where Island Dive has a big shop. Note: The shop may not be open in 2005 due to construction, so call ahead.

SWIMMING AND FITNESS

The YMCA's **Camp Orkila** (360/376-2678 or 206/382-5009, www.seattleymca.org) has an impressive Olympic-size heated outdoor swimming pool open to the public in the summer 1–1:45 P.M. daily (except Wednesday) for just $1/person. The pool has a wonderful beachside location. The camp is approximately two miles from Eastsound at the western end of Mount Baker Road. Families staying on Orcas for a week or more should be sure to get details on the Y's youth swim lessons, offered four times a week from late June to mid-August.

Three **Moran State Park** lakes—Mountain Lake, Cascade Lake, and Twin Lake—are popular summertime swimming destinations, but there are no lifeguards. Cascade Lake is the center of the action and a favorite for families. It has a roped-off swimming area and shallow water that warms up to swimmable level June–August. A snack bar is nearby, along with kid's playground and a boathouse that rents rowboats and paddleboats. Rowboats are also available at Mountain Lake.

There are no public pools on Orcas, but you can pay $15 for a day pass and use the lap pool at **Orcas Spa and Athletic Center** (188 A St. in Eastsound, 360/376-6361 or 800/322-3552, www.orcasspaandathletics.com) This is a full-service athletic club with racquetball court, saunas, Jacuzzi, weights, massage, racquetball, and a spa with massage, aromatherapy, facials, mud masks, and other body treats.

The Avanyu Spa at Rosario Resort (360/376-2152 or 800/562-8820, www.rosarioresort.com) is open to those who aren't staying at the resort for $25/day. This provides access to an indoor pool, Jacuzzi, sauna, exercise equipment, towels, and showers. Fitness classes, including yoga, aquatics, hiking, and strength training, are offered daily. For extra charges you can luxuriate with a professional massage, aromatherapy, body wrap, facial, manicure, or pedicure, or get the full treatment with a spa package. The spa is open daily year-round.

For less pretentious facilities, head a few miles beyond Rosario to **Doe Bay Resort & Retreat** (360/376-2291, www.doebay.com) with its au naturel sauna and hot tubs. A day pass is $10/person if you aren't staying here.

OTHER RECREATION
M The Funhouse

Founded by Jim Bredouw, who spent more than $1 million of his own money on the project, The Funhouse (30 Pea Patch Ln., 360/376-7177, www.thefunhouse.org, $5/person or $20/family; no charge for kids under five) is a nonprofit hands-on science discovery center housing dozens of educational exhibits. It provides a place to learn with other kids and acts as an after-school hangout and teen center on weekend evenings. With exhibits that challenge and interest all ages, The Funhouse isn't just for the youngsters. It includes a music studio, video production studio, climbing wall, pool table, foosball, ping pong, Internet access, physics demonstrations, a radio theater, and all sorts of other activities.

The center is open in July and August 11 A.M.–5 P.M. Monday–Saturday, and the rest of the year 3–5:30P.M. Monday–Friday and 10 A.M.–3 P.M. Saturday. It is also open for teens-only sessions Friday and Saturday 7–midnight.

Golf and Tennis
Golfers will enjoy a round at **Orcas Island Country Golf Club** (360/376-4400, www.orcasisland.com/golf) a nine-hole public course on Orcas Road southwest of Eastsound with a par 36 rating. Built in 1960 and reminiscent of the Scottish country clubs, the course challenges with gently rolling hills, cantankerous water hazards, and a quaint setting. It's easily the most interesting course in the San Juans. The course is a bit pricey at $22 for nine holes, but worth it. The pro shop rents clubs, pull carts, and electric carts, and offers personalized instruction.

Buck Park, just north of Eastsound along Mt. Baker Rd., has public tennis courts, baseball diamonds, and a big skateboard park.

Horseback Rides
Once in a Blue Moon Farm (360/376-7035, www.onceinabluemoonfarm.com) is a 35-acre farm a couple of miles up from the ferry dock on Orcas. Trail rides for experienced riders are $65/person for a 1.5-hour saunter through the woods and fields, and special learn-about-horses sessions are offered for kids over three in the arena: $50/family.

Walking Horse Country Farm (West Beach Rd. at Crow Valley Rd., 360/376-5306, www.walkinghorsefarm.com) is home to 10 Tennessee walking horses, along with Belgian draft horses and Shetland ponies. The owners operate a horsemanship experience program that is a great way to learn about horses, especially if your daughter is begging to get one. Three-hour programs ($75/person) include an introduction to handling, grooming, saddling, and at least a half-hour of riding in the arena. Kids over eight are welcome but a parent must be present.

Summer Camps and Retreats

CAMP ORKILA
Operated by the Seattle YMCA, Camp Orkila (206/382-5009, www.seattleymca.org) is the fifth largest summer camp in America, housing up to 450 kids at a time. The camp first opened in 1906, when 30 boys from Seattle spent a month on waterfront land belonging to Laurence Colman. The property was deeded to the Y in 1938. Located on the northwest shore of Orcas Island, with a spectacular sunset view across President Channel to the Gulf Islands of British Columbia, the 280-acre camp is one of four run by the Y in Washington. Forested grounds slope gently down to the water, with a half-mile of private beach and an ideal setting for outdoor activities.

Featured camp attractions include an Olympic-size heated outdoor pool, marine life touch tanks, a 150-foot dock, sea kayaks, BMX track, sailboats, rowboats, canoes, a 44-passenger power-boat, indoor climbing walls, ropes courses, sports fields, a craft center, pottery studio, horses and riding arena, vegetable garden, plus a model farm with chickens, goats, turkeys, sheep, and pigs. The Y also owns a mountain camp at Twin Lakes on the edge of Moran State Park, along with 107-acre Satellite Island, a favorite overnight boating trip for campers.

In addition to the camps listed below, Orkila is a popular place for scouting weekends, corporate retreats, and smaller gatherings, from weddings to quilting groups.

Summer Camp
Camp Orkila is the ideal place for an old-time summer camp, available for youths in grades 3–12. Depending on their age and abilities, kids can join in a wide range of activities, including sports, crafts, swimming, nature study, archery, riflery, ceramics, wilderness camping,

Orcas Island

skateboarding, pioneer farming, high-ropes training, horseback riding, bicycling, rock climbing, canoeing, and kayaking. Campers choose from a variety of skill clinics, sports, crafts, and activities each day.

Lodging is in rustic open-air Adirondack-style cabins with bathroom facilities a short walk away. Filling meals are served family style. The costs depend upon the length of the stay, the season, age group, and activities. Typical in-camp sessions for younger kids are around $530/week, and a horsemaster program for older youths costs $700/week. Camp spaces go fast, so make reservations for your child early—in January for the most popular programs.

Special teen adventure programs focus on building self-confidence and leadership skills through biking, sea kayaking, sailing, rock climbing, rafting, and backpacking trips that begin on the San Juans and head into the North Cascades and British Columbia. These last 1–3 weeks each and vary in cost, starting around $570 for a one-week kayaking camp.

Family Camps and Retreats

Camp Orkila isn't just for kids, offering both family camps and women's wellness retreats six weekends a year. The cost for family camps varies seasonally, with the highest rates over Labor Day: $144/adult and $117 each for ages 4–12; free for kids under four. Lodging is in rustic cabins that accommodate two or three families, with bathrooms a short walk away. Your fee includes lodging, meals, and activities. If you want to stay in something nicer, the camp also has a half-dozen deluxe fourplex cabins, but these cost an extra $162 for a family of four over Labor Day weekend.

Family camp activities include hikes, archery, arts and crafts, riflery, rowboats, climbing wall, campfires, games, farm and salmon hatchery visits, and more. There's a small extra fee to use the sea kayaks or to try out the daredevil high-ropes course. The women's wellness weekends provide time away from husbands, kids, dogs, phones, and mortgages in mid-March and early November, with yoga, kickboxing, massage, manicures, aromatherapy, sea kayaking, and other activities. These cost around $170; call 360/376-2678 for the complete story.

Day Camps

If you're bringing school-age children on vacation, this may be the hottest tip you'll find in this book. Camp Orkila operates an outstanding community day camp ($100/week) from mid-June through August, and it's open to anyone with kids in grades 1–5. The program operates 9 A.M.–5 P.M. Monday–Friday and includes swimming, arts and crafts, archery, games, field trips, and much more. A special marine-science day camp ($150/week) is also available. Call 360/376-2678 several weeks ahead of your visit to Orcas to be assured of space in the day-camp program.

FOUR WINDS–WESTWARD HO CAMP

In 1927, a young teacher named Ruth Brown established Four Winds Camp for girls at Four Winds Bay on the Orcas Island. Five years latter, she created Westward Ho Camp for boys on the opposite side of the bay. She ran the camp for many years, and in 1967 deeded the 150 acres of land, facilities, and equipment to a nonprofit foundation called Four Winds, Inc. (360/376-2277, www.fourwindscamp.org).

Camp Life

Today, all Four Winds–Westward Ho Camp activities are coed, but the boys and girls are still housed on separate sides of Four Winds Bay—to the relief of parents of teenage girls. The camp houses 180 kids at a time, with one counselor for every 4–6 children. Everyone wears a uniform (tennis shirts and hiking shorts for the boys and decidedly old-fashioned middies and bloomers for the girls) to cut down on teen fashion jealousies and make it easier to manage the laundry. Girls live in simple cedar cabins and wall tents, while boys stay in wall tents.

During their stay, campers learn horseback riding (25 horses, and both Western and English-style riding classes), sailing, tennis, archery, soccer, photography, arts and crafts, poetry, and many other activities. No candy, walkmans, or iPods are allowed, but music is a big part of camp life. In addition to dinghies and sailboats, the camp has a 61-foot yawl that is used to train older kids in the art of sailing. The sailboat, canoes, and kayaks are used for multi-night trips away from camp as kids explore the San Juan Islands.

Costs and More

Two one-month sessions are offered each summer for ages 9–16, followed by a one-week session that introduces younger kids (ages 7–10) to the wonders of camp life. These aren't cheap, $3,575 for the one-month sessions, or $825 for the one-week camps. Families without that kind of money can apply for a scholarship, and the staff strives to make this a noncompetitive experience that brings together campers from various racial, economic, and social backgrounds. Approximately 20 percent of the kids attend on full scholarships, and a few partial scholarships are available for middle-income families. Most of those who attend Four Winds–Westward Ho Camp come from San Francisco, Los Angeles, and Seattle—including quite a few children from famous families. Free transportation is provided from Sea-Tac Airport and Anacortes. In addition, a separate counselor-training program is available, giving young people the chance to take on greater responsibilities as they mature.

Four Winds–Westward Ho Camp is located along the southern end of West Sound, a couple of miles from Deer Harbor.

CAMP INDRALAYA

This is a camp unlike any other in the San Juan Islands. The camp was founded in 1927 by members of the Theosophical Society (www.theosophical.org), a religion with some similarities to Buddhism. The guiding principles of theosophy is that we are all one, and that everyone finds his or her own truth.

Indralaya (360/376-4526, www.indralaya.org) is one of just four Theosophical retreat centers in America; the others are in Arkansas, California, and New York. The 78-acre camp is on the northwest end of East Sound, just two miles from the village of Eastsound. The name Indralaya is derived from Sanskrit and means "a home for the spiritual forces in nature." Many types of programs are offered, particularly in the summer, when the facilities are almost always busy. The camp is open to all, so you don't need to be a member of the Theosophical Society. Campers stay in simple rustic cabins (bring your own bedding) with wood-burning stoves and separate bathhouses. Vegetarian meals are served in the dining hall, and all participants join in the cleanup. Indralaya also has a substantial metaphysical library and a small bookstore.

All sorts of classes and workshops take place here: silent meditations, deep singing workshops, family gatherings, therapeutic touch classes, yoga, and much more. Program fees are amazingly inexpensive, and lodging in simple cabins plus three meals a day are just $41–63/person per night ($30/night if you stay in a tent), with discounts for anyone under 25. Day visitors are welcome to attend programs and activities at Indralaya for a small charge.

Accommodations

Anyone planning to stay on Orcas in the summer—particularly on weekends—should make reservations several months ahead of time.

Call the Orcas Island Chamber of Commerce lodging hotline at 360/376-8888 or 888/376-8888 for current availability; it's updated daily June–August. Their website, www.orcasisland.org, has links to most local places. Only Doe Bay Resort & Retreat has hostel accommodations ($25/person).

The **Orcas Island Lodging Association** (866/376-5879, www.orcas-lodging.com) has online links to a dozen local places and a helpful calendar listing availability at the various bed-and-breakfasts, cottages, and inns.

WEEKLY RENTALS

If you plan to spend more than a few nights on Orcas, the best deal is often a vacation rental, especially for families needing space to spread out or folks looking to save money by cooking their own meals. **Cherie Lindholm Real Estate** (360/376-2204, www.orcashomes.com) offers 50 or so rental homes on Orcas Island. Most are two- or three-bedroom homes costing $900–2,000/week, but a few modest places can be found for under $700. The most elaborate waterfront mansions cost $2,500 or more weekly. The finest places go early, so book several months ahead if possible. Off-season (September–May) rates are typically far lower.

Windermere Real Estate (360/378-3601 or 800/391-8190, www.windermerevacationrentals .com) typically has 20 homes on Orcas, plus additional rentals on San Juan and Lopez Islands. There's a one-week minimum mid-June to mid-September, and three nights at other times.

Many of the resorts, inns, cottages, and bed-and-breakfasts described below also offer weekly rates; call them for specifics.

HOTELS AND INNS
Bartwood Lodge
Located off the beaten path amid a small luxury home development northeast of Eastsound, Bartwood Lodge (178 Fossil Bay Dr., 360/376-2242 or 866/666-2242, www.bartwoodlodge.com) is a beachfront hotel with 16 rather standard guest rooms containing small fridges and microwaves. The simplest rooms (no view) are $119 d, and waterfront view rooms with decks are $139. Fireplace suites cost $159–169 d, and suites with full kitchens and fireplaces are $229 d. Amenities include tennis courts, a boat launch, and private moorage for guests. Cormorants often sit on the pier out front. Kids are welcome.

Cascade Harbor Inn
The buildings at Cascade Harbor Inn (1800 Rosario Rd., 360/376-6350 or 800/201-2120, www.cascadeharborinn.com) were originally part of the adjacent Rosario Resort, so the facilities are similar, but you get a better bargain here. Furnishings are somewhat newer, prices are lower for equivalent rooms, and you can choose from 48 studio or one- and two-bedroom units, all with killer waterfront views from private balconies. A variety of configurations are available by com-

bining adjoining rooms into suites, making this spot ideal for families. The larger studios and suites contain full kitchens with dishes, plus Murphy beds and fireplaces. Rates are $129–149 d for small motel rooms, $199 d for studios and mini-suites, and $299–399 d (plus $25/person for extra guests) in spacious suites. During the summer, a continental breakfast is available, and a two-night minimum is required. The inn is entirely no-smoking and is AAA-approved.

The Inn at Ship Bay
Just a mile and a half out of Eastsound, The Inn at Ship Bay (326 Olga Rd., 360/376-3933 or 877/276-7296, www.innatshipbay.com, $150–195 d rooms, $250–295 d suite) houses one of the finest and most popular restaurants on Orcas. Behind the restaurant and facing the waters of Eastsound are recently built units containing 10 comfortable staterooms and an executive suite, all with king beds, covered balconies, gas fireplaces, and fridges. Rates include a light breakfast. The busy restaurant brings considerable traffic in the evenings, but mornings are quiet. Kids are welcome and the inn is open all year.

Landmark Inn
Landmark Inn (67 Main St. in Eastsound, 360/376-2423 or 800/622-4758, www.landmark inn.net) has 15 recently constructed and well-maintained condo units, all with private decks, fireplaces, and kitchens. Rates are $164–179 d for two-bedroom units that can sleep five, and $189 for up to eight people in three-bedroom condos. Kids are welcome, and a two-night stay is preferred in the summer. Weekly rates are also available. Landmark Inn is AAA-approved.

Orcas Hotel
For classic lodging, stay at Orcas Hotel (360/376-4300 or 888/672-2792; www.orcashotel.com), a 12-room Victorian inn overlooking the ferry landing in Orcas. Rates are just $85–109 d for nicely furnished old-style rooms with TVs and shared baths, or $139–169 d for those with private baths. The two finest rooms ($198 d) have decks and Jacuzzi tubs. For ease of access, the location can't be beat; just step off the ferry and

Orcas Hotel

you're there. Built in 1904, the hotel is also a popular place for weddings, family reunions, and office parties, though it isn't a quiet place due to the constant ferry traffic.

Outlook Inn

Outlook Inn (360/376-2200 or 888/688-5665, www.outlookinn.com) is a superbly restored 1888 hotel right in Eastsound with its own private beach. The historic main building features comfortable upstairs rooms with sinks and phones in the rooms (no TVs), and baths down the hall. They aren't spacious, but offer old-time hospitality for a budget price: $84 d. Larger rooms with private baths and TVs are $150 d, and the newest building contains exceptional suites with king beds, whirlpool tubs, radiant floor heat, small balconies overlooking the bay, three phones, and mini-bars for $245 d ($275 for four). Kids are welcome, and two rooms are wheelchair-accessible. Outlook Inn is AAA-approved.

RESORTS *weekly*

Beach Haven Resort

One of the hidden treasures in the San Juans, Beach Haven Resort (684 Beach Haven Rd., 360/376-2288, www.beach-haven.com) has a peaceful setting, old-time cabins, and reasonable prices. Located on the northwest side of Orcas Island, three miles from Eastsound, the resort consists of 11 log cabins—all built in the 1940s—along with a couple of newer units. Cabins front a long pebble beach and nestle beneath an old-growth forest of cedar and Douglas fir. Don't expect TVs, phones, or the latest furnishings here; the one- to four-bedroom cabins have rustic décor, full kitchens with dishes, woodstoves with firewood, private baths with showers, and decks with picnic tables and barbecues. There's a one-week minimum stay mid-June through Labor Day, with a three-night minimum for September and winter holidays, and a two-night minimum the rest of the year. Prices have hardly risen in a decade, making this one of the best deals going for family gatherings.

One-bedroom cabins are $840/week; two-bedroom cabins cost $1,015/week for up to five guests, and three-bedroom cabins are $1,225/week for eight. The resort's largest cabin holds up to 10 people in four bedrooms for $1,750/week and has tall picture window, a fireplace, and a large deck facing the bay. Also available is a modern honeymoon cottage ($875 d/week) with a jetted tub and heated tile floor, along with a pair of apartments with great waterfront decks. The smaller one sleeps two for $700 d/week, while the larger unit has space for six at $1,120/week. Children are welcome in most of Beach Haven Resort's cabins, and they will love the delightful playground. Guests can also rent canoes and rowboats, or hike the 1.5-mile wooded nature trail.

Don't tell anyone else about this place and maybe it'll stay a secret just between us. Sorry, but that was wishful thinking, since Beach Haven has been discovered for decades. Anyone looking for a cabin during July and August should look elsewhere; families return each year and the resort already has a 10-page waiting list! Space is, however, available at other times of the

Orcas Island

year, especially in the winter months when prices are lower and fellow travelers are scarce.

Doe Bay Resort & Retreat

Located on a 30-acre spread along a peaceful cove, Doe Bay Resort & Retreat (360/376-2291, www.doebay.com) is 20 miles from the ferry terminal. Don't let the "Resort" in the name fool you; this is an unpretentious place with cabins, yurts, a hostel, and tent sites. New owners took over a few years back, and they have made major renovations and upgrades—including the addition of several modern cabins—while keeping the emphasis on relaxation. A friendly New Age atmosphere still brings couples and families back year after year. You can sit inside the wood-fired sauna with its octagonal stained-glass windows, and then head to one of three soaking tubs right on a pretty creek with a waterfall that drops into Doe Bay. The clothing-optional sauna and tubs are open 10 A.M.–9 P.M. daily and cost $10 if you aren't a guest.

The six-bed coed **hostel** costs $25/person in a large room, or $65 d for a private room. Also at the budget end are summer-only tent and RV spaces ($35 d), miniscule units ($55 d) with simple furnishings, and in-the-trees yurts and domes ($75 d; summer only). These share a central shower house and communal kitchen. Considerably nicer are 20 or so cabins ($85–185) with full baths and kitchens; the largest of these can sleep eight in three bedrooms. Special **Ayurvedic retreats** provide the opportunity to regain wellness and balance in your life. One-week sessions cost $1,350 with meals; lodging is extra.

Resort headquarters is the historic Doe Bay General Store, built in 1908, and now home to a little store and the seasonal Doe Bay Café, serving vegetarian meals for brunch and dinner, with most dinner entrées under $12.

Lieber Haven Resort

A small out-of-the-way place, Lieber Haven Resort (360/376-2472, www.lieberhavenresort.com) occupies a protected cove on the southern edge of Orcas Island near Obstruction Pass. A county boat ramp and dock are right across the road, and one of the only sandy beaches on the island

is out front. Lodging is in a dozen simple studio units and one- and two-bedroom cottages that are fine for families on a budget. Most units have a small kitchen (with dishes, pots, and pans), queen bed, and sofa bed, along with a deck just a few steps from the water. Studio units are $115 d, and one- and two-bedroom cottages cost $125; one larger unit ($145) also has a fireplace. No minimum stay, and the friendly owners welcome sailors and kayakers. A little store sells snacks, and you can check out the collection of nautical antiques, rent kayaks, rowboats, sailboats, and motorboats at the marina, or go along on whale-watching and sailing trips, sea-kayak tours, or fishing charters.

North Beach Inn

A mile west of Eastsound, North Beach Inn (650 Gibson Rd., 360/376-2660, www.northbeach inn.com) is something of a misnomer, since this is actually a quaint family resort where a dozen housekeeping cottages face a very private beach. Most date from the 1930s and '40s, and each unit contains a full kitchen, fireplace, Adirondack chairs, and a barbecue. The furnishings are showing their age. Kids are welcome and so are dogs ($10 extra/day).

Older studio cabins are $750 d/week, and two-bedroom cottages cost $1,025/week for four people. The resort has three more recently built, larger cottages—one even has a loft—that go for $1,400/week for four guests, or $1,600/week for six. Reserve far ahead for any of these popular cottages; try to book in September for the following July or August. A one-week minimum stay is required in July and August, with a two-day minimum rest of year. The resort is closed late November to mid-February.

Resort at Deer Harbor

A popular west side option, Resort at Deer Harbor (200 Deer Harbor Rd., 360/376-4420 or 888/376-4480, www.deerharbor.com) has a variety of cedar-sided cottages arranged on a hillside facing Deer Harbor. An outdoor swimming pool (seasonal) is centrally located, and all units include private Jacuzzis on the porches, TVs, VCRs, and stereos, plus a light breakfast served in the lobby.

The resort's deluxe units ($279 d) are modern and very nicely appointed, each with a queen bed, fridge and microwave, gas fireplace, and a large bath with jetted tub. The "historical" units ($189 d) are small, with a double bed, fridge and microwave, little woodstove, and shower. A number of other suites are also available; $219–299 for up to four people. The finest option is the "grand suite" ($410 for up to five guests), a small home with two bedrooms, two baths, a wood fireplace, kitchen, and a wrap-around deck where you can soak in the Jacuzzi while tall Pacific madrone trees frame the harbor. A couple of drawbacks are that most of the cottages are crowded together, and some face onto the backside of other cabins. A two-night minimum is required in summer, and children are welcome.

Rosario Resort & Spa

Built between 1905 and 1909 and now on the National Register of Historic Places, famous Rosario Resort (1400 Rosario Rd., 360/376-2222 or 800/562-8820, www.rosarioresort.com) is five miles south of Eastsound near Moran State Park. The striking mansion at the center of Rosario was once the home of Robert Moran, a shipping magnate, Seattle mayor, and philanthropist; he donated the land for nearby Moran State Park. Today the resort is owned by Rock-Resorts, which also operates resorts in Vail, Jackson Hole, Santa Fe, and other trendy spots.

This is the largest lodging place on Orcas, with 116 guest rooms. Moran's grand white mansion serves as a centerpiece for the resort and is a great place to explore even if you aren't staying here. Free organ concerts are given at 6 P.M. Monday, Wednesday, and Saturday in the grand music room (Saturday only in winter), or you can take a self-guided tour at other times. The lush grounds and sprawling veranda, backdropped by boat-filled Cascade Bay, are popular for summer weddings. The mansion also houses a restaurant, along with a fascinating collection of historic items and photos. Downstairs is a full-service spa with professional massage, body wraps, facials, manicures, and pedicures, plus an indoor pool, Jacuzzi, sauna, exercise equipment, plus daily yoga and fitness classes.

On the 30 acres of manicured grounds and gardens you'll find a large outdoor pool facing the harbor and a separate pool for kids, plus tennis courts, horseshoes, croquet, shuffleboard, bocce, and other lawn games. Head to the marina for sea kayaking (through Shearwater Adventures), sailboat and fishing charters, boat rentals, and whale-watching trips (through Deer Harbor Charters). A concierge and gift shop are available. The resort's Moran Lounge has romantic music most summer weekends. Scheduled floatplane flights directly to Rosario are provided by Kenmore Air out of Seattle's Lake Union.

Room rates at Rosario vary depending on occupancy at the resort and the season. The least expensive rooms cost $249 d on weekends, while remodeled and spacious suites go for $349 d. A $10 "resort fee" is added to these rates for access to the pools, spa, and other facilities. Extra guests (other than kids) are $20/person. Wheelchair-accessible rooms are available.

Rosario rooms vary greatly in size and amenities, with some remodeled rooms featuring full kitchens, gas fireplaces, large waterside decks, and Jacuzzi tubs; others have worn, plain-Jane furnishings that look like they haven't been updated in many years. They're a major disappointment given the beauty of the historic mansion at Rosario. In general, you'll find nicer rooms for less cash elsewhere on Orcas. One real exception is the luxurious and modern Cliff House honeymoon suite that goes for $650 d. As this was written, a new management team promises much-needed improvements at Rosario. For the latest on conditions, visit one of the online lodging review sites, such as www.tripadvisor.com.

Smuggler's Villa Resort

Located on the north side of Orcas Island along Haro Strait, Smuggler's Villa Resort (360/376-2297 or 800/488-2097, www.smuggler.com) consists of modern two-bedroom townhouses with full kitchens and fireplaces for $199–299 d/night or $1,300–2,000/week. Some units can sleep six for no additional charge. A four-night minimum is required in the summer. Amenities at Smuggler's Villa include a year-round outdoor pool, two hot tubs, a sauna, tennis and basketball courts, playground, and a private pebble beach. Kids are welcome.

West Beach Resort

A busy waterside spot, West Beach Resort (three miles west of Eastsound off Enchanted Forest Rd., 360/376-2240 or 877/937-8224, www.westbeachresort.com) opened in 1939, and is still popular with families today. Cabins face west along a gravely beach, offering sunset vistas in a peaceful setting. Several types of cottages are available, and guests appreciate the central hot tub.

Most of the 19 cottages are right along the shore—we're talking 20 feet to the water—and have one or two bedrooms with double beds, full kitchens, woodstoves, private baths with showers, hide-a-bed sofas, and covered porches with barbecue grills. Many of these are plain older units with a mismatched and funky decor that isn't for everyone, but several modern ones are nicer and have large decks. The cottages rent for $1,200–1,500/week for up to four guests, plus $18/person for additional guests. Two modern cabins ($1,500/week for seven) are perfect for groups and family gatherings, and an adorable little honeymoon cottage ($145 d/night) faces a small pond. In addition, West Beach Resort has tent and RV spaces, a small store selling limited supplies, espresso, and gas, plus a marina with boat and canoe rentals and kayak tours.

None of the West Beach cottages include phones or TVs, though you can rent TV/VCRs to watch videos. The resort caters to families and offers an array of kid activities daily in the summer. Cribs are also available, and pets are allowed in some of the cottages for an extra $16/day. West Beach Resort requires a one-week minimum stay for July and August, and a two- or three-night minimum in June and September. The resort is open year-round.

BED-AND-BREAKFASTS

Orcas has quite a few luxurious bed-and-breakfasts for discriminating travelers looking for a sanctuary from the hustle and bustle. Be sure to book several months ahead for summertime rooms.

Anchorage Inn

Anchorage Inn (249 Bronson Way, east of the Orcas Golf Course, 360/376-8282, www.anchorageonorcas.com, $189 d) is definitely out of the way, hidden among tall Douglas firs along East Sound at the end of a dirt road. Three modern townhouse-style units are available on a 16-acre parcel with a pebbly beach out front—perfect for launching kayaks—and a Jacuzzi to enjoy those romantic starry nights. Bald eagles nest close by, and you may also see herons, seals, loons, and other critters. Each unit has a private stairway and entrance, queen bed, bath, fireplace, kitchenette, and small cedar deck. The fridge is stocked with fixins for a make-it-yourself breakfast. No children allowed, and a two-night minimum stay is required in the summer. Check in with owners Dick and Sandra Bronson, who live in the house next door.

Buck Bay Farm B&B

Set on five acres near Moran State Park, Buck Bay Farm (716 Point Lawrence Rd., 360/376-2908 or 888/422-2825, www.buckbayfarm.com) began life as a 1920s barn. Today it has been transformed into a comfortable country farmhouse surrounded by forest, pasture, and a pond. Four guest rooms ($119–135 d) have queen beds and private baths, while two other rooms share a bath and are rented either separately ($99 d) or as a suite ($188 for four people). Amenities include two relaxing hot tubs, a solarium, home-style breakfasts, evening wine and cheese, plus badminton and horseshoes on the lawn. Kids of all ages are welcome—the owners have two children—and the bed-and-breakfast is AAA-approved.

Deer Harbor Inn

A variety of lodging options exist at Deer Harbor Inn (360/376-4110 or 877/377-4110, www.deerharborinn.com) located eight miles west of the ferry dock and just above Deer Harbor. The inn buildings surround an old apple orchard (gravenstein and king trees) that was planted in 1906; it's one of many still scattered around Orcas. A contemporary log lodge contains eight comfy but rather small rooms ($125 d) with tables, chairs, queen beds, and

Deer Harbor Inn

other furnishings crafted from lodgepole pine logs. Each also has a fridge and private bath. No TVs in the rooms, but a central sitting area has sofas, a woodstove, and television.

Four attractive, modern cottages ($189–299 d; $10 for additional guests) are also on the grounds. Each is a bit different: the largest (1,100 square feet, with room for eight people) has two bedrooms, a full kitchen, and covered deck, while the other three units are smaller, but have decks with private Jacuzzis, gas fireplace, fridge, microwave, TV/VCR, and log furnishings. Pets are $25 extra. Across the road is a small remodeled house ($350 for up to eight guests) with a king bed in one of the three bedrooms, plus a log fireplace, full kitchen, hot tub and BBQ grill on the wraparound deck, and even a telescope for checking out boats in the harbor.

All guests at Deer Harbor Inn (including those staying in the lodge) can hop in the Jacuzzi behind the lodge, but it can get a bit busy. Massage is also available. A two-night minimum stay is required in the summer, and no young kids are allowed in the lodge, though they're welcome in the cottages and houses. Deer Harbor Inn is also home to a fine restaurant, run by the owners'

sons and housed in a farmhouse built in 1915. The bed-and-breakfast is AAA-approved.

Double Mountain B&B

Enjoy a panoramic view of the San Juans from the deck of Double Mountain B&B (Double Hill Rd., 360/376-4570, www.doublemountainbandb.com), a contemporary home atop a 750-foot hill, two miles out of Eastsound. Inside are two guest rooms ($90–125 d), and a two-room suite ($149 d or $209 for four) with its own kitchen and entrance. All rooms have private baths, and a full breakfast is served. No kids under 10, and a two-night minimum is required in July and August.

Hazelwood B&B

A remote lodging place, Hazelwood B&B (Victorian Valley Rd., 360/376-6300 or 888/360-6300, www.hazelwoodbandb.com, $125–145 d) sits atop a hill on a 12-acre spread, but is just a few miles from the ferry dock at Orcas. The home itself is a geodesic dome. A large deck faces Victorian Valley—with glimpses of the distant Olympic Mountains—and tall trees border the sides. Two of the three rooms share a bath and the other has its own. Guests are served a big continental breakfast and kids are accepted. A two-night minimum stay is required in the summer.

Hollyhock Inn

A pretty blue house, Hollyhock Inn (252 Deer Harbor Rd., 360/376-3745) is located on seven lovingly landscaped acres near West Sound; the long driveway is lined with you-guessed-it, hollyhocks. There's a guest room in the house ($85 d) with a private bath, and an apartment ($100 d) that includes a private bath, full kitchen, and hide-a-bed sofa. No hot tubs or fancy hors d'oeuvres, but rates are reasonable and the owner prepares a gourmet breakfast each morning. Children are welcome. The bed-and-breakfast is open summers only.

The Inn on Orcas Island

Nestled along a meadow at the head of Deer Harbor, The Inn on Orcas Island (114 Channel Rd., 360/376-5227 or 888/886-1661, www.theinnonorcasisland.com) is the newest and one of the finest places to stay on Orcas. This eight-room luxury inn caters to couples in search of a romantic escape; no kids allowed. Most rooms have fireplaces, and all include Jacuzzi tubs and decks. Guest are treated to a multi-course breakfast, and can hop on the bikes to explore the area. Rooms start at $185 d (queen bed with water view) to $225 for a king suite. Two cottages ($245–285 d) provide more private luxury.

Kangaroo House B&B

Kangaroo House (just north of Eastsound, 360/376-2175 or 888/371-2175, www.kangaroohouse.com, $115–160 d) was built in 1907 and bought in the '30s by a sea captain, Harold Ferris, who picked up a young female kangaroo on one of his Australian voyages. The kangaroo is long gone, but the name remains on this attractive old home with a big fireplace, period furnishings, decks, and a garden hot tub. The five guest rooms and suites all have private baths. Ultra-friendly owners Peter and Helen Allen are retired Park Service employees with a strong knowledge of the area; Peter actually grew up in Australia. They produce a memorable multi-

course breakfast each morning, and bird-watchers will appreciate the many species that come to the backyard feeders. Families are welcome, and the bed-and-breakfast is AAA-approved.

Kingfish Inn B&B

Built around 1915, Kingfish Inn (Deer Harbor and Crow Valley Rds., 360/376-4440, www.kingfishinn.com) sits directly across the road from West Sound. The four small but nicely remodeled guest rooms exhibit a Victorian charm. Each has a private bath, TV, and VCR, and two have king beds. Rates are $150–160 d; one room sleeps four people for $180. The building also houses popular West Sound Café, where your hearty breakfast is served each morning. Kids are accepted, and bike and sea-kayak rentals are available for guests.

Massacre Bay B&B and Cottage

Situated in a rural area near West Sound, Massacre Bay B&B (2098 Deer Harbor Rd., 360/376-2766 or 877/248-7833, www.interisland.net/massacrebayb&b) has a large grassy lawn facing the bay, and a small private beach right across the road. Inside are three reasonably priced guest rooms ($105–135 d, plus $20 for extra guests), all with private baths. Two have tiny private balconies, and the largest is in the daylight basement with a queen bed and sleeper sofa. Breakfast is brought to your room each morning, or you can eat on the deck. A studio cottage ($129 d, plus $10 for extra guests without breakfast or $145 d with breakfast) is perfect for small families, with a bed and sleeper sofa, full kitchen, private bath with shower, woodstove, TV/VCR, and barbecue. All guests can use the living room with TV and VCR in the house. Hosts Ray and Karen Brown provide free golf clubs for use at the local course, have mountain bikes for rent, and welcome children. A two-night minimum is generally required in the summer.

Old Trout Inn B&B

For a bit of France on Orcas Island, stay at Old Trout Inn (5272 Orcas Rd., 360/376-7474, www.oldtroutinn.com), an elegant country home just three miles from the ferry dock. The pond

Orcas Island

out back attracts birds, and you can fish (catch-and-release only) for trout, carp, or bluegills. Two suites ($150 and $185 d) with private baths and Jacuzzis, mini-fridges, and separate entrances are in the house, and the larger unit features a fireplace and deck facing the pond. A separate cottage ($195 d) is next door, with a full kitchen, gas fireplace stove, private bath, covered porch, and hot tub along the pond. Extra guests are $25 each. Also here is an exercise facility and massage room. Owners Henri and Nicole de Marval once ran a French restaurant and offer dinners by reservation for $45/person. Because of the unfenced pond, young children aren't allowed.

Otter's Pond B&B

A modern country home near Moran State Park, Otter's Pond B&B (360/376-8844 or 888/893-9680, www.otterspond.com, $135–195 d) faces a 20-acre pond. Five elegantly furnished rooms each have a private bath and access to the shoji screen–enclosed Jacuzzi. The more expensive rooms are quite spacious, with king beds, skylights, and clawfoot tubs, but the smallest "hummingbird" room is equally popular and offers views of the pond. Innkeepers Carl and Susan Sil-

vernail are fine hosts who create a five-course breakfast that is certain to please. Behind the home is a large deck and several birdfeeders that attract a flittering crowd most mornings. The pond is home to nesting mallards and wood ducks during the summer, and migrating flocks at other times. This is a place to escape, so young children are not allowed. The bed-and-breakfast has wireless Internet access throughout and is AAA-approved.

The Place at Cayou Cove B&B

The Place at Cayou Cove B&B (Deer Harbor, 360/376-3199 or 888/596-7222, www.cayoucove.com) has three luxurious private cottages and two delightful rooms in a restored 1913 home. Guests have access to a private beach, and the deck overlooks a harbor full of bobbing boats. Rates are $180–245 d in the home, including a full breakfast, along with wine and cheeses each evening. Cottages ($275–295 d) contain full kitchens, wood-burning fireplaces, private outdoor hot tubs, and a morning basket of breakfast goodies. Children and dogs are welcome in the cottages. A two-night minimum stay is required for the summer; three nights on holidays. Cayou Cove is closed December–January.

Orcas Island

© DON PITCHER

Otter's Pond B&B

APPLE WALNUT GORGONZOLA OMELET

This makes 1 serving.

1 ounce blue cheese or Gorgonzola

1 tablespoon sour cream

2 tablespoons toasted walnuts, coarsely chopped and bounced around in a
   sieve to remove skin

2 eggs

2 drops Tabasco sauce

2 teaspoons cold water

4 or 5 thin slices of apple, about ¼ of an apple

2 teaspoons butter

2 tablespoons cooked crumbled bacon (1 piece per serving)

Mix the blue cheese or Gorgonzola, sour cream, and walnuts together to make filling and set aside. Beat eggs with Tabasco and water until blended. Heat an 8-inch omelet pan, melt butter, and pour egg mixture into pan when butter is sizzling. When eggs begin to firm up, place apple slices along one side and then cook at medium heat. When eggs are no longer liquid, add filling. Fold omelet in half and top with crumbled bacon.

Recipe courtesy of Otter's Pond B&B

Sand Dollar Inn B&B

Sand Dollar Inn B&B (Point Lawrence Rd. near Olga, 360/376-5696, www.sdollar.com, $135 d) is a 1920s home with three large upstairs rooms, all with private baths and sweeping views of Buck Bay, Lopez Island, and the Olympic Mountains. Moran State Park is just up the road, making this a good base for hiking and biking. The house is furnished with Japanese antiques and woodblock prints, and a full breakfast is served. No kids under age 14.

Spring Bay Inn B&B

A secluded lodge, Spring Bay Inn (near Obstruction Pass, 360/376-5531, www.springbayinn.com, $220–260 d) is surrounded by 57 acres of woods and waterfront. The five guest rooms all include private baths, wood stoves, wireless Internet, and access to the hot tub; two of them also have private balconies and king beds. A continental breakfast is followed by a big brunch. In between, co-owner Carl Burger, a retired park ranger, takes guests on a two-hour sea-kayak paddle around nearby Obstruction Island for no

extra charge. There's a two-night summer minimum, and kids are accepted. This bed-and-breakfast is AAA-approved.

M Turtleback Farm Inn

Orcas Island's most famous bed-and-breakfast, Turtleback Farm Inn (1981 Crow Valley Rd., 360/376-4914 or 800/376-4914, www.turtlebackinn.com) began life as a simple 1910 farmhouse in the shadow of Turtleback Mountain. Innkeepers Susan and Bill Fletcher bought the rundown old farmhouse, restored and expanded the building, added hardwood floors, and then opened the doors to Orcas Island's first bed-and-breakfast. The inn is approximately six miles from the ferry landing near the center of Orcas. Its two-level back deck overlooks a bucolic pasture, part of this 80-acre farm. Cows and sheep graze below, and a crowing rooster might waken you in the morning. Birdwatchers will enjoy exploring the farm's six ponds.

The farmhouse features seven guest rooms, each furnished with a Victorian-inspired décor that deftly balances luxury and comfort. One minuscule room, barely big enough for the double bed and your shoes, is an inexpensive ($90 d) option, and has a small private bath. The others are substantially larger with queen beds and claw-foot tubs in the private baths; $145–175 d. Nicest is the Valley Room, with antique furnishings and a private deck overlooking the farm. No televisions or phones here; the emphasis is on relaxation and getting away from it all. Kids over eight are welcome in the house. A substantial breakfast is served downstairs each morning, or on the deck when weather permits. End the day sipping sherry by the fireplace.

Adjacent to the historic farmhouse is the recently built **Orchard House,** a cedar barn-like structure where the emphasis is on privacy. Each of the four plush guest rooms has a king-size bed, gas fireplace, private deck, sitting area, bath with clawfoot tub, and separate shower. Breakfast is delivered to your room, making this spot popular with couples who just want to be alone for a quiet morning. It's perfect for honeymooners, but families are also welcome. One of the rooms has been set up to accommodate travelers with disabilities; it's the most popular room here. Orchard House rooms go for $250 d. A two-night minimum is required in the summer and on many weekends and holidays at other times. This bed-and-breakfast is AAA-approved.

GUEST HOUSES AND COTTAGES

A number of the bed-and-breakfasts described above also have guest cottages available, including Deer Harbor Inn, Old Trout Inn B&B, and Massacre Bay B&B and Cottage.

Aerie on Orcas Guest House

Located on the north side of Orcas, Aerie (991 Bartel Rd., 360/376-6307, www.aerieonorcas.com, $140 d or $160 for four) is a one-bedroom guesthouse with a full kitchen, fireplace, private deck (great water views), and private beach. Kids are welcome, and a two-night minimum is required in the summer.

Bayside Cottages

Bayside Cottages (65 Willis Ln., 360/376-4330,

www.orcas1.com) consists of eight vacation cottages and houses on 14 waterfront acres near the village of Olga. All include full kitchens and private baths, with access to a private beach and fine views east to Mt. Baker. The cottages range from a nicely appointed loft in the upper level of a converted barn ($145 d) to a newly built 2,000-square-foot three-bedroom home that sleeps six for $325 d. Also available is a small cottage ($145 for up to five) in the heart of Eastsound that's fine for families. Weekly rates are available and kids are welcome. A two-night minimum is required in the summer.

⚑ Beach House on Orcas

A newly built north shore home, Beach House on Orcas (64 Fox Cove Court, 360/376-4679, www.beachhouseonorcas.com) has a sunny guest cottage with private deck, big windows on all sides, living room with pull-out sofa, and gas fireplace; $189 d or $229 for four. Also available is a room in the main house with its own entrance and yard; $139 d. Guests have access to the private beach, dock, and tennis court. The real treat is the spectacular ocean view, especially at sunset. This is a delightful romantic getaway.

Boardwalk Waterfront Cottages

Right next to the busy Orcas ferry landing, Boardwalk Waterfront Cottages (360/376-2971, www.orcasislandboardwalk.com) consists of two small cottages ($150–160 d) with fridges and microwaves, and two others ($225–260 d) that have separate bedrooms and full kitchens. Kids are welcome in one of the units. The owner's son and daughter-in-law operate Orcas Outdoors, with kayak trips departing from the adjacent dock.

Buckhorn Farm Bungalow

If you're looking for a place that exemplifies island living, be sure to check out Buckhorn Farm Bungalow (17 Jensen Rd., 360/376-2298, www.buckhornfarm.com, $125 d, $10/person for additional guests) a cute one-bedroom cottage on the north side of Orcas near Eastsound. Step inside to find a full kitchen, woodstove, and private bath. Step

Orcas Island

WARM CHOCOLATE-ESPRESSO PUDDING CAKES

¾ cup butter or margarine

6 ounces bittersweet chocolate, chopped

2 teaspoons freeze-dried espresso powder, or 2 tablespoons hot espresso

4 ½ tablespoons unbleached white flour

2 tablespoons unsweetened cocoa

5 large eggs, separated

⅛ cup sugar

1 ½ tablespoons Kahlua

½ teaspoon vanilla

Preheat oven to 375°F.

In a small pan, combine butter and chocolate. Heat over low flame until melted and smoothly mixed. Add espresso and mix. Mix together flour and cocoa. In a large bowl beat the 5 egg whites until they become white. Beat in 1 tablespoon sugar at a time until the eggs hold stiff and shiny, but not dry, peaks.

Blend together the yolks, liqueur, vanilla, and the cocoa and flour mixture, then add the chocolate and butter mixture. Gently fold in the egg whites.

Pour about ½ cup batter into each of 8 buttered ramekins or custard cups. For ease of handling, place the ramekins on a cookie sheet before placing in the oven to bake. Bake until the edges begin to firm but the center is still soft when pressed, 11–12 minutes. Let cool for a few minutes, then invert onto serving plates. Serve with coffee ice cream.

Recipe courtesy of Turtleback Farm Inn

outside to take in the peaceful orchard setting. There's a two-night minimum in the summer, and kids are welcome.

Cabins-on-the-Point

Cabins-on-the-Point (360/376-4114, www.cabinsonthepoint.com) consists of Cape Cod–style cabins facing Massacre Bay and West Sound from a rocky point of land. It's a wonderful spot for weddings or yoga retreats. Four cabins are available, each with a woodstove (wood provided) and full kitchen. Guests have access to the hot tub and a private beach where kayaks are available to borrow. The Heather Cabin ($225 for up to three) is a premier choice, with windows just a few feet from the water. The nearby Primrose cabin ($195 d) features skylights, French doors leading into the sitting room, and a little garden. Willow ($235 for up to five) is a two-bedroom cottage with a sun porch that fronts the bay.

Owner Jennifer Fralick also has two great family-friendly lodging options on Orcas, both with full kitchens, down comforters, and antique furnishings. **Highlands House** is a large two-bedroom, two-bath hilltop home that includes a spacious great room with cathedral ceiling and fireplace, an open kitchen, and a deck affording stunning vistas across East Sound from the Jacuzzi. The house is located above Rosario Resort and costs $325 d for up to six guests. This is one of the most private places on the island, and works well for two couples. **Sunset House** is a large waterside home close to Eastsound with three bedrooms and two baths, a big deck, floor-to-ceiling windows, and a full kitchen—all in a woodsy setting. It sleeps six comfortably for $395, or four for $325.

A three-night stay is required in the summer for all of these, or two nights at other times. Kids are accepted in the houses and two of the cottages, and pets are also allowed in some units with prior arrangement. All of these fill fast, so call well ahead of your visit.

Camp Moran Vacation House

Set in a forest on the south end of Cascade Lake within Moran State Park, Camp Moran Vacation House (details at 360/376-2326, reservations at 800/360-4240, www.parks.wa.gov/vacationhouses) sleeps up to eight guests for an amazingly reasonable $100. Inside this wheelchair-accessible structure are two bedrooms with a mix of full-size and bunk beds (bring your own linen and towels), a full bathroom, a full kitchen with cooking utensils, and a spacious living room with TV/VCR. Guests have access to a dock on the lake (not open to general park users). This is a fine base from which to explore the park and Orcas Island and can be reserved up to one year in advance.

Heartwood House

A beautiful handcrafted post-and-beam home, Heartwood House (360/376-8220, www.heartwoodhouse.com) is just a short walk from Eastsound. The home includes two bedrooms and baths, a full kitchen, two wood-burning stoves, and a large deck with a hot tub. It can sleep 10 and rents for $2,300/week.

Isle Dream Cottage

An idyllic spot to escape the stresses of city life, Isle Dream Cottage (Sunderland Rd., 360/376-2500, www.isledreamorcas.com, $205 d) occupies three wooded acres along the west shore of East Sound. A deck encompasses the cottage on three sides, and guests can follow the path to a private beach with a hammock and dock. The cottage has an open floor plan and a queen bed along the bay window, a small kitchen area, and two-person shower with skylight. A two-night minimum stay is required.

The Homestead

Located on three acres of waterfront property along West Sound, The Homestead (360/376-5284, www.homesteadorcas.com, $235 d or $275 for four) consists of two very comfortable cottages in a peaceful setting. One cottage began life as barn, but has been transformed into a delight home with large windows facing the water, a deck, full kitchen and bath, and modern furnishings. The second is a newer place with pine floors and rustic wood beams, and a small covered porch facing the garden. Guests have access to a large Jacuzzi and a dock where they can hop in a rowboat and head over to nearby Skull Island. There's a three-night minimum stay in the summer or two nights the rest of the year. Kids are welcome. The Homestead is a popular spot for weddings.

Maggie's Manor and Gnome House

Maggie's Manor (Deer Harbor, 360/376-4223, www.orcasrec.com) is a beautiful waterfront home on a 110-acre estate. The front porch and outdoor Jacuzzi provide picture-postcard vistas, while inside are four bedrooms and baths, a full kitchen, and a living room with a concert grand piano. The house rents for $2,250/week, and sleeps up to eight.

Also on the estate is a unique little place called the Gnome House, a handcrafted cottage that looks like it belongs in a fairy tale. It's a delightful honeymoon spot. You'll find a spiral staircase, sleigh bed, sunken tub bath, full kitchen, and a bay window facing the surrounding flower gardens. Outside is a private hot tub. The Gnome House rents for $185 d/day ($205 for four people) or $1,110/week. A two-night summertime minimum is required.

Meadowlark Guest House

An antique-filled home, Meadowlark Guest House (Pt. Lawrence Rd. in Olga, 360/376-3224, www.sanjuanweb.com/meadowlark, $149 for up to four) provides a quiet country setting facing Buck Bay. The bedroom has a queen bed, with a pull-out sofa in the living room, private bath, full kitchen, washer/dryer, and deck where you can watch the ferries go by. Children and dogs are welcome, and there's a two-night summer minimum.

North Shore Cottages

North Shore Cottages (271 Sunset Ave., 360/376-5131, www.northshore4kiss.com) has three

cottages with kitchens, private
woodstoves, and access to a de-
una. Each cottage has its own
Jacuzzi. Rates are $225–285 d.
elcome, and a two-night mini-
d in summer (three nights on holidays). This is a great place to get pampered.

Once in a Blue Moon Farm

On the south end of Orcas, a couple of miles
from the ferry dock, Once in a Blue Moon Farm
(412 Eastman Rd., 360/376-7035, www.once
inabluemoonfarm.com) is a peaceful 35-acre
farm with three places available for rent. Largest
is a 5,000-square-foot three-bedroom home with
complete kitchen, deck, and 1.5 baths: $295 for
four people. It can sleep eight comfortably, with
additional guests at $35 each. Also on the farm is
a separate carriage house loft ($265 for four peo-
ple) and a two-bedroom home ($260 for four);
both of these have full kitchens and baths. When
space is available, Blue Moon rents individual
rooms for $150 d.

This is one of the few places on the islands
that allows visitors to bring along their pets (with
advance notice). The owners have their own
menagerie of goats, llamas, horses, ducks, geese,
turkeys, guinea hens, and chickens—not to mention wild deer and rabbits—plus an old orchard
with apple, plum, cherry, and pear trees. Kids
love the chance to pet animals and feed the chickens, and horseback rides are available. The rural
setting works well for family reunions and wedding parties, and many groups rent all three
homes at once. The owners also have a separate
beach house for rent by the week on the north
side of Orcas.

Orcas Cottages

Orcas Cottages (Olga Village, 360/779-1296
www.orcascottages.com) are two charming places
with panoramic water views. Most impressive is
the Island Cottage, which is actually a comfortable home built in 1884. It offers three bedrooms, a full kitchen, and delightful views of
Rosario Strait; $200 for up to six people. Smaller
but still delightful is a second cottage that runs
$115 for three people.

Rose Arbor Cottage

A cozy little home, Rose Arbor Cottage (16 Sunset St. in Eastsound, 503/635-8834, www.rose
air.com, $165 for four people or $185 for six)
contains two bedrooms, a bath and a half, plus a
full kitchen, wood stove, and washer/dryer. A
four-night summertime minimum is required.
Owner Jane Rosevelt has a one-woman air taxi service and flies to Orcas from Portland, Oregon.

Swannie's Inn

Swannie's (24 Shady Ln. in Eastsound, 360/376-
5686, www.sanjuanweb.com/swannies, $90 d)
is a one-bedroom suite in a century-old home
with a private entrance, fridge, microwave, bath,
and patio. Kids are accepted, but a two-night
summer minimum is required.

CAMPGROUNDS

Orcas Island has the vast majority of public campsites on the San Juans, nearly all of which are in
Moran State Park on the east end of the island.

If you aren't interested in roughing it, contact **Trailers to Go** (360/376-3033 or 888/317-
6516, www.trailerstogo.com) for vacation camp
trailers with all the basics, from linen to silver-
ware. These 19- and 25-foot campers ($60–
75/day or $325–400/week) are delivered to any-
place on Orcas, including Moran State Park.
Call ahead for reservations.

Showers are available at Moran State Park, or
pay $2 at Deer Harbor Marina.

Moran State Park

One of the most popular camping areas in
Washington, Moran State Park (360/376-2326,
www.parks.wa.gov) has 151 campsites scattered
across three campgrounds along Cascade Lake,
with a fourth along Mountain Lake, and a separate bike-in area. These comprise some of the
finest camping opportunities in the San Juans,
and fill early during July and August. Tent sites
cost $16 (max eight people/site), including hot
showers. No RV hookups, though there is a
dump station. The four standard campgrounds
all accommodate trailer campers and RVs, but
some campsites will not fit large motor homes.

Orcas Island

Camping is not allowed outside established park campgrounds.

North End Campground is across the road from the swimming beach area, and several of these sites are quite private. **Midway Campground** is near the Cascade Lake boat launch, and its most popular sites are right on the lakeshore (but also next to the sometimes noisy road). **South End Campground** is the park's most popular, with almost all of the sites located right along the shore. This area has a wheelchair-accessible campsite and restroom. **Mountain Lake Campground** is one mile up Mount Constitution Road on the shores of Mountain Lake, the park's largest lake. In addition, for those who arrive by bicycle or on foot, 15 primitive campsites ($11) are located in a small site on the road to Mount Constitution.

Due to Moran State Park's popularity, camping reservations are highly advised in July and August when the sites are perpetually full seven days a week. (You may find a space without a reservation, but get there early if you want to risk it.) All sites are pre-assigned in the summer, so check in at the pay station across from Cascade Lake when you arrive. Campground reservations can be made as little as two days in advance, or as much as nine months ahead. Make reservations ($7 extra) at 888/226-7688, www.parks.wa.gov/reserve.asp. The website also includes a campsite availability map. From September 16 to May 14, camping is on a first-come, first-served basis with no reservations. At least one of the campgrounds remains open year-round.

Obstruction Pass State Park

This 80-acre park sits on the south end of Orcas Island, two and a half miles southeast of Olga and 17 road miles from the ferry dock. A one-mile dirt road heads off Obstruction Pass Road and ends at a parking lot where a pleasant half-mile hike takes you to nine campsites (360/376-2326, www.parks.wa.gov, $10) with pit toilets. The location is very scenic, with tent sites facing nearby Obstruction and Blakely Islands, but there's no vehicle access, reservations, or potable water. The campsites fill fast and it's illegal to camp elsewhere nearby, so get there early on summer weekends to be sure of a space following

your hike. Avoid the crowds by coming in mid-week or the off-season. A county boat ramp is available at Obstruction Pass, and it's just a short paddle to privately owned Obstruction Island.

Point Doughty Marine State Park

Located on the northeast end of Orcas, this 60-acre park has four primitive water-accessible Cascadia campsites (206/545-9161, www.wwta.org, $10). No drinking water, but vault toilets are provided. You'll need a kayak to camp here since there's no road or trail access. The point faces west to British Columbia's Gulf Islands, making for magnificent sunsets. Only the four acres at the very tip of Point Doughty are open to the public.

Doe Bay Resort & Retreat

Funky Doe Bay Resort (360/376-2291, www.doebay.com, $35) is a couple of miles east of Olga (20 miles from the ferry terminal), and has walk-in tent sites and RV spaces (but no hookups). Campers can join other resort guests in the popular creekside hot tubs at no extra charge, take a kayak tour (fee), or enjoy a vegetarian meal in the café.

West Beach Resort

A cozy family place, West Beach Resort (360/376-2240 or 877/937-8224, www.westbeachresort.com) is three miles west of Eastsound off Enchanted Forest Road, and offers both lodging and campsites in a setting that delivers great sunsets. Tent spaces are $25 for up to three people, while RV sites with water and electricity cost $30–35 for up to three. A shower house is nearby and pets are an extra $5. Daily kid activities are offered, and parents will appreciate the big hot tub ($4).

The store sells firewood, groceries, gas, and other supplies, while the marina here rents motorboats, rowboats, canoes, and kayaks, and offers sea-kayaking tours. Guest moorage is available (fee charged) for campers. Reservations are highly advised for July and August and on holidays and busy weekends. Call two weeks ahead of your visit if you're bringing an RV, and a year ahead for the ocean-view sites near the beach! If you show up without a reservation in the peak summer season, you may well be out of luck. West Beach Resort's tent and RV sites are open mid-May to mid-October.

Orcas Island

Food

Eastsound, the "big city" on Orcas, has the best choice of food on the island, though you'll find a scattering of fine restaurants and cafés elsewhere.

EASTSOUND AREA

Breakfast and Lunch

Eastsound's old firehouse has been thoroughly transformed into a bright and delightful deli-restaurant called **M Roses Bakery Café** (382 Prune Alley, 360/376-5805). The café serves some of the best local espresso coffees, but other breakfast offerings are limited (they open at 10 A.M.). Lunch brings out the crowds for made-to-order sandwiches (including pan-seared halibut), soups, salads, and thin-crust pizzas from the woodstove oven. The adjacent deli houses wines, artisan breads, gourmet cheeses, and a freezer packed with homemade soups, pot pies, and fruit pies to take home. Roses dinner menu ($10–16) stars a changing selection of specialties, such as oven-roasted oysters, Provencal seafood soup, or a simple penne pasta with roasted tomatoes.

Eastsound's best latte spots are Roses and **Strait Shots** (296 Main St., 360/376-2177) inside Darvill's Bookstore.

Popular for old-fashioned breakfasts, soup-and-sandwich lunches, and carnivorous dinners is **Vern's Bayside** (246 Main St., 360/376-2231). It's right on the water with a downstairs lounge filled with tobacco puffers. Reservations advised for dinners, with entrées costing $20–27.

Quick Bites

Get quick Asian-influenced take-away fare—including hot and sour soup, potstickers, veggie burgers, and teriyaki chicken—at **The Kitchen** (249 Prune Alley, 360/376-6958). Nothing is over $8 in this tiny walk-up spot popular with locals. A few picnic tables sit next to a flower-filled yard. Closed Sundays.

Another good spot for finger food is **The Lower Tavern** (Prune Alley, 360/376-4848), where the tasty bar meals include the best fish and chips in town, along with hamburgers and soups. The television has sports on most afternoons, making this a popular rainy-day retreat. Cigarette smoke can be annoying inside, but the patio is available.

Get very good pizzas by the slice or pie, along with calzones and sandwiches at **Portofino Pizzeria** store (A St., 360/376-2085, www.portofinopizzeria.com). This kid-friendly spot is upstairs behind the Village Stop convenience store. The second-floor deck affords a view across Eastsound.

International Food

A local legend, **M Bilbo's Festivo** (310 A St., 360/376-4728), has been attracting locals and visitors since 1974. Owners Cy and Julie Fraser deliver traditional Mexican and Southwest favorites with a touch of the Northwest. House specialties include mesquite-grilled meats, such as cordero Roberto (grilled marinated leg of lamb), seafood, and fresh-fruit margaritas. Crab enchiladas are especially good, and the chips and salsa are made in the kitchen. Bilbo's is open daily for lunch and dinner, with distinctive handcrafted furniture and large servings. Outside dining is available in the courtyard. The setting is fun and friendly, but drinks are surprisingly expensive. It's easy for two people to drop $50 with drinks. Reservations are advised in the summer. Servings are substantial, and as with other Mexican eateries, this is not a place for those on a diet. No lunches in the off-season.

Callaloo Caribbean Kitchen (Prune Alley and A St., 360/376-5375, $12–16) is a friendly and colorful café with spicy lunches and dinners. Its funky atmosphere make it a favorite of travelers and locals. Patio dining adds to the summertime appeal. Start out with Bahamian conch fritters or curried squash soup before settling down to entrées, such as Trinidadian curried chicken, BBQ pork spareribs, or Cuban-style steaks. Be sure to sample a piece of the moist and flavorful cornbread.

Fine Dining

Ask locals where they go for special occasions and you're certain to hear one place near the top of everyone's list: **ℕ Inn at Ship Bay** (326 Olga Rd., 360/376-5886, www.innatshipbay.com, $19–27). Chef-owner Geddes Martin prepares a variety of fresh-from-the-sea specials—including Judd Cove oysters harvested that morning—and uses fresh organic ingredients from the garden and orchard out front. The menu is updated frequently and includes an impressive wine list. Located a mile east of Eastsound at an old farmhouse, this comfortably upscale restaurant is the sort of place where the knowledgeable staff stays year after year. Inn at Ship Bay has attracted the likes of Al Gore and Conan O'Brien in the past, so check nearby tables for a recognizable face. The restaurant is closed January to mid-February.

Enjoy an ever-changing choice of Northwest cuisine at **ℕ Christina's** (310 Main St., 360/376-4904, www.christinas.net, $25–38), where the patio out back overlooks East Sound. Christina's has been here for more than two decades, so you know they're doing something right. Diners will appreciate the cozy atmosphere, attention to detail, and excellent service. It's a fine special-occasion spot, and children are welcome. Be sure to try the famous Chocolate blackout torte—the ultimate killer chocolate dessert.

Housed within the historic Outlook Inn, **Sunflower Café** (171 Main St., 360/376-2335, www.outlookinn.com, $20–25) serves ample and nicely presented Northwest meals, with specialties like garlic-infused pork loin or artichoke and mushroom lasagna. The café is open for brunch, lunch, and dinner, and dinner entrées include a fresh-greens salad or house soup. An open-air porch overlooks the bay, and it's just a block from the shops of Eastsound.

Markets and Bakeries

For groceries, film, and other essentials, stop by **Orcas Island Market** (469 Market St., 360/376-6000). This is the largest market in the San Juans, and has an in-store bakery, deli, ATM, and video rentals. It's open 8 A.M.–9 P.M. Monday–Saturday, and 10 A.M.–8 P.M. Sunday.

Homegrown Market (8 North Beach Rd.,

360/376-2009), has natural foods and a deli with daily specials and salads, plus fresh crab and salmon in season. This is the place to buy ultra-fresh Judd Cove oysters harvested at nearby Crescent Beach; $6 for a dozen big ones.

The **Orcas Island Farmers Market** (360/376-4594, www.orcasislandfarmersmarket.org) is held at Eastsound's Village Square May through early October 10 A.M.– 3 P.M. Saturdays. Come here for local produce, flowers, crafts, clothing, and more.

For the finest breads, cheeses, and gourmet deli foods, don't miss **Roses Bakery Café.**

THE WEST END

Orcas Village

When you step off the ferry at Orcas, the grand old Orcas Hotel faces you. Inside is **Octavia's Bistro** (360/376-4300 or 888/672-2792, www.orcashotel.com, $17–25), open for breakfast and dinner. Evening entrées include a mix of meats, seafood, pasta, and vegetarian dishes. Outdoor seating is available. Also within the hotel is **Orcas Hotel Café,** with burgers, fish and chips, wraps, sandwiches, and salads, plus Starbucks iced mochas. Eat inside or on the covered patio.

Right next to the ferry landing is **Orcas Village Store** (360/376-8860) with a good selection of groceries and a deli that cranks out outstanding sandwiches ($6–7) and lattes. Stop here for a last-minute take-aboard lunch before walking on the ferry.

Deer Harbor

Housed in a 1915 farmhouse, **Deer Harbor Inn** (Deer Harbor, 360/376-4110 or 877/377-4110, www.deerharborinn.com, $17–24), is a spacious and comfortable place with outstanding meals. It's a bit off the beaten path if you're staying near Eastsound, but worth the drive. You can get something as simple as freshly baked bread and homemade soups, or choose a full dinner from the blackboard listing the day's specials. Meals come with soup, bread, salad, and veggies. There's always grilled seafood and a vegetarian choice, along with a full bar. The homemade apple pie à la mode is made from apples picked in the old orchard out front. A large outdoor deck opens seasonally. The restaurant serves breakfast in the summer, and is open daily till 9 P.M. so arrive early for an evening meal. In the winter, it's open for dinners several days a week. Reservations advised.

Open for breakfast and lunch, homey **M** **West Sound Café** (Crow Valley and Deer Harbor Rds., 360/376-4440, www.kingfishinn.com), occupies a historic waterside building; the upstairs operates as Kingfish Inn B&B. The café is a family show, and you're likely to find Bob Breslauer in the kitchen while his wife Lori runs the café and cash register. Jazz tunes spill from the stereo as patrons pull up high-back chairs and settle in for a relaxing morning. Try the huevos rancheros or wild mushroom omelet for breakfast. Lunches run $8–11, and include such specialties as fish tacos, halibut fish and chips, and bacon cheeseburgers, plus espresso. Dinner entrées are $11–15. Outside seating is available on a delightful little deck facing the harbor. The café is closed mid-December to mid-February.

The striking harbor-front location of **Starfish Grill** (360/376-2482, www.deerharbor.com) is reason enough to visit this relaxing bistro at Deer Harbor, but the food is also of note. The deck out front faces a bevy of boats in the harbor. The café is open for lunch (clam chowder, burgers, fish tacos, Caesar salads, and more) and dinner (steaks, pizzas, king salmon, and Jamaican Jerked pork ribs); evening entrées run $15–20. Off-season Sunday dinners are served family style. Starfish is closed November–March, but the adjacent **High Tide Pub** (built in 1893) stays open year-round with beer, wine, and a finger-licking menu.

THE EAST END

Café Olga (Horseshoe Hwy. and Doe Bay Rd., 360/376-5098) is housed within the Orcas Island Artworks building. A well-known brunch and lunch stop, the café closes at 6 P.M. In addition to sandwiches and salads, the restaurant serves up a range of daily seafood specials, vegetarian items, and espresso, but save room for the justly famous blackberry pie. Their monster cinnamon roll could feed a small nation. The out-of-the-way

The historic Olga Store is also home to Café Olga.

location keeps the crowds at bay. Open daily, except January to mid-February when the café shuts down for a vacation.

Rosario Resort & Spa (downhill from Moran State Park, 360/376-2222 or 800/562-8820, www.rosarioresort.com), has spectacular views and romantic dining at this historic building five miles south of Eastsound. The Compass Room serves dinners for $18–30; reservations required. Popular with locals is the less-formal Orcas Dining Room, best-known for its Friday night seafood buffet ($42), which includes fresh crab, oysters, smoked salmon, salads, desserts, and vegetarian choices. Sunday champagne brunches are $38. Buffets are offered year-round, and reservations are recommended. For seasonal dining with a view, try lunch at the resort's outdoor pool: alfresco dining overlooking Cascade Bay.

Located at Doe Bay Resort & Retreat, **Doe Bay Café** serves vegetarian (and some seafood) meals in a rustic and out-of-the-way location. The café features local organic produce and is open for brunch and dinner (summers only), with most dinner entrées under $12. After dinner, head up the creek for a soak in the hot tub ($10 day pass if you aren't a guest).

Arts and Entertainment

GALLERIES

The arts are very important on Orcas, with nearly 10 percent of locals listing "artist" as their profession. The island boasts an abundance of galleries and craft shops. The fascinating **Lambiel Museum** (near Eastsound, 360/376-4544, www.lambielmuseum.com) is packed with works from island artists (see *Sights*).

Orcas Island Artworks

The barn-like structure that houses Orcas Island Artworks (Horseshoe Hwy. and Doe Bay Rd., 360/376-4408, www.orcasisland.com/artworks) was built in 1936, and originally served as a processing plant for strawberries picked on nearby farms. The gallery has been here since 1982, making this one of the oldest artist-owned cooperatives in the Pacific Northwest. More than 65 artists and crafts workers display their pieces on two levels, and the back corner houses Café Olga, a popular lunch spot. The gallery is approximately eight miles south of Eastsound.

A mile away in Olga, visit **Studio 4:20** (1179 Pt. Lawrence Rd.), with pottery, candles, leather, and jewelry.

Crow Valley Pottery

Housed within the oldest building on the island, an 1866 log cabin, tiny Crow Valley Pottery (2274 Orcas Rd., 360/376-4260, www.crow-valley.com) contains works by four local potters, plus paintings, jewelry, sculpture, cards, baskets, and glass from regional artists. The studio has been here since 1959 and mounts four different exhibits throughout the summer. It is located along the main road connecting Orcas Village and Eastsound. Closed in January.

Orcas Island Pottery

This out-of-the-way studio should not be missed. The oldest pottery studio in the Northwest—it opened in 1945—Orcas Island Pottery (360/376-2813, www.orcasislandpottery.com) sits atop a high bluff overlooking President Channel, and is a quarter-mile drive through tall Douglas firs off West Beach Road. The inspiring setting alone makes it worth the side trip, but the wheel-thrown and hand-built pottery is equally notable. This is a laid-back and friendly place and you're welcome to bring a picnic lunch and relax on the benches or have your kids try out the swings with a million-dollar view. Two rustic log buildings feature the works of 26 potters, many of whom fire their pieces here. Dozens of colorful plates and pots sit outside on the grounds, filling with water when it rains. Be sure to check out the surprising not-for-sale window.

The Right Place

Trudy Erwin runs The Right Place (2915 Enchanted Forest Rd., 360/376-4023, www.rightplacepottery.com), a small and seasonal Westside pottery studio near West Beach Resort. She owned Orcas Island Pottery for many years—it's now run by her daughter and grandson—and continues to produce an assortment of local crafts, from personalized plates to blown glass. In the summer, she'll introduce you to the potter's wheel with make-it-yourself pieces for a mere $5. These crafts are a longtime Orcas tradition and are always a big hit with children.

Howe Art Gallery

As visitors approach Eastsound from the ferry, they are surprised to see several tall silvery sculptures twirling in the wind alongside the road. Just a quarter-mile from town is the turnoff to Howe Art Gallery & Kinetic Sculpture Garden (360/376-2945, www.howeart.net). Follow Double Hill Road uphill to the home of Tony Howe, a transplant from the New York City art scene. Many of his whimsically playful welded-metal mobiles and kinetic art pieces fill the grounds and an adjacent gallery. The gallery is open daily (except Mondays) in the summer and by appointment the rest of the year. Don't miss this place!

Orcas Island

PERFORMANCE

The **Orcas Theatre & Community Center** (North Beach and Mount Baker Rds. in Eastsound, 360/376-2281, www.orcascenter.org) hosts a variety of events year-round, from concerts by nationally known musicians like Taj Mahal or Wynton Marsalis to local theatrical performances and productions for kids. There's also a monthly gallery show by local artists. The theater was constructed solely from local contributions, not government grants.

Check out the latest movies at **Sea View Theatre** (A St. in Eastsound, 360/376-5724).

NIGHTLIFE

Anyone coming to Orcas for the nightlife will find slim pickings, though you might find the occasional weekend band in the summer at **The Lower Tavern,** (Prune Alley, 360/376-4848) or **Vern's Bayside** (246 Main St., 360/376-2231). Over at **Rosario Resort & Spa** (360/376-2222 or 800/562-8820, www.rosarioresort.com), the seasonal music is on the mellow side, with live piano music in the main dining room and easy-listening tunes at Moran Lounge.

FESTIVALS

See the Orcas Island Chamber's website (www.orcasisland.org) for information on upcoming island events. Start the summer off with the **Bite of Orcas** on Memorial Day weekend, a great chance to taste foods prepared by local restaurants to benefit Wolf Hollow Wildlife Rehabilitation Center.

Small **Summer Solstice** festivities take place in Eastsound and Deer Harbor on June 21. Every Thursday at noon during July and August, head to the waterside Emmanuel Episcopal Church in Eastsound for a free **Brown Bag Concert.** Over in **Deer Harbor Marina,** find live music on the dock all summer 4–7 P.M. Fridays.

Eastsound—like nearly every small town in the United States—has a fun parade on the Saturday nearest the **4th of July.** Other holiday weekend festivities include a community band concert, a pancake breakfast, and salmon barbecue in Eastsound, plus fireworks at three locations: Eastsound, Rosario Resort, and Deer Harbor on three different nights.

The first weekend of August brings a popular **Orcas Island Fly-In** (www.orcasisland.org/flyin), which features many antique planes. It's followed on the second Saturday of August by the **Library Fair** (360/376-4985, www.orcaslibrary.org), a big arts and crafts fair and book sale.

Labor Day weekend brings the always-sold-out **Orcas Island Chamber Music Festival** (360/376-6636 or 866/492-0003, www.oicmf.org). You'll hear the works of Mozart, Bach, Schubert, Tchaikovsky, and others.

In early September, the **Wooden Boats Rendezvous** (360/376-3037, www.deerharbormarina.com) exhibits wood boats, and features a sailing race and live music at Deer Harbor.

Information and Services

Get island information at the **Orcas Island Chamber of Commerce Visitor Center** (113 A St., 360/376-2273, www.orcasisland.org), located next to the post office. Summer hours are 10:30 A.M.–3:30 P.M. Monday–Saturday; October–April 10 A.M.–2 P.M. Monday–Friday. An information kiosk at **Moran State Park** is open Memorial Day–Labor Day 9:30 A.M.–1:30 P.M. Monday–Saturday.

Orcas Isle (www.orcasisle.com) is a helpful Web source with links to many local businesses.

LAUNDRY AND SHOWERS

Airport Center Self Service Laundry (360/376-2678) is located on the southwest side of the airport in Eastsound. **Country Corner Laundry** (Crescent Beach and Terrill Beach Rds., 360/376-6900) is a half-mile east of Eastsound. Additional washers and driers are at the Rosario Resort Marina.

The marinas at Rosario Resort, Deer Harbor, and West Sound all have coin-op showers.

CLEANING UP

If you're staying in a rental house on the island, you'll need to haul garbage to the **Solid Waste Transfer Facility** (along Orcas Rd., 360/376-4089) on the west side of the island. You can recycle many items here, including mixed paper, tin cans, aluminum, plastic bottles, cardboard, and newspapers. Don't bother to sort your recyclables; they all go in one bin and are sorted later. Dumping garbage costs $6/bag.

SHOPPING

Eastsound is the primary shopping center on Orcas, with a number of pricey boutiques, galleries, antique shops, and gift shops. One place worth a look is **Monkey Puzzle Curiosities** (432 North Beach Rd., 360/376-2275 or 800/273-4055, www.monkeypuzzle.com), with objets d'art, designer clothing, knitwear, handbags, home accessories, and more. Check out **Rutabaga** (Deer Harbor, 360/376-5737, www.rutabaga.biz) for distinctive gifts, handcrafted items, folk art, baskets, and items for the home and garden.

Darvill's Rare Print Shop & Fine Art Gallery (296 Main St. in Eastsound, 360/376-2351, www.darvillsrareprints.com) is famous for original antique prints, maps, old manuscripts, vintage calendar art, postcards, botanicals, and much more—some of which date back to the 18th century. There's bound to be something of interest here; it's a great spot to explore on a rainy afternoon. Also available are limited-edition prints by contemporary Northwest artists, including Rie Muñoz. Darvill's has been around since 1942.

BOOKSTORES AND LIBRARIES

Eastsound is home to the attractive and modern **Orcas Island Library** (500 Rose St., 360/376-4985, www.orcaslibrary.org), a great place to relax on a drizzly afternoon. The public is welcome at the 11 A.M. preschool story hour every Tuesday, and for the noontime first Friday book discussions for adults. A half-dozen computers are available to surf the web or check your email, but you may need to wait a bit for a machine. Non-locals pay $50 for a library card if you want to check something out. Library hours are 10 A.M.–7 P.M. Monday–Thursday, 10 A.M.–5 P.M. Friday–Saturday.

Darvill's Bookstore (296 Main St. in Eastsound, 360/376-2135), has the finest selection of books on Orcas, with a knowledgeable staff and many regional titles. The little coffee shop in the back cranks out some of the best espresso on the island.

Pyewacket Books (Main St. and Prune Alley in Eastsound, 360/376-2043), is packed with used titles.

INTERNET ACCESS

In addition to the free computers at the library, **Orcas Online** (254 North Beach Rd. in Eastsound, 360/376-4124, www.orcasonline.com) lets you surf the Web; $5 for 20 minutes. **The Mail Depot/Kiki's Kafé** (432 North Beach Rd., 360/376-6230 or 866/342-6245, www.themaildepot.us) is an Internet café with high-speed Internet access ($2.50 for 15 minutes), plug-ins for laptops (free Internet for first 15 minutes), espresso, and fresh baked goods.

KIDS STUFF

Weekday childcare is available on a drop-in basis at **Orcas Island Children's House** (36 Peapatch Ln., 360/376-4744, www.rockisland.com/childrenshouse) and **Kaleidoscope** (1292 North Beach Rd., 360/376-2484). Call ahead for age requirements and to make sure they have space.

One of the most popular child and teen attraction is The Funhouse (see *Sights*). **Orcas Island Skateboard Park** on Mt. Baker Road (see *Recreation*) is one of the finest such parks in the Northwest, and a big draw for teenagers.

Looking for a kid's playground? The best ones are outside The Funhouse and at Cascade Lake in Moran State Park. **Wildlife Cycles** in Eastsound (350 North Beach Rd., 360/376-4708, www.wildlifecycles.com) has baby joggers, trail-a-bikes, and kid trailers for rent.

MEDICAL AND VETERINARY CARE

Call 911 on a regular phone for medical emergencies or fires; on a cell phone, dial 360/378-4141.

Orcas Island Family Medicine (7 Deye Ln., 360/376-2561), has two physicians available in the summer (one the rest of the year), along with two physician assistants, two acute-care beds, and x-rays. Just up the way is **Orcas Family Physicians** (1286 Mt. Baker Rd., 360/376-7778, www.orcasfamilyphysicians.com) with two physicians. Both facilities can provide urgent care and lab tests, and are open weekdays, with a physician on call after hours and on weekends. Orcas Island has a paramedic system, but the closest hospital is in Anacortes, and serious medical problems require a medivac flight to Seattle.

For a New Age take on health—including a naturopath, massage therapists, acupuncture, life coaching, and intuitive counselors—visit **The Healing Arts Center** (304 North Beach Rd., 360/376-4002). Get prescription medicines at **Ray's Pharmacy** in Eastsound (Templin Center, 360/376-2230; after hours call 360/376-3693).

Take sick or injured pets to **Orcas Animal Clinic** (429 Madrona St. in Eastsound, 360/376-7838).

BANKING AND MAIL

Eastsound's three banks all have ATM machines: **Islanders Bank** (475 Fern St., 360/376-2265 or 800/843-5441, www.islandersbank.com), **Key Bank** (210 Main St., 360/376-2211, www.keybank.com), and **Washington Federal Savings** (Eastsound Square, 360/376-2218, www.washingtonfederal.com). You'll also find ATMs at the Orcas Island Market and Ray's Pharmacy in Eastsound, and the Orcas Village Store at the ferry landing.

Post offices can be found on A Street in Eastsound (360/376-4121), at Deer Harbor (360/376-2548), Olga (360/376-4236), and Orcas (360/376-4254). **The Mail Depot** (432 North Beach Rd., 360/376-6230 or 866/342-6245, www.themaildepot.us) has private mail boxes, packaging material, and shipping services for Fed Ex.

Transportation

STATE FERRY SERVICE

Washington State Ferries (360/376-6253 for the Orcas ferry terminal, 206/464-6400 for general info, or 888/808-7977 in Washington and British Columbia) dock at Orcas Village on the south end of the island. Find all the details—including current ferry wait times—on their website: www.wsdot.wa.gov/ferries. The fare for a car and driver to Friday Harbor is $15.75; walk-ons and passengers ride free. Vehicles and passengers traveling east from Orcas to Shaw, Lopez, or Anacortes do not need tickets and there is no charge. Peak-season weekend fares from Anacortes to Orcas are $11.40 for passengers and walk-ons, $37.50 for car and driver. Bikes are $4 extra, and kayaks cost $18 more. Reservations are not available for any of these runs, so you'll need to get in line and wait. Vehicle reservations *are*, however, required at least 24 hours in advance if you're heading west on the runs from Orcas Island to Sidney, British Columbia. These tickets to Vancouver Island cost $23.75 for a car and driver or $5 for passengers or walk-ons.

WATER TAXIS

Marty Mead of **North Shore Charters** (360/376-4855, www.sanjuancruises.net), offers day trips and drop-offs to state marine parks on Stuart, Sucia, Matia, Patos, and other islands. Rates are $135/hour for up to six passengers, and trips depart from Deer Harbor Marina. There's also space for kayaks and bikes. North Shore Charters also has a boat based at Rosario Resort that can carry up to six passengers for $185/hour (no kayaks or bikes). The latter is especially popular for sunset cruises and charters to Bellingham or Anacortes. Fishing charters are also available.

ORCAS ISLAND MILEAGE

	Orcas Village Ferry Dock	Deer Harbor	Doe Bay	Eastsound	Moran State Park	Olga
Deer Harbor	8					
Doe Bay	20	22				
Eastsound	9	11	11			
Moran State Park	14	15	7	4		
Olga	17	18	3	8	4	
West Sound Marina	4	4	18	7	12	15

BY AIR

Floatplanes

Operating out of Lake Union in Seattle, **Kenmore Air** (425/486-1257 or 800/543-9595, www.kenmoreair.com), has daily scheduled floatplane flights to Rosario Resort, Deer Harbor, and West Sound on Orcas Island. A 24-pound baggage weight limit is in effect on these flights, and excess baggage costs $1/pound.

Airport Services

San Juan Airlines (360/376-4176 or 800/874-4434, www.sanjuanairlines.com) has scheduled daily wheeled-plane service to Eastsound Airport from Seattle, Anacortes, and Bellingham, plus connecting service to San Juan and Lopez Islands. Flightseeing and air charters are also available.

Rose Air (503/675-7673, www.roseair.com), is a one-woman operation with charter flights between Portland, Oregon, and Orcas Island aboard Jane Rosevelt's Cessna 182.

Rugby Aviation (360/376-7139, www.rugby aviation.com) provides flightseeing tours ($150/hour for up to three people), along with air taxi and charter flights ($85 to Bellingham, $74 to Friday Harbor, or $239 to Seattle for up to three people) from the Eastsound airport. Owner-operator Frank Cantwell also offers aviation rental and instruction.

Biplane Rides

For a ride into the past, hop aboard the gorgeous biplane flown by effusive Rod Magner, an ex-Navy pilot who has flown since age 14. His **Magic Air Tours** (360/376-2733 or 800/376-1929, www.magicair.com) depart from Eastsound Airport. The plane is officially a 1929 TravelAir (one of just 40 still flying), but only a few pieces remain from the original fuselage. Rebuilt from the ground up in 1984, the plane looks brand new, and is decked out in glistening red and yellow that bring out the "wow" factor. Rod compares a flightseeing trip to "flying in an old Buick convertible." There's room for two in the open front cockpit, and he narrates the sights along the way. The cost for two people is $200 for a half-hour flight, including leather helmets, goggles, and headsets. Flights are offered April–October, and are available for ages three and up. Even if you aren't planning to fly, you may want to check out the plane at the airport. His old-fashioned hangar, filled with flying memorabilia, is fun to see, and the plane itself is a stunner. Kids love to play on his pedal planes, one of which is an exact copy of the TravelAir.

RENTAL CARS

Rent cars seasonally at Orcas Village from **M&W Auto Rentals** (360/376-3883 or 800/323-6037, www.sanjuanauto.com) or at Eastsound Airport

Orcas Island

© KATIE WOODS/MAGIC AIR TOURS

Based on Orcas Island, Magic Air Tours offers biplane tours over the San Juan Islands.

year-round from **San Juan Airlines** (360/293-4691 or 800/874-4434, www.sanjuanairlines.com). Expect to pay around $50/day for a small car or $70/day for an SUV.

Gas is available at two stations east of Eastsound along Crescent Beach Drive and from the hardware store at the junction of West Beach Road and Crow Valley Road. In a pinch, you can also get fuel from the various boat harbors, including West Beach Resort and Deer Harbor Marina. Fuel prices are a rip-off on Orcas, so fill up on the mainland before you get on the ferry.

SHUTTLES AND TAXIS

Orcas Island Shuttle (360/376-3414 or 800/516-9010, www.orcasislandshuttle.com) is a godsend for travelers to Orcas, with scheduled bus service from the Orcas ferry landing to West Sound, Deer Harbor, Eastsound, Moran State Park, Rosario Resort, Olga, and Obstruction Pass. Buses run four times a day in each direction, and cost $5 one-way or $10 for an all-day pass. Kids under 12 are half-price, and those under five are free. Add $1 to transport a bike. You can get off the bus anywhere along the route, and can flag it down on a later run. Buses operate on these scheduled runs daily May–September. Charter service is available any time of the year.

Orcas Island Taxi (360/376-8294 or 800/942-1926), provides service to Eastsound ($19), Moran State Park ($24), Rosario Resort ($27), Doe Bay ($35), and other places on the island.

Lopez Island

If you're venturing out to the San Juans from Anacortes, Lopez Island (population 2,200) is the first place the ferry stops. The third largest island in the archipelago, it covers almost 30 square miles. Pastoral farmland and water vistas predominate, especially on the southern end of the island.

Because of its lack of both steep hills and traffic, Lopez is very popular with cyclists, including many groups of touring bikers. The roads are mostly paved, and views of the surrounding islands and mountains to the east and west jut out from every turn.

Along the west side of Lopez just north of Fisherman Bay is the island's quaint business center, little **Lopez Village.** Here you'll find a scattering of cafés, shops, a museum, grocery store with gas, a post office, pharmacy, medical clinic, and several real estate offices—which should tell you something about the island's newfound popularity. The Islandale convenience store is on the south end of the island. A few more businesses cluster along pretty **Fisherman Bay,** filled with sailboats and other craft, but the rest of the island is essentially undeveloped. Many Lopez businesses are shuttered during the winter.

© DON PITCHER

Must-Sees

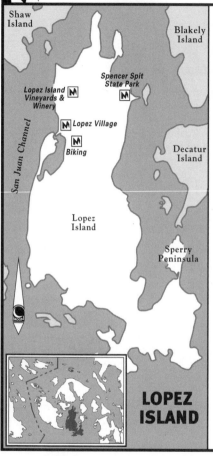

Lopez Village

ⓜ **Lopez Village:** The center of commerce on Lopez, this little business center has a small museum, galleries, good food, and more (page 166).

ⓜ **Lopez Island Vineyards & Winery:** This little six-acre farm eschews pesticides in the production of their madeleine angevine and siegerrebe wines. Locals pick the grapes each fall in a harvest party (page 167).

ⓜ **Spencer Spit State Park:** Excellent camping, kayaking, beachcombing, and clamming attract the crowds to this park on the east side of Lopez (page 168).

ⓜ **Biking:** Biking the 30-mile loop is a favorite form of recreation and a perfect way to explore the farms, fields, forests, and bays (page 171).

Often called "The Friendly Isle" or "Slow-pez," Lopez is an easy-going place with gently rolling terrain, old farms with buildings in various states of disrepair, shaggy black dogs, and a famously friendly populace. Waving to passing cars and bicycles is a time-honored local custom, and failure to wave back will label you a tourist as surely as a camera around your neck and rubber flip-flops.

Lopezians are an odd amalgamation of carpenters, retirees, back-to-the-land organic farmers, fishermen, artists and musicians, bed-and-breakfast owners, and more than a few eccentrics. This is the kind of place where the bumper stickers poke fun at the NRA ("National Waffle Association") and conservative Christians (a fish-shaped symbol surrounding the word "Gefilte"). Lopez also has homes that belong to the rich and famous. The singer Jewel and Microsoft billionaire Paul Allen own homes on the island. (Allen's purchase of Sperry Peninsula for a private,

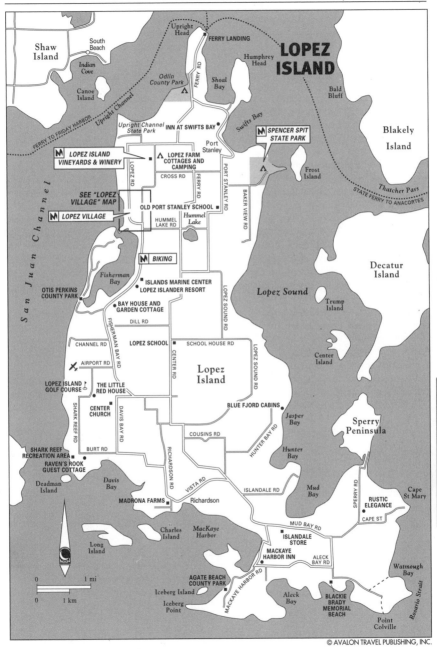

Shaw Island

South Beach

Indian Cove

Canoe Island

Upright Head

FERRY LANDING

LOPEZ ISLAND

Humphrey Head

Bald Bluff

Odlin County Park

Shoal Bay

Upright Channel

FERRY TO FRIDAY HARBOR

Upright Channel State Park

INN AT SWIFTS BAY

Swifts Bay

SPENCER SPIT STATE PARK

Blakely Island

LOPEZ ISLAND VINEYARDS & WINERY

LOPEZ FARM COTTAGES AND CAMPING

Port Stanley

Frost Island

Thatcher Pass

STATE FERRY TO ANACORTES

San Juan Channel

LOPEZ RD

CROSS RD

FERRY RD

PORT STANLEY RD

BAKER VIEW RD

SEE "LOPEZ VILLAGE" MAP

LOPEZ VILLAGE

OLD PORT STANLEY SCHOOL

HUMMEL LAKE RD

Hummel Lake

Decatur Island

BIKING

Lopez Sound

Fisherman Bay

ISLANDS MARINE CENTER
LOPEZ ISLANDER RESORT

LOPEZ SOUND RD

Trump Island

OTIS PERKINS COUNTY PARK

BAY HOUSE AND GARDEN COTTAGE

DILL RD

CHANNEL RD

FISHERMAN BAY RD

LOPEZ SCHOOL

SCHOOL HOUSE RD

CENTER RD

Center Island

AIRPORT RD

Lopez Island

LOPEZ SOUND RD

Sperry Peninsula

LOPEZ ISLAND GOLF COURSE

THE LITTLE RED HOUSE

SHARK REEF RD

CENTER CHURCH

DAVIS BAY RD

BLUE FJORD CABINS

Jasper Bay

COUSINS RD

HUNTER BAY RD

Hunter Bay

SHARK REEF RECREATION AREA

BURT RD

Cape St Mary

RAVEN'S ROOK GUEST COTTAGE

Davis Bay

RICHARDSON RD

VISTA RD

ISLANDALE RD

Mud Bay

SPERRY RD

RUSTIC ELEGANCE

Deadman Island

MADRONA FARMS

Richardson

MUD BAY RD

CAPE ST

MOON

Charles Island

MacKaye Harbor

ISLANDALE STORE

ALECK BAY RD

Watmough Bay

Long Island

MACKAYE HARBOR RD

MACKAYE HARBOR INN

0   1 mi

0   1 km

AGATE BEACH COUNTY PARK

Iceberg Island

Iceberg Point

Aleck Bay

BLACKIE BRADY MEMORIAL BEACH

Point Colville

Rosario Strait

N Lopez Island

© AVALON TRAVEL PUBLISHING, INC.

guarded estate in the 1990s forced out the beloved Camp Nor'wester and created a major rift in the community.)

PLANNING YOUR TIME

Lopez reaches nine miles north to south, and approximately four miles across. Flat or gently rolling terrain, open country, and relatively straight roads make it easy to cover the island in a day—even on a bike. It's the first ferry stop heading west from Anacortes and has a couple of campgrounds near the ferry landing on the north end, making it perfect for relatively short visits, such as a weekend.

Because it's so easy to get around, you can stay almost anywhere on the island and still be just a few miles from the main settlement of **Lopez Village.** There aren't a lot of "sights" to discover, but the rural, farming island is a perfect place to explore by **bicycle.** Most of the land is privately owned, but a handful of small parks and preserves remain in public hands, including **Spencer Spit State Park** on the northern end of the island. This park is popular not only for beachcombing, camping, and picnicking, but also as a launching point for sea kayaks. A number of mooring buoys are just offshore. Other small but interesting parks include **Hummel Lake Preserve, Shark Reef Park, Odlin County Park,** and **Agate Beach County Park.**

One of the few commercial places in Washington that grows pesticide-free grapes, **Lopez Island Vineyards & Winery** has madeleine angevine and siegerrebe plants and a small winery where locals pitch in for the fall harvest.

HISTORY

Lopez is named in honor of Lopez Gonzales de Haro, the first European to discover the San Juans. He served as sailing master during the 1791 expedition of explorer Francisco Eliza. Haro Strait is another of his namesakes.

Lopez was occupied for thousands of years by the Coast Salish people, and the coastline is littered with archaeological sites. Whites first settled the island in the 1850s. They found incredible forests covering a rich land that would prove perfect for farming, a heritage that continues today. By the middle of the 20th century, Lopez was known as the "Guernsey Island," and more than 130 farms produced milk, eggs, poultry, veal, pork, peas, vetch, oats, barley, and wheat. Nearly all of the big farms are gone, but agriculture is still important. Today the farms are smaller and more specialized, offering everything from organic beef to wild sea vegetables.

Sights

Lopez's main attraction is its rural, pastoral countryside. The long stretches of hills, fields, orchards, and woods could just as well be rural Vermont, complete with contented cows. You might even see flocks of sheep being driven along local roads. Bucolic Lopez Island is a delightful place to explore, but unfortunately, much of the shoreline and many of the beaches are privately owned and closed to the public.

Picturesque **Fisherman Bay** is the boating center for Lopez, with two marinas and a small fleet of commercial fishing boats, including a number of distinctive reefnet boats that are unique to this area.

LOPEZ VILLAGE

This small settlement near Fisherman Bay is as developed as things get on Lopez, with all the "necessities" of life: real estate offices, fresh baked goods, espresso, video rentals, art galleries, books, a farmers market, and ice cream. Like the rest of the island, it's laid back, and stores may or may not open at the set hours.

Lopez Historical Museum

The Lopez Historical Museum (on Weeks Road in Lopez Village, 360/468-2049, www.rock-island.com/~lopezmuseum) is open July and

August noon–4 P.M. Wednesday–
Sunday; May, June, and September noon–4 P.M. Friday–Sunday;
and by appointment only the rest
of the year. The museum contains
local flotsam and jetsam: the first
car driven on the island, old farm
equipment, a captain's gig from a
19th-century sailing ship, a stuffed
albino red-tailed hawk, and historical photos. Outside, find a
reefnet fishing boat, a gillnetter,
and an aging tractor.

Historic Buildings

A number of other buildings are
worth a gander around the island. Pick up a historical landmark tour brochure from the
museum for all the details. The
white New England–style **Lopez
Island Community Church** in
Lopez Village was built in 1904
and is notable for its steeple,
which splits into four cupolas.
Center Church, built in 1887,
is a simple white structure surrounded by a picket fence and
next to a hilltop cemetery. The
church is home to both Catholics
and Lutherans (what would Martin Luther say?) and is about two
miles south of Lopez Village on
Fisherman Bay Road. It's a favorite spot for island weddings.

The **Lopez Library** (just east
of Lopez Village) is housed in a
bright red and white building that began life
in 1894 as a schoolhouse. Built in 1917 and
used until 1940, the recently restored **Port Stanley School** is on Port Stanley Road near Hummel Lake; call the museum at 360/468-2049
for tours.

TOURING THE ISLAND
Lopez Island Vineyards & Winery
Head a mile north of Lopez Village on Fisherman

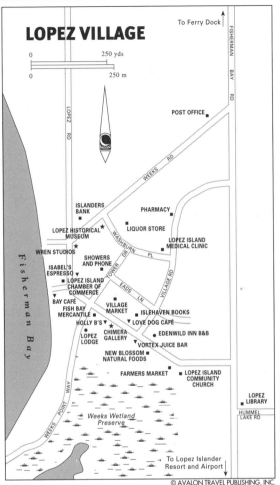

Bay Road to Lopez Island Vineyards & Winery
(724 B Fisherman Bay Rd., 360/468-3644,
www.lopezislandvineyards.com), a family operation that grows pesticide-free grapes on six acres
of land. The grapes grown here are madeleine
angevine (a white-wine grape from the Loire Valley of northern France) and siegerrebe (a cross between Madeleine Angevine and gewürtztraminer). In addition to producing award-winning wines from local grapes, winemaker Brent
Charnley, trained in enology at the University

© DON PITCHER

Lopez Village

of California Davis, uses grapes from Washington's hot and dry Yakima Valley for his chardonnay, merlot, and cabernet sauvignon–merlot wines. Lopez Island Winery also produces several fruit wines—primarily from locally grown organic fruits—including raspberry, blackberry, and apple-pear wines. Lopezians harvest all of the grapes by hand at a community picking party in early October.

The winery is open for tastings and self-guided tours July to early September noon–5 P.M. Wednesday–Saturday, and in fall and spring noon–5 P.M. Friday–Saturday. It's open only by appointment Christmas–March. **Lopez Island Kiwi** (360/468-3243) is right next door; kiwi fruits are picked in late October, but don't ripen till December. They're sold in Larry's Markets in the Seattle area.

Other Lopez Farms

Several dozen farms dot the Lopez Island landscape, producing such specialty products as blackberry jams, chili peppers, Arabian horses, mohair yarn, organic garlic, and cut flowers. Many local farm products are sold at the Lopez Farmers Market, held on summer Saturdays and Wednes-

days in Lopez Village. For a complete list, pick up the *Lopez Island Farm Products Guide* (360/378-4414, http://sanjuan.wsu.edu) at the museum or chamber of commerce office.

PARKS

🅽 Spencer Spit State Park

On the east side of Lopez Island, the 130-acre Spencer Spit State Park (360/468-2251, www .parks.wa.gov, $5 day use), has a half-mile beach with good clamming, beachcombing, hiking, and picnicking. The sandy shoreline is strewn with driftwood, and a reconstructed cabin—part of an old homestead belonging to the Spencer family—sits at the end of the spit. The spit points like an arrow to nearby **Frost Island,** less than a hundred feet from its tip. Frost is private and rocky, with a handful of homes. Spencer Spit hems in a brackish lagoon that frequently hosts ducks, herons, gulls, and shorebirds. Rabbits and black-tailed deer are common evening sights in the park.

Spencer Spit State Park has excellent campsites, but if you're pitching a tent here, you won't be the first person to do so. Not only is it a very

© DON PITCHER

Lopez Island Vineyards and Winery

popular destination today, but the Coast Salish people also used it for at least 3,000 years as a seasonal fish camp. Other park facilities include 16 very popular mooring buoys ($10), drinking water, restrooms, and an RV dump station. Spencer Spit doesn't have a boat ramp or dock, but the beach is a launching spot for sea kayaks; ask at the park office for access via a service road so you don't have to carry your kayaks and gear too far. Kayakers heading out overnight will need to get a parking permit ($10/night). The park is closed November–February.

Odlin County Park

Located on the north end of Lopez just a mile from the ferry landing, Odlin County Park (360/468-2496, www.co.san-juan.wa.us/parks) has a sandy beach along Upright Channel with views of nearby Shaw Island.

Two short paths provide a bit of diversion here: **Big Tree Trail** leads through a stand of giant old-growth Douglas firs and **Little Bird Trail** offers up bluff-top viewpoints. Campsites, picnic areas, a boat launch, and a baseball field are also in the park, and abundant rabbits are a treat for kids.

Upright Channel State Park

This 20-acre park is accessible from a parking area ($5 day use) on Military Road. A short, wooded walk takes you to four picnic tables on the beach, but public access is limited to the immediate area since adjacent beaches are private property. Four mooring buoys ($10) are just offshore.

Agate Beach County Park

Very few of Lopez's beaches are open to the public. One exceptional exception is Agate Beach, on the south end of the island at the end of MacKaye Harbor Road. Across the road from the beach are a few parking spaces, a picnic area, and outhouses. The pebbly beach is filled with colorful wave-rounded stones. I've never found agates here, but persistent rock hounds might find a few. At larger low tides, you can scramble onto a big rock for a view of Iceberg Point, which is owned by the Bureau of Land Management but lacks legal road access.

Otis Perkins County Park

This scenic beach—one of the longest on the islands—is located along Bayshore Road on the south end of Fisherman Bay. The west-facing

Lopez Island

Agate Beach County Park

location makes this a fine sunset stroll, with San Juan Island and the Olympic Mountains accenting the horizon. A couple of picnic tables are also here. The beach (day use only) is public north from the parking area, but to the south it becomes private property.

Shark Reef Park

Another fine small natural area is Shark Reef Park, at the end of Shark Reef Road on the southwest side of Lopez. An easy half-mile path takes you through one of the few old-growth stands of trees (including Douglas fir and Pacific yews) left on the island. It ends at a rocky coastline, a good place to look for harbor seals and sea lions sunning on nearby rocks, while bald eagles wheel through the sky. Less than a mile away is the southern end of San Juan Island, with the grassy slopes of American Camp capped by Cattle Point Lighthouse. The narrow passage frequently develops turbulent flows when the tide is changing. Tiny **Deadman Island** is just offshore south of

Shark Reef and is owned by The Nature Conservancy (206/343-4344, www.tnc-washington.org); no public access.

Weeks Wetland Preserve

This 22-acre saltwater marsh is on the north end of Fisherman Bay and adjacent to Lopez Village. A short loop trail leads to an observation deck overlooking this important resting area for migrating birds. Interpretive signs describe the animals and plants that live here.

Watmough Bay and Point Colville

The Bureau of Land Management (509/665-2100) owns several easily accessible natural areas on the southeast end of Lopez Island near the terminus of Watmough Bay Road. No motorized vehicles or camping are allowed. Look for the unmarked side road to Watmough Bay on the left—near a cluster of mailboxes—at the bottom of a hill in the woods. The road leads to a parking area where a quarter-mile trail continues to a Watmough Bay beach hemmed in by rocky cliffs. Find more impressive views atop nearby **Chadwick Hill,** a scramble from the west side of the beach.

Point Colville is a bit farther out Watmough Bay Road, and a quarter-mile beyond the sign that marks the end of county maintenance. Pull into the little parking area on the left for access to a half-mile trail leading downhill to a grassy area along the Strait of Juan de Fuca.

Hummel Lake Preserve

A pleasant loop trail takes you through the woods to a tiny dock along this lake near the middle of Lopez. The trail starts off Center Road, where you'll find picnic tables and an outhouse. This 79-acre preserve is one of many areas protected by the San Juan County Land Bank.

Blackie Brady Memorial Beach

Find this little county-owned beach on the south end of Lopez along Hughes Bay; turn right on Huggins Road off Aleck Bay Road. Huggins ends at a couple of parking spaces with stairs leading to this gorgeous cove. It's a fine, out-of-the-way place to escape.

Recreation

N BIKING

A favorite local activity is pedaling the 30-mile loop around Lopez Island. Once you get beyond the steep initial climb from the ferry dock, the rest of the island consists of gently rolling hills, making Lopez ideal for family rides. Center Road is relatively busy and best avoided, but most of the others don't see a lot of traffic.

Lopez Bicycle Works (just south of Lopez Village at 2847 Fisherman Bay Rd., 360/468-2847, www.lopezbicycleworks.com) is the oldest bike shop on the San Juans—it opened in 1978. Mountain bikes rent for $30/day, including a helmet. Tandem and recumbent bikes, along with trailer carts and panniers, are also available. Reservations are recommended, especially for midsummer weekends. The shop is open daily May–September, but bikes are also available in the off-season if you call ahead. The shop can drop off or pick up bikes at your lodging place or the ferry early in the morning for a small fee. No tours, but the island is easy enough for almost anyone, and it's hard to get lost. If you need a lift, A Lopez Cab Courier (360/468-2227) will carry your bike.

SEA KAYAKING

If you're taking your kayak on the ferry to Lopez, note that you can't access the water near the ferry terminal. The closest put-in is Odlin County Park, a mile away. Other commonly used places to put your kayak in the water include Spencer Spit State Park, the marinas on Fisherman Bay, and boat ramps at MacKaye Harbor and Hunter Bay.

Kayak Rentals and Trips

Located on the grounds of Lopez Islander Resort, **Lopez Kayaks** (2845 Fisherman Bay Rd., 360/468-2847, www.lopezkayaks.com) rents and sells sea kayaks and runs tours from its waterside location on Fisherman Bay. Double plastic kayaks go for $60/day ($80/day for fiberglass touring doubles). Two types of kayak tours are offered. A 3.5-hour trip off the south end of Lopez ($75) provides

the chance to explore unusual rock formations and to see a variety of birds and other wildlife. Two-hour sunset tours ($35) are a popular way to end the day. No experience necessary. The shop is open May to early October. Lopez Bicycle Works (same family) is right next door.

Based along Fisherman Bay, **Elakah Expeditions** (360/734-7270 or 800/434-7270, www.elakah.com) guides sea kayaking trips of varying lengths. Day trips (4–5 hours on the water) cost $75 including a big lunch. The departure point depends upon weather and winds; trips that take off from MacKaye Harbor are particularly scenic. Elakah also leads multi-day kayaking-and-camping tours to the outlying islands: $325 for three days or $525 for five days. For something more comfortable, take a three-day Lopez-based trip ($475) that includes two nights at Edenwild Inn.

BOATING AND FISHING

Lopez's two marinas are next to each other along Fisherman Bay. Both offer guest moorage, boat launching ramps, and restrooms with showers. It's less than a mile from the marinas to "downtown" Lopez Village. **Islands Marine Center** (360/468-3377, www.islandsmarinecenter.com) has a 100-slip marina, the largest marine repair operation in the San Juans, plus a chandlery, marine supplies, boat launch ramp, and apartment rentals. Immediately to the south is **Lopez Islander Resort and Marina** (360/468-2233 or 800/736-3434, www.lopezislander.com) with a 60-slip marina, boat fuel, propane, laundry, and groceries, plus a small resort with lodging, camping, RV sites, a restaurant, gift shop, and lounge.

Patrick Cotton of **Harmony Charters** (360/468-3310, www.interisland.net/countess) rents a luxurious 65-foot motor yacht, the *Countess,* for $200/person per day including meals and crew. Patrick's sister—Jackie Ashe—operates **Kismet Sailing Charters** (360/468-2435, www.rock-island.com/~sailkismet), with a gorgeous custom-built 36-foot sailing yacht available for skippered charters.

© DON PITCHER

Fisherman Bay

You'll find public boat-launch ramps at Odlin County Park on the north end of the island, and at MacKaye Harbor and Hunter Bay on the south end.

Anglers may want to drop a line at **Hummel Lake,** just a mile east of Lopez Village along Hummel Lake Road. The largest freshwater lake on Lopez, this is also a fine spot for a picnic lunch if you're cycling around the island. A trail leads into a small cedar grove and eventually winds up at the floating dock.

GOLF

Lopez Island Golf Club (360/468-2679) is a nine-hole, par-35 public course along Airport Road. Greens fee is $18 for nine holes. The course is open year-round.

Accommodations

Only 80 or so rooms are available on Lopez Island, so it's a good idea to make reservations a month or more ahead of time to be assured of a space, particularly on summer weekends. If you want to stay at a specific place, make reservations in January or February for a midsummer date. Many of the resorts, inns, and cottages also offer weekly rates. The Lopez Chamber of Commerce's website (www.lopezisland.com) has links to local lodging places.

WEEKLY RENTALS

For furnished homes available on a weekly basis, contact **Lopez Village Properties** (360/468-

5055 or 888/772-9735, www.lopezproperties .com), with more than 30 vacation rental properties on Lopez. These vary greatly, starting at $500/week for a simple place, up to $2,500/week for a large and luxurious home. **Windemere Real Estate** (360/468-3344 or 866/468-3344, www.wrelopez.com) also has a handful of weekly rentals available on Lopez.

RESORT
Lopez Islander Resort

Less than a mile south of Lopez Village along Fisherman Bay Road, Lopez Islander Resort (2864 Fisherman Bay Rd., 360/468-2233 or

800/736-3434, www.lopezislander.com) offers both motel-style units ($100–143 d) with decks and three-bedroom suites with full kitchens ($250–260 for up to eight people). Room rates are approximately 20 percent lower Monday–Thursday nights. Also here are a seasonal outdoor pool, year-round Jacuzzi, volleyball court, and marina. A free shuttle is available to the ferry, airport, vineyard, or golf course, and Kenmore Air has direct floatplane flights from Seattle. This is a favorite place for boaters to pull in and dry out awhile. Lopez Islander Resort is AAA-approved.

BED-AND-BREAKFASTS
Edenwild Inn B&B
Edenwild Inn (132 Lopez Rd., 360/468-3238 or 800/606-0662, www.edenwildinn.com, $135–175 d) is a modern and elegant Victorian-style inn in the heart of Lopez Village. Rose arbors and floral gardens fill the yard, and the home itself features eight spacious and distinctive rooms, all with private baths. One room is wheelchair-accessible, and four of them have fireplaces that actually burn wood (this is getting to be a rarity in our turn-on-the-gas era). A continental breakfast buffet is included and kids are welcome, but call at least two weeks ahead of your visit.

Inn at Swifts Bay
Located a mile south of the ferry, Inn at Swifts Bay (856 Point Stanley Rd., 360/468-3636 or 800/903-9536, www.swiftsbay.com) is a gorgeous out-of-the-way Tudor-style home behind a large lawn and tall trees. Two guest rooms ($110–125 d) share a bath, and three suites ($175–210 d) include private baths, separate entries, and fireplaces. Guests sit down to a European-style gourmet breakfast each morning, and also appreciate the private beach (right across the road), Jacuzzi, exercise room, and sauna at this romantic getaway. No kids under 16.

Lopez Farm Cottages and Tent Camping
For delightful in-the-country lodging, stay at the fairy-tale Lopez Farm Cottages (555 Fish-

erman Bay Rd., 360/468-3555 or 800/440-3556, www.lopezfarmcottages.com, $150 d) just up the way from Lopez Island Vineyards. The four immaculate and modern cottages include kitchenettes, gas fireplaces, a continental breakfast basket, private baths with dual showerheads, and a delightful outdoor Jacuzzi. Guests walk in the last 100 yards or so, and the intentional lack of phones and TVs—not to mention children (no kids under 14)—helps preserve the quiet character. The adjacent pasture has several sheep and you're almost guaranteed to see rabbits hopping around the grounds in the morning. Also here is a fifth cottage that is larger and more luxurious, with a king bed and private outdoor Jacuzzi ($175 d). You can drive up to this one, and it is wheelchair-accessible. Lopez Farm Cottages are especially popular with honeymooners and couples celebrating anniversaries. They're also AAA-approved.

MacKaye Harbor Inn
This stately white farmhouse sits near the southernmost end of Lopez, and directly across the road from protected Barlow Bay. Originally constructed in 1904, MacKaye Harbor Inn (949 MacKaye Harbor Rd., 360/468-2253 or 888/314-6140, www.mackayeharborinn .com) was the first place on Lopez to have electric lights. Today, four guest rooms and a suite are available, starting with two rooms ($99 s or $109 d) that share a bath. Two others are $135–150 s or $145–160 d, and offer harbor views and private baths. Largest is a suite ($169 s or $179 d) that features a fireplace, private deck facing the sunset, antique Italian furnishings, and bath. The inn is just a stone's throw from a sandy beach where seals, otters, and eagles are common sights. Rent sea kayaks ($25/day) to explore nearby waters, or borrow a mountain bike to ride around the island. Guests are served a gourmet breakfast, along with port and chocolates in the evening. Children 12 and up are welcome. The inn is a dozen miles from the restaurants in Lopez Village, though the Islandale store is relatively close for groceries and deli meals.

FINNISH PANCAKES (PANNUKAKKU)

8 eggs
¼ cup honey
½ teaspoon salt
2 ½ cups milk
⅔ cup flour
4 tablespoons butter

Blend all ingredients in a blender, alternating flour and milk last. Melt 4 tablespoons of butter in a large baking dish or pan (9x13 inches). Pour blended mixture into this dish and bake at 425°F for 20–25 minutes until puffed and golden. Serves 6–8 people. Drizzle with hot jam or sprinkle with nutmeg or powered sugar. This recipe is almost like having custard for breakfast, something gentle for the awakening tummy and tongue.

Recipe courtesy of MacKaye Harbor Inn

GUEST HOUSES AND COTTAGES

Bay House and Garden Cottage

Located along Fisherman Bay, Bay House and Garden Cottages (360/468-4889, www.interisland.net/cc) consists of a two-bedroom home ($175 d plus $15/person for additional guests) and two guest cottages ($135 d). All three have full kitchens and private baths. The home contains a fireplace and the cottages have wood stoves. They are located on a beautifully accented and flower-filled yard—the owners are professional landscapers.

Blue Fjord Cabins

Blue Fjord Cabins (862 Elliot Rd., 360/468-2749 or 888/633-0401, www.interisland.net/bluefjord, $98 d) consists of two secluded chalet-style log cabins in a quiet, wooded setting on the east side of the island. Each has a queen bed, full kitchen, skylight, covered deck, and TV/VCR. A short walk away is a gazebo set on the shore of pristine Jasper Cove. This is a fine place to relax and soak up the quietude. A three-night summer minimum is required (two nights the rest of the year).

Islands Marine Center

Islands Marine Center (360/468-3377, www.is-landsmarinecenter.com) is the boating center for Lopez, but it also rents out two apartments over the store and right across the road from Fisherman Bay. Each has a full kitchen with dishes, private bath, woodstove, TV, and VCR. The smaller unit rents for $85 d, and the larger one goes for $95 d. A third room can be combined with either apartment for an additional $35, and extra guests are $10 each. This is a good deal for families and groups, since doors open between all the apartments, creating a unit that includes three bedrooms, two kitchens, two baths, and two living rooms; it can sleep up to 13 guests at once! A barbecue pit and picnic tables are out front, and Lopez Island Resort is next door.

The Little Red House

Charming is a word that comes immediately to mind when you see the aptly named Little Red House (177 Starkman Ln., 360/468-2903, www.lopezvacationrental.com, $135 d or $150 for four). Guests have the run of a nicely maintained, small two-bedroom, one-bath furnished home with a full kitchen, TV/VCR, washer, and dryer. Relax on the old-fashioned porch swing and take in the serenity. There's a two-night minimum, and families are welcome. Lopez Island Golf Course is just across the road.

© DON PITCHER

farm on Lopez Island

Lopez Lodge

Three options are available at Lopez Lodge (Weeks Point Rd., 360/468-2777, www.lopez lodge.com) in the heart of Lopez Village: a studio apartment and two guest rooms. The studio ($125 for up to four) includes two queen beds and a full kitchen, while the rooms ($60–90 d) are simpler, with a bath, fridge, and microwave.

Raven's Rook Guest Cabin

A unique in-the-trees option, Raven's Rook Guest Cabin (58 Wildrose Ln., 360/468-2838 or 888/314-6140, www.rockisland.com/~ravens rook, $105 for up to four) is on the south end of Lopez, and just a short hike from Shark Reef Park. Inside this post-and-beam cabin, you'll find skylights, two queen beds, a full kitchen, and bath. There's a two-night minimum stay required in the summer. Families are welcome, but no toddlers. Bikes are available to rent. A larger octagonal house ($150 with a four-night minimum) is sometimes available; call for details.

Rustic Elegance

Built like a water tower, this wood-shingled home (90 Sperry Place, 360/435-8065, www.lopezrus

ticelegance.com, $115 for up to four, $15/person for additional guests) occupies a remote corner of Lopez. Inside are two guest rooms (one with a king bed), a full kitchen and bath, and living room with a pullout sofa. A hot tub is on the deck, with a hammock in the yard. There's a two-night minimum, and kids are welcome. Billionaire Paul Allen's wall-of-glass house is just up the road next to a small public beach.

View Cabin on Lopez

Located on the southern part of the island, View Cabin on Lopez (1005 Richardson Rd., 360/468-2088, www.rockisland.com/~stonem, $125 d or $135 for four) is a good spot for a weekend escape. Tall windows and a big deck provide a fine view west to the lights of Victoria, and the cabin has two queen beds, a TV, and kitchen, but no phone. It has a three-night minimum in the summer and over holidays (two nights at other times).

CAMPGROUNDS

Camping is available at four places on Lopez, but the two public campgrounds do not have

Lopez Island

© DON PITCHER

Lopez Farm Cottages and Tent Camping

showers. Coin-operated showers are available at the public restrooms near Lopez Village Market and the marinas on Fisherman Bay.

Trailers to Go (360/376-3033 or 888/317-6516, www.trailerstogo.com) will rent and deliver a vacation trailer anyplace on Lopez. It's a good deal if you have a camping spot and want to stay in pseudo-luxury without bringing along your own RV or travel trailer.

Odlin County Park

Odlin County Park (360/468-2496, www.co.san-juan.wa.us/parks) just a mile south of the ferry landing, has year-round waterfront campsites ($19), wooded sites ($16), and walk-in or bike-in sites ($11; no vehicles and max of four people). No RV hookups or showers, but the park does have a boat ramp, a long sandy beach, and hiking trails. Call 360/378-1842 for reservations ($6 fee) April–October. These sites are available five days to three months ahead and are a good idea on weekends.

◼ Spencer Spit State Park

Spencer Spit State Park (360/468-2251), five miles from the ferry landing on the east end of

Baker View Road, has standard campsites ($16) and Adirondack-style shelters for groups. No showers or RV hookups, but there are restrooms and a dump station. The delightful sandy spit is a short walk from the campground. All sites fill early on summer weekends, so make reservations in advance ($7 fee) at 888/226-7688 or www.parks.wa.gov. A separate Cascadia Marine Trail campsite (206/545-9161, www.wwta.org, $10) within the park is accessible by kayak or other beachable boat only. Spencer Spit State Park is closed November–February.

◼ Lopez Farm Cottages and Tent Camping

Located on a 30-acre spread, Lopez Farm Cottages and Tent Camping (555 Fisherman Bay Rd., 360/468-3555 or 800/440-3556, www.lopezfarmcottages.com, $33 d) has 13 nicely designed walk-in "gourmet" campsites in the woods. The offer hammocks and Adirondack chairs, plus a central building for cooking and showers. Other amenities include barbecues, a fireplace, croquet, and badminton. These tent sites are perfect for couples, but no children under 14 or RVs are allowed. Parking is in a separate location to cut down on noise and nighttime headlights. The campground is open May–October.

Lopez Islander Resort
A short walk from Lopez Village, this centrally located resort (2877 Fisherman Bay Rd., 360/468-2233 or 800/736-3434, www.lopezislander.com)

has an abundance of in-the-open tent sites ($25) on the lawn, and woodsy RV sites ($35 with water and electricity) near Fisherman Bay. The shower house is next to a seasonal pool and year-round Jacuzzi, and campers can hop on a free shuttle to the ferry, airport, vineyard, or golf course. Kayak and bike rentals are available at the resort, which also has a full-service marina and motel.

Food

Dining choices on Lopez are good, but a bit limited, particularly in the winter when many places are shuttered. Get there on a Tuesday evening in November and you'll find only a couple of places open.

Bakeries, Cafés, and Sweets
M Holly B's Bakery (Lopez Village, 360/468-2133), begun by Holly Bower in 1978, is *the* place to go for great breads, cookies, butterhorns, raspberry scones, chocolate croissants, and enormous cinnamon rolls, plus focacia and pizza. Check out the "Holly's Buns Are Best" T-shirts. The bakery is open mid-April–November. Holly is the author of *With Love and Butter,* a beautiful cookbook–*cum*–island history. Closed Tuesdays.

Isabel's Espresso (Lopez Village, 360/468-4114), just up the street, is a relaxed hangout with a large outdoor deck that attracts locals. The tasty pastries served here come from La Vie en Rose French Bakery of Anacortes. It's open daily year-round. Isabel's also houses a video exchange, an only-on-Lopez library of sorts where locals pay $45 a year and can swap a hundred or so videos and DVDs among themselves. Watch out, Blockbuster!

Lopez Island Creamery, near the center of the island (986 Dill Rd., 360/468-2051, www.lopezislandcreamery.com), is locally famous for ultra-creamy (16 percent milk fat) gourmet ice creams. The cream comes from Skagit Valley Holsteins, and the ingredients include fresh berries from Washington, along with imported nuts and chocolates. Established in 1993, Lopez Island Creamery sells its ice cream by the pint throughout the San Juans and in Anacortes, Bellingham, and Mount Vernon. Try the wild

blackberry, cappuccino chunk, or lemon raspberry swirl. You can get it by the scoop from the little seasonal stand near Lopez Market, or in local restaurants.

Quick Bites
Located in the Homestead Building in Lopez Village, **Vortex Juice Bar** (360/468-4740) serves healthy food using organic produce and ingredients whenever possible. On the menu are burritos, wraps, salads, soups, smoothies, teas, and a big choice of fruit and vegetable juice combinations. There are a few indoor seats, plus a couple of tables outside on the deck facing the old apple orchard.

Ferry passengers will be pleased to discover **Fogged Inn** (360/468-4330) right next to the dock on the north end of Lopez. This hole-in-the-wall joint cranks out hamburgers piled high with all the fixings, along with halibut burgers, halibut and chips, and other notable fast finger food. It closes by 3:30 P.M. even in the summer, so get here early. Locals claim this is the best burger place on Lopez.

Open for lunches and dinners to go, **Vita's Wildly Delicious** (360/468-4268) is right across from the farmers market on Village Road North. Get gourmet paninis, salads, and a variety of entrées (including vegetarian specials), plus a surprising selection of wines. No seating, and closed January–February.

American
Love Dog Café (Lopez Village, 360/468-2150) is named for a poem by the Islamic spiritual master Rumi, who lived in what is now Afghanistan during the 13th century. The lunch and dinner menu is sprinkled with a number

Lopez Island

of salad entrées, including marinated flank steak salad and chicken fajita salad. Also available are soups, pastas, seafood, steaks, eggplant parmesan, sandwiches, and Lopez's best pizzas. The setting is pleasant, with tall plants, taller windows, and a woodstove with overstuffed chairs and a couch nearby for relaxing. Love Dog is open for all three meals year-round, and has a few tables on the patio for summertime dining.

Galley Restaurant and Lounge (3365 Fisherman Bay Rd., 360/468-2713, www.rock-island.com/~galley) is right across the street from Fisherman Bay, and even has a dock for customers. In business since 1971, the restaurant is known for fresh seafood—particularly halibut tacos—along with mouthwatering steaks, pasta and chicken dishes, Mexican specialties, and double-size bacon cheeseburgers. There's a salad bar if you're counting calories, and a bar with a pool table and sports on the television. The restaurant is open three meals a day.

If you're looking for a real slice of life on the "rock," drop by **Lopez Island Pharmacy** (157 Village Rd. in Lopez Village, 360/468-4511, www.lopezislandpharmacy.com). The old-fashioned soda fountain here fills with locals at lunchtime, and serves soups, sandwiches, malts, sundaes, ice cream sodas, and banana splits. They'll put together a box lunch if you call ahead. Closed Sundays.

Fine Dining

M The Bay Café (Lopez Village, 360/468-3700, www.bay-cafe.com, $19–33) is Lopez Island's four-star restaurant, with Northwest cuisine that includes seafood and grilled meats. Chef and co-owner Daren Holscher is particularly known for his memorable seafood curry. The café is only open for dinner, and reservations are essential. All seats face Fisherman Bay, and the deck opens when the weather approves. Bay Café is open all year, but only on weekends in mid-winter.

Markets and Produce

Get groceries and general merchandise from **Village Market** (Lopez Village, 360/468-2266). The store also sells beer, wine, firewood, gas, and propane, and has an ATM. It's open daily all year. **Lopez Liquor Store** (Lopez Village, 360/468-2407) sells the hard stuff, along with beer and wine; closed Sundays and Mondays.

Also in Lopez Village, **Blossom Natural Foods** (360/468-2204) focuses on organic fare, including cheeses, milk, bulk foods, nuts, herbs, and local organic produce and meats.

On the south end of the island, the **Islandale** store (Mud Bay Rd., 360/468-2315) has a fair choice of groceries, supplies, beer, wine, and gas. In the rear of the store, **Southend Deli** (360/468-3982) cranks out burgers, fish and chips, soup, salmon burgers, pre-made sandwiches, and evening pizzas, plus breakfasts—including biscuits and gravy. The back deck and lawn are fun on a warm summer afternoon.

The **M Lopez Island Farmers Market** comes to the village mid-May to Labor Day 10 A.M.–2 P.M. Saturdays. Drop by for fresh garden produce, flowers, and eggs, along with arts and crafts.

Arts and Entertainment

The modern **Lopez Center for Community and the Arts** (204 Village Rd., 360/468-2203, www.lopezcenter.com) was built entirely with local funding and is used for concerts, art exhibitions, theatrical productions, and other activities. Outdoor pavilion concerts are a staple in the summer months here.

Located at Lopez Islander Resort (2877 Fisherman Rd., 360/468-2233 or 800/736-3434, www.lopezislander.com), **Tiki Cocktail Lounge** has two pool tables and live music on summer weekends. **Galley Restaurant and Lounge** (3365 Fisherman Bay Rd., 360/468-2713, www.rockisland.com/~galley) has a pool table and live music on an irregular basis.

EVENTS

Held the last Saturday of April, the **Tour de Lopez** is a non-competitive 10-mile or 26-mile ride around the island, with a big community barbecue lunch afterwards. This is a great family event. The big event in Lopez Village comes, not surprisingly, on the **4th of July,** with a corny parade, fun run, salmon barbecue, live music, arts fair, library book sale, and a big display of fireworks over Fisherman Bay (said to be the largest private fireworks display in Washington). An **Artists' Studio Tour** (360/468-2157, www.sanjuanartistcommunity.com) takes place on Labor Day weekend, with 15 or so artists participating.

You can also join in the fun at the annual **Harvest Festival** at Lopez Island Vineyards & Winery (360/468-3644, www.lopezislandvineyards.com) in early October. It's a combination party and community grape harvest.

SHOPPING

Note that many Lopez businesses are closed Mondays (and some also on Tuesdays) in the summer and aren't open in the winter. Don't miss **Chimera Gallery** (Lopez Village Plaza, 360/468-3265, www.chimeragallery.com), a cooperatively run gallery with unusual blown-glass pieces, etchings, ceramics, watercolors, pottery,

sweaters, cedar baskets, and jewelry. Also of interest in the village is **Gallery 10 Fine Art** (265 Lopez Rd., 360/468-4910, www.gallery-10.com), offering works from local artists and a little boutique for clothing and accessories.

Also in Lopez Village is **Fish Bay Mercantile** (360/468-2811, www.fishbaymercantile.com), a whimsical shop next to Holly B's filled with all sorts of objets d'art, decorative gifts, and other "cool Lopez stuff."

Lopez's most ostentatious artist space is **Wren Studios** (352 Lopez Rd., 360/468-3368, www.leonardwren.com), where Leonard Wren creates impressionist paintings of the Pacific Northwest. His reproductions are displayed at more than 350 galleries in the United States. The studio is worth a visit even if the paintings aren't to your taste, but hours are sporadic. Outside is Wren's classic '37 Ford.

Get books and cards from cozy **Islehaven Books** (Lopez Village, 360/468-2132). Owner Phyllis Potter is a great source not only for book recommendations, but also for information on the island. You're likely to meet one of her borzoi (Russian wolfhound) assistants, who rotate duty at the shop.

Information and Services

Get local information at the **Lopez Island Chamber of Commerce** (16A Old Post Rd., 360/468-4664, www.lopezisland.com) across from Bay Café. The office is open Memorial Day–Labor Day 11 A.M.–3 P.M. Wednesday–Saturday, with reduced hours the rest of the year. Be sure to pick up the free *Map and Guide of Lopez Island* here or at the museum. In addition to the chamber's website, another useful Web source for local info is www.lopezisland.net.

Quaint **Lopez Island Library** (Fisherman Bay and Hummel Lake Rds., 360/468-2265, www.lopezlibrary.org) is close to Lopez Village. The library gets more usage per capita than any other in Washington. Hours are 10 A.M.– 6 P.M. Tuesday, Thursday, and Friday, 10 A.M.–9 P.M. Wednesday, and 10 A.M.–5 P.M. Monday and Saturday. Use the computers here to check your email.

Lopez does not have a movie theater.

KIDS STUFF

Activities for kids are mostly do-it-yourself on Lopez, though they will certainly appreciate the downtown ice cream shop. Lopez Elementary School has a **playground,** and **Lopez Children's Center** (160 Village Rd., 360/468-3896) provides day care on a space-available basis in a wonderful setting. The island's beaches, bike routes, and wooded trails provide popular family activities.

BANKING AND MAIL

Get cash from ATMs at **Islanders Bank** (45 Weeks Rd., 360/468-2295, www.islandersbank.com) or **Village Market** (Lopez Village, 360/468-2266, www.lopezvillagemarket.com). Take care of your mailing needs at the **Lopez**

Post Office (Weeks Rd., 360/468-2282) in Lopez Village.

MEDICAL CARE

Call 911 on a regular phone for medical emergencies or fires; on a cell phone, dial 360/378-4141. **Lopez Island Medical Clinic** in Lopez Village (157 Village Rd., 360/468-2245) has a physician or nurse practitioner on duty, along with a lab and x-ray services. The clinic is open for primary care and emergencies Monday–Friday. The closest hospital is in Anacortes.

Fill your prescriptions at **Lopez Island Pharmacy** next door to the clinic (360/468-2616, www.lopezislandpharmacy.com).

LAUNDRY AND SHOWERS

Wash clothes at the self-service **Keep It Clean Laundry** (864 Fisherman Bay Rd., 360/468-3466), a mile north of Lopez Village; it's open daily. **Showers** are available at the public restrooms near Lopez Village Market and the marinas on Fisherman Bay.

Transportation

WASHINGTON STATE FERRIES

Washington State Ferries (360/468-4095 for the Lopez ferry terminal; 206/464-6400 for general info, or 888/808-7977 in Washington and British Columbia only) dock at the north end of Lopez Island at Upright Head, about four miles from Lopez Village. Find all the details—including current ferry wait times—on their website: www.wsdot.wa.gov/ferries. Tickets are needed if you're heading west from Lopez to Shaw, Orcas, or San Juan Islands, but not for travel east to Anacortes (even with a vehicle). Peak-season weekend fares from Anacortes to Lopez are $11.40 for passengers and walk-ons, or $31.25 for a car and driver. Bikes are $4 extra, and kayaks cost $16.70 more. The fare for a car and driver to any of the other islands is

$15.75; walk-ons and passengers ride free between the islands. Reservations are not available for any of these runs, so you'll need to get in line and wait.

If you're on Lopez and want to take a look around Orcas before continuing to Friday Harbor (or want a quick stop on Shaw before continuing to Orcas), be sure to request a free vehicle transfer. These are good for 24 hours, and getting one saves you $15.75 for each stop, but you must ask for it on your departure island.

PRIVATE FERRY

The **San Juan Island Commuter** (360/734-8180 or 888/734-8180, www.islandcommuter.com) departs Bellingham daily in the summer for Friday Harbor. Upon request, the passenger ferry

LOPEZ ISLAND MILEAGE

	Ferry Landing	Spencer Spit State Park	Lopez Village	Agate Beach	Islandale Store
Spencer Spit State Park	3				
Lopez Village	4	4			
Agate Beach	15	10	11		
Islandale Store	14	15	12	7	
Shark Reef	9	19	6	5	5

© DON PITCHER

The state ferry docks at Upright Head on the north end of Lopez Island.

will stop at Odlin County Park on Lopez for $39 rt ($20 kids). Kayaks ($20) and bikes ($5) can also be transported.

AIR SERVICE

Floatplanes
Operating out of Seattle's Lake Union, **Kenmore Air** (425/486-1257 or 800/543-9595, www.kenmoreair.com) has daily scheduled floatplane flights to the Lopez Islander Resort Marina. A 24-pound baggage weight limit is in effect on these flights, and excess baggage costs $1/pound.

Wheeled-Plane Flights
San Juan Airlines (360/293-4691 or 800/874-4434, www.sanjuanairlines.com), has scheduled daily service to Lopez Airport from Seattle, Anacortes, and Bellingham. Flightseeing and air charters are also available.

TAXIS AND HITCHING
There is no bus service or car rentals on Lopez, but **A Lopez Cab Courier** (360/468-2227) has taxi service and can carry bikes if you need a sag wagon.

Hitchhiking is not uncommon on Lopez Island, but you might end up in the back of a pickup atop a load of hay. It's relatively easy to get a ride from the ferry to Lopez Village if a ferry is off-loading.

Lopez Island

Other San Juan Islands

In addition to the three main islands, the San Juan archipelago contains a myriad of smaller ones, including some islets that only appear at low tide. Shaw Island is served by the ferry system but has limited services. Lummi Island is just a short distance from the mainland, and is served by an hourly ferry. Of the remaining islands, only Blakely and Decatur Islands have stores. The rest are either marine state parks, part of the San Juan Islands National Wildlife Refuge, or dominated by private property.

This chapter begins with coverage of Shaw and Lummi Islands, and then shifts to descriptions of the various marine state parks and private islands. Even though these islands are not widely known outside the region, many still see large numbers of boat-in visitors, especially on summer weekends. This is particularly true for the marine state parks on Clark, James, Jones, Matia, Patos, Stuart, Sucia, and Turn Islands, where the campsites fill quickly and protected coves are dotted with motor yachts and sailboats. (See *Hiking and Birding* in the *Orcas Island* chapter for information on Point Doughty Marine State Park and *Camgrounds* in the *San Juan Island* chapter for information about Griffin Bay Marine State Park.)

Must-Sees

Look for **M** to find the sights and activities you can't miss and **N** for the best dining and lodging.

M Cedar Rock Biological Preserve: Owned by the University of Washington, this little-known gem is located on the south side of Shaw Island (page 191).

M Jones Island Marine State Park: A quick water-taxi ride from Orcas Island, this easily accessible marine park has fun hikes and semi-tame deer (page 199).

M Stuart Island: Take a water taxi from Friday Harbor to this island, where you can hike to one of the most picturesque lighthouses in the San Juans (page 203).

M Sucia Island Marine State Park: An exceptionally popular marine park, this diverse island is a favorite of kayakers, sail boaters, campers, and hikers (page 205).

M Yellow Island: The Nature Conservancy allows daytime access to this 10-acre jewel, where more than 150 species of flowers bloom each spring (page 212).

© DON PITCHER

Cedar Rock Biological Preserve

Sucia Island Marine State Park

Stuart Island

Jones Island Marine State Park

Yellow Island

Cedar Rock Biological Preserve

Padilla

Bay

San Juan Channel

Rosario Strait

USA

CANADA

OTHER SAN JUAN ISLANDS

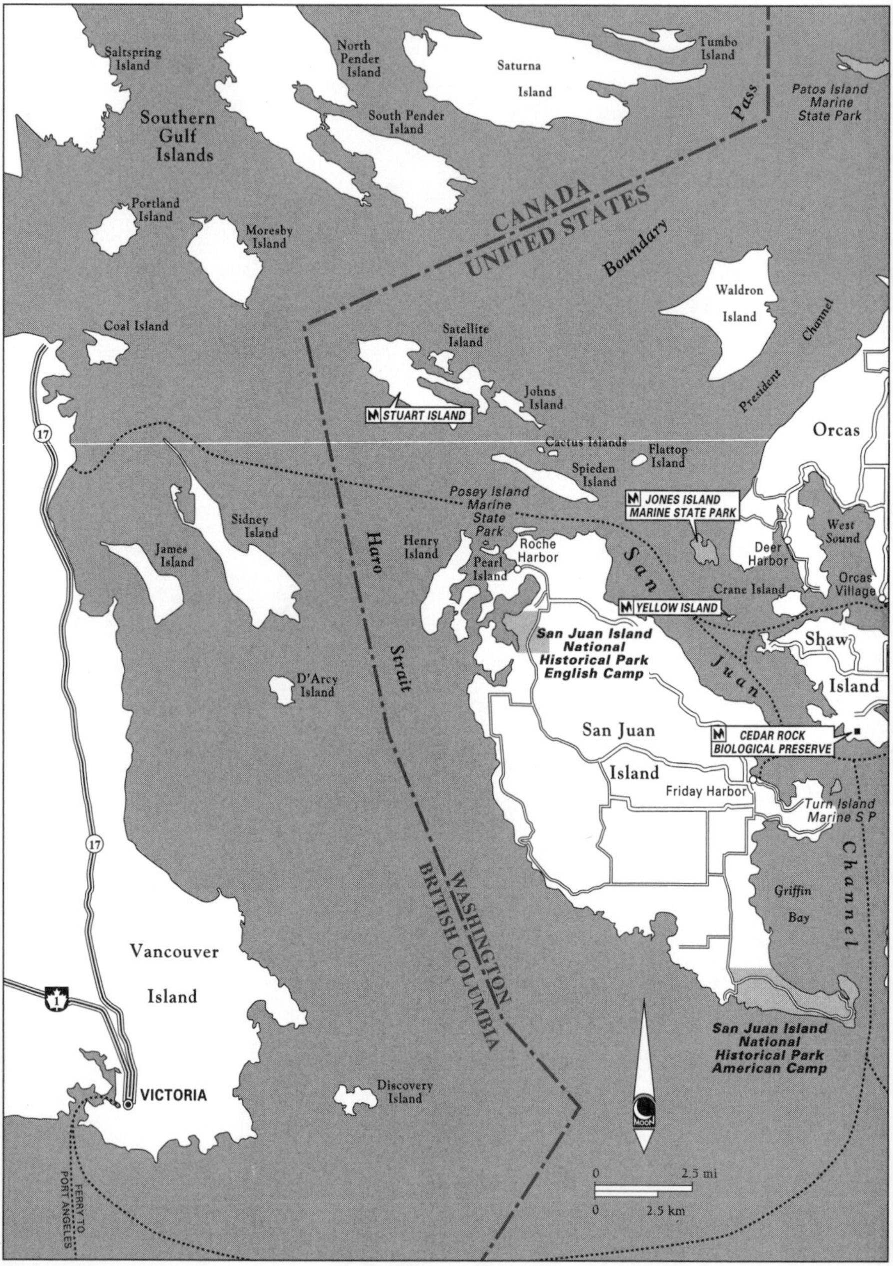
Saltspring Island
North Pender Island
Saturna Island
Tumbo Island
Patos Island Marine State Park
Southern Gulf Islands
South Pender Island
Pass
CANADA
UNITED STATES
Boundary
Portland Island
Moresby Island
Waldron Island
President Channel
Coal Island
Satellite Island
Johns Island
STUART ISLAND
17
Orcas
Cactus Islands
Flattop Island
Spieden Island
Posey Island Marine State Park
JONES ISLAND MARINE STATE PARK
Sidney Island
James Island
Henry Island
Haro Strait
Roche Harbor
Pearl Island
San Juan
Deer Harbor
West Sound
Crane Island
Orcas Village
YELLOW ISLAND
Shaw Island
San Juan Island National Historical Park English Camp
D'Arcy Island
San Juan Island
CEDAR ROCK BIOLOGICAL PRESERVE
Friday Harbor
Turn Island Marine S P
Channel
Griffin Bay
WASHINGTON
BRITISH COLUMBIA
Vancouver Island
1
San Juan Island National Historical Park American Camp
VICTORIA
Discovery Island
MOON
FERRY TO PORT ANGELES
0
2.5 mi
0
2.5 km

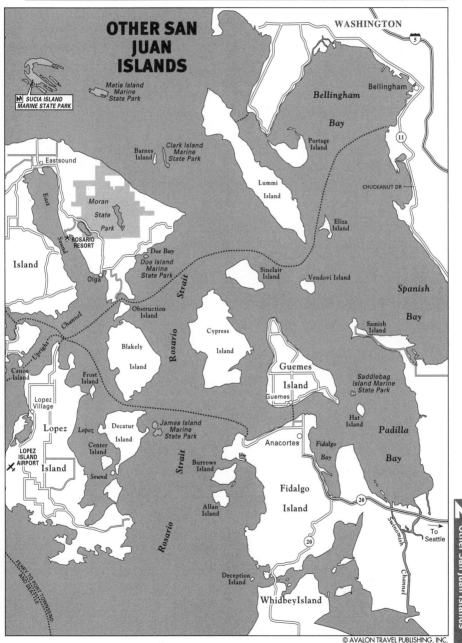

OTHER SAN JUAN ISLANDS

WASHINGTON

5

SUCIA ISLAND
MARINE STATE PARK

Matia Island
Marine
State Park

Bellingham

Bellingham
Bay

11

Eastsound

Barnes
Island

Clark Island
Marine
State Park

Portage
Island

CHUCKANUT DR

Lummi

Island

Moran

State

Park

East

Sound

Eliza
Island

ROSARIO
RESORT

Doe Bay

Doe Island
Marine
State Park

Sinclair
Island

Vendovi Island

Spanish

Island

Olga

Bay

Obstruction
Island

Rosario

Strait

Samish
Island

Cypress

Upright

Channel

Blakely

Island

Island

Saddlebag
Island Marine
State Park

Canoe
Island

Frost
Island

Guemes

Island

Lopez
Village

Guemes

Hat
Island

Padilla

Lopez

Lopez

Decatur

Island

James Island
Marine
State Park

Anacortes

Fidalgo

LOPEZ
ISLAND
AIRPORT

Center
Island

Island

Bay

Bay

Island

Burrows
Island

Sound

Fidalgo

20

Rosario

Strait

Allan
Island

Island

20

To
Seattle

Samish

Channel

FERRY TO PORT TOWNSEND
AND SEATTLE

Deception
Island

WhidbeyIsland

N

Other San Juan Islands

© AVALON TRAVEL PUBLISHING, INC.

National Wildlife Refuge

The San Juan Islands National Wildlife Refuge encompasses 84 islands, islets, and reefs within the archipelago. The largest, Matia Island, covers 145 acres, while many more are just tiny rocky points. These islands are vital nesting areas for bald eagles and seabirds, including pelagic and double-crested cormorants, pigeon guillemots, rhinoceros auklets, black oystercatchers, and glaucous-winged gulls. Tufted puffins are also present in these waters, but they only breed on one undisclosed island in the San Juans. The NWR islands are also used as haul-outs for harbor seals, California and Steller sea lions, elephant seals, and other animals.

Boaters—including sea kayakers—must stay at least 200 yards offshore from these islands, and no landings are permitted except at designated areas on Turn and Matia Islands. The U.S. Fish & Wildlife Service office (Port Angeles, 360/457-8451, http://pacific.fws.gov) manages the refuge and can provide a small map of the islands. Marine navigation charts also denote islands within the refuge.

PLANNING YOUR TIME

Most travelers to the San Juans don't get beyond the three main islands: San Juan, Orcas, and Lopez, but the lesser-known islands also have much to offer, especially for those who love wild places. These less-visited islands are scattered across the archipelago, and include a mix of public and private lands.

Best-known of these "other islands"—and the only one visited by the state ferry system—is **Shaw Island,** home to a little country store,
many well-heeled land owners, and a couple of natural areas: **Cedar Rock Biological Preserve,** with day use only, and Shaw Island County Park, with a handful of campsites.

Lummi Island is just west of Bellingham, with access via a county-run ferry. The island has very little public land, but lodging and cafés are available.

Quite a few of the more remote islands in the San Juans are marine state parks. They are popular with boaters, kayakers, campers, and day hikers, and are accessible by water taxi from the main islands, Anacortes, or Bellingham. **Jones Island Marine State Park** is a short boat ride from Deer Harbor on Orcas Island, and features good mooring, camping, and easy hikes. **Stuart Island** lies northwest of San Juan Island. Much of the island is privately owned, but the main harbors are public, and a pleasant day hike takes you to a lighthouse overlooking Boundary Pass. **Sucia Island Marine State Park** is north of Orcas Island, with wonderful protected coves, miles of hiking and biking trails, good campsites, and a couple of sandy beaches. It's an especially popular place for sailboats to drop anchor.

A scattering of islands in the San Juans are privately owned, or with only limited public access. Two of the islands (Canoe and Johns Island) have summer camps open to the public, and two others (Blakely and Decatur) have general stores and limited access or lodging. Sinclair Island has a boat dock and dirt roads leading to a 35-acre public park. The Nature Conservancy owns several San Juan Islands, the best-known being tiny **Yellow Island,** a short water taxi from Friday Harbor. It's famous for springtime floral displays and is open to the public during the day.

Shaw Island

The smallest and least visited of the ferry-served islands, Shaw is a primarily residential island where locals jealously guard their privacy. Around 200 people live here year-round, with two or three times that in the summer. The island covers a bit less than eight square miles, making it the fifth largest of the San Juans (after Orcas, San Juan, Lopez, and Cypress). It sits at the center of the San Juan archipelago, with the Orcas ferry landing just a mile and a half away from the Shaw ferry dock. A number of well-known and wealthy business leaders have homes on the island, including Bill Gates Sr., members of the Kaiser family, and executives from Boeing and the *Seattle Times*. Bill Gates Jr. (www.microsoft .com/billgates), also owns a sizable chunk of land on Shaw.

HISTORY

Shaw Island received its appellation during the 1841 Wilkes Expedition, and was named for U.S. naval captain John Shaw, who fought against the Barbary pirate states in 1815. The island was home to the Coast Salish people for thousands of years; one archaeological site at Blind Bay is 9,000 years old. The island supported far more people than now live here, with almost 750 Native Americans living here in the 1700s. Many of them died from diseases brought by Europeans or from raids by the Haidas, but some remained on the island. A few Salish women married American settlers.

ISLAND LIFE

Shaw Island remains essentially undeveloped, with second-growth forests, old orchards, and pastures covering most of the land. Prominently posted No Trespassing signs limit access to all but a few beaches. To outsiders, Shaw Islanders appear insular (guess that shouldn't be surprising, given their location) and anxious to keep the rest of the world—and you in particular—away. Too bad they couldn't take a few lessons from their friendly Lopez Island neighbors! But

© DON PITCHER

Shaw Island

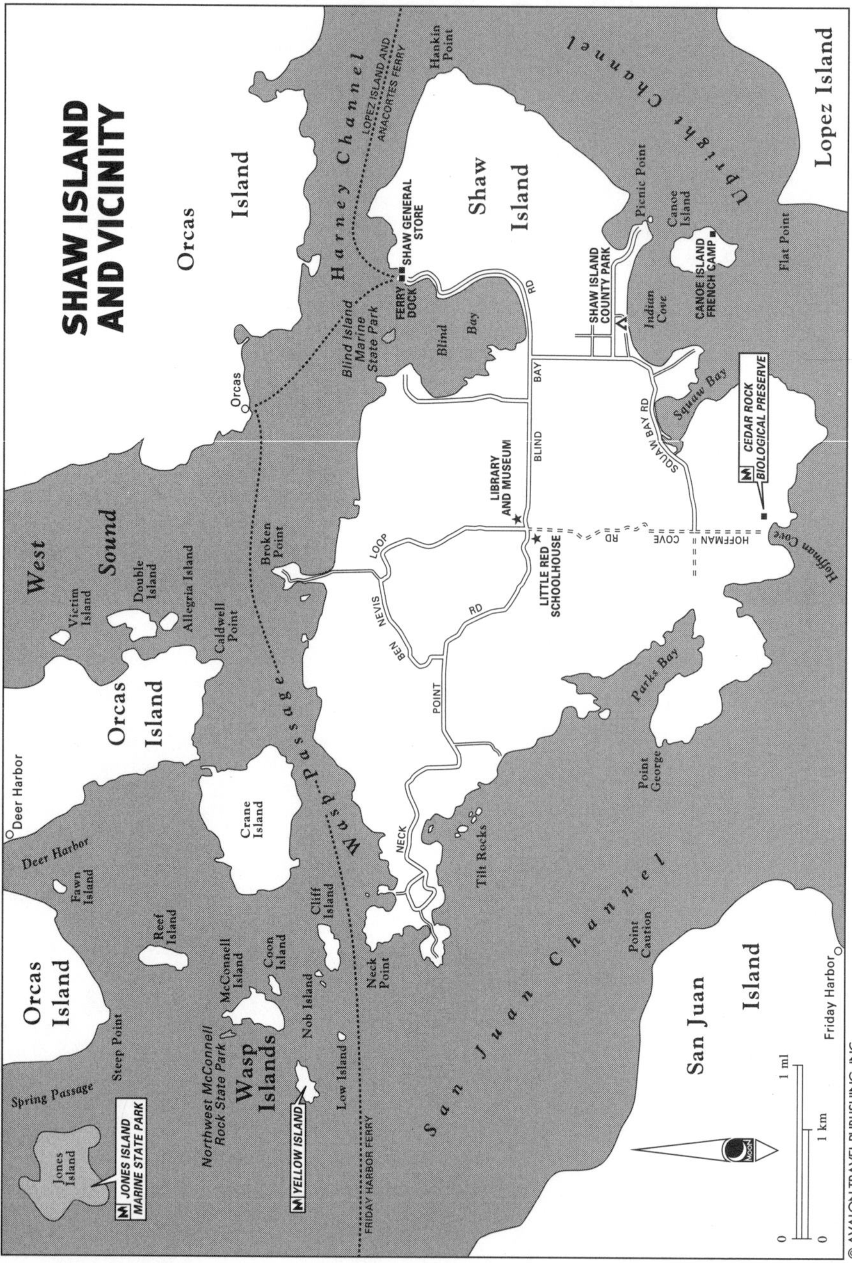

SHAW ISLAND AND VICINITY

Orcas Island

West Sound

Orcas Island

Deer Harbor

Deer Harbor

Spring Passage

Steep Point

Orcas Island

JONES ISLAND MARINE STATE PARK

Jones Island

Wasp Islands

Northwest McConnell Rock State Park

McConnell Island

Coon Island

Nob Island

Low Island

YELLOW ISLAND

FRIDAY HARBOR FERRY

Fawn Island

Reef Island

Cliff Island

Neck Point

Wasp Passage

Crane Island

Victim Island

Double Island

Allegria Island

Caldwell Point

Broken Point

Blind Island Marine State Park

FERRY DOCK

SHAW GENERAL STORE

Orcas

Harney Channel

LOPEZ ISLAND AND ANACORTES FERRY

Hankin Point

Shaw Island

Blind Bay

BAY RD

LIBRARY AND MUSEUM

LITTLE RED SCHOOLHOUSE

LOOP RD

BEN NEVIS RD

POINT RD

NECK RD

BLIND COVE RD

HOFFMAN COVE

Hoffman Cove

SQUAW BAY RD

SHAW ISLAND COUNTY PARK

Indian Cove

Squaw Bay

CEDAR ROCK BIOLOGICAL PRESERVE

Picnic Point

Canoe Island

CANOE ISLAND FRENCH CAMP

Flat Point

Upright Channel

Lopez Island

Parks Bay

Point George

Tilt Rocks

Point Caution

San Juan Channel

San Juan Island

Friday Harbor

1 mi

1 km

© AVALON TRAVEL PUBLISHING, INC.

Shaw Islanders really don't care what the rest of the world does. They relish their peaceful and slow-paced life, the lush landscape, and a grade school where the student-to-teacher ratio is 1:6. The island has a general store, a little post office, and two private airstrips, but no medical facility.

Only one commercial business is headquartered on Shaw Island, **Northwest Marine Technology** (www.nmt.com), the manufacturer of fish tags used all over the world. The tags themselves are made elsewhere.

There are no bed-and-breakfasts, bike rental shops, kayak companies, or galleries on Shaw, and none are likely to appear. When kayakers started launching from a dock next to the ferry landing, Shaw Islanders purchased the land and posted signs to keep commercial kayak companies away. Sky-high land prices, minimal turnover, and locals who snatch up whatever comes on the market make it virtually impossible to buy property or a house here.

Independence Day on July 4th brings a little parade that features a children's kazoo band, lawnmower drill team, auction, and potluck dinner. In early August, the **Row Around Shaw** hosts rowboats, kayakers, and canoeists in a fun race around the island. You can learn a bit more about life on Shaw at the **Shaw Island Association** website (www.shawislanders.org).

SIGHTS AND RECREATION

General Store

"Downtown" Shaw consists of the ferry dock, the Shaw General Store (360/468-2288), and a couple of adjacent buildings. For almost three decades, the island's claim to fame was the Franciscan Catholic nuns who operated the ferry dock and store. They left in 2004 when the nuns grew too old to continue their work. Today, the store and adjacent ferry terminal are run by friendly Steve and Terri Mason, along with their four kids. Step inside the store for basic supplies, local produce, ice cream, and espresso, or next door for gifts, light meals, and pizzas (whole or by the slice); they'll even deliver to boats in nearby Blind Bay. The store is open daily in the summer;

closed Sundays in the off-season. You'll find restrooms, a pay phone, and gas pump out front, and the little marina has a couple of slots for guest mooring.

Monastery

The store still sells Mother Prisca's Hot Mustard, herbal vinegars, teas, and spices made by a Catholic order called **Our Lady of the Rock Monastery** (360/468-2321, www.rockisland.com/~mhildegard). Founded in 1977, the monastery is home to eight Benedictine nuns who live on an immaculate 300-acre spread of forests and farmland. The nuns are sometimes called the "spinning nuns," and you might see them spinning and weaving hand-dyed yarn on the ferry to Shaw. Guest mistress Mother Hildegard George has a Ph.D. in child and adolescent psychology and is a leader in the field of animal-assisted therapy. The priory raises long-haired Scottish Highlands cattle, black Cotswold sheep, llamas, alpacas, and a menagerie of pigs, turkeys, chickens, geese, ducks, peacocks, and other critters—all of which have names. The farm's raw milk is sold to folks on Shaw and Orcas, but is not available in the store. Tours of Our Lady of the Rock are available, but call ahead. The order also has a small guesthouse for religious retreats.

Shaw Island Historical Museum

This tiny museum (Blind Bay and Hoffman Cove Rds., 360/468-4068) is housed in a log cabin (two miles from the ferry landing). Inside you will find historical photos and various farming and fishing implements, along with arrowheads and other Coast Salish artifacts. Out front is a reefnet fishing boat like those still used to fish for salmon in nearby waters. The museum is open 2–4 p.m. Tuesday, 11 a.m.–1 p.m. Thursday, and 11 a.m.–noon and 2–4 p.m. Saturday. Next door is **Shaw Island Library** (360/468-4068); same hours.

Little Red Schoolhouse

Across the intersection from the museum and library is a red one-room grade school that is now on the National Register of Historic Places. It's still in use today, with 20 or so students in

REEFNET FISHING

When we went out there and put in those reef nets, we caught fish right off starting the first day and the white fishermen never had one to eat. They didn't know how to catch them. They didn't know how to use a reef net. Every night when we'd go home, you could go down and sit on the beach and see them out there measuring our reef net and copying it.

Herman Olsen, quoted in *Lummi Elders Speak*, edited by Ann Nugent

This unique and ingenious way to catch salmon originated with the Coast Salish people around the San Juans. Today, fewer than a dozen commercial reefnet operations remain in Washington, all run by non–Native Americans. Each summer, salmon return from the Pacific Ocean to spawn in British Columbia's Fraser River. Their migration takes them past the San Juan Islands, where reefnet fishermen work from a pair of small scows with a net strung between them. (The Salish originally used large dugout canoes for this purpose.) Salmon are directed into the net through an artificial reef covered with plastic ribbons that simulate reef grasses. The open end of the "reef" is held on the bottom by heavy concrete anchors, and at the back is a 50-foot-long windsock-shaped net.

Each boat has a tall ladder that allows spotters to see salmon as they enter the net and to alert crewmembers below to close the net. Timing is tricky, and precautions must be taken to keep from spooking the salmon. Within 15–30 seconds the net is winched up, pulling the boats together and forcing the fish into a pocket. The fish are lifted onboard and dumped into a water-filled tank called a live box. They remain in the tank until sold to a fish buyer, who selects the salmon he wants and immediately puts them on ice. Everything else in the live box is released back into the sea. Reefnet fishing results in the highest-quality fish, since the netted salmon stay alive longer and are kept in much better condition than those caught using other fishing methods. In addition, there is no bycatch (taking of unwanted or prohibited species of fish).

You'll see reefnet boats anchored or in use at a couple of places around the San Juans. The little Shaw Island Museum has one out front, and others are often visible in Fisherman Bay on Lopez Island, in Reid Harbor on Stuart Island, and along Lummi Island's Legoe Bay. Find out more on the web at www.leoslive.com/reefnet.

reefnet fishing boat, Shaw Island Historical Museum

© DON PITCHER

© DON PITCHER

Little Red Schoolhouse

grades K–8; a second building has been added in the back with computers. Shaw's count-them-on-one-hand high-school students commute by ferry to Orcas or San Juan Islands.

Shaw Island County Park

Also known as South Beach County Park (www.co.san-juan.wa.us/parks), this 65-acre park is one of the few public spots on the Shaw shoreline. It is two miles south of the ferry landing off Squaw Bay Road, and faces Canoe Island, home to a French-language summer camp. The park is best known for its beautiful sandy beach—one of the best in the islands—where you'll sometimes find sand dollars. By midsummer, the shallow waters of Indian Cove are warm enough for a swim, and a picnic area and boat launch are available, along with outhouses.

The park includes six waterfront ($16) and five in-the-trees ($13) campsites, along with one site that is for kayakers, hikers, or cyclists willing to share ($4 per person with a maximum of 10 people; no vehicles). The park has a cooking shelter and limited drinking water, but no showers. There are no other camping or lodging options on Shaw, so reserve ahead for peak-season

weekends unless you want to catch the next ferry back to Anacortes. Call 360/378-1842 for campground reservations; a $6 fee is charged and you can reserve from five days to three months in advance. The campground is open year-round.

Cedar Rock Biological Preserve

The University of Washington's Cedar Rock Biological Preserve is a quiet off-the-beaten-path place on the south side of Shaw along Hoffman Cove. Open to the public, it covers approximately 1,000 acres with rocky shorelines and forests dominated by stately Pacific madrones and Douglas firs. Get there from the ferry by following Blind Bay Road to the schoolhouse, and turning left (south) on Hoffman Cove Road. The road ends near the water's edge at the preserve, but parking is almost nonexistent, so bikes are a better way to get here. Sign in at the entrance box and head up the path to an old field with several homestead buildings and out to a small rocky point. Stop awhile to soak up the view across San Juan Channel and to watch the ferries steaming into Friday Harbor. From here, the rough trail continues east along the shore to small coves with gravely beaches, through pristine forests with

Other San Juan Islands

© DON PITCHER

Cedar Rock Biological Preserve

periodic openings, and up rocky knolls. The route dwindles away, becoming little more than a game trail, but ambitious hikers could continue along the shore a mile and a half to Squaw Bay, where you run into private land again. Most folks turn back before this, but even a short hike at Cedar Rock offers a relaxing respite. You may want to time your hike to coincide with low tide, making it easier to walk the beaches.

More Exploring

Besides the preserve and county park, nearly all of Shaw is a look-only place. Despite this, the roads are quiet and the countryside is very scenic, making Shaw a wonderful place to explore by bicycle. You'll find old orchards, some beautiful homes, and peaceful vistas of nearby islands. From the ferry, Blind Bay Road follows the shore of this pasture-and-forest-bordered bay, with Blind Island Marine State Park in the middle. The westernmost end of Shaw Island, **Neck Point,** is especially picturesque, with the road passing over a slender peninsula where waves lap on both sides.

Kayaking, Boating, and Biking

The relatively protected waters and undeveloped shores of Shaw Island are very popular with sea kayakers. Randel Washburne's *Kayaking Puget Sound, the San Juans, and Gulf Islands* (The Mountaineers, www.mountaineers.org) has details on a 14-mile circumnavigation of Shaw Island. Unfortunately, you can't launch sea kayaks from the Shaw Island ferry landing; the closest place to do so is Shaw Island County Park, two miles away, or from Odlin County Park on Lopez Island.

The island's shoreline is also popular with sailors and motorboaters, and each August the San Juan Island Yacht Club (360/378-3434, www.sjiyc.com) sponsors a popular **Shaw Island Classic** yacht race that circles the island.

Shaw Island, with its paved roads, bucolic country, and paucity of cars, is a delight for cyclists. Unfortunately, even Shaw can get busy in midsummer, particularly when large touring groups of cyclists roll off the ferry. Because of the island's small size, some cyclists arrive in the morning, pedal around, take a lunch break, and are off to another island when it comes time to pitch their tents.

FERRIES

Washington State Ferries (360/468-2142 for Shaw ferry terminal, 206/464-6400 for general info, or 888/808-7977 in Washington and British Columbia, www.wsdot.wa.gov/ferries) ply the waters around Shaw almost constantly, en route to Anacortes, Lopez Island, Orcas Island, San Juan Island, or Vancouver Island. Quite a few of these also stop at Shaw Island's little dock. Peak-season interisland service costs $15.75 for a car and driver if you're heading west to Orcas Village or Friday Harbor; eastbound service to Lopez or Anacortes is free. There's never a charge for walk-on passengers commuting between the islands. Peak-season weekend fares from Anacortes to Shaw Island are $11.40 for passengers and walk-ons, or $37.50 for a car and driver. Bikes are $4 extra, and kayaks cost $18 more. Reservations are not available, just get in the queue and wait.

Lummi Island

Lummi (pronounced "LUM-ee," as in "tummy") is only an eight-minute ferry ride from the mainland, but since it is some distance from other islands in the San Juans, it doesn't get a lot of attention. Lummi Island lies within Whatcom County, not San Juan County, and many people do not consider it part of the archipelago. At the peanut-shaped island's southern end is a steeply wooded mountain that slopes down abruptly to more or less level land on the north end, which is where nearly all the residents live. Most of the island is private property with no public access, but you can ride the roads to a few public areas.

Lummi is a quiet island, home primarily to artists, weekenders, and a few salmon fishermen, some of whom fish with reefnets.

Lummi Reservation

The Lummi people were the first inhabitants of the island, but they abandoned it after Haidas raided their village to capture slaves. By the time the first whites arrived in the 1870s, the Lummi had moved to the mainland. Today, 600 people live in scattered homes on the 13,000-acre Lummi Reservation at Gooseberry Point, where the ferry departs for the island.

ACCOMMODATIONS

Lummi Island has a church, school, library, grocery store, espresso joint, post office, and community hall, along with a couple of nice bed-and-breakfasts and one of the best restaurants in the region.

On the west side of the island, **The Willows Inn B&B** (2579 W. Shore Dr., 360/758-2620 or 888/294-2620, www.willows-inn.com) has five rooms in the inn ($125–140 d), a honeymoon cottage ($155 d), and a guest house ($290 for up to six people). All include a fine three-course breakfast, private baths, and an outdoor Jacuzzi. The honeymoon cottage provides additional privacy and a magnificent view of the San Juans, plus a jetted tub.

West Shore Farm B&B (2781 West Shore Dr., 360/758-2600) offers accommodations in a handcrafted octagonal home. The 21-acre spread features sweeping Georgia Strait views and private beach access. The two guest rooms have king-size beds and private baths, and cost $90 d, including a full breakfast. The owners are very friendly, and kids are welcome.

Cottage by the Sea (3869 Legoe Bay Rd., 360/758-7144) is a two-bedroom cottage with a kitchen and Jacuzzi bath; $150 d plus $15/person (maximum of six).

Campgrounds

The **Washington Department of Natural Resources** (360/856-3500, www.dnr.wa.gov) maintains a free kayak-accessible campground near the south end of the island. This delightful spot is the only camping place on Lummi Island.

ARTS AND EVENTS

Good Thunder Arts (2307 Tuttle Ln., 360/758-7121) has handcrafted pottery, sculptures, and other artwork.

The **Lummi Stommish Water Festival** in mid-June is held on the Lummi Reservation and features competitive war-canoe races over a five-mile course, with up to 11 people in a canoe. Other activities include arts and crafts sales, Native American dancing, and a salmon bake. For details, call the tribal office at 360/384-1489.

Local artists offer studio tours on Memorial Day and Labor Day weekends, and the first weekend of December; call 360/758-7121.

Get additional Lummi Island info on the Web at www.lummi-island.com.

FOOD

The owners of Willows Inn—Riley Starks and Judy Olsen—also run an organic farm (www.nettlesfarm.com) with seasonal produce, eggs, chicken, fresh pastas, and even reefnet-caught salmon. You can savor some of this and other local fare upstairs at **Willows Inn Supper Club** (2579 W. Shore Dr., 360/758-2620 or

888/294-2620, www.willows-inn.com), a fine dining restaurant open for dinner Thursday–Sunday, plus Sunday brunch. The menu changes weekly, but always includes vegetarian entrées, organic Kobe beef, and homemade ravioli. Be sure to ask about their fresh spot prawns, served on the deck. Downstairs at Willows Inn is a little coffeehouse/pub that's open all day with pot pies, quiche, soup, and sandwiches.

Just south of the ferry dock, the **Islander Store** (360/758-2190) sells beer, soda pop, ice cream, and other necessities of life; it's open daily. North of the dock is **Beachstore Café** (360/758-2233), a casual bistro with an award-winning seafood chowder, pizzas, burritos, salads, beer on tap, fresh baked breads, and pastries. Same owners as Willows Inn, so you know the food is good. Closed Monday and Tuesday.

TRANSPORTATION

From I-5, go west on Slater Road to Haxton Way on the Lummi Reservation and follow it to the **ferry landing.** The county-owned ferry (360/676-6692) makes eight-minute trips back and forth from Gooseberry Point on the mainland to Lummi Island every hour on the hour from 7 a.m. to midnight (more frequently during the commute period). Round-trip cost is $4 for car with driver, $1 for passengers, $1 for bikes, and free for kids.

Because Lummi is nearly all in private hands, access is quite limited. You can ride bikes or cars on the island's roads, but the undeveloped mountainous southern end of the island is off-limits. The only readily accessible public beach is just north of the ferry dock.

Marine State Parks

A number of the smaller islands in the San Juan archipelago are preserved as marine state parks and are largely undeveloped. The parks are very popular with boaters and sea kayakers looking for a summertime island escape. In addition to these, The Nature Conservancy's Yellow Island is also open to the public. The **San Juan Islands National Wildlife Refuge** is made up of 84 islands, almost all off-limits. Be sure to avoid these refuge islands, as they provide vital breeding and resting areas for birds and marine mammals. Boaters—including kayakers—must stay at least 200 yards away.

Off-Limits Parks

Several small island state marine parks are closed to the public to protect them from being damaged. Three of these undeveloped parks are offshore from Orcas Island: **Freeman Island State Park** near Point Doughty, **Skull Island Marine State Park** at the head of Massacre Bay, and **Victim Island Marine State Park** in West Sound. Another closed area, **Iceberg Island State Marine Park,** sits near the southwest end of Lopez Island.

CAMPGROUNDS AND MOORINGS

Most marine state parks have primitive campsites for $10 a night, available on a first-come basis. At the most popular parks—Clark, James, Jones, Matia, Patos, Stuart, Sucia, and Turn Islands—campsites often fill on weekends between mid-July and mid-August or over summer holiday weekends. There's generally space midweek.

Kayakers will find Cascadia Marine Trail sites on Blind, Cypress, James, Jones, Posey, Strawberry, and Stuart Island. These sites are generally shared if more than one group arrives. Park rangers try to prevent overcrowding, but won't make folks move off-island if the sea conditions are unsafe. Campsite reservations are only available for group sites on Clark, Jones, and Sucia Islands.

Most of these marine parks contain relatively protected coves with mooring buoys ($10 a night). Other attractions include hiking trails and picnic tables, while some islands also have drinking water, docks, or floats. Most islands have outhouses, but you'll need to haul out any garbage. Pets are allowed in the marine parks, but must be on a leash at all times.

SEA KAYAKING

Quite a few companies lead sea-kayaking trips of varying lengths to the marine state parks. The San Juan Island chapter has details on a half-dozen companies, including: **Outdoor Odysseys** (360/378-3533 or 800/647-4621, www.outdoorodysseys.com), **Sea Quest Expeditions** (360/378-5767 or 888/589-4253, www.sea-quest-kayak.com), and **San Juan Kayak Expeditions** (360/378-4436, www.sanjuankayak.com). Orcas Island–based kayak companies are **Shearwater Adventures** (360/376-4699, www.shearwaterkayaks.com), and **Osprey Tours** (360/376-3677 or 800/529-2567, www.ospreytours.com). **Elakah Expeditions** (360/734-7270 or 800/434-7270, www.elakah.com) operates from Lopez Island, **Island Outfitters** (360/299-2300 or 866/445-7506, www.seakayakshop.com) is based in Anacortes, and **Moondance Sea Kayaking Adventures** (360/738-7664, www.moondancekayak.com) leads sea-kayak tours from Bellingham.

Sea kayaks are a popular island-hopping mode of transportation, but since some of the smaller islands are several miles out, be careful not to overestimate your ability. If you're planning a kayak trip to the islands, get a copy of Randel Washburne's *Kayaking Puget Sound, the San Juans, and Gulf Islands* (The Mountaineers, www.mountaineers.org). It contains information on destinations, safety, difficulty ratings, and launching points.

MOUNTAIN BIKING

Mountain bikes are allowed year-round on all marine state park trails, but cyclists need to avoid conflicts with other users. This means staying on trails, looking out for others, and riding slowly around camping areas. Bikes aren't allowed on piers, ramps, or floats. Local water taxis will transport bikes, and bike rentals are available from the three main islands: Orcas, Lopez, and San Juan.

INFORMATION

For additional information on the marine parks, call 360/376-2073, or visit the state park website, www.parks.wa.gov. Another useful online source for the San Juan Islands marine parks is www.sjmp.org, maintained by the Friends of San Juan Marine Parks.

See Ken Wilcox's helpful *Hiking the San Juan Islands* (Northwest Wild Books) for details on marine state park hiking trails.

Boaters heading out on their own to these smaller islands will want to pick up one of the cruising guides to the islands.

Gunkholing the San Juans by Jo Bailey and Carl Nyberg (San Juan Enterprises) is packed with details on all the islands in the archipelago, and is interesting even if you don't have a boat or kayak. On the Web, visit *Northwest Boating's* homepage, www.nwboating.com, for brief island descriptions.

TRANSPORTATION

The state ferry does not stop on any of the marine state parks, and access is limited to water taxi, airplane, private boat, or sea kayak.

Water Taxis

A number of companies provide water taxi service to the more remote islands. Most operate seasonally, but **Paraclete Charters** (360/293-5920 or 800/808-2999, www.paracletecharters.com) provides year-round service. In business since 1992, the company runs three boats (the largest can carry 64 passengers) from Anacortes to anywhere in the San Juans. They serve homeowners on islands not on the ferry system, along with other folks wanting to reach the islands. Prices depend on your destination and number of people, but you don't need to charter an entire boat, and they have room for kayaks, bikes, and pets. As an example, Anacortes to Clark Island costs $53 for one person each way, or $32 per person for five folks. Add $5 each way for bikes, or $10 for kayaks.

Based at Cap Sante Marina in Anacortes, **Island Express Charters** (360/299-2875 or 877/473-9777, www.islandexpresscharters.com) has a high speed landing craft with space for kayaks, bikes, and gear. Rates depend upon the number of passengers; $240 round-trip for two people. Add $12 round-trip for bikes or $20 for kayaks.

KING OF THE SMUGGLERS

Smuggling along the United States–Canadian border has always been a fact of life, and the items transported back and forth have always been the same: liquor (particularly during the United States's foray into prohibition), illegal drugs, illegal Chinese immigrants, and even Canadian wool and silks.

An Irishman named Larry Kelly was the most infamous of all the smugglers, though perhaps not the most successful at staying away from the law. Kelly arrived in America simply by jumping ship in New Orleans. He fought in the Civil War on the Confederate side. Not long after the war, he arrived in Seattle. He had heard about the "hole in the fence," meaning the easy smuggling across the Canadian border—especially through Puget Sound—of liquor, opium, and Chinese laborers.

Kelly bought an old sailboat in 1872 and sailed north to Guemes Island, where he set up shop. He learned it was easy to hide from the revenue cutters because they ran on a set schedule. Kelly made a nice profit smuggling opium, which he bought at $15 a pound from factories in Victoria and sold for three times that in Seattle.

The opium was packed in watertight tin cans, and to each can Kelly tied a chunk of salt as a sinker in case he was caught. After the salt dis-solved, the can would float to the surface so Kelly could go back out and retrieve it. Kelly charged about $50 for smuggling a Chinese laborer out of Canada into the United States. Although he denied ever killing one, other smugglers weren't averse to chaining a boatload of immigrants together and dumping them overboard to drown if a revenue cutter approached. It is likely he did do some of the things common among his fellow smugglers, such as putting laborers down on a beach in British Columbia and telling them they were in America.

Kelly was caught in 1882 with 40 cases of Canadian whiskey, and fined. He wasn't caught again for another four years, but that time he had 567 tins of opium. For this he was sent to McNeil Island Federal Penitentiary. In 1891 he was caught for the final time, on a train with opium in his traveling bag. He was put away again, and while in prison decided to change his life. He wrote to the Louisiana Chapter of the Daughters of the Confederacy to see if any of his old friends from the Civil War were still alive. He found some in a Confederate old soldiers' home in New Orleans, and it was there he went on his release from prison, never to smuggle again.

At least, he was never caught at it.

Based at Deer Harbor on Orcas Island, **North Shore Charters** (360/376-4855, www.sanjuancruises.net) offers day trips and drop-offs to state marine parks on Stuart, Matia, Patos, Sucia or other islands. The 26-foot boat costs $135/hour, and can hold six people plus kayaks or bikes. Owner Marty Mead is an experienced captain with years of experience in local and Alaskan waters.

Located at Deer Harbor Marina, **Orcas Boat Rentals** (360/376-7616, www.orcasboats.com) provides a quick ride to Jones Island, Yellow Island, and the Wasp group of islands. Owner Marc Broman can haul up to six folks on his 17-foot Boston Whaler.

Based in Bellingham, the **San Juan Island Commuter** (360/734-8180 or 888/734-8180, www.islandcommuter.com) has daily summer-time passenger-ferry service to Friday Harbor, and will stop at Lopez, Blakely, Eliza, or Sinclair Islands with advance notice. The cost is $35–39 rt, $20 kids.

By Air

San Juan Airlines (360/293-4691 or 800/874-4434, www.sanjuanairlines.com) has scheduled daily wheeled-plane service to the three main San Juan Islands, and will stop at most other island runways, including Blakely, Center, Crane, Decatur, Eliza, Sinclair, Stuart, and Waldron Islands on a charter basis.

Based at San Juan Island Airport, **Island Air** (360/378-2376 or 888/378-2376, www.sanjuan-islandair.com) provides charter flights to most islands.

Kenmore Air (425/486-1257 or 800/543-

9595, www.kenmoreair.com) has charter float-plane flights from Lake Union in Seattle to Sucia and Jones Islands in the San Juans.

BLIND ISLAND MARINE STATE PARK

Blind Island (360/378-2044, www.parks.wa.gov or www.sjmp.org) is a three-acre grassy island within Blind Bay on the north side of Shaw Island. It's a great place to watch the ferries pass, with the Shaw ferry dock just a quarter-mile away, and Orcas Village less than a mile away. Facilities are limited to four mooring buoys, picnic tables, fire pits, and a composting toilet. Bring your own water. The island's four primitive campsites (206/545-9161, www.wwta.org, $10) are part of the Cascadia Marine Trail, and are available only for the use of sea kayakers.

In the early 1900s, Blind Island was occupied by a squatter family who built several buildings and rock cisterns and had a garden. The buildings are long gone, but you will see the cherry, apple, and hazelnut trees they planted.

CLARK ISLAND MARINE STATE PARK

Two miles northeast of Orcas Island, Clark Island (360/376-2073, www.parks.wa.gov or www.sjmp.org) is a narrow 55-acre island. It's relatively close to the western shore of Lummi Island, making it a destination for sea kayakers and boaters. The island has pretty sand and gravel beaches for walking, sunbathing, fishing, or scuba diving, plus a 100-foot-high hill in the middle. Droopy madrone trees line the water, framing dramatic views of the Cascades to the east or Georgia Strait and the setting sun to the west. Short paths connect the two sides of the island, but the once-popular south end trail has been closed to protect nesting seabirds.

Currents can be strong on the west side of the island, and storms often bring big waves and powerful currents that create hazardous conditions. The island is popular for day use, but not advisable if it's blowing. In addition, there's heavy tanker traffic in the channel east of Clark Island.

Nearby is privately owned **Barnes Island,** with a few homes, plus a cluster of rocky islets just southeast of Clark Island called **The Sisters Islands.** These are frequently crowded with nesting gulls, cormorants, and other seabirds. Two of them lie within the San Juan Islands National Wildlife Refuge, and boaters must stay 200 yards away.

Camping and Moorage

On shore are nine primitive campsites ($10) with pit toilets but no water. Most of these are on-the-beach sites open only April–September, but two are in the trees and available year-round. Groups can reserve one of the campsites by calling the park.

Mooring buoys are available on both sides of Clark Island, but buoys on the west side are exposed.

Transportation

Paraclete Charters (360/293-5920 or 800/808-2999, www.paracletecharters.com) runs boats from Anacortes throughout the San Juan Islands. Prices depend upon the number of folks; to Clark, it's $168 round-trip for two people. Add $10 round-trip for bikes, or $20 for kayaks.

Also based in Anacortes, **Island Express Charters** (360/299-2875 or 877/473-9777, www.islandexpresscharters.com) has a high speed landing craft with plenty of room for kayaks, bikes, and gear. Rates depend upon the number of passengers; $164 round-trip for two people. Add $12 round-trip for bikes or $20 for kayaks.

CYPRESS ISLAND

The fourth largest island in the San Juans, Cypress is just three miles northeast of Anacortes. It is surprisingly wild, with excellent recreational opportunities and beautifully rugged scenery. Featured attractions include tall stands of old-growth trees, more than 25 miles of hiking trails, along with campsites, pretty beaches and coves, a couple of small lakes, abundant wildlife, and some stunning hilltop viewpoints.

There are no cypress trees on Cypress Island. Captain George Vancouver named the island in 1792, but misidentified the trees; they're actually Rocky Mountain junipers. Coast Salish peoples once occupied the island seasonally, and a number of archaeological sites have been identified. American settlers came to homestead, farm, log, fish, or mine, but most of them gave up almost a century ago. In the 1970s, local environmentalists prevented the island from being developed into a planned resort and residential area. Today, the four-and-a-half mile-long island is mostly in public hands and managed as a natural area by the Washington Department of Natural Resources (360/856-3500, www.dnr.wa.gov).

Campgrounds

Free campsites are located at **Cypress Head DNR Recreation Site** on the east side of the island, where you will also find five mooring buoys and outhouses, but no drinking water—so bring plenty with you. The bay at Cypress Head is peaceful and gorgeous. **Pelican Beach DNR Recreation Site** is another picturesque place, with six mooring buoys, free campsites, a shelter, picnic tables, and outhouses, but no water. It is located on the northeast side of Cypress. Additional free campsites can be found at **Strawberry Island DNR Recreation Site,** a rocky-sided islet just off the western shore of Cypress Island. Here you'll find three campsites with picnic tables, fire grates, and vault toilets, but no water. Camping is only allowed in designated campsites on Cypress and Strawberry Islands.

Hiking

For a truly incredible view, climb to the 800-foot summit of **Eagle Cliff** on the northern end of Cypress Island. The shortest trail begins from Pelican Beach and is a bit less than three miles round-trip. As might be surmised from the name, this is a bald eagle nesting area. To protect them, the trail is closed February to mid-July. Other trails and dirt roads lace the island, going all the way from Pelican Beach to the southern tip of Cypress Island. Mountain bikes and motorized vehicles are not allowed on any of these. See Ken Wilcox's *Hiking the*

San Juan Islands for complete details on your hiking options.

Transportation

Kayakers and boaters typically head to Cypress from Anacortes, but small vessels need to take precautions due to difficult currents and tide rips in Bellingham Channel.

Based in Anacortes, **Island Express Charters** (360/299-2875 or 877/473-9777, www.island-expresscharters.com) has a high-speed landing craft with plenty of room for kayaks, bikes, and gear. Rates depend upon the number of passengers; $116 round-trip for two people. Add $12 round-trip for bikes or $20 for kayaks.

Paraclete Charters (360/293-5920 or 800/808-2999, www.paracletecharters.com) runs three boats from Anacortes throughout the San Juan Islands. For the west side of Cypress, it's $104 round-trip for two people, or $128 to the east side. Add $10 round-trip for bikes, or $20 for kayaks.

DOE ISLAND MARINE STATE PARK

Doe Island (360/376-2073, www.parks.wa.gov or www.sjmp.org) is a delightful six-acre escape. The secluded island is heavily forested and has both rocky shorelines and a gravel beach. It is located just southeast of Orcas Island, and less than a half-mile kayak paddle from the hot tubs at Doe Bay Resort & Retreat on Orcas. There are no mooring buoys, but a seasonal float extends from the north shore. Hiking trails circle and cross the island, and five simple campsites ($10) are available. No drinking water, but it does have picnic tables and pit toilets. Be sure to check out the archaeological site in a little pocket cove on the north side; you can still see the place where the Lummi cleared rocks to beach their canoes.

Guided kayak trips to Doe Island depart Doe Bay Resort & Retreat on a regular basis in the summer; contact **Shearwater Adventures** (360/376-4699, www.shearwaterkayaks.com) for details. The closest access point for boaters and kayakers heading to Doe Island is the county's Obstruction Pass boat ramp.

JAMES ISLAND MARINE STATE PARK

Less than a half mile east of Decatur Island and just four miles from the Anacortes ferry terminal along Rosario Strait, James Island (360/376-2073, www.parks.wa.gov or www.sjmp.org) is a cliff-faced and scenic little place. The island was named for an American sailor, Reuben James, who died during a naval battle in Tripoli while saving the life of Stephen Decatur. It was one of many places named during the 1841 Wilkes Expedition.

Covering 114 acres, James Island is shaped like an hourglass, with coves and mooring buoys ($10) on both sides of the "waist." The east cove offers a better anchorage for boats if the buoys are already taken, and the west cove has a floating dock. Beaches on both sides are steep. Kayakers need to be especially cautious in the waters north of the island, where deadly rip currents can form.

Two Anacortes-based companies provide transport to James Island: **Island Express Charters** (360/299-2875 or 877/473-9777, www.island-expresscharters.com) and **Paraclete Charters** (360/293-5920 or 800/808-2999, www.paracletecharters.com). Bikes and kayaks are extra.

Campgrounds

Pitch a tent at one of 13 primitive campsites ($10), or at the Cascadia Marine Trail campsite (206/545-9161, www.wwta.org, $10) if you're in a kayak. The island has the usual complement of deer, birds, and raccoons, the last of which can be a real pest when the sun goes down. You'll need to bring your own water. Picnic tables, a shelter, and pit toilets are present, however, and a network of short trails traverses the forests and twin 200-foot-high hills of James Island.

JONES ISLAND MARINE STATE PARK

One of the most heavily visited of the San Juan marine parks, Jones Island (360/376-2073, www.parks.wa.gov or www.sjmp.org) is a 188-acre island just a mile from the southwestern tip of Orcas Island, or a two-mile boat ride from Friday Harbor. The island is named for Jacob Jones, an American naval captain during the War of 1812, and is yet another place named during the 1841 Wilkes Expedition. It is a wonderful destination, either as a day trip or a multinight family adventure. Two coves provide boat

Hundreds of rocky islets surround the San Juan Islands.

© DON PITCHER

Other San Juan Islands

anchorage and access to the island's pleasures, and boaters can tie onto one of seven mooring buoys ($10). The north cove is a better anchorage and also has both a dock and seasonal moorage float. Local boaters recommend avoiding the north cover in high-pressure conditions, when winds blow from the north; avoid the south cove during low-pressure systems, when winds are reversed.

Exploring the Island

Jones Island features a mixture of old-growth forests (some of which were flattened in a fierce 1990 windstorm), stands of stately madrone, oak, and juniper trees, and grassy meadows. The shoreline is equally diverse, containing both rocky stretches and sandy beaches in pocket-sized coves. The island's abundant (and tiny) black-tailed deer are very habituated to people, making them a favorite of children. But please don't feed them. Two unusual plants—prickly pear cactus and Garry oak—are also present in protected areas on Jones Island.

Two miles of trails traverse Jones Island, with one path leading across the island to the south cove, passing an old apple orchard along the way. The southern shore has interesting tidepools. Other trails take you to the scenic western side of the island (also great tidepools) and to the northern end, where vistas extend to the Gulf Islands of British Columbia.

Campgrounds

The state park has 21 primitive campsites ($10) with picnic tables, pit toilets, and potable water, though the well may run dry in late summer. Because of its beauty and proximity to Friday Harbor and Deer Harbor, Jones Island is often crowded. Camping is only allowed at designated sites, and these fill quickly on summer weekends. Reservations are only available for a special group campsite on Jones Island; call 360/378-2044 for details. Kayakers will find a Cascadia Marine Trail campsite (206/545-9161, www.wwta.org, $10) on a cozy southwestern beach facing San Juan Channel. For additional Jones Island information, see www.parks.wa.gov or www.sjmp.org.

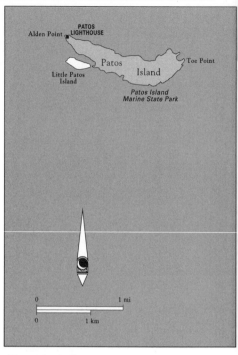

Transportation

Jones Island is exceptionally popular with boaters, sailors, and sea kayakers. Several water-taxi companies are happy to get you to the island.

Located at Deer Harbor Marina, **Orcas Boat Rentals** (360/376-7616, www.orcasboats.com) is just a five-minute boat ride from Jones Island. Owner Marc Broman will take a load of up to six people to the island for $60 rt.

North Shore Charters (360/376-4855, www.sanjuancruises.net) offers day trips and drop-offs to Jones Island from Deer Harbor on Orcas Island; $135 round-trip for up to six passengers.

Two Anacortes-based companies also provide transport to Jones Island: **Island Express Charters** (360/299-2875 or 877/473-9777, www.islandexpresscharters.com) and **Paraclete Charters** (360/293-5920 or 800/808-2999, www.paracletecharters.com).

Natalie Herner of **Gnat's Nature Hikes** (360/376-6629, www.orcasislandhikes.com) leads boat-and-hike trips to Jones Island in the summer from

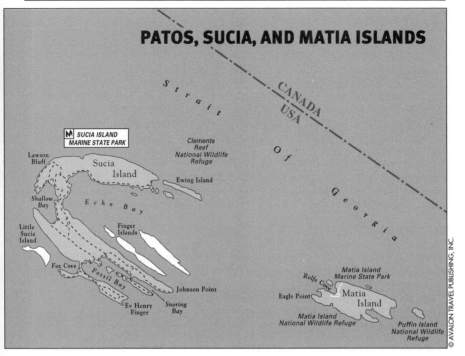

PATOS, SUCIA, AND MATIA ISLANDS

Orcas Island. These half-day trips cost $65/person, including the boat ride. There's a three-person minimum and a six-person maximum.

Kenmore Air (425/486-1257 or 800/543-9595, www.kenmoreair.com) has charter float-plane flights from Lake Union in Seattle to Jones Island.

MATIA ISLAND MARINE STATE PARK

Located three miles northeast of Orcas Island and a mile from Sucia Island, Matia (pronounced ma-TEE-uh; 360/376-2073, www.parks.wa.gov or www.sjmp.org) Island is a mile long and covers 145 acres. Sandstone bluffs line the shore, and tall old-growth forests of Douglas fir, Western hemlock, and western red cedar fill the center of the island. It's a beautiful and essentially undeveloped place. Matia received its name from the 1791 expedition of Francisco Eliza; in Spanish, the word means no protection.

Matia was for decades the quiet home of a Civil War veteran, Elvin Smith, who got a regular workout rowing the three miles to Orcas and walking another two miles to Eastsound to buy his groceries. On his last trip in 1921, he and another elderly friend headed out from Eastsound in seas that suddenly turned rough. Pieces of the boat were later discovered near the Canadian border, but the two men were never found. For a riveting account of Elvin Smith, see *Pig War Islands* by David Richardson (Orcas Publishing Company).

Campgrounds and Exploring

Most of Matia Island lies within the **San Juan Islands National Wildlife Refuge,** but the five-acre **Matia Island Marine State Park** centers around Rolfe Cove on the western end. Here you'll find a seasonal dock (generally April–September), two mooring buoys ($10), six primitive campsites ($10), and a composting toilet. No water is available, and wood fires aren't allowed on

Other San Juan Islands

Matia, though you can use charcoal briquettes in the fire stands.

A scenic one-mile **hiking trail** starts at Rolfe Cove and loops across the island, passing scattered remnants of Smith's old homesite and taking you through dense forests and along rocky shores. This is all part of the National Wildlife Refuge, so stay on the trails to protect the land and wildlife. Pets are not allowed on Matia Island trails. Boaters cannot approach Matia closer than 200 yards, except at the state park.

Immediately east of Matia is **Puffin Island,** with an active eagle nest, various nesting seabirds, seals, and sea lions. Puffins no longer nest there, though they apparently did in the past.

Transportation

Matia Island is popular with kayakers and boaters, but has potentially treacherous currents. **North Shore Charters** (360/376-4855, www.sanjuancruises.net) offers day trips and drop-offs to Matia Island from Deer Harbor on Orcas Island; $540 round-trip for up to six passengers and kayaks.

Paraclete Charters (360/293-5920 or 800/808-2999, www.paracletecharters.com) runs boats from Anacortes to Matia. Prices depend upon the number of folks; it's $204 round-trip for two people. Add $10 round-trip for bikes, or $20 for kayaks.

Also based in Anacortes, **Island Express Charters** (360/299-2875 or 877/473-9777, www.islandexpresscharters.com) has rates that depend upon the number of passengers; $240 round-trip for two people. Add $12 round-trip for bikes or $20 for kayaks.

PATOS ISLAND MARINE STATE PARK

Northernmost of the San Juan archipelago, Patos (properly pronounced PAW-tohs, though you'll also hear PAY-tohs; 360/376-2073, www.parks.wa.gov or www.sjmp.org) covers 208 acres and is six miles north of Orcas Island or two miles northwest of Sucia Island. The Southern Gulf Islands of British Columbia are only a few miles away. Wild, remote, and quiet Patos Island was named during a Spanish expedition in 1792.

The name means duck, and may have possibly come from a rock formation on the east side of the island that resembles the head of a duck.

The lack of a dock on Patos limits access, but you can anchor at two mooring buoys ($10) in **Active Cove.** Located on the southwestern side of Patos, it's sheltered behind **Little Patos Island.** During high-pressure systems the moorage is exposed to winds blowing down the Strait of Georgia, creating a rough anchorage; otherwise it's fairly protected.

Campgrounds and Hiking

Seven primitive campsites (free) on Patos have picnic tables, fire pits, and outhouses, but no water. A 1.5-mile loop trail circles the western side of the island, passing through dense forests before opening onto the barren northwest tip at Alden Point. A quarter-mile spur leads to picturesque **Patos Lighthouse.** Built in 1893 and now automated, the lighthouse sits atop a rocky bluff. For a lovingly written reminiscence of growing up on Patos in the early 1900s, see *Light on the Island* by Helene Glidden (San Juan Publishing). The author was raised as a lighthouse-keeper's daughter and tells of her adventures with scoundrels, Native peoples, and even Teddy Roosevelt.

Transportation

Patos is not the place for novice kayakers or folks in small boats. There are few areas offering any protection, and the currents and tide rips can be treacherous. Kayakers typically head to Patos from Sucia Island, rather than attempting the four-mile open-water crossing from Point Doughty on Orcas Island.

North Shore Charters (360/376-4855, www.sanjuancruises.net) has day trips and drop-offs to Patos from Deer Harbor on Orcas Island; $400 round-trip for up to six passengers.

Based in Anacortes, **Island Express Charters** (360/299-2875 or 877/473-9777, www.islandexpresscharters.com) has a high-speed landing craft with plenty of room for kayaks, bikes, and gear. Rates depend upon the number of passengers; $240 round-trip for two people. Add $12 round-trip for bikes or $20 for kayaks.

Paraclete Charters (360/293-5920 or 800/808-2999, www.paracletecharters.com) also runs boats from Anacortes to Patos. Prices depend upon the number of folks; it's $204 round-trip for two people. Add $10 round-trip for bikes, or $20 for kayaks.

POSEY ISLAND MARINE STATE PARK

This pinprick of an island covers just one acre and is located a quarter-mile north of San Juan Island's Roche Harbor. Posey Island (360/378-2044, www.parks.wa.gov or www.sjmp.org) is named for the small and abundant wildflowers that carpet the ground in mid-summer. Shallow waters and two Cascadia Marine Trail campsites (206/545-9161, www.wwta.org, $10) make this a favorite spot for folks on kayaks and canoes in search of their own island. It's a great place to watch the parade of boats heading into or out of this busy harbor.

The island sees heavy daytime use by kayakers, and camp spaces fill quickly. Limit your stay to one night to give someone else a chance. Because of its location close to numerous summer homes and the harbor entrance, you shouldn't expect a quiet night during the summer season. No water is available on the island, but picnic tables and a composting toilet are here. A maximum of 16 people are allowed to camp on Posey, which is really far too many for such a tiny spot.

SADDLEBAG ISLAND MARINE STATE PARK

This 24-acre island in Padilla Bay is just two miles northeast of Anacortes and half a mile east of Guemes Island. It might be a stretch to call Saddlebag part of the San Juan archipelago, but the island is a marine state park. Facilities include five primitive campsites ($10) and an outhouse, but no drinking water, buoys, or floats are available. A Cascadia Marine Trail campsite (206/545-9161, www.wwta.org, $10) is available for sea kayakers. The southeast corner of Saddlebag Island almost touches tiny **Dot Island,** part of the San Juan Islands National Wildlife Refuge. To protect nesting sites for seabirds, boaters aren't allowed within 200 yards of Dot Island. **Hat Island,** a larger island southeast of Saddlebag, is also closed to the public to protect wildlife.

Get additional Saddlebag Island park information at 360/757-0227, www.parks.wa.gov or www.sjmp.org.

🅜 STUART ISLAND

Stuart Island, five miles northwest of San Juan Island's Roche Harbor, has two bucolic harbors just a stone's throw apart, along with a densely forested, hilly landscape and a classic old lighthouse. The island sits in the middle of Haro Strait, where killer whales are a common summertime sight. Canadian waters are less than a mile from the western end of Stuart Island. The three-mile-long island is predominately private, but **Stuart Island Marine State Park** (360/378-2044, www.parks.wa.gov or www.sjmp.org) covers 88 prime acres, including 4,000 feet of shoreline. There are no stores of any kind on the island, so bring whatever you need when you come.

The island has two large and well-protected harbors—both within the state marine park—that are favorites of boaters. Located on the southeast end of Stuart Island, **Reid Harbor** has 15 mooring buoys, linear moorage, and a dock, along with two floats at the head of the bay and a marine pump-out station. The 640-foot summit of Tiptop Hill (no public access) rises to the south, with a small road providing access to other parts of the island. A wide path leads north from Reid Harbor dock to **Prevost Harbor.** It's an easy 200-yard walk, but boats enter Prevost Harbor from the north side of Stuart Island. This harbor has seven mooring buoys, linear moorage, and a dock.

History

The 1841 Wilkes Expedition named Stuart Island for the captain's clerk, Fredrick D. Stuart. Loggers, fishermen, and a few farmers later settled the island. Today, Stuart is home to 40 or so year-round residents, augmented by another 150 folks with summer homes. Privacy is a priority here, and many areas are posted with No Trespassing signs. Fortunately, some of the most interesting sights are accessible by public trails or county roads, including Stuart Island Marine State Park and a beautiful lighthouse on the westernmost end.

Exploring the Island

Several relatively short trails (two miles maximum) loop through the marine state park, offering ridge-crest views, open forests of madrone and Douglas fir, and rocky shorelines along the way. Check the information kiosks at either harbor for details. For something a bit more ambitious, head up the county road that begins on public land at the head of Reid Harbor. This narrow dirt road climbs uphill for three-quarters of a mile to a white one-room schoolhouse. Built in 1902, it now serves as a library. Nearby is a much newer school with a handful of local students in K–8 grades, some of whom arrive by boat. It's certainly one of the last American public schools without electricity or flush toilets!

Continue a quarter-mile past the school to a road junction, and turn right. A short distance beyond is an unmarked road on the left leading to the **Stuart Island Cemetery,** with graves dating to 1904. Look for the distinctive headstone of Littlewolf, a local character who crafted copper bracelets that supposedly offered medical benefits. Back on the main road, you pass an airstrip and some placidly grazing cows before a road junction. Turn left at the sign to reach **Turn Point Lighthouse.** Completed in 1893, it has been automated since 1939. The lighthouse and surrounding 53 acres are owned by the Bureau of Land Management, which allows day use only. The last portion of this hike is delightful, and the trail eventually emerges atop a tall cliff (stay away from the edge) where the panorama encompasses Haro Strait, the Southern Gulf Islands, and Vancouver Island. You'll see a parade of freighters, tankers, and smaller boats, and might even spot a pod of killer whales.

Turn Point marks the transition between Haro Strait to the south and Boundary Pass to the north. Large ships threading these channels must make a sharp turn here, and so do the often-turbulent tidal currents. The boundary waters are the deepest in the San Juan archipelago, reaching a maximum of 1,200 feet. It's a six-mile round-trip hike from Reid Harbor to the lighthouse.

Campgrounds

Stuart Island Marine State Park straddles the isthmus between Prevost and Reid Harbors, and includes 19 campsites ($10), picnic tables, seasonal drinking water, fireplaces, and pit toilets. Drinking water is limited and the system often runs dry by mid-July, so call ahead to make sure it's available. Two Cascadia Marine Trail campsites (206/545-9161, www.wwta.org, $10) are available for sea kayakers at the head of Reid Harbor.

Boats and Kayaks

Powerful currents and tidal rips make the waters around Stuart Island challenging for small boats and kayaks; paddling here is not for beginners or the faint of heart. The closest access is Roche Harbor on San Juan Island, but you'll need to pass through the frequently swirling flows of Spieden Channel. For details on the best way to proceed, see Randel Washburne's *Kayaking Puget Sound, the San Juans, and Gulf Islands.*

Transportation

North Shore Charters (360/376-4855, www .sanjuancruises.net) offers day trips and drop-offs to Stuart Island from Deer Harbor on Orcas Island; $250 round-trip for up to six passengers.

Based in Anacortes, **Island Express Charters** (360/299-2875 or 877/473-9777, www.island-expresscharters.com) has a high-speed landing craft with space for kayaks, bikes, and gear. Rates depend upon the number of passengers; $240 round-trip for two people. Add $12 round-trip for bikes, or $20 for kayaks.

Paraclete Charters (360/293-5920 or 800/808-2999, www.paracletecharters.com) provides service to Stuart from Anacortes. Prices depend upon the number of folks; it's $204 round-trip for two people. Add $10 round-trip for bikes, or $20 for kayaks.

San Juan Airlines (360/293-4691 or 800/ 874-4434, www.sanjuanairlines.com) will land at Stuart Island on a charter basis.

Nearby Islands

Johns, Satellite, Sentinel, and Spieden Islands are nearby, and **Cactus Island** and several surrounding tiny islets are within the San Juan Islands National Wildlife Refuge. Boats aren't allowed within 200 yards of refuge islands to protect habitat for seals, sea lions, and seabirds. Cactus Island, along with a few other places in the San Juans, has Puget prairie vegetation, with native grasses and various rare plants, including the prickly pear cactus—the only species of cactus native to western Washington. You'll also find these unusual conditions at minuscule **Gossip** and **Cemetery Islands,** near the mouth of Reid Harbor. The latter two islands are undeveloped state parks with day use only allowed and no picnics. There's a pretty white beach at Gossip Island.

⋈ SUCIA ISLAND MARINE STATE PARK

Sucia Island (360/376-2073, www.parks.wa.gov or www.sjmp.org) is the gold standard for Wash-

ington's marine state parks, with something for almost everyone. The shoreline has delightful sandy beaches for sunbathing, exploring, clamming, and crabbing, plus bizarre water-carved sandstone formations and lounging seals. Offshore, you can scuba dive on an artificial reef created by three sunken wrecks. Hikers and mountain bikers will find 10 miles of scenic trails, campers revel in the many primitive campsites, and boaters tie up at buoys, linear moorage, or docks in a half-dozen small bays. Picnic tables and shelters dot the coves. Note: The island is commonly pronounced SUE-sha, but many folks now prefer the original Spanish pronunciation, sue-SEE-uh.

Shaped like a horseshoe, Sucia Island is 2.5 miles north of Orcas Island and almost to the Canadian border. In addition to the main island of Sucia, nine smaller islands (some privately owned) are adjacent, including the Finger Islands, Little Sucia Island (closed to public access when bald eagles are nesting here), Justice Island, and Ewing Island. Altogether, the islands cover almost 750 acres. Two other popular marine destinations are nearby: Patos and Matia Islands.

Sucia Island is the largest and one of the most popular marine state parks in Washington, with more than 100,000 boaters annually. Don't expect

© DON PITCHER

North Shore Charters

© DON PITCHER

China Caves along Shallow Bay

to be the only visitor on Sucia Island; on a summer weekend, the waters around the island are jam-packed with U.S. and Canadian vessels of all descriptions. You can avoid some of the mob scene in midweek or during the slower spring and fall.

History

The first European to discover Sucia Island was explorer Francisco Eliza in 1791. He named it for the Spanish word that means dirty or foul, a nautical reference to the shoal-filled waters surrounding Sucia.

The San Juans have long been a haven for smuggling, and its multitude of coves and sculpted sandstone rocks made Sucia Island a center for everything from illegal booze during Prohibition to Chinese laborers in the late 19th century. During the early 1900s, sandstone quarried from Sucia was used to pave Seattle's streets. In the 1950s, a wealthy Californian prepared to

buy Sucia Island from its local owners, intending to subdivide it for vacation homes. Word quickly spread in the Puget Sound yachting and boating community, and a drive was mounted to raise $25,000 to purchase the island. In 1960, the Puget Sound Interclub Association donated Sucia to the state of Washington, thus preserving this marvelous island for the public.

Anchorages

Sucia Island wraps its two long arms around **Echo Bay,** where you'll find 14 mooring buoys and two sets of linear moorage ($10). **Shallow Bay** is right across a narrow isthmus from the head of Echo Bay, and has a pleasant beach, eight buoys, and colorful sunsets. An eroded sandstone cliff, filled with many small nooks and crannies, borders the northeast side of Shallow Bay. Known as **China Caves,** these niches were supposedly used by 19th-century smugglers to hide illegal Chinese laborers from immigration officials. It's a good tale, but probably apocryphal.

On the southern end of the island is **Fossil Bay**—named for marine fossils scattered along the beach—with 16 buoys, two docks, and a park ranger's station. Families have fun finding the fossils, but it's illegal to take them. A low, sandy isthmus (great for hanging out on a sunny day) separates it from **Fox Cove,** which has four buoys. **Snoring Bay** (two buoys) is near the south end of the island, while **Ewing Cove** (four buoys) occupies the northeast end of the island facing Ewing Island.

Hiking and Biking

Despite the abundance of summertime boaters in Sucia, it is easy to escape the crowds by simply heading inland on one of the trails that lace the island. The land is surprisingly diverse, with a variety of forests—including Douglas fir, shore pine, Pacific madrone, and Rocky Mountain juniper—along with sea cliffs (use caution hiking with small children), sandy beaches, odd rock formations, and all-encompassing seascapes.

Trails start from all of the popular bays and coves, offering options of varying lengths. If you were to hike from Johnson Point on the southern end of the island to Ewing Cove on the northern end, it would be a round-trip walk of nine miles. Of note is the one-mile hike from Fossil Bay to the end of **Ev Henry Finger,** a narrow peninsula with steep cliffs and killer views of Orcas Island and points south. The hike to **Ewing Cove** is another delightful option, with a wooded trail that follows the shoreline to this beautiful and out-of-the-way cove. There are some steep drops along the way, so watch your step.

All of these trails are also open to mountain bikers, and biking the main roads is quite easy, but it's best to leave the narrower trails to hikers. North Shore Charters will haul you out to Sucia for a day trip from Orcas Island; add $35 for a high-quality mountain bike.

Campgrounds

A total of 55 primitive campsites ($10) are located at Echo Bay, Fossil Bay, Shallow Bay, Fox Cove, Ewing Cove, and Snoring Bay. Picnic shelters, fireplaces, and composting toilets are all available at the various campgrounds. Drinking water is here early, but the system often runs dry by mid-July; so call ahead to make sure, or bring your own. Camping is only allowed at designated sites. The campsites at Ewing Cove and Snoring Bay are a bit more isolated, and may be a better choice in the peak summer season when the island is a frenzy of activity. Reservations are available for three group campsites on Sucia Island; call 360/376-2073 for details. Groups can also reserve a picnic area along Fossil Bay.

Transportation

It's relatively easy to get to Sucia via sailboat or motorboat, and many others paddle kayaks from North Beach or Bartwood Lodge on Orcas Island. A number of regional kayak companies offer guided trips to Sucia for those who prefer a knowledgeable guide when crossing these sometimes-difficult waters filled with odd currents, sudden winds, and dangerous reefs. Don't take chances! **Shearwater Adventures** (360/376-4699, www.shearwaterkayaks.com) sometimes leads kayaking day trips from Orcas to Sucia when conditions are calm enough.

North Shore Charters (360/376-4855, www .sanjuancruises.net) offers day trips and drop-offs to Sucia Island from Deer Harbor on Orcas Island; $400 round-trip for up to six passengers.

Based in Anacortes, **Island Express Charters** (360/299-2875 or 877/473-9777, www.island-expresscharters.com) has a high-speed landing craft. Rates depend upon the number of passengers; $240 round-trip for two people. Add $12 round-trip for bikes, or $20 for kayaks.

Paraclete Charters (360/293-5920 or 800/808-2999, www.paracletecharters.com) provides service to Sucia Island from Anacortes. Prices depend upon the number of folks; it's $204 round-trip for two people. Add $10 round-trip for bikes, or $20 for kayaks.

Kenmore Air (425/486-1257 or 800/543-9595, www.kenmoreair.com) provides charter floatplane flights from Seattle to Sucia Island.

TURN ISLAND MARINE STATE PARK

Turn Island (360/378-2044, www.parks.wa.gov or www.sjmp.org) is just a quarter mile from San Juan Island's east shore and within easy kayaking distance of Friday Harbor. The 35-acre island is both a marine state park and a part of the San Juan Islands National Wildlife Refuge. The island was named by the British in 1858 to denote the abrupt change in course required when navigating the San Juan Channel here.

For such a little place, Turn Island has more than its share of attractions, including three mooring buoys, two pebbly beaches, camping, nearby scuba diving, and three miles of hiking trails. One path completely circles Turn Island, with another cutting through its densely forested center.

Campers can pitch a tent at one of 10 primitive campsites ($10), which fill quickly. The island has picnic tables, fire pits, and compost toilets, but no water. The proximity to Friday Harbor makes this both easy to reach and close to the noises caused by all that activity in the summertime, making it something less than a remote experience.

Transportation

Turn Island is a very popular place for day-use

Turn Point Lighthouse

picnickers and hikers who arrive by small boat or sea kayak. The closest access is from a little parking lot on Turn Point Road just a mile and a half east of Friday Harbor; it is locally called Pinedrona Cove. From here, it's less than a quarter mile to the island. Note, however, that the channel between Turn Island and San Juan Island can have strong currents and wakes from passing ferries. You can also put in at the Friday Harbor dock.

Private Islands

Scattered across the San Juans are islands that are predominately—or entirely—owned by private individuals or non-profit organizations. Not all of these islands are restricted to landowners, however, and a number of these have at least some publicly accessible areas.

Some islands have only a single home, others a few dozen residences and an unpaved airstrip. None have more than 80 or so people. Privacy is closely guarded on many of these islands, and visitors—particularly those who trespass on private land—are not appreciated.

Anyone interested in buying their own island should look over local real estate publications. When I last checked, Reef Island was for sale at the bargain price of $5.5 million.

Public Tidelands

Note that even those islands that are entirely in private hands may have beaches and tidelands that are accessible to the public if you arrive by boat. The Washington Department of Natural Resources (360/856-3500, www.dnr.wa.gov) produces detailed State Public Lands Quadrangle Maps showing public beaches in the San Juans and elsewhere.

BLAKELY ISLAND

As the state ferry heads west from Anacortes to the San Juans, it threads its way between two large and privately owned islands, Blakely and Decatur. Blakely is the namesake of Johnston Blakely, a U.S. naval commander in the War of 1812, and was named during the 1841 Wilkes Expedition. Today, Blakely is known as the "Flying Island." Many residents are pilots whose homes are adjacent to the airstrip; they taxi right up their driveways and park.

Blakely has a heavily wooded interior (all second-growth forests from logging in the 1950s), two lakes, a 100-foot-high waterfall, several large hills (one is 1,042 feet), and miles of private roads. A public marina is located on the northern tip of Blakely across from Obstruction Island. Visitors are welcome here, and guest moorage is available, along with fuel, showers, and washers and driers. A good little general store (360/375-6121, www.rock-island.com/~blakely) and post office are on the shore. Beyond this, almost the entire island is private and completely off limits. A handful of locals live on the island year-round, with more flying or boating in seasonally. In addition, Seattle Pacific University (360/375-6224, www.spu.edu) owns 967 acres on Blakely, which it uses as a marine biology and ecological research area; no public access.

Transportation

You can't stay on Blakely without permission, but you can at least get there and check out the marina. The **San Juan Island Commuter** (360/734-8180 or 888/734-8180, www.islandcommuter.com) departs Bellingham daily in the summer for Friday Harbor. The passenger ferry will stop at Blakely for $39 round-trip ($20 for kids) with advance notice.

Paraclete Charters (360/293-5920 or 800/808-2999, www.paracletecharters.com) provides service to Blakely Island from Anacortes. Prices depend upon the number of folks; it's $104 round-trip for two people. Add $10 round-trip for bikes, or $20 for kayaks.

Also based in Anacortes, **Island Express Charters** (360/299-2875 or 877/473-9777, www.islandexpresscharters.com) has a high-speed landing craft. Rates depend upon the number of passengers; $116 round-trip for two people.

San Juan Airlines (360/293-4691 or 800/874-4434, www.sanjuanairlines.com) has charter flights to Blakely Island.

CANOE ISLAND

Halfway between Shaw and Lopez Islands is this privately owned 50-acre island, home to the **Canoe Island French Camp** (360/468-2329, www.canoeisland.org), a nonprofit language and culture summer camp that attracts children from around the nation. The coed camp opened in 1969 and is staffed by French speakers who work with the 40 or so campers, ages 9–15. Kids don't need to know any French to attend, and there's a 1:3 counselor-to-camper ratio.

Campers stay in teepees and mornings are filled with French-language classes and activities, such as theater, fencing, music, and French cooking. Afternoons center around sports, swimming, and boating. Three-week sessions at Canoe Island cost $2,550, and a two-week session is $1,850. The island is not open to the general public, though the tidelands are public below mean high tide.

DEADMAN AND GOOSE ISLANDS

These two little islands are sandwiched between Lopez and San Juan Islands and are owned by The Nature Conservancy (206/343-4344, www.tnc-washington.org). Deadman Island is just west of Shark Reef along Lopez, while Goose Island sits off Cattle Point on San Juan Island. They are not generally open to the public, but access may be allowed if you contact TNC in advance.

The Conservancy also owns the publicly accessible **Chuckanut Island** within Chuckanut Bay just south of Bellingham. This five-acre island is popular with kayakers and features graceful madrone trees and a short trail.

DECATUR AND CENTER ISLANDS

Decatur Island is just east of Lopez Island and immediately south of Blakely Island. This large island is privately owned and home to 60 or so people year-round and hundreds more seasonally. The island has a small store, post office, grade school, boat launch, airport, and even a shipyard, plus miles of scenic county roads open to the public. The island is not on most travelers' agendas because you can't get off the roads to explore the private lands, and the beaches are not readily accessible. Experienced kayakers sometimes visit pretty **White Cliff Beach** on the southeastern side of Decatur, walking the public tidelands.

Decatur Island received its name during the 1841 Wilkes Expedition, and is named for Stephen Decatur, a famous U.S. naval officer during the War of 1812 and various skirmishes in northern Africa. He is best known for his nationalist maxim that has become a right-wing standby, "Our country, right or wrong." Decatur was killed in a duel with a fellow captain at the age of 40.

Center Island is a 222-acre private island sandwiched between Decatur and Lopez Islands. It has quite a few summer homes and an airstrip.

Food and Lodging

Near the center of Decatur Island and just up from the school, **Alma's Country Store** (360/375-6090, www.interisland.net/almas) carries all the basics, from plumbing supplies to soda pop. The store is open year-round, but closed Mondays and Tuesdays, with sit-down lunches and locally famous milkshakes. The top level houses a comfortable 700-square-foot apartment ($65 for up to four) with a double bed, futon couch, bath, and full kitchen.

Getting There

Paraclete Charters (360/293-5920 or 800/808-2999, www.paracletecharters.com) provides service to Decatur and Center Islands from Anacortes. Prices depend upon the number of folks; it's $104 round-trip for two people.

Anacortes-based **Island Express Charters** (360/299-2875 or 877/473-9777, www.island-expresscharters.com) has a high-speed landing craft, and rates depend upon the number of passengers; $116 round-trip for two people to Decatur or Center Islands.

Both **San Juan Airlines** (360/293-4691 or 800/874-4434, www.sanjuanairlines.com) and **Kenmore Air** (425/486-1257 or 800/543-9595, www.kenmoreair.com) will land at Decatur Island on a charter basis.

JOHNS ISLAND

A little more than a mile long, this privately owned island has a mixture of rocky bluffs and

quiet beaches, but no public facilities—unless you count the popular summer camp. The island lies immediately east of Stuart Island and north of Spieden Island.

Two Anacortes-based companies provide water-taxi service to the island: **Island Express Charters** (360/299-2875 or 877/473-9777, www.islandexpresscharters.com) and **Paraclete Charters,** 360/293-5920 or 800/808-2999, www.paracletecharters.com).

Camp Nor'wester

Johns Island is the home of Camp Nor'wester (360/468-2225 or 360/472-1382, www.norwester.org), a coed summer camp for ages 9–16. The camp has been in existence since 1935, though it only recently moved to the beautiful 132-acre Johns Island site from Lopez Island; billionaire Paul Allen bought the old camp site.

Kids take part in such traditional summer-camp activities as camping, sailing, canoeing (on a 35-foot Haida-style canoe), and natural history, along with a ropes course, biking, and arts and crafts. The emphasis is on working with peers to develop friendships and to learn together rather than independently. Sessions include a maximum of 170 campers with a staff of 70. Four-week sessions for ages 11–16 cost $3,000, and two-week camps for ages 9–10 are $1,500; prices include transportation to and from Seattle. In late August, a special four-day "preview session" provides an introduction for parents and kids ages 6–12. The cost is just $150/person, including transportation from Friday Harbor. This is a great way to introduce your child to summer camp.

OBSTRUCTION ISLAND

This triangular island is wedged between Blakely and Orcas Islands. The state park campsites at Obstruction Pass on Orcas are less than 400 yards away. Entirely private, Obstruction Island has rocky shores, tiny beaches, and a dozen or so homes. Public access is not allowed. The island covers 217 acres, and is heavily forested. Even though you can't go ashore, kayakers often put in at Obstruction Pass and paddle around the island.

SATELLITE ISLAND

The Seattle YMCA's Camp Orkila (206/382-5009, www.seattleymca.org) owns 107-acre Satellite Island, located just off the north side of Stuart Island at Prevost Harbor. The island was named for H.M.S. *Satellite*, a steamship used for surveys by the British during the Pig War. Satellite Island has no permanent structures, and is not open to the general public. (The only exceptions are areas below mean high water, which are publicly accessible at low tides.)

SENTINEL ISLAND

Owned by The Nature Conservancy (206/343-4344, www.tnc-washington.org), Sentinel Island is a 15-acre forested island immediately south of Spieden Island. The island is preserved as eagle habitat today, but was once the home of June and Farrar Burn, who homesteaded here in 1940. June went on to write about life here in the autobiographical *Living High* and described their adventures sailing around the San Juans in *100 Days in San Juans*. Both books make for interesting reading if you're looking for a taste of a quieter era. Sentinel Island is not generally open to the public, but access may be allowed if you contact TNC in advance.

SINCLAIR ISLAND

Sinclair Island was named during the Wilkes Expedition of 1841 for Arthur Sinclair Sr., a U.S. naval captain during the War of 1812. During his heyday as a smuggler, Larry Kelly owned a third of Sinclair Island.

This small and mostly private island is less than a mile northeast of Cypress Island. A county dock extends from the southwest end of the island, providing access to the little village called Urban and to the dirt roads that crisscross Sinclair. It's a two-thirds mile walk to **Sinclair Island Natural Wildlife Area**, a 35-acre beachfront parcel on the southeast end of the island. By combining beach walks with the island's quiet back roads, you can spend an enjoyable afternoon wandering the island while remaining on public lands.

Transportation

The **San Juan Island Commuter** (360/734-8180 or 888/734-8180, www.islandcommuter.com) departs Bellingham daily in the summer for Friday Harbor. Upon request, the passenger ferry

---

GUMDROP ISLANDS

Boats for the San Juans leave the Quackenbush Dock in Bellingham at seven. On a Puget Sound morning in winter, seven is pitch-dark night. In summer, it has been full day for two hours or more. In the fall and spring, it is pale dawn. That is how it was on this September day, but fresh and clear, as though the world had got up on the right side of the bed.

Little fishing boats rolled sleepily against their moorings. Another passenger-and-freight boat was loading. It left just before us. I watched its keel rip open the bright silk of the bay.

Later, I learned the names of the dark green islands we passed, but that morning they were mysterious and dreamlike. Eliza slipped behind. Lummi Island, elephant-big, reared up on its haunches in front of the boat, but we sidestepped it and went on. Eagle Cliff on Cypress, Blakely Island, Lopez, Shaw, Orcas, Deer Harbor, Waldron, Stuart Island.

From the narrow channel between Johns and Stuart, we saw a tall, long, lovely island just ahead. "That's Spieden," the captain said. "Ed Chevalier lives there. His wife's father homesteaded part of it, and Ed has gradually got it all. Just on the other side of Spieden is the little island you are looking for."

Across another channel, seagulls screaming. Around the immense hip of Spieden—and there was Sentinel Island, like a green gumdrop, fir trees lifting their beautiful crowns into the sky, sedum-covered bluffs shearing straight down into the rich, green-blue water.

from June Burn's *Living High*, an autobiography published by Griffin Bay Bookstore on San Juan Island

will stop at Sinclair or nearby Eliza Island for $35 round-trip ($20 for kids).

Paraclete Charters (360/293-5920 or 800/808-2999, www.paracletecharters.com) provides service to Sinclair Island from Anacortes. Prices depend upon the number of folks; it's $128 round-trip for two people.

Based in Anacortes, **Island Express Charters** (360/299-2875 or 877/473-9777, www.island-expresscharters.com) has a high-speed landing craft with space for kayaks, bikes, and gear. Rates depend upon the number of passengers; $116 round-trip for two people.

San Juan Airlines (360/293-4691 or 800/874-4434, www.sanjuanairlines.com) will land at Sinclair Island on a charter basis.

SPIEDEN ISLAND

Located between Stuart and San Juan Islands, Spieden (pronounced SPY-den) Island covers 480 acres and is privately owned with no public access. In the early 1970s, two taxidermists bought the island and began importing exotic animals for wealthy trophy hunters to bag. Environmentalists protested the sham and forced an end to the game farm three years later. The axis deer, Japanese sika deer, Spanish goats, Corsican mouflon sheep, Barbary sheep, Indian blackbuck, and other animals gradually disappeared, though a few survivors may be seen grazing in the open grasslands on the south side of Spieden. Forests carpet the north side of the island, and Steller sea lions are often seen on rocks off the eastern end of Spieden.

WALDRON ISLAND

This large, mostly private island is a mile and a half northwest of Orcas. The locals don't generally take kindly to outsiders, but the roads are open to the public, along with the dock at Cowlitz Bay. There are no stores, electricity, or phone service on the island, though it does have a small post office, cemetery, grade school, and landing strip. The year-round population is around 100, but it doubles when summer residents show up. Waldron Island was named for two members of the

1841 Wilkes Expedition: Thomas W. Waldron and R.R. Waldron.

Much of Waldron Island is flat and marshy, though the south end rises to 600 feet at Disney Mountain. The **Waldron Island Preserve** encompasses some 480 acres along Cowlitz Bay and Disney Mountain. These lands are jointly managed by The Nature Conservancy (www.tnc-washington.org) and the San Juan Preservation Trust (www.sjpt.org), with day use only allowed. The Conservancy has a steward on the island; call 206/343-4344 for access information.

Transportation

North Shore Charters (360/376-4855, www.sanjuancruises.net) offers day trips and drop-offs to Waldron Island from Deer Harbor on Orcas Island; $200 round-trip for up to six passengers.

Paraclete Charters (360/293-5920 or 800/808-2999, www.paracletecharters.com) provides service to Sucia Island from Anacortes. Prices depend upon the number of folks; it's $204 round-trip for two people.

Also based in Anacortes, **Island Express Charters** (360/299-2875 or 877/473-9777, www.islandexpresscharters.com) has a high-speed landing craft with space for kayaks, bikes, and gear. Rates depend upon the number of passengers; $240 round-trip for two people.

San Juan Airlines (360/293-4691 or 800/874-4434, www.sanjuanairlines.com) will land at the Waldron Island airstrip on a charter basis.

◪ YELLOW ISLAND

This 10-acre slice of paradise is virtually equidistant from San Juan, Shaw, and Orcas Islands. Yellow Island (206/343-4344, www.tnc-washington.org) is famous for its lush wildflower displays that peak from mid-April to early June, when more than 150 species are in bloom. The lack of deer and strong preservation efforts keep the island in a pristine state. Long and thin, Yellow Island has sand spits and grassy meadows on both ends, with a belt of evergreens across the middle.

Yellow Island was home for many years to Lewis and Tib Dodd, who lived a life that followed Henry David Thoreau's philosophy of self-sufficiency and harmony with nature. Allen died in 1960, and Tib continued to spend summers on the island for many more years before donating the land to The Nature Conservancy in 1980. The simple driftwood and rock cabin built by the Dodds now serves as the caretaker's seasonal home.

Visiting the Preserve

Today, Yellow Island is managed as an ecological preserve with a very stringent set of regulations. Visitors can only come between the hours of 10 a.m. and 4 p.m. daily, and will generally need to land their kayak or small boat on the southeast beach. No camping or overnight mooring is allowed, and you can't bring pets, food, or beverages to the island. Groups larger than six people will need written permission to visit. A half-mile trail rings the small island; pick up an interpretive brochure before heading out.

Most visitors to Yellow Island arrive by sea kayak or motorboat from Friday Harbor or Deer Harbor. Located at Deer Harbor Marina, **Orcas Boat Rentals** (360/376-7616, www.orcasboats.com) is a fairly short boat ride from Yellow Island. Owner Marc Broman will take a load of up to six people to the island for $100 round-trip.

North Shore Charters (360/376-4855, www.sanjuancruises.net) has day trips to Yellow Island from Deer Harbor on Orcas Island; $135 round-trip for up to six passengers.

Island Outfitters (360/299-2300 or 866/445-7506, www.seakayakshop.com) leads spring wildflower tours from Anacortes for $149/person. These include boat transport to Jones Island and a kayak paddle to Yellow Island, where you can hike around before returning to Anacortes by boat.

Other Wasp Islands

Yellow Island is one of the Wasp Islands. Others in the group include Bird Rock, Cliff, Coon, Crane, Low, McConnell, Nob, and Shirt Tail Reef. Crane Island is the largest of these, covering 222 privately owned acres. McConnell Island is also private, but a tombolo (narrow sandy strip) links it to diminutive **Northwest McConnell Rock State Park,** a popular lunch spot for kayakers. Look along the shore of McConnell for remains of an old miniature railroad that was once used to entertain kids. Contact Orcas Boat Rentals for access to the Wasp Islands.

Other San Juan Islands

Victoria and the Southern Gulf Islands

Many people view Victoria for the first time from the Inner Harbour, coming in by boat the way people have for almost 150 years; on rounding Laurel Point, the city sparkles into view. Ferries, fishing boats, and seaplanes bob in the harbor, with a backdrop of manicured lawns and flower gardens, quiet residential suburbs, and striking inner-city architecture. Despite the pressures that go with city life, easygoing Victorians still find time for a stroll along the waterfront, a round of golf, or a night out at a fine dining restaurant. Discovering Victoria's roots has been a longtime favorite with visitors, but some locals find the "more English than England" reputation tiring. Yes, there's a tacky side to some traditions, but high tea, double-decker bus tours, and formal gardens remain some of the true joys in Victoria.

Part of the same archipelago as the San Juan Islands, but separated by an international border,

© ANDREW HEMPSTEAD

Must-Sees

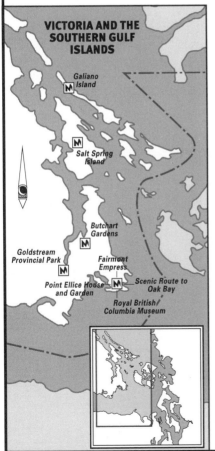

M Fairmont Empress: You don't need to be a guest of the Fairmont to admire this hotel's grandeur. Plan on eating a meal here for the full effect (page 219).

M Royal British Columbia Museum: If you only visit one museum in Victoria, make it this one. The collection spans the centuries, from wooly mammoths and First Peoples to modern day explorers (page 222).

view from Maple Ridge Cottages on Salt Spring Island

M Scenic Route to Oak Bay: Take this by route by car, bike, or even on foot to get a feeling for the natural splendor of Victoria (page 225).

M Point Ellice House and Garden: A standout among many dotting the city, this tearoom offers tours of the historic home and its grounds for CAN$17 (page 226).

M Goldstream Provincial Park: Laced with hiking trails, this park offers a fine escape from the city. If you're visiting in late fall, a trip here is worthwhile to view the spectacle of spawning salmon (page 227).

M Butchart Gardens: Even if you only have one day in Victoria, make time to visit Butchart, one of the world's most delightful gardens (page 228).

M Salt Spring Island: Largest of the Southern Gulf Islands, this is a wonderful place to explore, particularly the main settlement of Ganges and its colorful waterfront area (page 256).

M Galiano Island: This long, narrow island has some delightful beaches and good kayaking, especially around Montague Harbour Provincial Park (page 259).

VICTORIA AND THE SOUTHERN GULF ISLANDS

Galiano Island

Salt Spring Island

Butchart Gardens

Goldstream Provincial Park

Fairmont Empress

Point Ellice House and Garden

Scenic Route to Oak Bay

Royal British Columbia Museum

Victoria and the Southern Gulf Islands

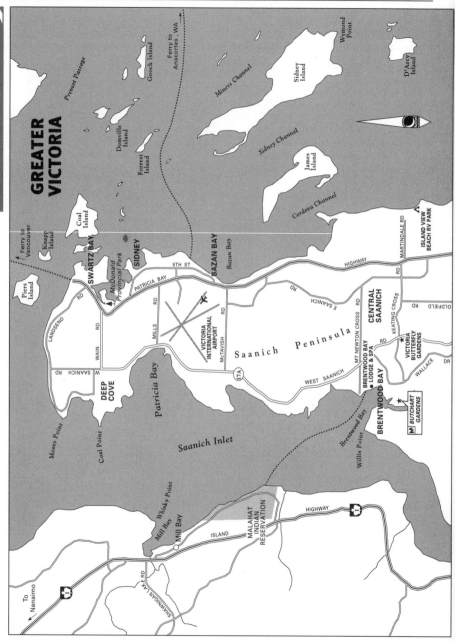

GREATER
VICTORIA

Prevost Passage

Gooch Island

Ferry to
Anacortes, WA

Miners Channel

Sidney
Island

Wymond
Point

D'Arcy
Island

Domville
Island

Sidney Channel

Forrest
Island

James
Island

Cordova Channel

Coal
Island

SWARTZ BAY

Knapp
Island

Ferry to
Vancouver

McDonald
Provincial Park

SIDNEY

BAZAN BAY

Bazan Bay

MARTINDALE RD

ISLAND VIEW
BEACH RV PARK

Piers
Island

5TH ST

Highway

RD

LANDSEND
RD

PATRICIA BAY

RD

RD

E SAANICH

RD

KEATING CROSS RD

OLDFIELD RD

CENTRAL
SAANICH

MILLS
RD

VICTORIA
INTERNATIONAL
AIRPORT

McTAVISH
RD

Saanich   Peninsula

MT NEWTON CROSS RD

BRENTWOOD BAY
LODGE & SPA

VICTORIA
BUTTERFLY
GARDENS

WALLACE
DR

WAIN

W SAANICH RD

17A

WEST SAANICH

BRENTWOOD BAY

BUTCHART
GARDENS

DEEP
COVE

Patricia Bay

Brentwood Bay

Moses Point

Coal Point

Saanich   Inlet

Willis Point

Whisky Point

Mill Bay

Mill Bay

MALAHAT
INDIAN
RESERVATION

HIGHWAY

ISLAND

SHAWNIGAN LAKE RD

To
Nanaimo

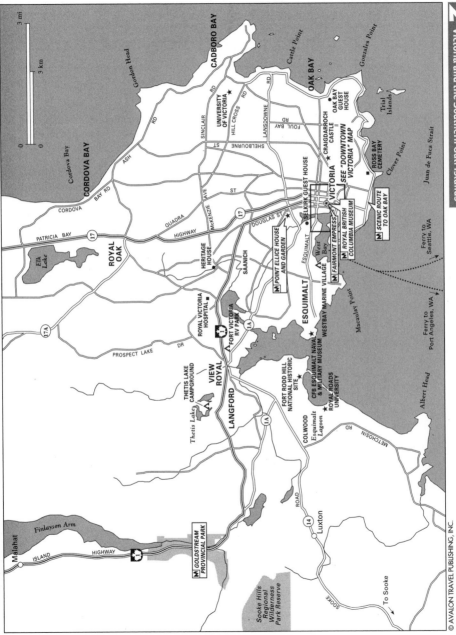

the Southern Gulf Islands are a natural addition to your Victoria vacation. Five of the islands—Salt Spring, North Pender, Galiano, Mayne, and Saturna—are populated. The largest of the islands, Salt Spring, is home to more than triple the population of the other four combined.

Note: Coverage of Victoria and the Southern Gulf Islands follows Canadian spellings and prices are in Canadian dollars (CAN$). This chapter is taken from *Moon Handbooks Vancouver & Victoria* by Andrew Hempstead. If you're planning to travel to other parts of Vancouver Island or the city of Vancouver, be sure to get this guidebook.

PLANNING YOUR TIME

Many visitors to Victoria spend a few nights in the city as part of a longer vacation that includes the rest of Vancouver Island. At an absolute minimum, plan on spending two full days in the capital, preferably overnighting at a characterful bed-and-breakfast. If this type of lodging doesn't appeal to you, book a room in one of the many historic hotels. Regardless of how long you'll be in the city, much of your time will be spent in and around the **Inner Harbour,** a busy waterway surrounded by the city's top sights and best restaurants. At the top of the must-see list is the **Royal British Columbia Museum,** which will impress even the biggest museophobes. The adjacent **Thunderbird Park** holds a collection of totem poles, making it a worthwhile stop. Unless you're traveling with the family in tow, give the commercial attractions a miss and spend your money on afternoon tea at an Oak Bay tearoom or a whale-watching trip. Victoria's most-visited attraction is Butchart Gardens, an absolutely stunning collection of plants that deserves at least half a day of your time. **Goldstream Provincial Park** and the scenic waterfront drive between downtown and Oak Bay are two outdoor destinations you should figure into your schedule.

The Southern Gulf Islands are linked to Victoria by ferry and floatplane, with ferries departing from Swartz Bay, north of downtown. If you have more than three days in Victoria, you should

plan on including the islands in your itinerary. Ferry service is frequent and hassle-free—simply roll up at the terminal and drive (or walk) aboard. **Salt Spring** is the closest populated island to Victoria and therefore not surprisingly the busiest. Here, the laid-back town of **Ganges** is well worth a stop for its scenic waterfront location and profusion of crafty shops. To experience the less touristy side of island life, you'll want to travel beyond Salt Spring to the other islands.

HISTORY

In 1792, Captain George Vancouver sailed through the Strait of Georgia, noting and naming Vancouver Island. But this had little effect on the many indigenous communities living along the shoreline. Europeans didn't see and exploit the island's potential for another 50 years, when the Hudson's Bay Company established control over the entire island and the mainland territory of "Columbia."

Fort Victoria

Needing to firmly establish British presence on the continent's northwest coast, the Hudson's Bay Company built Fort Victoria—named after Queen Victoria—on the southern tip of Vancouver Island in 1843. Three years later, the Oregon Treaty fixed the U.S./Canada boundary at the 49th parallel, with the proviso that the section of Vancouver Island lying south of that line would be retained by Canada. To forestall any claims that the United States may have had on the area, the British government went about settling the island. In 1849, the island was gazetted as a Crown colony and leased back to the Hudson's Bay Company. Gradually, land around Fort Victoria was opened up by groups of British settlers brought to the island by the company's subsidiary, Puget Sound Agricultural Company. Several large company farms were developed, and Esquimalt Harbour became a major port for British ships.

The Growth of Victoria

In the late 1850s, gold strikes on the mainland's Thompson and Fraser Rivers brought thousands of gold miners into Victoria, the region's only port and source of supplies. Overnight, Victoria became a classic boomtown, but with a distinctly British flavor; most of the company men, early settlers, and military personnel firmly maintained their homeland traditions and celebrations. Even after the gold rush ended, Victoria remained an energetic bastion of military, economic, and political activity. It was officially incorporated as a city in 1862. In 1868, two years after the colonies of Vancouver Island and British Columbia were united, Victoria was made capital. Through the two World Wars, Victoria continued to grow. The commencement of ferry service between Tsawwassen and Sidney in 1903 created a small population boom, but Victoria has always lagged well behind Vancouver in the population stakes.

Sights

The best way to get to know this compact city is on foot. All the downtown attractions are within a short walk of one another, and the more remote sights are easily reached by road or public transit. In summer, various tours are offered, giving you the choice of seeing Victoria by horse-drawn carriage, bus, boat, bicycle, limo—you name it. But if you still feel the need to have a car readily available, you'll be pleased to know that parking is plentiful just a few blocks from the Inner Harbour.

Victoria doesn't have as many official sights as Vancouver, but this isn't a bad thing. Once you've visited "must-sees" like the Royal British Columbia Museum and Butchart Gardens, you can devote your time to outdoor pursuits, such as whale-watching, a bike ride through Oak Bay, or something as simple as enjoying high tea in an old-fashioned tea room. You will be confronted with oodles of ways to trim bulging wallets in Victoria. Some commercial attractions are worth every cent, others are routine at best. The latter, though, may be crowd pleasers with children, which makes them worth considering.

INNER HARBOUR

The epicenter of downtown Victoria is the foreshore of the Inner Harbour, which is flanked by the parliament buildings, the city's main museum, and the landmark Fairmont Empress Hotel. Government Street leads uphill from the waterfront through a concentration of touristy shops and restaurants, while parallel to the west, Douglas Street is the core street of a smallish Central Business District.

Above the northeast corner of the harbor is the **Victoria Visitor Info Centre** (812 Wharf St., 250/953-2033, www.tourismvictoria.com), the perfect place to start your city exploration. Be sure to return to the Inner Harbour after dark, when the parliament buildings are outlined in lights and the Empress Hotel is floodlit.

Fairmont Empress

Overlooking the Inner Harbour, the pompous, ivy-covered 1908 Fairmont Empress is Victoria's most recognizable landmark. Its architect was the

Fairmont Empress

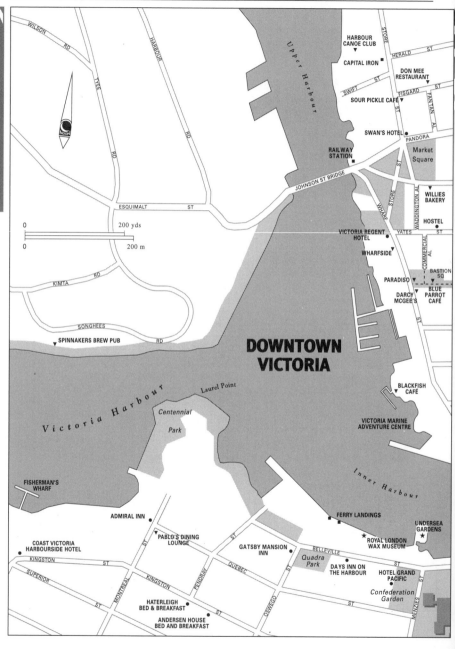

HARBOUR CANOE CLUB

CAPITAL IRON

DON MEE RESTAURANT

SOUR PICKLE CAFÉ

SWAN'S HOTEL

RAILWAY STATION

Market Square

WILLIES BAKERY

HOSTEL

VICTORIA REGENT HOTEL

WHARFSIDE

PARADISO

DARCY MCGEE'S

BLUE PARROT CAFÉ

SPINNAKERS BREW PUB

DOWNTOWN VICTORIA

BLACKFISH CAFÉ

VICTORIA MARINE ADVENTURE CENTRE

Victoria Harbour

Laurel Point

Centennial Park

Inner Harbour

FISHERMAN'S WHARF

ADMIRAL INN

PABLO'S DINING LOUNGE

GATSBY MANSION INN

FERRY LANDINGS

UNDERSEA GARDENS

ROYAL LONDON WAX MUSEUM

COAST VICTORIA HARBOURSIDE HOTEL

Quadra Park

DAYS INN ON THE HARBOUR

HOTEL GRAND PACIFIC

Confederation Garden

HATERLEIGH BED & BREAKFAST

ANDERSEN HOUSE BED AND BREAKFAST

WILSON RD

TYEE RD

HARBOUR RD

Upper Harbour

STORE ST

HERALD ST

SWIFT ST

FISGARD ST

FAN TAN AL

PANDORA

ESQUIMALT ST

WHARF ST

STORE ST

WADDINGTON AL

YATES ST

COMMERCIAL AL

BASTION SQ

JOHNSON ST BRIDGE

0   200 yds

0   200 m

KIMTA RD

SONGHEES RD

KINGSTON ST

SUPERIOR ST

MONTREAL ST

KINGSTON ST

PENDRAY ST

QUEBEC ST

OSWEGO ST

BELLEVILLE ST

MENZIES ST

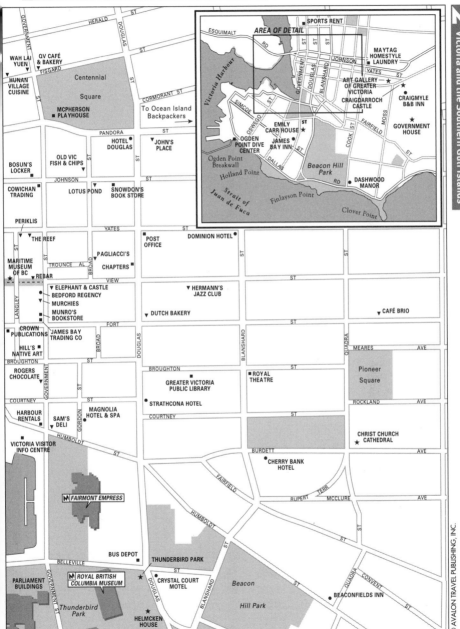

© AVALON TRAVEL PUBLISHING, INC.

well-known Francis Rattenbury, who also designed the parliament buildings, the CPR steamship terminal (now housing the wax museum), and Crystal Garden. It's worthwhile walking through the hotel lobby to gaze—head back, mouth agape—at the interior razzle-dazzle, and to watch people-watching people partake in traditional afternoon tea (see *Food*). Browse through the conservatory and gift shops, drool over the menus of the various restaurants, see what tours are available, and exchange currency if you're desperate (banks give a better exchange rate). Get a feeling for the hotel's history by joining a tour.

Behind the Empress Hotel is **Miniature World** (649 Humboldt St., 250/385-9731), a longtime favorite among Victoria's many commercial attractions. Featuring 80 settings—from the historic Canadian Pacific Railway to a futuristic space—admission is adult CAN$9.50, child CAN$6.50.

Royal British Columbia Museum

Canada's most-visited museum and easily one of North America's best, the Royal British Columbia Museum (675 Belleville St., 250/356-7226, summer 9 A.M.–6:30 P.M. daily, the rest of the year 9 A.M.–5 P.M. daily) is a must-see attraction for even the most jaded museum-goer. Its fine Natural History Gallery displays are extraordinarily true to life, complete with appropriate sounds and smells. Come face-to-face with an ice-age woolly mammoth, stroll through a coastal forest full of deer and tweeting birds, meander along a seashore or tidal marsh, then descend into the Open Ocean Exhibit via submarine—a very real trip not recommended for claustrophobics. The First Peoples Gallery holds a fine collection of artifacts from the island's first human inhabitants, the Nuu-chah-nulth (Nootka). Many of the pieces were collected by Charles Newcombe, who paid the Nuu-chah-nulth for them on collection sorties in the early 1900s. More modern human history is also explored here in creative ways. Take a tour through time via the time capsules; walk along a turn-of-the-century street; and experience hands-on exhibits on industrialization, the gold rush, and the exploration of British Columbia by land and sea in the Modern History and 20th Century Galleries.

The main gift shop stocks an excellent collection of books on Canadiana, wildlife, history, and indigenous art and culture, along with postcards and tourist paraphernalia, while the Out of the Mist gift shop sells indigenous arts and crafts. Next door, the tearoom is always crowded. A new addition to the museum is the **National Geographic Theatre,** showing nature-oriented IMAX films 9 A.M.–8 P.M. daily (additional charge).

Admission outside of summer is a very worthwhile adult CAN$11, senior and youth CAN$7.70. In summer, admission jumps to around CAN$23 for adults, which includes access to a traveling exhibit.

Surrounding the Museum

In front of the museum, the 27-meter (89-foot) high **Netherlands Centennial Carillon** was a gift to the city from British Columbia's Dutch community. The tower's 62 bells range in weight from eight to 1,500 kilograms (3,300 pounds) and toll at 15-minute intervals 7 A.M.–10 P.M. daily.

On the museum's eastern corner, at Belleville and Douglas Streets, lies **Thunderbird Park,** a small green spot chockablock with authentic totem poles intricately carved by northwest coast native peoples. Best of all, it's absolutely free.

Beside Thunderbird Park is **Helmcken House** (10 Elliot St., 250/361-0021, summer 10 A.M.–5 P.M. daily, the rest of the year noon–4 P.M. daily, adult CAN$5, senior CAN$4, child CAN$3), the oldest house in the province still standing on its original site. It was built by Dr. J.S. Helmcken, pioneer surgeon and legislator, who arrived in Victoria in 1850 and aided in negotiating the union of British Columbia with Canada in 1870. Inside this 1852 residence you'll find restored rooms decorated with Victorian period furniture, as well as a collection of the good doctor's gruesome surgical equipment (which will help you appreciate modern medical technology).

Parliament Buildings

Satisfy your lust for governmental, historic, and architectural knowledge all in one go by taking a free tour of the harborside Provincial Legislative Buildings, a.k.a. the parliament buildings. These prominent buildings were designed by Francis

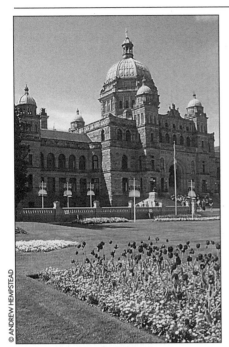

© ANDREW HEMPSTEAD

Parliament Buildings in Victoria

Rattenbury and completed in 1897. The exterior is British Columbia Haddington Island stone, and if you walk around the buildings you'll no doubt spot many a stern or gruesome face staring down from the stonework.

On either side of the main entrance stand statues of Sir James Douglas, who chose the location of Victoria, and Sir Matthew Baillie Begbie, who was in charge of law and order during the gold-rush period. Atop the copper-covered dome stands a gilded statue of Captain George Vancouver, the first mariner to circumnavigate Vancouver Island. Walk through the main entrance and into the memorial rotunda, look skyward for a dramatic view of the central dome, then continue upstairs to peer into the legislative chamber, the home of the democratic government of British Columbia. Free guided tours are offered every 20 minutes, 9 A.M.–noon and 1–5 P.M. in summer, less frequently (Monday–Friday only) in winter. Tour times differ ac-

cording to the goings-on inside; for current times, call the tour office at 250/387-3046.

Laurel Point

For an enjoyable short walk from downtown, continue along Belleville Street from the parliament buildings, passing a conglomeration of modern hotels, ferry terminals, and some intriguing architecture dating back to the late 19th century. A path leads down through a shady park to Laurel Point, hugging the waterfront and providing good views of Inner Harbour en route. If you're feeling really energetic, continue to **Fisherman's Wharf,** where an eclectic array of floating homes are tied up to floating wharves.

Commercial Attractions

Along the waterfront on Belleville Street, across the road from the parliament buildings, is the former CPR steamship terminal, now the **Royal London Wax Museum** (470 Belleville St., 250/388-4461, 9 A.M.–5 P.M. daily, until 7:30 P.M. in summer). As you enter the grandly ornate building, pay the admission (adult CAN$9, senior CAN$8, child CAN$5) to the cashier on the right. Inside the attraction proper is a series of galleries filled with around 300 wax figures—British Royalty, famous folks such as Mother Teresa and Albert Einstein, Canadian heroes like courageous cancer victim Terry Fox, and Arctic explorers. About half-way through, choose between Storybook Land or the Chamber of Horrors. If you have children (or even if you don't), you may want to bypass the latter. The hideous story of Madame Tussaud and her work that led to the famous London wax museum is interesting, but other displays are gruesome at best. By the time I'd watched the workings of the Algerian Hook and emerged at the gallery of movie stars, even Goldie Hawn was looking creepy.

On the water beside the wax museum, **Pacific Undersea Gardens** (490 Belleville St., 250/382-5717, summer 9 A.M.–6 P.M. daily, the rest of the year 9 A.M.–5 P.M. daily, adult CAN$9, senior CAN$8, child CAN$5) is of dubious value. Local species on display include tasty snapper, enormous sturgeon, schools of salmon, and scary wolf eels. Scuba divers miked for sound make regular appearances at the far end.

OLD TOWN

The oldest section of Victoria lies immediately north of the Inner Harbour between Wharf and Government Streets. Start by walking north from the Inner Harbour along historic Wharf Street, where Hudson's Bay Company furs were loaded onto ships bound for England, gold seekers arrived in search of fortune, and shopkeepers first established businesses. Cross the road to cobblestoned **Bastion Square,** lined with old gas lamps and decorative architecture dating from the 1860s to 1890s. This was the original site chosen by James Douglas in 1843 for Fort Victoria, the Hudson's Bay Company trading post. At one time the square held a courthouse, jail, and gallows. Today, restored buildings house trendy restaurants, cafés, nightclubs, and fashionable offices.

Maritime Museum of British Columbia

At the top (east) end of Bastion Square, the Maritime Museum of British Columbia (250/385-4222, daily 9:30 A.M.–4:30 P.M., until 6 P.M. in summer, adult CAN$8, senior CAN$5, child CAN$3) is housed in the old provincial courthouse building. It traces the history of seafaring exploration, adventure, commercial ventures, and passenger travel through displays of dugout canoes, model ships, Royal Navy charts, figureheads, photographs, naval uniforms, and bells. One room is devoted to exhibits chronicling the circumnavigation of the world, and another holds a theater. The museum also has a nautically oriented gift shop.

Other Old Town Sights

Centennial Square, bounded by Government Street, Douglas Street, Pandora Avenue, and Fisgard Street, is lined with many buildings dating from the 1880s and '90s, refurbished in recent times for all to appreciate. Don't miss the 1878 **City Hall** (fronting Douglas Street) and the imposing Greek-style building of the Hudson's Bay Company. Continue down Fisgard Street into colorful **Chinatown,** one of Canada's oldest Chinese enclaves. It's a delicious place to breathe in the aroma of authentic Asian food wafting from the many restaurants. Chinese prospectors and laborers first brought exotic spices, plants, and a love of intricate architecture and bright colors to Victoria in the 19th century. Poke through the dark little shops along Fisgard Street, where you can find everything from fragile paper lanterns and embroidered silks to gingerroot and exotic canned fruits and veggies. Then cruise Fan Tan Alley, the center of the opium trade in the 1800s. Walk south along Store Street and Wharf Street back to Bastion Square.

SOUTH OF THE INNER HARBOUR

Emily Carr House

In 1871, artist Emily Carr was born in this typical upper-class 1864 Victorian-era home (207 Government St., 250/383-5843, mid-May to mid-Oct. 10 A.M.–5 P.M. daily, adult CAN$5.50, senior and student CAN$4.50, child CAN$3.25). Carr moved to the mainland at an early age, escaping the confines of the capital to draw and write about the British Columbian native peoples and the wilderness in which she lived. She is best remembered today for her painting, a medium she took up in later years.

Beacon Hill Park

This large, hilly city park—a lush, sea-edged oasis of grass and flowers—extends from the back of the museum along Douglas Street out to cliffs that offer spectacular views of Juan de Fuca Strait and, on a clear day, the distant Olympic Mountains. Add a handful of rocky points to scramble on and many protected pebble-and-sand beaches and you've found yourself a perfect spot to indulge your senses. Catch a sea breeze and gaze at all the strolling, cycling, dog-walking, and pram-pushing Victorians passing by. On a bright sunny day you'll swear that most of Victoria is here, too. The park is within easy walking distance from downtown and can also be reached by bus no. 5. For a tidbit of history, walk through the park to rocky Finlayson

Point, once the site of an ancient fortified indigenous village. Between 1878 and 1892, two enormous guns protected the point against an expected but unrealized Russian invasion.

ROCKLAND

This historic part of downtown lies behind the Inner Harbour, east of Douglas Street, and is easily accessible on foot.

Christ Church Cathedral

On the corner of Quadra and Courtney Streets, Christ Church Cathedral (250/383-2714) is the seat of the Bishop of the Diocese of British Columbia. Built in 1896, in 13th-century Gothic style, it's one of Canada's largest churches. Self-guided tours are possible 8:30 A.M.–5 P.M. Monday–Friday and 7:30 A.M.–8:30 P.M. Sunday. In summer, the cathedral sponsors free choral recitals each Saturday at 4 P.M. The park next to the cathedral is a shady haven to rest weary feet, and the gravestones make fascinating reading.

Art Gallery of Greater Victoria

From Christ Church Cathedral, walk up Rockland Avenue through the historic Rockland district, passing stately mansions and colorful gardens on tree-lined streets. Turn left on Moss Street and you'll come to the 1889 Spencer Mansion and its modern wing, which together make up the Art Gallery of Greater Victoria (1040 Moss St., 250/384-4101, 10 A.M.–5 P.M. daily, 10 A.M.–9 P.M. Thursday, adult CAN$6, senior and child CAN$4). The gallery contains Canada's finest collection of Japanese art, a range of contemporary art, Emily Carr pieces, and traveling exhibits, as well as a Japanese garden with a Shinto shrine. The Gallery Shop sells art books, reproductions, and handcrafted jewelry, pottery, and glass.

Government House

Continue up Rockland Avenue from the art gallery to reach Government House, the official residence of the lieutenant governor, the queen's representative in British Columbia. The surrounding gardens, including an English-style garden, rose garden, and rhododendron garden, along with green velvet lawns and picture-perfect flower beds, are open to the public throughout the year. On the front side of the property, vegetation has been left in a more natural state, with gravel paths leading to benches that invite pausing to take in the city panorama.

Craigdarroch Castle

A short walk up (east) from the art gallery along Rockland Avenue and left on Joan Crescent brings you to the baronial four-story mansion known as Craigdarroch Castle (1050 Joan Crescent, 250/592-5323, summer 9 A.M.–7 P.M. daily, the rest of the year 10 A.M.–4:30 P.M. daily, adult CAN$10, child CAN$6). From downtown, take bus no. 11 (Uplands) or no. 14 (University) to Joan Crescent, then walk 100 meters (110 yards) up the hill. The architectural masterpiece was built in 1890 for Robert Dunsmuir, a wealthy industrialist and politician who died just before the building was completed. For all the nitty-gritties, tour the mansion with volunteer guides who really know their Dunsmuir, then admire at your leisure all the polished wood, stained-glass windows, Victorian-era furnishings, and the great city views from upstairs.

SCENIC ROUTE TO OAK BAY

This route starts south of the Inner Harbour and follows the coastline all the way to the University of Victoria. If you have your own transportation, this is a "must-do" in Victoria; if you don't, most city tours take in the sights detailed below. You can take Douglas Street south alongside Beacon Hill Park to access the coast, but it's possible to continue east along the Inner Harbour to the mouth of Victoria Harbour proper, passing the Canadian Coast Guard Base and the **Ogden Point Breakwall,** the official start of the Scenic Drive (marked by blue signs). The breakwater is only three meters (10 feet) wide, but extends for 800 meters (half a mile) into the bay. It's a super-popular stroll, especially in the early morning.

For the first few kilometers beyond the breakwater, the Olympic Mountains in Washington State are clearly visible across the Strait of Georgia, and many lookouts allow you to stop and take in the panorama, including **Clover Point.** A few hundred meters beyond Clover Point, **Ross Bay Cemetery** is the final resting place of many of early Victoria's most prominent residents. Volunteer hosts are on hand through summer to point out the graves of Emily Carr; British Columbia's first governor, Sir James Douglas; members of the coal-baron Dunsmuir family; and Billy Barker, of gold-rush fame. The gates are open weekdays through daylight hours.

Continuing east, Dallas Road takes you through quiet residential areas, past small pebble beaches covered in driftwood, and into the ritzy mansion district east of downtown, where the residents have grand houses, manicured gardens, and stunning water views.

Continue through the well-manicured fairways of Victoria Golf Club on Gonzales Point to Tudor-style **Oak Bay Beach Hotel,** a rambling old building with an English pub serving up hearty fare in an old-fashioned dining room or out on a patio with water views. From the nearby marina, the coastal road continues north to Cadboro Bay, home to the **Royal Victoria Yacht Club.** The **University of Victoria** lies on a ridge above Cadboro Bay; from here, head southwest along Cadboro Bay Road then Yates Street to get back downtown. To head north, take Sinclair Road then Mackenzie Avenue to reach Highway 17, the main route up the Saanich Peninsula toward famous Butchart Gardens.

THE GORGE WATERWAY

This natural canal leads north from the Inner Harbour to Portage Inlet, a small saltwater lake beside Highway 1. The best way to see the Gorge is from sea level, aboard a **Victoria Harbour Ferry** (250/708-0201). This company runs funky little 12-passenger vessels to a turnaround point at Gorge Park by the Tillicum Road Bridge. The round trip is CAN$16 pp.

Point Ellice House and Garden

Built in 1861, this restored mansion (250/380-6506, May to mid-Sept. 10 A.M.–4 P.M. daily, CAN$5, senior CAN$4, child CAN$3) sits amid beautiful gardens along the Gorge on

Point Ellice, less than two kilometers (1.2 miles) from the Inner Harbour. The house's second owner, Peter O'Reilly, a successful entrepreneur and politician, bought it in 1868 and entertained many distinguished guests there. Original Victorian-era artifacts clutter every nook and cranny of the interior. The best reason to visit is to enjoy a traditional English afternoon tea served 11 A.M.–3 P.M. (CAN$16.95 includes admission). To get there from the Inner Harbour, jump aboard a Victoria Harbour Ferry (10 minutes and CAN$3 each way). By road, take Government or Douglas Street north from downtown, turn left on Bay Street, and turn left again on Pleasant Street.

Craigflower Manor

Completed in 1856 using local lumber, this stately home (250/479-8053, May–Sept. Wed.–Sun. 1–5 P.M., grounds open year-round for self-guided tours, CAN$5 adults, CAN$3 students, free admission for children under 12) on the Gorge Waterway was built for Kenneth McKenzie, who employed colonists to farm the surrounding land. It was one of the island's first farms, and helped in the transition of the area from a fur-trading camp to a permanent settlement. Surrounded by commercial and residential sprawl, the scene today is a far cry from the 1800s, when the grand home was a social hub for Victorian socialites and naval officers from nearby Esquimalt. You can wander through the grounds and ask questions of volunteers who tend to gardens filled with the same vegetables and herbs that the original owners planted and ask to peek inside the main residence. Directly across the Gorge Waterway is Craigflower Schoolhouse, dating from a similar era as the manor and built from lumber cut from a steam-powered sawmill operated by the Mackenzie family. It served children from the adjacent farm while the second floor provided living quarters for the teacher's family. To reach Craigflower, take Gorge Road (Highway 1A) north from downtown to the Craigflower Bridge (around four km/2.5 miles). The schoolhouse is on the left; the manor is across the bridge on the right.

WEST OF DOWNTOWN

CFB Esquimalt Naval & Military Museum

This small museum (250/363-4312, 10 A.M.–3:30 P.M. Mon.–Fri., adult CAN$2, senior and child CAN$1) lies within the confines of **CFB Esquimalt,** on Esquimalt Harbour west of downtown. A couple of buildings have been opened to the public, displaying naval, military, and general maritime memorabilia. To get there from downtown, take the Johnson Street Bridge and follow Esquimalt Road to Admirals Road; turn north, then take Naden Way and you're on the base; follow the museum signs.

Fort Rodd Hill National Historic Site

Clinging to a headland across the harbor entrance from CFB Esquimalt, this picturesque site (603 Fort Rodd Hill Rd., Colwood, 250/478-5849, March–Oct. 10 A.M.–5:30 P.M. daily, Nov.–Feb. 9 A.M.–4:30 P.M. daily, adult CAN$4, senior CAN$3, child CAN$2) comprises **Fort Rodd,** built in 1898 to protect the fleets of ships in the harbor and **Fisgard Lighthouse,** which dates to 1873. It's an interesting place to explore; audio stations bring the sounds of the past alive, workrooms are furnished as they were at the turn of the century, and the lighthouse has been fully restored and is open to visitors. To get there from downtown, take the Old Island Highway (Gorge Road) and turn left on Belmont Road, then left onto Ocean Boulevard. By bus, take no. 50 from downtown, then transfer to no. 52.

While you're in the vicinity, continue down the forested road beyond the historic site turnoff to **Esquimalt Lagoon,** a haven for a great variety of bird life. The lagoon is separated from the open water by a narrow 1.5-kilometer (0.9-mile) causeway. An unpaved road leads along its length, providing access to a driftwood-strewn beach that is a popular swimming and sunbathing spot in summer.

Goldstream Provincial Park

Lying 20 kilometers (12 miles) from the heart of Victoria, this 390-hectare (960-acre) park straddles Highway 1 northwest of downtown.

The park's main natural feature is the Goldstream River, which flows north into the Finlayson Arm of Saanich Inlet. Forests of ancient Douglas fir and western red cedar flank the river; orchids flourish in forested glades; and at higher elevations, forests of lodgepole pine, western hemlock, and maple thrive.

The park's highlight event occurs late October through December, when chum, coho, and chinook salmon fight their way upriver to spawn themselves out on the same shallow gravel bars where they were born four years previously. Bald eagles begin arriving in December, feeding off the spawned-out salmon until February. From the picnic area parking lot, two kilometers (1.2 miles) north of the campground turnoff, a trail leads 400 meters (440 yards) along the Goldstream River to **Freeman King Visitor Centre** (250/478-9414, 9 A.M.–5 P.M. daily), where the life cycle of salmon is described.

Even if the salmon aren't spawning, Goldstream is a great place to visit at any time of year, with a hike for you no matter what your fitness level. Starting from the visitor center, the 200-meter (220-yard) **Marsh Trail** will reward you with panoramic water views from the mouth of the Goldstream River. Another popular destination is **Goldstream Falls,** in the south end of the park. This trail leaves from the back of the park campground and descends to the picturesque falls in around 300 meters (200 yards). Non-campers should park at the campground entrance, from which it's 1.2 km (0.7 miles) to the falls. One of the park's longer hikes is the **Goldmine Trail,** which begins from a parking lot on the west side of Highway 1 halfway between the campground and picnic area. This trail winds two kilometers (1.2 miles) each way through a mixed forest of lodgepole pine, maple, and western hemlock, passing the site of a short-lived gold rush and coming to **Niagara Falls,** a poor relation of its eastern namesake but still a picturesque flow of water. Of a similar length but more strenuous, is the trail to the summit of 419-meter (1370-foot) **Mt. Finlayson,** which takes around one hour each way and rewards successful summiteers with views back across the city and north along Saanich Inlet. The trail is accessed from

Finlayson Arm Road. (For details about camping in Goldstream Provincial Park, see *Campgrounds* in the *Accommodations* section.)

SAANICH PENINSULA

The Saanich Peninsula is the finger of land that extends north from downtown. It holds Victoria's most famous attraction, Butchart Gardens, as well as Victoria International Airport and the main arrival point for ferries from Tsawwassen. If you've caught the ferry over to Vancouver Island from Tsawwassen, you'll have arrived at **Swartz Bay,** on the northern tip of the Saanich Peninsula; from here, it's a clear run down Highway 17 to downtown Victoria. If you've been in Goldstream Provincial Park or are traveling down the island from Nanaimo on Highway 1, head north and south, respectively, to **Mill Bay,** where a ferry departs regularly for **Brentwood Bay** on the Saanich Peninsula. (Brentwood Bay is home to Butchart Gardens.) Ferries run in both directions nine times daily between 7:30 A.M. and 6 P.M. Peak one-way fares for the 25-minute-long crossing are adult CAN$5, child CAN$2.75, vehicle CAN$13.50. For exact times, contact **BC Ferries** (250/386-3431, www.bcferries.com).

Butchart Gardens

Carved from an abandoned quarry, these delightful gardens are Victoria's best-known attraction. They're approximately 20 kilometers (12 miles) north of downtown (800 Benvenuto Dr., Brentwood Bay, 250/652-4422, www.butchart-gardens.com). The gardens are open every day of the year from 9 A.M., closing in summer at 10 P.M. and in winter at 4 P.M., with varying closing hours in other seasons. Admission in summer is adult CAN$21, child CAN$10.50; admission is much lower in winter.

A Canadian cement pioneer, R.P. Butchart, built a mansion near his quarries. He and his wife, Jennie, traveled extensively, collecting rare and exotic shrubs, trees, and plants from around the world. By 1904, the quarries had been abandoned, and the couple began to beautify them by transplanting their collection into a number of formal gardens interspersed with concrete foot-paths, small bridges, waterfalls, ponds, and fountains. The gardens now contain more than 5,000 varieties of flowers, and the extensive nurseries test-grow some 35,000 new bulbs and more than 100 new roses every year. Go there in spring, summer, or early autumn to treat your eyes and nose to a marvelous sensual experience (many a gardener would give both hands to be able to work in these gardens). Highlights include the Sunken Garden (the original quarry site) with its water features and annuals; the formal Rose Garden, set around a central lawn; and the Japanese Garden, from which views extend to Saanich Inlet. In winter, when little is blooming and the entire landscape is green, the basic design of the gardens can best be appreciated. Summer visitors are in for a special treat on Saturday nights (July and August only), when a spectacular fireworks display lights up the garden.

As you may imagine, the attraction is extremely busy throughout spring and summer. For this reason, try to arrive as early as possible, before the tour buses arrive. Once through the tollgate and in the sprawling parking lot, make a note where you park your vehicle. Once on the grounds, pick up a flower guide and follow the suggested route. After you've done the rounds (allow at least two hours), you can choose from a variety of eateries. You'll also find a gift shop specializing in—you guessed it—floral items as well as a store selling seeds.

To get there from downtown, take Highway 17 north to the Brentwood–Butchart Gardens turnoff, turn left on Keating Crossroad, and follow the signs. **Island Coachlines** (250/388-6534) runs a regular shuttle out to the gardens from its downtown depot at 700 Douglas St. for CAN$4 each way, or join one of the many guided tours of Victoria that include this famous attraction. Bus nos. 74 and 75 from downtown go to Brentwood Bay.

Victoria Butterfly Gardens

In the same vicinity as Butchart Gardens, Victoria Butterfly Gardens (corner of Benvenuto and W. Saanich Rds., 250/652-3822, summer 9 A.M.–5 P.M. daily, March to mid-May and October 9:30 A.M.–4:30 P.M. daily, adult CAN$8.75, senior

CAN$7.75, child CAN$5) offers you the opportunity to view and photograph some of the world's most spectacular butterflies at close range. Thousands of these beautiful creatures—species from around the world—live here, flying freely around the enclosed gardens and feeding on the nectar provided by colorful tropical plants. You'll also be able to get up close and personal with exotic birds, such as parrots and cockatoos.

Sidney

The small town of Sidney lies on the east side of the Saanich Peninsula, overlooking the Strait of Georgia. As well as being the departure point for ferries to Washington's San Juan Islands, the waterfront area is a pleasant spot to spend a sunny day exploring bustling Port Sidney Marina and the many outdoor cafés. From the marina, the **Sidney Harbour Cruise** (250/655-5211) runs four tours daily around the harbor and to a couple of the inner Gulf Islands; CAN$15 pp. The only official attraction is **Sidney Museum** (9801 Seaport Place, at the end of Beacon Ave., 250/656-2140, 10 A.M.–4 P.M. daily, donation). The highlight is a display pertaining to whales, which includes skeletons.

Recreation

All of Vancouver Island is a recreational paradise, but Victorians find plenty to do around their own city. Walking and biking are especially popular, and from the Inner Harbour, it's possible to travel on foot or by pedal power all the way along the waterfront to Oak Bay. The best place to get information on a wide variety of commercial-activity operators is the **Inner Harbour Centre,** based on a floating dock just around the corner from the information center (Wharf St., 250/995-2211 or 800/575-6700, www.marine-adventures.com).

HIKING AND BIKING

If you're feeling energetic—or even if you're not—plan on walking or biking at least a small section of the Scenic Marine Drive, which follows the shoreline of Juan de Fuca Strait from Ogden Point all the way to Oak Bay. The section immediately south of downtown, between Holland Point Park and Ross Bay Cemetery is extremely popular with early rising locals, who start streaming onto the pedestrian pathway before the sun rises. Out of town, **Goldstream Provincial Park,** beside Highway 1, and **East Sooke Regional Park,** off Highway 14 west of downtown, offer the best hiking opportunities.

The **Galloping Goose Regional Trail** follows a rail line that once linked Victoria and Sooke. For 55 kilometers (34 miles), it parallels residential back streets, follows waterways, and passes through forested parkland. The rail bed has been graded the entire way, making it suitable for both walkers and cyclists. The official starting point is the disused railway station at the top end of downtown where Wharf and Johnson Streets merge. From the end of the trail in Sooke, bus no. 1 will bring you back to the city. Obviously, you can't walk the entire trail in a day, but even traversing a couple of short sections during your stay is worthwhile for the variety of landscapes en route.

Biking

For those keen on getting around by bike, it doesn't get much better than the bike path following the coastline of the peninsula on which Victoria lies. From downtown, ride down Government Street to Dallas Road, where you'll pick up the separate bike path running east along the coast to the charming seaside suburb of Oak Bay. From there, Oak Bay Road will take you back into the heart of the city for a round-trip of 20 kilometers (12 miles). You can rent bikes at **Sports Rent,** just north of downtown (1950 Government St., 250/385-7368, CAN$6–8 per hour, CAN$25–35 per day).

WATER SPORTS
Kayaking

Daily through summer, **Ocean River Sports** (Market Square, 1824 Store St., 250/381-4233 or

© ANDREW HEMPSTEAD

Sea kayaking is a great way to experience the Southern Gulf Islands.

To access the great diving in the Straits of Georgia and Juan de Fuca, you'll need to charter a boat. One particularly interesting site lies in the shallow waters off Sidney, just north of Victoria, where a 110-meter (360-foot) destroyer escort was scuttled especially for divers.

Swimming and Sunbathing

The best beaches are east of downtown. At **Willows Beach,** Oak Bay, most of the summer crowds spend the day sunbathing, although a few hardy individuals brave a swim; water temperature here tops out at around 17°C (63°F). Closer to downtown, at the foot of Douglas Street, the foreshore is mostly rocky, but you can find a couple of short, sandy stretches here and there. **Elk Lake,** toward the Saanich Peninsula, and **Thetis Lake,** west of downtown along Highway 1, are also popular swimming and sunbathing spots. Within walking distance of downtown, **Crystal Pool** (2275 Quadra St., 250/361-0732) has an Olympic-size pool as well as diving facilities, a kids' pool, sauna, and whirlpool.

TOURS

The classic way to see Victoria is from the comfort of a horse-drawn carriage. Throughout the day and into the evening, **Victoria Carriage Tours** (250/383-2207 or 877/663-2207) has horse carriages lined up along Menzies Street at Belleville Street awaiting passengers. A 30-minute tour costs CAN$80 per carriage (seating up to six people), a 45-minute tour costs CAN$120, or take a 60-minute Royal Tour for CAN$160. Tours run 9 A.M.–midnight and bookings aren't necessary, although there's often a line.

Big red double-decker buses are as much a part of the Victoria tour scene as horse-drawn carriages. These buses are operated by **Gray Line** (250/388-6539 or 800/663-8390) from beside the Inner Harbour. There are many tours to choose from, but to get yourself oriented while also learning some city history, take the 90-minute Grand City Drive Tour. It departs from the harborfront every half hour 9:30 A.M.–4 P.M., adult CAN$18, child CAN$9. The most popular of Gray Line's other tours is the one to

800/909-4233, www.oceanriver.com, CAN$60 pp) organizes guided three-hour paddles in the Inner Harbour. They also offer kayaking courses, sell and rent kayaks and other equipment, and offer overnight tours as far away as the Queen Charlotte Islands. **Sports Rent** (1950 Government St., 250/385-7368) rents canoes, kayaks, and a wide range of other outdoor equipment. Expect to pay about CAN$35 per day and from CAN$145 per week for a canoe or single kayak.

Scuba Diving

Close to downtown Victoria lie a number of good dive sites, notably the Ogden Point breakwater. At the breakwater, **Ogden Point Dive Center** (199 Dallas Rd., 250/380-9119, www.divevictoria.com) offers rentals, instruction, and a daily (10 A.M.) guided dive. Other amenities include lockers and showers. Another recommended Victoria dive shop for sales, service, and rentals, is **Ocean Sports** (800 Cloverdale Ave., 250/475-2202).

WHALE-WATCHING FROM VICTORIA

Once nearly extinct, gray whales now number an estimated 20,000. Their biannual migration between Baja Mexico and the Bering Sea takes them along the length of the British Columbia coast twice each year. The spring migration (March–April) is close to the shore, with whales stopping to rest and feed in places such as Clayoquot Sound and the Queen Charlotte Islands. Orcas (best known as killer whales) are also sighted often along the coast of British Columbia. Orcas are not actually whales, but the largest members of the dolphin family. Adult males can reach ten meters (33 feet) in length and up to 10 tons in weight but their most distinctive feature is a dorsal fin that protrudes more than 1.5 meters (five feet) from their back. Orcas are widespread in oceans around the world, but especially common in the waters between Vancouver Island and the mainland.

Taking a Tour
For a chance to see both resident and transient whales, along with sea lions, porpoises, and seals, choose from a number of operators heading out from Victoria. Trips last 2–3 hours, are generally made in sturdy inflatable boats with an onboard naturalist, and cost $75–100 pp. Recommended operators departing from the Inner Harbour include **Cuda Marine** (250/995-2832 or 866/995-2832), **Great Pacific Adventures** (250/386-2277 or 877/733-6722), **Orca Spirit Adventures** (250/383-8411 or 888/672-6722), **Prince of Whales** (250/383-4884 or 888/383-4884), and **Sooke Coastal Explorations** (250/642-2343, www.sookewhalewatching.com). **Sea Quest Adventures** (250/655-4256 or 888/656-7599) is based in Sidney, on the Saanich Peninsula, and offers whale-watching cruises on the Strait of Georgia. The waters here are calmer than those experienced from trips departing the Inner Harbour. The local whale-watching season runs from mid-April to October.

Butchart Gardens (CAN$42.50, including admission price).

On the Water
Victoria Harbour Ferry (250/708-0201) offers boat tours of the harbor and Gorge Waterway. The company's funny-looking boats each seat around 20 passengers and depart regularly 9 A.M.–8:15 P.M. from below the Empress Hotel. The 45-minute loop tour allows passengers the chance to get on and off at will; adult CAN$14, senior CAN$12, child CAN$7, or travel just pieces of the entire loop for CAN$3 per sector.

Arts and Entertainment

Victoria has a vibrant performing-arts community, with a number of unique events designed especially for the summer crowds. The city lacks the wild nightlife scene of neighboring Vancouver, but a large influx of summer workers keeps the bars crowded and a few nightclubs jumping during the busy season. The city does have more than its fair share of British-style pubs, and you can usually get a good meal along with a pint of lager. The magazine *Monday* (www.mondaymag.com) offers a comprehensive arts and entertainment section.

PERFORMING ARTS
Theater
Dating to 1914 and originally called the Pantages Theatre, the grand old **McPherson Playhouse** (Centennial Square, at Pandora Ave. and Government St.) is known lovingly as the "Mac" by local theater goers. The Mac went through hard times during the 1990s but has seen a recent revival of fortunes and now hosts a variety of performing arts. Its sister theater,

the **Royal Theatre** (805 Broughton St.), began life as a roadhouse and was used as a movie theater for many years. Today it hosts stage productions and a variety of musical recitals. For schedule information and tickets at both theaters, contact the Royal & McPherson Theatres Society (250/386-6121 or 888/717-6121, www.rmts.bc.ca).

Performing arts on a smaller scale can be appreciated at the **Belfry Theatre** (in a historic church at 1291 Gladstone St., 250/385-6815, CAN$26–33 pp), which offers live theater October–April.

Music and Dance

Pacific Opera Victoria (250/385-0222, www.pov.bc.ca) performs three productions each year (usually October–April) in the McPherson Playhouse. Tickets run CAN$20–65. The **Victoria Operatic Society** (250/381-1021), presents opera year-round; call for the current schedule.

At the **Symphony Splash** on the first Sunday of August, the **Victoria Symphony** performs on a barge moored at the Inner Harbour. This kicks off the performing-arts season, with regular performances through May at the Royal Theatre and other city venues. Tickets range CAN$16–32. For details call 250/385-9771 or the box office at 888/717-6121.

DRINKING AND DANCING

Bars

The **Strathcona Hotel** (919 Douglas St., 250/383-7137) is Victoria's largest entertainment venue, featuring four bars, including one serving a magnificent rooftop patio, and the Sticky Wicket, an English bar complete with mahogany paneling.

Closer to the Inner Harbour and converted from an old grain warehouse is **Swans Hotel** (506 Pandora St., 250/361-3310, from 11 A.M. daily), which brews its own beer. Unlike many other smaller brewing operations, this one uses traditional ingredients and methods, such as allowing the brew to settle naturally rather than be filtered. The beer is available at the hotel's bar, in its restaurants, and in the attached

liquor store. The main bar is a popular hangout for local businesspeople and gets busy weeknights 5–8 P.M.

A few blocks farther north and right on the water is the **Harbour Canoe Club** (450 Swift St., 250/361-1940), housed in an 1894 red-brick building that was at one time home to generators that powered Victoria's street lights. This place is popular with the downtown crowd and has a great deck.

Also offering magnificent water views is **Spinnakers Brew Pub,** across the Inner Harbour from downtown (308 Catherine St., 250/384-6613, 11 A.M.–10 P.M. daily). Opening in 1984 as Canada's first brewpub, Spinnakers continues to produce its own European-style ales, including the popular Spinnakers Ale. The original downstairs brewpub is now a restaurant, while upstairs is now the bar. Most importantly, both levels have outdoor tables with water views. The classic Spinnakers combo is a pint of India Pale Ale (CAN$5.50) and a half dozen local oysters (CAN$8).

Victoria's many English-style pubs usually feature a wide variety of beers, congenial atmosphere, and inexpensive meals. The closest of these to downtown is the **James Bay Inn** (270 Government St., 250/384-7151). Further out, **Six Mile House** (494 Island Hwy., 250/478-3121) is a classic Tudor-style English pub that was extensively restored in 1980. To get there, head west out of the city along Highway 1 and take the Colwood exit.

Nightclubs and Live Music Venues

Most of Victoria's nightclubs double as live-music venues attracting a great variety of acts. **Legends,** in the Strathcona Hotel (919 Douglas St., 250/383-7137), has been a city hotspot for more than 30 years. It comes alive with live rock'n' roll some nights and a deejay spinning the latest dance discs on other nights. In the same hotel, **Big Bad John's** is the city's main country-music venue. Known locally as the "Ingy," the **Ingraham Hotel,** north of downtown (2915 Douglas St., 250/385-6731) has cover bands playing Wednesday–Saturday and a country jam on Sunday afternoon. At the bottom of Bastion Square, **D'Arcy McGee's** (1127 Wharf St., 250/380-

1322) offers live music—Celtic sounds draw the biggest crowds—Friday and Saturday night. Below street level at the Wharfside complex, the **Boom Boom Room** (1208 Wharf St., 250/381-2331, closed Sunday), with bright lights and a large dance floor, is the city's most popular dance-only club.

Victoria boasts several good jazz venues. The best of these is **Hermann's Jazz Club** (753 View St., 250/388-9166). **Steamers** (570 Yates St., 250/381-4340) draws diverse acts, but generally features jazz and blues on Tuesday and Wednesday night. Check the Victoria Jazz Info Line (250/388-4423, www.vicjazz.bc.ca) for a schedule of local jazz performances.

SHOPPING

Victoria is a shopper's delight. Most shops and all major department stores are generally open 9:30 A.M.–5:30 P.M. Monday–Saturday and stay open for late-night shopping Thursday and Friday nights until 9 P.M. The touristy shops around the Inner Harbour and along Government Street are all open Sunday. Government Street is the main strip of tourist and gift shops. The bottom end, behind the Empress Hotel, is where you'll pick up all those tacky T-shirts and such. Farther up the street are more stylish shops, such as **James Bay Trading Co.** (1102 Government St., 250/388-5477), which specializes in indigenous arts from coastal communities; **Hill's Native Art** (1008 Government St., 250/385-3911), selling a wide range of authentic indigenous souvenirs; and **Cowichan Trading** (1328 Government St., 250/383-0321), featuring Cowichan sweaters. Traditions continue at **Rogers Chocolates** (913 Government St., 250/384-7021), which is set up like a candy store of the early 1900s, when Charles Rogers first began selling his homemade chocolates to the local kids.

Old Town

In Old Town, the colorful, two-story **Market Square** courtyard complex was once the haunt of sailors, sealers, and whalers, who came ashore looking for booze and brothels. It's been jazzed up, and today shops here specialize in everything from kayaks to condoms. Walk out of Market Square on Johnson Street to find camping-supply stores and the interesting **Bosun's Locker** (580 Johnson St., 250/386-1308), filled to the brim with nautical knick-knacks. Follow Store Street north from Market Square for a concentration of arts and crafts shops along Herald Street. In the vicinity, **Capital Iron** (1900 Store St., 250/385-9703 or 877/385-9703, www.capitaliron.net) is the real thing. Housed in a building that dates to 1863, this business began in the 1930s by offering the public goods salvaged from ships. In the 70-odd years since, it's evolved into a department store stocking an eclectic variety of hardware and homeware products.

Festivals and Events

The birthday of Queen Victoria has been celebrated in Canada since 1834, and is especially relevant to those who call her namesake city home. The Inner Harbour is alive with weekend festivities that culminate on Monday in a downtown **Victoria Day Parade.** It can take two hours to pass a single spot. (Although Queen Victoria's actual birthday was May 24, the event is celebrated with a public holiday on the Monday preceding May 25.)

During **Jazzfest International** (250/388-4423, www.vicjazz.bc.ca), more than 200 musicians from around the world descend on the capital for this week-long celebration at various city venues at the end of June.

While most visitors associate Victoria with afternoon tea at the Empress, cowboys know Victoria as an important early-season stop on the rodeo circuit. The **Luxton Pro Rodeo** (250/478-4250, www.rodeocanada.com) features all traditional events as well as mutton-busting for the kids. It takes place the third weekend of May. Access to the grounds, west of the city toward Sooke, is free, with admission to the rodeo itself costing CAN$12.

Hosted by the Royal Victoria Yacht Club and with more than 60 years of history behind it, the **Swiftsure International Yacht Race** (250/592-9098, www.swiftsure.org) in late May attracts thousands of spectators to the shoreline of the Inner Harbour to watch a wide variety of vessels cross the finish line in six different classes, including the popular pre-1970 Classics division.

For 10 days in late June and early July, **FolkFest** (250/388-4728, www.icafolkfest.com) features contemporary and traditional, professional and amateur jazz centered on the Wharf Street waterfront. An arts and crafts market, a harborfront beer garden, and an International Food Village complete the festi-val. The best part is that entry to most performances is free.

On the first Sunday in August, the local symphony orchestra performs **Symphony Splash** (250/385-9771, www.symphonysplash.ca) from a barge moored in the Inner Harbour. This unique musical event attracts upwards of 40,000 spectators who line the shore or watch from kayaks.

Running 10 days in late August, the **Victoria Fringe Festival** (250/383-2663, www.victoriafringe.com) is a celebration of fringe theater, with more than 350 acts performing at six venues throughout the city, including outside along the harbor foreshore and inside at the Conservatory of Music on Pandora Street. All tickets are less than CAN$10.

Accommodations

Victoria accommodations come in all shapes and sizes. A couple of downtown hostels cater to travelers on a budget, while there are also a surprising number of convenient roadside motels with rooms for less than CAN$100, including one right off the Inner Harbour. Bed-and-breakfasts are where Victoria really shines, with more than 300 at last count. You'll be able to find bed-and-breakfast rooms for less than CAN$100, but to fully immerse yourself in the historic charm of the city, expect to pay more. In the same price range are boutique hotels, such as the Bedford Regency—older hotels that have been restored and come with top-notch amenities and full service. Finally, if you have wads of cash to spare or are looking for a splurge, the surrounding area is blessed with two lodges (Sooke Harbour House and the Aerie Resort) that regularly garner top rankings in all the glossy travel magazine polls and a third (Brentwood Bay Lodge & Spa) of equal quality that opened in 2004.

In the off season (October–May), nightly rates quoted below are discounted up to 50 percent, but again, occupancy rates are high as Canadians flock to the country's winter hot spot. No matter what time of year you plan to visit, arriving in Victoria without a reservation is unwise, but especially in the summer months, when gaggles of tourists compete for a relative paucity of rooms. As a last resort, staff at the **Victoria Tourist Info Centre** (812 Wharf St., 250/953-2022 or 800/663-3883, www.victoriatourism.com) can offer help finding a room.

DOWNTOWN

All but a couple of the accommodations in this section are within easy walking distance of the Inner Harbour. If you're traveling to Victoria outside of summer, don't be put off by the quoted rates—it is the downtown hotels that offer the biggest off-season discounts.

If you're simply looking for a motel room and don't want to pay for the location, there are options along the routes leading into downtown from the north. Locally owned **Traveller's Inn** (www.travellersinn.com) has a number of motels for less than CAN$100, while along Gorge Road (Hwy. 1A), you'll find a Days Inn and Howard Johnson.

Under CAN$50

Budget travelers are well catered to in Victoria, and while the accommodation choices in the capital are more varied than in Vancouver, there is no one backpacker lodge that stands out above the rest.

In the heart of downtown Victoria's oldest section is **Hostelling International Victoria** (516 Yates St., 250/385-4511 or 888/883-0099, www.hihostels.ca). The totally renovated hostel enjoys a great location only a stone's throw from the harbor. Separate dorms and bathroom facilities for men and women are complemented by two fully equipped kitchens, a large meeting room, lounge, library, game room, travel services, public Internet terminals, and an informative bulletin board. Members of Hostelling International pay CAN$20 per night, nonmembers CAN$24; private rooms range CAN$48–60 s or d.

Housed in the upper stories of an old commercial building, **Ocean Island Backpackers Inn** (791 Pandora Ave., 250/385-1788 or 888/888-4180, www.oceanisland.com) lies just a couple of blocks from downtown. This a real party place—exactly what some young travelers are looking for, but annoying enough for some to generate letters to harried travel writers. On the plus side, the lodging is clean, modern, and welcoming throughout. Guests have use of kitchen facilities, a laundry, and a computer for Internet access. There's also plenty of space to relax, such as a reading room, music room (guitars supplied), television room, and street-level bar open until midnight. Dorm beds are CAN$21–24 pp while private rooms are CAN$52 s or d. Parking is an additional CAN$5 per day, or the owners will make pick-ups from the bus depot.

If you have your own transportation, **M Selkirk Guest House** (934 Selkirk Ave., 250/389-1213 or 800/974-6638, www.selkirk guesthouse.com) is a good choice. This family-run accommodation is in an attractive historic home on the south side of the Gorge Waterway just under three kilometers (1.9 miles) from downtown (cross the Johnson Street Bridge from downtown and take Craigflower Road). It has all the usual facilities, as well as a private dock, waterfront hot tub, and pleasant gardens. Dorm beds are CAN$22 and breakfast is an additional CAN$5.

CAN$50–100

The centrally located **Hotel Douglas** (1450 Douglas St., 250/383-4157 or 800/332-9981, www.hoteldouglas.com) is one of Victoria's many old hotels, this one dating to 1911 and five stories high. Guests have use of a coin laundry, and downstairs is a 24-hour café and an old-fashioned lounge with food service. The rooms are basic and small but comfortable. One drawback is that half the rooms share bathrooms (CAN$55 s, CAN$65 d). Larger en suite rooms are CAN$80 s, CAN$90 d.

In a quiet residential area immediately east of downtown, **Craigmyle B&B Inn** (1037 Craigdarroch Rd., Rockland, 250/595-5411 or 888/595-5411, CAN$65–175 s or d) has been converted from part of the original Craigdarroch Estate (it stands directly in front of the famous castle). This rambling 1913 home is full of character, comfortable furnishings, and lots of original stained-glass windows. Rooms include singles, doubles, and family suites; some share bathrooms while others have en suites. An inviting living room with a TV, a bright sunny dining area, and friendly longtime owners make this a real home-away-from-home. Check in is 2–6 P.M.

Another excellent choice at the lower end of the price spectrum is **Selkirk Guest House** (934 Selkirk Ave., Esquimalt, 250/389-1213 or 800/974-6638, www.selkirkguesthouse.com), on the Gorge Waterway three kilometers (1.9 miles) from the Inner Harbour. While the house has been extensively renovated and offers comfortable accommodations, it's the location that sets this place apart from similarly priced choices. The only thing separating the house from the water is the manicured garden, complete with a hot tub that sits under an old willow tree. Three of the guest rooms share bathrooms and a kitchen (CAN$80–90 s or d), while the more spacious Rose Room has an en suite bathroom, fireplace, its own kitchen, and a verandah overlooking the garden (CAN$95 s or d). Breakfast is an additional CAN$5 per person. Younger travelers will love the trampoline and treehouse.

Just one block from the Inner Harbour and kitty-corner to the bus depot is the old **Crystal Court Motel** (701 Belleville St., 250/384-0551,

CAN$98 s, CAN$104 d, CAN$114 for a kitchenette), with 56 park-at-the-door-style motel rooms, half with kitchenettes. As you'd expect with any accommodation falling into this price category in such a prime position, the rooms are fairly basic. Ask for a non-smoking room when making your reservation.

Farther from the harbor, but still within walking distance, is the 1897 **Cherry Bank Hotel,** across Douglas St. in a quiet location (825 Burdett Ave., 250/385-5380 or 800/998-6688, CAN$79–99 s or d). Be sure to request a room in the original wing, otherwise you'll pay the same for a motel-like room lacking character. The rooms have no TV or phone. Downstairs is a lounge and a restaurant known for excellent ribs. Rates include a full breakfast served in a wonderfully old-fashioned dining room.

CAN$100–150

Value wise, you'll get the biggest bang for your buck with the first two choices in this price range. On the downside, you'll be a little way from the waterfront.

M Heritage House (3808 Heritage Ln., 250/479-0892 or 877/326-9242, www.heritage housevictoria.com), a beautiful 1910 mansion surrounded by trees and gardens, sits in a quiet residential area near Portage Inlet, five kilometers (3.7 miles) northwest of city center. Friendly owners Larry and Sandra Gray have lovingly restored the house to its former glory. Guests choose from several outstanding rooms, one with a view of Portage Inlet from a private veranda. Enjoy the large communal living room and a cooked breakfast in the elegant dining room. It's very busy in summer but quieter November–April. Reservations are necessary year-round. Rooms vary in size and furnishings; from CAN$135 s or d. Heritage Lane is not shown on any Victoria maps; from city center, take Douglas Street north to Burnside Road East (bear left off of Douglas). Just across the TransCanada Highway, Burnside makes a hard left. (If you continue straight instead, you'll be on Interurban Road). Make the left turn and continue down Burnside to just past Grange Road. The next road on the right is Heritage Lane.

East of downtown in the suburb of Oak Bay, the Tudor-style **Oak Bay Guest House,** one block from the waterfront (1052 Newport Ave., 250/598-3812 or 800/575-3812, www.beds-breakfasts.com, CAN$135–180 s or d), has been taking in guests since 1922. It offers 11 smallish antique-filled rooms, each with a private balcony and a bathroom. The Sun Lounge holds a small library and tea- and coffee-making facilities, while the Foyer Lounge features plush chairs set around an open fireplace. Rates include a delicious four-course breakfast.

Dating to 1911 and once home to artist Emily Carr, **James Bay Inn** (270 Government St., 250/384-7151 or 800/836-2649, www.james-bayinn.com) is five blocks from the harbor and within easy walking distance of all city sights and Beacon Hill Park. From the outside, the hotel has a clunky, uninspiring look, but a bright and breezy décor and new beds in the simply furnished rooms make it a pleasant place to rest your head. Summer rates range CAN$120–179 s or d, discounted as low as CAN$60 in winter. All guests enjoy discounted food and drink at the downstairs restaurant and pub.

Away from the water, but still just one block from Douglas Street, is the 1876 **Dominion Hotel** (759 Yates St., 250/384-4136 or 800/663-6101, www.dominion-hotel.com), Victoria's oldest hotel. Millions of dollars have been spent restoring the property with stylish wooden beams, brass trim and lamps, ceiling fans, and marble floors reminiscent of the Victorian era. The restored Boutique Rooms (CAN$149–249 s or d) are absolutely charming with large beds and lovely furnished bathrooms. Some rooms at the Dominion haven't been renovated in years. These are sold as Standard Rooms (you won't find pictures on the Dominion website) and are a little overpriced at CAN$89–119 s, CAN$99–139 d. Tea and toast is included in all these rates. The Dominion offers some attractive off-season, meal-inclusive deals—just make sure you know which class of room you'll be in.

CAN$150–200

If you're looking for a modern feel, centrally located **M Swans Suite Hotel** (506 Pandora Ave.,

250/361-3310 or 800/668-7926, www.swans hotel.com) is an excellent choice. Located above a restaurant/pub complex that was built in the 1880s as a grain storehouse, each of the 30 split-level suites holds a loft, full kitchen, dining area, and bedroom. The furnishings are casual yet elegantly rustic, with West Coast artwork adorning the walls and fresh flowers in every room. The rates of CAN$159 for a studio, CAN$189 for a one-bedroom suite, and CAN$259 for a two-bedroom suite are a great value. In the off-season, all rooms are discounted up to 50 percent.

A few blocks back from the Inner Harbour is **Andersen House Bed and Breakfast** (301 Kingston St., 250/388-4565 or 877/264-9988, www.andersenhouse.com). Built late last century for a retired sea captain, the house features large high-ceilinged rooms all overlooking gardens that supply the kitchen with a variety of berries and herbs. Each has an en-suite bathroom, private entrance, and CD player (complete with CDs). In the tradition of its original owner, the house is decorated with furnishings from around the world, including contemporary paintings. My favorite of the four guest rooms is the Garden Studio, an oversized space with stained-glass windows, a jetted tub, and doors that open to a private corner of the garden. Summer rates range CAN$195–275 s or d, while in the cooler months, these same rooms run CAN$95–175.

Separated from downtown by Beacon Hill Park, **Dashwood Manor** (1 Cook St., 250/385-5517 or 800/667-5517, www.dashwoodmanor .com), a 1912 Tudor-style heritage house on a bluff overlooking Juan de Fuca Strait, enjoys a panoramic view of the entire Olympic mountain range. The 14 rooms are elegantly furnished, and hosts Dave and Sharon Layzell will happily recount the historic details of each room. Rates range from CAN$155 s or d up to CAN$295 for the Oxford Grand, which holds a chandelier, stone fireplace, and antiques. Off-season rates range CAN$75–145.

Yes, it's a chain hotel, but **Days Inn on the Harbour** (427 Belleville St., 250/386-3451 or 800/665-3024, www.daysinnvictoria.com) has a prime waterfront location that will make you feel like you're paying more than you really are.

Befitting the location, rooms have a subtle nautical feel, and like all Days Inns, practical yet comfortable furnishings. Standard rooms start at CAN$169 s or d, but it's well worth the extra CAN$10 for a harbor view. In winter, you'll pay just CAN$100 for a suite with a view. Year-round bonuses include free parking, in-room coffeemakers, and complimentary newspapers and bottled water.

In the oldest section of downtown, surrounded by the city's best dining and shopping opportunities, is the **Bedford Regency** (1140 Government St., 250/384-6835 or 800/665-6500), featuring 40 guest rooms of varying configurations. Stylish, uncluttered Art Deco furnishings and high ceilings make the standard rooms (CAN$165 s or d) seem larger than they really are. A better deal are the deluxe rooms and suites, which provide more space and better amenities for only slightly more money (from CAN$180 s or d). The downstairs Belingo Lounge is the perfect place to relax with a glass of Pacific Northwest wine.

CAN$200–250
Right on the Inner Harbour, **Gatsby Mansion Inn** (309 Belleville St., 250/388-9191 or 800/ 563-9656, www.bellevillepark.com) has a very central position across from the water. Dating to 1897, this magnificent 20-room property has been elegantly restored, with stained-glass windows, a magnificent fireplace, lots of exposed wood, crystal chandeliers under a gabled roof, and antiques decorating every corner. Afternoon tea is served in a comfortable lounge area off the lobby, and the restaurant has a nice veranda. Through summer, rooms start at CAN$235 s, CAN$245 d; the biggest and best of these, with a king bed and harbor view, is CAN$309 s, CAN$319 d. Packages make staying at the Gatsby Mansion more reasonable, or visit in winter for as little as CAN$129 s, CAN$139 d.

Just four blocks from the Inner Harbour, the 1905 **Beaconsfield Inn** (988 Humboldt St., 250/384-4044 or 888/884-4044, www.beaconsfieldinn.com, CAN$219–359 s or d) is exactly what you may imagine a Victorian bed-and-breakfast should be. Original mahogany floors, high ceilings, classical moldings, imported antiques,

© ANDREW HEMPSTEAD

Gatsby Mansion Inn

and fresh flowers from the garden create an upscale historic charm throughout. Each of the nine guest rooms is individually decorated in a style matching the Edwardian era. I stayed in the Emily Carr Room. Named for the renowned artist who spent her early years in the city, this room has a rich burgundy-and-green color scheme, Emily Carr prints on the walls, a regal mahogany bed topped by a goose-down comforter, an oversized bathroom and double jetted tub, and a separate sitting area with a fireplace. After checking in, you'll be invited to join other guests for high tea in the library, then encouraged to return for a glass of sherry before heading out for dinner. As you may expect, breakfast—served in a formal dining room or more casual conservatory—is a grand affair, with multiple courses of hearty fare delivered to your table by your impeccably presented host.

Around the southern end of the Inner Harbour, the **Admiral Inn** (257 Belleville St., 250/388-6267 or 888/823-6472, www.admiral.bc.ca,

CAN$219–249 s or d, CAN$129–159 in winter) has been creeping up in price. Nonetheless, it's an excellent place to stay away from the downtown crowd, while still within walking distance of the main attractions and best restaurants. Spacious rooms come with a balcony or patio, and extras include free parking, a light breakfast, kitchens in many rooms, and discount coupons for local attractions. Throw in friendly owner-operators, and you have good value.

Enjoying an absolute waterfront location right downtown is the **Victoria Regent Hotel** (1234 Wharf St., 250/386-2211 or 800/663-7472, www.victoriaregent.com). The exterior of this renovated building is nothing special, but inside, the rooms are spacious and comfortable. The best value rooms at the Regent are the suites, which include a full kitchen, balcony, and a daily newspaper; CAN$269 s or d, or CAN$299 with a water view. Regular rooms are CAN$200 s or d.

CAN$250–300

The  **Magnolia Hotel & Spa** (623 Courtney St., 250/381-0999 or 877/624-6654, www.magnoliahotel.com, CAN$269 s or d) is a European-style boutique hotel just up the hill from the harbor. It features an elegant interior with mahogany-paneled walls, Persian rugs, chandeliers, a gold-leafed ceiling, and fresh flowers throughout public areas. The rooms themselves are each elegantly furnished and feature floor-to-ceiling windows, heritage-style furniture in a contemporary room layout, richly-colored fabrics, down duvets, a work desk with cordless phone, and coffee-making facilities. Many also feature a gas fireplace. The bathrooms are huge, each with marble trim, a soaker tub, and separate shower stall. The Magnolia is also home to an AVEDA Lifestyle Spa, two restaurants, and a small in-house brewery. Rates include a light breakfast, daily newspaper, passes to a nearby fitness facility, and unlike most other downtown hotels, free parking. Off-season rates range CAN$169–209 s or d.

Holding a prime waterfront position next to the Parliament Buildings is the **Hotel Grand Pacific** (463 Belleville St., 250/386-0450 or 800/228-5151, www.hotelgrandpacific.com).

First opened in 1989, the Grand Pacific has been an ongoing construction project, with extra wings added through the ensuing 15 years. Aside from more than 300 rooms, this property is also home to Spa at the Grand, a health club, a variety of restaurants and lounges, and a currency exchange. Standard rooms, with king or twin beds, cost CAN$259 s or d (check the Internet for these same rooms sold for less than CAN$200), or pay CAN$329 for water views. All rooms are well appointed, spacious, and have small private balconies.

Over CAN$300

The grand old **Fairmont Empress** (721 Government St., 250/384-8111 or 800/257-7544, www.fairmont.com) is Victoria's best-loved accommodation. Covered in ivy and with only magnificent gardens separating it from the Inner Harbour, it's also in the city's best location. Designed by Francis Rattenbury in 1908, the Empress is one of the original Canadian Pacific Railway hotels. Rooms are offered in 90 different configurations, but like other hotels of the era, most are small. Each is filled with Victorian period furnishings and antiques. The least expensive Fairmont rooms start at CAN$299, but if you really want to stay in this Canadian landmark, consider upgrading to an Entrée Gold room. Although not necessarily larger, these rooms have views, a private check-in, nightly turn-down service, and a private lounge where hors d'eouvres are served in the evening; CAN$429–499 includes a light breakfast. If you can't afford to stay at the Empress, plan on at least visiting one of the restaurants or the regal Bengal Lounge.

Campgrounds

The closest camping to downtown is at **Westbay Marine Village** (453 Head St., Esquimalt, 250/385-1831, www.westbay.bc.ca), across Victoria Harbour from downtown. Facilities at this RV-only campground include full hook-ups and a laundry facility. It is part of a marina complex comprising floating residences and commercial businesses, such as fishing charter operators and restaurants. Water taxis connect the "village" to downtown. Rates range CAN$25–40 per night,

depending on the view (the CAN$40 sites have unobstructed views across to the Inner Harbour).

Fort Victoria RV Park (340 Island Hwy., 250/479-8112, www.fortvicrv.com) is six kilometers (3.7 miles) northwest of city center on Highway 1A. This campground provides hookups, free showers, laundry facilities, and opportunities to join charter salmon-fishing trips. Tenting sites are CAN$24, hookups are CAN$28–30.

Continuing west along Highway 1, take Exit 10 (stay in the Colwood Lane), and then take Six Mile Road back under the highway to reach **Thetis Lake Campground** (West Park Ln., 250/478-3845). The grounds feature pleasant shaded sites, coin-operated showers, and laundry facilities. It adjoins Thetis Lake Park, which is crisscrossed by hiking trails and holds one of the city's favorite swimming and sunbathing spots. Unserviced sites are CAN$22, hookups CAN$25–30.

Continuing west from Thetis Lake Campground, Highway 1 curves north through **Goldstream Provincial Park** (19 kilometers/11 miles from downtown) and begins its up-island journey north. The southern end of the park holds 161 well-spaced campsites scattered through an old-growth forest—it's one of the most beautiful settings you could imagine close to a capital city. The campground offers free hot showers but no hookups. Sites are CAN$22 per night. While the park's interpretive center is further north along the highway, many trails lead off from the campground, including a five-minute walk to photogenic Goldstream Falls. The campground is also within walking distance of a grocery store.

SAANICH PENINSULA

With the exception of the sparkling new Brentwood Bay Lodge & Spa, the accommodations detailed below are along Highway 17, the main route between downtown Victoria and the BC Ferries terminal at Swartz Bay. These properties are best suited to travelers arriving at or departing from the airport or ferry terminal, but are also handy to Butchart Gardens.

CAN$50–100

Right beside the highway, **Western 66 Motel**

(2401 Mt. Newton Cross Rd., 250/652-4464 or 800/463-4464, www.western66travel.com) has a large variety of affordable rooms, English-style gardens, complimentary coffee in the lobby each morning, and an inexpensive restaurant on the premises. Rooms start at CAN$90 s or d but traveling families will want to upgrade to the super-spacious family rooms that sleep up to six people.

CAN$100–150

Just off the main highway between the ferry terminal and downtown, on the road into downtown Sidney, is **M Cedarwood Inn & Suites** (9522 Lochside Dr., 250/656-5551 or 877/656-5551, www.cedarwoodinnandsuites.com) highlighted by a colorful garden with outdoor seating overlooking the Strait of Georgia. Regular motel rooms go for CAN$109 s or d, but a better deal are the individually furnished cottages, some with full kitchens (from CAN$139 s or d).

At the same intersection as the Western 66 is **Quality Inn Waddling Dog** (2476 Mt. Newton Cross Rd., 250/652-1146 or 800/567-8466, www.qualityinnvictoria.com, CAN$120–130 s or d), styled as an old English guesthouse complete with an English pub. The Waddling Dog offers a number of well-priced packages that include admission to Butchart Gardens.

Over CAN$300

You'll feel like you're a million miles from the city at **Brentwood Bay Lodge & Spa** (849 Verdier Ave., Brentwood Bay, 250/544-2079 or 888/544-2079, www.brentwoodbaylodge.com, CAN$495 s or d in summer, CAN$300 between mid-Oct. and April), an upscale retreat overlooking Saanich Inlet. One of only three Canadian properties with Small Luxury Hotels of the World designation, you will want for nothing. You can learn to scuba dive, take a water taxi to Butchart Gardens, enjoy the latest spa treatments, or join a kayak tour. The 33 rooms take understated elegance to new heights. Filled with natural light, they feature contemporary West Coast styling (lots of polished wood and natural colors), the finest Italian sheets on king-size beds, and private balconies. Modern conveniences like DVD entertainment systems,

high-speed Internet access, and free calls within North America are a given. Dining options include a wood-fired grill, an upscale restaurant, a coffee bar, and a deli serving up picnic lunches.

Campgrounds

If you're coming from or heading to the ferry terminal, consider staying at **McDonald Provincial Park,** near the tip of the Saanich Peninsula 31 kilometers (19 miles) north of the city center. Facilities are limited (no showers or hookups); campsites are CAN$14 per night.

Also on the peninsula, halfway between downtown Victoria and Sidney, is **Island View Beach RV Park** (Homathko Dr., 250/652-0548, CAN$22–27), right on the beach, three kilometers (1.9 miles) east of Highway 17. You'll need quarters for the showers.

SOOKE

The seaside township of Sooke lies 34 kilometers (21 miles) west of downtown. Just a 40-minute drive from the city, the atmosphere is very uncity-like, with hiking in East Sooke Regional Park, fishing charters down at the marina, and a beautiful coastal drive beginning from town.

CAN$150–200

M Sooke River Estuary Bed & Breakfast (2056 Glenidle Rd., 250/642-4655 or 888/681-4677, www.sookeriver.com, CAN$159–169 s or d) takes full advantage of its waterfront location at the mouth of the Sooke River. The two suites and one cottage are comfortable and come with niceties such as robes, fireplaces, and roomy bathrooms with top-notch amenities. The Harbourside Cottage is a real treat—jetted tub with water views, laundry facilities, basic cooking facilities, and a private deck. The rates include a generous, multi-course breakfast delivered to your room. This is a professionally run bed-and-breakfast with hosts that will fill you with ideas for local sightseeing and dining.

Over CAN$250

M Sooke Harbour House (1528 Whiffen Spit Rd., 250/642-3421 or 800/889-9688, www

.sookeharbourhouse.com, CAN$375–575 s or d) combines the elegance of an upscale country-style inn with the atmosphere of an exclusive oceanfront resort. The restaurant attracts discerning diners from throughout the world, and the accommodations are equally impressive. The sprawling waterfront property sits on a bluff, with 28 guest rooms spread through immaculately manicured gardens. Each of the rooms reflects a different aspect of life on the West Coast, and all have stunning views, a wood-burning fireplace, and deck or patio. Rates include breakfast and a picnic lunch; off-season rates are reduced up to 40 percent.

MALAHAT

This small community is strung out along the main route up the island 25 kilometers (15.5 miles) from downtown Victoria, making it a good place to spend the night for those who want to get an early start on northward travel.

CAN$50–100

If you just need somewhere to spend the night, it's hard to go past the eight-room **Malahat Oceanview Motel** (Hwy. 1, 250/478-9231 or 877/478-8181, CAN$65–105 s or d). No surprises here—expect fairly basic motel rooms with distant water views from private and semi-private balconies.

Over CAN$250

For a splurge, consider **The Aerie** (600 Ebedora Ln., 250/743-7115 or 800/518-1933, www.aerie .bc.ca, CAN$295 s or d), a sprawling complex of Mediterranean-style villas high above the waters of Saanich Inlet and surrounded by well-manicured gardens. No expense has been spared fitting out the 23 units. Each features a king-size bed, private balcony, lounge with fireplace, and luxurious bathroom complete with soaker tub. Upon arrival, guests receive fresh flowers and gourmet chocolates. The resort also has an indoor pool, outdoor hot tub, hiking trails leading through the forested hillside, tennis courts, and a restaurant considered one of the province's best. Rates include a small hamper of breakfast treats delivered to the room followed by a full breakfast in the dining room. To get there take the Spectacle Lake Provincial Park turnoff from Highway 1, then take the first right and follow the winding road up to the resort.

Campgrounds

In Malahat, seven kilometers (4.3 miles) farther north along Highway 1, is **Victoria West KOA** (250/478-3332 or 800/562-1732, www.victoriakoa.com, May–Sept.). Facilities include free showers, an outdoor pool, laundry, store, and game room. Unserviced sites are CAN$30, hookups CAN$32–38, and Kamping Kabins from CAN$66.

Food

While Victoria doesn't have a reputation as a culinary hot spot, for the past decade things have improved greatly with the opening of numerous restaurants serving top-notch internationally accented cuisine. Local chefs are big on produce organically grown and sourced from island farms. Seafood—halibut, shrimp, mussels, crab, and salmon—also features prominently on many menus.

Because of a thriving tourist trade centered on the Inner Harbour, chances are you will find something to suit your tastes and budget close at hand—Italian, Mexican, Californian, and even

vegan cuisine. Mixed in with a few tourist traps (that advertise everywhere) are a number of excellent harborfront choices that are as popular with the locals as with visitors. Unlike many cities—and aside from the small Chinatown—ethnic restaurants are not confined to particular streets. On the other hand, Fort Street east of Douglas has a proliferation of restaurants that are as trendy as it gets on the island.

You still find great interest in traditional English fare, including afternoon tea, which is served everywhere from motherly corner cafés to the grand Fairmont Empress. English cooking in general is

TREATING YOURSELF TO AFTERNOON TEA

Afternoon tea, that terribly English tradition that started in the 1840s as a mid-meal snack, is one ritual you should definitely partake in while visiting Victoria. Many North Americans don't realize that there is a difference between afternoon tea and high tea, and even in Victoria the names are sometimes used in place of one another. Afternoon tea is the lighter version, featuring fine teas (no tea bags) accompanied by delicate crustless sandwiches, scones with clotted cream and preserves, and a selection of other small treats. High tea (traditionally taken later in the day, around 6 P.M.) is more substantial—more like dinner in North America.

The best place to immerse yourself in the ritual is at one of the smaller tearooms scattered around the outskirts of downtown. You can order tea and scones at the **James Bay Tea Room** (332 Menzies St., 250/382-8282), but apart from the faux-Tudor exterior, it's not particularly English inside. Instead, continue on to Oak Bay to the **Blethering Place Tearoom** (2250 Oak Bay Ave., 250/598-1413, 11 A.M.–6 P.M. daily), which looks exactly like a tearoom should, right down to the regulars blethering (chatting) away with the friendly staff in white aprons. Tea and scones is CAN$6, a full afternoon tea is CAN$15, or pay CAN$17 and end the procession of food with a slab of trifle. **Windsor House Tea Room** (2540 Windsor Rd., Oak Bay, 250/595-3135, noon–5 P.M. Mon.–Sat.) has an authentic feeling (note the picture of the Queen Mother hanging from the wall). As well as afternoon tea favorites, full meals such as quiche and meat pies are available. **White Heather Tea Room** (1885 Oak Bay Ave., 250/595-8020, 9:30 A.M.–5 P.M. Tues.–Sat., 10 A.M.–5 P.M. Sunday) features a smaller, more homely setting, with a great deal of attention given to all aspects of afternoon tea—down to the handmade tea cozies.

If the sun is shining, a pleasant place to enjoy afternoon tea is **Point Ellice House,** a historic waterfront property along the Gorge Waterway (250/380-6506, May to mid-Sept. 11 A.M.–3 P.M. daily). The price of CAN$16.95 includes a tour of the property. As you'd expect, it's a touristy affair at **Butchart Gardens** (see *Sights;* 800 Benvenuto Dr., Brentwood Bay, 250/652-4422, www.butchartgardens.com); afternoon tea is CAN$20 and high tea (with Cornish pastries, quiche, and more) is CAN$27.

The **Fairmont Empress** (721 Government St., 250/389-2727) offers the grandest of grand afternoon teas, but you pay for it—CAN$50 pp. Still, it's so popular you must book at least a week in advance through summer and reserve a table for one of seven sitting times between noon and 5 P.M.

Finally, **Murchies** (1110 Government St., 250/381-5451), in the heart of the tourist precinct, sells teas from around the world as well as tea paraphernalia, such as teapots, gift sets, and collector tins. The adjacent café pours teas from around the world in a North American–style coffeehouse.

much maligned, but worth trying. For the full experience, choose kippers and poached eggs for breakfast, a ploughman's lunch (crusty bread, a chunk of cheese, pickled onions), and then roast beef with Yorkshire pudding (a crispy pastry made with drippings and doused with gravy) in the evening.

BAKERIES AND CAFÉS

Murchies (1110 Government St., 250/381-5451) began as an importer of fine teas but has branched into the coffee business, with a popular café adjacent to a shop selling teas and coffees from around the world.

At the foot of Bastion Square, a cobbled pedestrian mall, quiet **Paradiso** (10 Bastion Square, 250/920-7266, 7 A.M.–6 P.M. Mon.–Fri., 8 A.M.–6 P.M. Sat., 9 A.M.–6 P.M. Sun.) serves a range of coffees, pastries, and muffins. The Paradiso's outdoor tables are reason enough to stop by. Tucked into a Bastion Square alley, **Blue Carrot Café** (18 Bastion Square, 250/381-8722) is a quieter spot with similar hours.

In Old Town, **Willies Bakery** (537 Johnson St., 250/381-8414) is an old-style café offering cakes, pastries, and sodas, with a quiet cobbled courtyard in which to enjoy them. Ignore the dated furnishings at the **Dutch Bakery** (718 Fort

St., 250/383-9725, closed Sunday) and tuck into freshly baked goodies and handmade chocolates.

QUICK BITES

While tourists flock to the cafés and restaurants of the Inner Harbour and Government Street, Douglas Street remains the haunt of lunching locals. Reminiscent of days gone by, **John's Place** (723 Pandora Ave., 250/389-0711, 7 A.M.–9 P.M. Mon.–Fri., 8 A.M.–10 P.M. Sat.–Sun.), just off Douglas St., serves up excellent value for those in the know. The walls are decorated with movie posters, old advertisements, and photos of sports stars, but this place is a lot more than just another greasy-spoon restaurant. The food is good, the atmosphere casual, and the waitresses actually seem to enjoy working here. It's breakfast, burgers, salads, and sandwiches through the week, but weekend brunch is busiest, when there's nearly always a line spilling onto the street.

The **James Bay Inn** (270 Government St., 250/384-7151l, 7 A.M.–9 P.M. daily) has a downstairs restaurant with disco decor, friendly staff, and a wide-ranging menu that suits the tastes of in-house guests (who receive a 15-percent discount on their food) and hungry locals avoiding the waterfront area.

Right across from the information center, and drawing tourists like a magnet, is **Sam's Deli,** (805 Government St., 250/382-8424, 7:30 A.M.–10 P.M. daily). Many places nearby have better food, but Sam's boasts a superb location and a casual, cheerful atmosphere that makes it perfect for families. The ploughman's lunch, a staple of English pub dining, costs CAN$8.50, while sandwiches (shrimp and avocado is the in-house feature) are in the range CAN$5.50–9 and salads are all around CAN$6–9. Wondering how the weather is in Victoria? Check out the Sam Cam at www.samsdeli.com—and then, when you're in town, try to spot it high above the sidewalk tables. In Old Town, the small **Sour Pickle Cafe** (1623 Store St., 250/384-9390, 7:30 A.M.–4:30 P.M. Mon.–Fri.) comes alive with funky music and an enthusiastic staff. The menu offers bagels from CAN$2, full cooked breakfasts from CAN$7, soup of the day CAN$4, healthy

sandwiches CAN$7–8.50, and delicious single-serve pizzas for around CAN$9.

SEAFOOD

Victoria's many seafood restaurants come in all forms. Fish and chips is a British tradition and is sold as such at **Old Vic Fish & Chips** (1316 Broad St., 250/383-4536, open 11 A.M.–7 P.M. Mon.–Thurs., 11 A.M.–8 P.M. Fri.–Sat.).

Occupying a prime location on a floating dock amid whale-watching boats, seaplanes, and shiny white leisure craft, the **Blackfish Cafe** (Wharf St., 250/385-9996, hours may vary per season) is just steps from the main tourist trail, but it's far enough removed to make it a popular haunt with locals wanting a quiet, casual, waterfront meal. The setting alone makes the Blackfish a winner, but the menu is a knockout. Choose pan-fried oysters (CAN$9) or grilled chili-lime marinated prawns to share, then move onto mains like seafood risotto (CAN$23). The Blackfish opens at 6:30 A.M. Monday–Saturday and at 7:30 A.M. on summer weekends, closing between 6:30 and 9 P.M. depending on the season. To get there, walk north along the harbor from the information center.

Chandlers (1250 Wharf St., 250/385-3474, 11:30 A.M.–10 P.M. daily) is on the main strip of tourist-catching restaurants along the waterfront, but is generally regarded as Victoria's finest seafood restaurant. The stately setting is a lot quieter that the nearby Wharfside, and the dishes a little more inventive. Salmon, a menu staple, comes in a variety of ways, including poached with a maple glaze (CAN$23). Lunches, such as smoked salmon pasta, range CAN$7–13.

Away from the tourist-clogged streets of the Inner Harbour is **Barb's Place** (Fisherman's Wharf, at the foot of St. Lawrence St., 250/384-6515, from 8 A.M. daily), a sea-level eatery on a floating dock. It's not a restaurant as such, but a shack surrounded by outdoor tables, some protected from the elements by a canvas tent. The food is as fresh as it gets. Choose cod and chips (CAN$7), halibut and chips (CAN$9.50), clam chowder (CAN$6), or splash out on a steamed crab (CAN$16).

Adding to the charm are surrounding floating houses and seals that hang out waiting for handouts. An enjoyable way to reach Barb's is by ferry (CAN$3 from the Inner Harbour).

Touristy **Wharfside Eatery** (1208 Wharf St., 250/360-1808) is a bustling waterfront complex with a maritime theme and family atmosphere. Behind a small café section and a bar is the main dining room and a two-story deck, where almost every table has a stunning water view. The lunch menu covers all bases, with dishes in the CAN$10–19 range. Seafood starters to share include a tasting plate of salmon and mussels steamed in a creamy tomato broth. The lunchtime appetizers runs through to the evening menu (same prices), which also includes wood-fired pizza (CAN$18–20 for two people), standard seafood dishes under CAN$30, and a delicious smoked chicken and wild mushroom penne (CAN$20). The cheesecake is heavenly.

PUBS

Right in the heart of downtown is the **Elephant and Castle** (Government and View Sts., 250/383-5858). This English-style pub features exposed beams, oak paneling, and traditional pub décor. A few umbrella-shaded tables line the sidewalk out front. You'll find all the favorites, such as steak and kidney pie and fish and chips, which range CAN$8–14.50. Open daily for lunch and dinner.

As well as the Fowl & Fish Café, **Swan's Hotel** (506 Pandora St., 250/361-3310, daily 7 A.M.–1 A.M.) is home to an English-style pub with matching food, such as bangers and mash (sausages and mashed potatoes) and Shepherd's Pie, all around CAN$10–12. Along with the typical pub pews, a glass-enclosed atrium covers a section of the sidewalk.

M **17 Mile House** (5126 Sooke Rd., 250/642-5942, 11 A.M.–10 A.M. daily) is a charming relic from the past. It dates from an era when travelers heading to Sooke would stop for a meal 17 miles from Victoria's City Hall. The walls are decorated in a century's worth of memorabilia and there's still a hitching post out back. The rotating nightly specials haven't changed for years,

but no one seems to mind, especially on Saturday, when a prime rib dinner is served up for CAN$18. One thing that definitely wasn't on the menu 100 years ago is a delicious sesame teriyaki grilled salmon dish (CAN$16).

While all of these pubs exude the English traditions for which Victoria is famous, **Spinnakers Brew Pub** (308 Catherine St., Esquimalt, 250/386-2739, from 11 A.M. daily) is in a class by itself. It was Canada's first in-house brew pub, and it's as popular today as when it opened in 1985. The crowds come for the beer, but also for great food served up in a casual, modern atmosphere. British-style pub fare, such as a Ploughman's Lunch, is served in the bar while West Coast and seafood dishes, such as sea bass basted in an ale sauce, are offered in the downstairs restaurant.

ITALIAN

The energetic atmosphere at **M** **Café Brio** (944 Fort St., 250/383-0009, from 5:30 P.M. daily) is contagious and the food is as good as anywhere in Victoria. The Mediterranean-inspired dining room is adorned with lively artwork and built around a u-shaped bar, while out front are a handful of tables on an alfresco terrace. A creative menu combines local, seasonal produce with Italian expertise and flair. The crab salad is always a good choice to begin with, followed by wild salmon prepared however your server suggests. Order the chocolate cake smothered in chocolate espresso sauce, even if you're full. Mains range CAN$9–28, with side dishes, such as grilled asparagus and mushroom fricassee, extra.

One of the most popular restaurants in town is **Pagliacci's** (1011 Broad St., 250/386-1662, 11:30 A.M.–midnight daily), known for hearty Italian food, homemade bread, great desserts, and loads of atmosphere. Small and always busy, the restaurant attracts a lively local crowd, many with children; you'll inevitably have to wait for a table during the busiest times (no reservations taken). Pastas, including a prawn fettuccine topped with mint chutney, range between CAN$10 and CAN$14. A jazz combo plays Wednesday–Sunday nights.

OTHER EUROPEAN RESTAURANTS

A good place to go for a menu of well-rounded Greek favorites is **Periklis** (531 Yates St., 250/386-3313). Main courses range CAN$14–25, and almost anything might be happening on the floor—from exotic belly dancing to crazy Greek dancing.

Beyond the west end of Belleville Street is **Pablo's Dining Lounge** (225 Quebec St., 250/388-4255, from 5 P.M. daily), a long-time Victorian favorite serving a variety of European cuisines. Atmosphere in the Edwardian house is relaxed yet intimate, and the dishes are all well prepared and well presented. Everything is good, but the beef tenderloin topped with crabmeat and béarnaise sauce (CAN$34) is simply the best.

CARIBBEAN

The Reef (533 Yates St., 250/388-5375, daily lunch and dinner) is as un-Victoria-like as one could imagine, but it's incredibly popular, both for its upbeat atmosphere, tasty food, and is-land-friendly service. The kitchen concentrates on the classics, with jerk seasoning and tropical-fruit juices featured in most dishes. Highlights include any of the West Indian curries, *ackee* (fruit) with salted cod fish, plantain chips with jerk mayo, and chicken marinated in coconut milk then roasted. Of course, you'll need to order a fruity drink—a traditional favorite like a piña colada or something a little more hip, like a rum-infused banana smoothie—for the full effect.

VEGETARIAN

Green Cuisine, at the courtyard level of Market Square (560 Johnson St., 250/385-1809, 10 A.M.–8 P.M. daily) takes the vegetarian theme to the fullest, with a vegan menu that uses no oils, sugars, or refined flours. A small buffet is offered, but the regular menu provides many choices, from chili to fruit juices.

N Rebar (50 Bastion Square, 250/361-9223, 8:30 A.M.–9 P.M. Mon.–Sat., 8:30 A.M.–3:30 P.M. Sun.) is a 1970s-style vegetarian restaurant with a loyal local following. Dishes, such as the almond burger (CAN$7.50) at lunch and Thai tiger prawn curry (CAN$16) at dinner, are full of flavor and made with only the freshest ingredients. Still hungry? Try the nutty carrot cake (CAN$5.50). Children are catered to with fun choices, such as banana and peanut butter on sunflower seed bread (CAN$4). It's worth stopping by just for juice; vegetable and fruit juices, power tonics, and wheatgrass infusions are made to order for less than CAN$5.

CHINESE

Victoria's small Chinatown surrounds a short, colorful strip of Fisgard Street between Store and Government Streets. The restaurants welcome everyone and generally the menus are filled with all the familiar westernized Chinese choices. Near the top (east) end of Fisgard is **QV Cafe and Bakery** (1701 Government St., 250/384-8831) offering inexpensive western-style breakfasts in the morning and Chinese delicacies the rest of the day. One of the least expensive places in the area is **Wah Lai Yuen** (560 Fisgard St., 250/381-5355, 10 A.M.–9 P.M. daily), a large, simply decorated, well-lit restaurant with fast and efficient service. The wonton soups (from CAN$3) are particularly good, or try the hearty chicken hot pot (CAN$8.50) or scallops and broccoli (CAN$14.50).

Named for the Chinese province renowned for hot and spicy food, **Hunan Village Cuisine** (546 Fisgard St., 250/382-0661, Mon.–Sat. for lunch and daily for dinner) offers entrées ranging CAN$8–15. Down the hill a little is **Don Mee Restaurant** (538 Fisgard St., 250/383-1032, Mon.–Fri. for lunch, daily for dinner), specializing in the cuisine of Canton. Entrées run about CAN$7 each, while four-course dinners for two or more diners are a good deal at less than CAN$15 pp.

A few blocks from Chinatown and just off Douglas Street is **Lotus Pond** (617 Johnson St., 250/380-9293, 11 A.M.–8 P.M. Mon.–Sat.), a no-frills vegetarian Chinese restaurant.

OTHER ASIAN RESTAURANTS

Step into the world of British colonialism at the **N Bengal Lounge,** in the Fairmont Empress

© ANDREW HEMPSTEAD

Victoria's Chinatown is small, but it boasts a variety of inexpensive resaurants.

(721 Government St., 250/389-2727). The curry lunch buffet (11:30 A.M.–3 P.M. daily, CAN$23) and curry dinner buffet (6–9 P.M. Sun.–Thurs., CAN$28) come with the three condiments I love to have with curry—shaved coconut, mango chutney, and mixed nuts. Friday and Saturday evenings, an à la carte East Indian menu is offered, with live background jazz; prices range from CAN$6.50 for soup to a reasonable CAN$14–23 for main courses. As a lounge bar, it does not permit anyone younger than 19. If you're traveling as a family and want to dine at the Empress, consider a meal at **Kipling's,** which serves up buffets for breakfast (CAN$23), lunch (CAN$21), and dinner (CAN$29)in a casual atmosphere.

If you've never tried Thai cuisine, you're in for a treat at **Sookjai Thai** (893 Fort St., 250/ 383-9945, 11:30 A.M.–2:30 P.M., Mon.–Fri. and 5–9 P.M. Mon.–Sat.). The tranquil setting is the perfect place to sample traditional delights, such as *Tom Yum Goong,* a prawn and mushroom soup with a hint of tangy citrus (CAN$9), and baked red snapper sprinkled with spices from Thailand (CAN$16). The snapper is the most expensive main, with a number of inspiring vegetarian choices all under CAN$10.

OUT-OF-TOWN SPLURGES

The following two restaurants are out of town but well worth the drive. Both also provide accommodations.

Sooke Harbour House

One of Canada's, finest dining experiences can be had at Sooke Harbour House (34 kilometers/21 miles west of downtown at 1528 Whiffen Spit Rd., Sooke, 250/642-3421 or 800/889-9688, from 5 P.M. daily). In a magnificent setting atop a seaside bluff, three rooms of what was originally a private residence have been converted to a restaurant. The décor is country-style simple, not that anything could possibly take away from the food and views. The menu changes daily, but most dishes feature local seafood, prepared to perfection with vegetables and herbs picked straight from the surrounding garden. Many diners disregard the cost and choose the eight-course Gastronomical Tasting Menu (CAN$100 pp), which represents a wide variety of seafood, including wild sea asparagus harvested from tidal pools below the restaurant. Otherwise, dinner entrées range CAN$28–40, with vegetarians offered at least one choice. The cellar is almost as renowned as the food—it holds upward of 10,000 bottles. Make reservations before taking the 40-minute trip out to Sooke.

The Aerie

The restaurant at The Aerie (25 kilometers/15.5 miles north from downtown Victoria, Malahat, 250/743-7115, noon–1:30 P.M. and 6–8:30 P.M. daily) is equally popular but more pretentious than Sooke Harbour House. In a delightful hillside location, surrounded by forest and grazing wildlife, diners are treated to almost over-the-top extravagance in the dining room, which features a gold-leafed ceiling, faux-marble columns, crystal chandeliers, and elegant table settings with high-backed chairs. The cuisine is traditional French and is accompanied by a French-influenced wine list. Stick to the menu and pay CAN$37–41 for a main, or try the seven-course table d'hôte menu for CAN$95 pp. Also at The Aerie is Bonelli, casual Mediterranean-style dining that sprawls onto a huge terrace.

Information and Services

INFORMATION CENTERS

Tourism Victoria (250/953-2033 or 800/663-3883, www.tourismvictoria.com) runs the bright, modern **Victoria Visitor Info Centre,** which overlooks the Inner Harbour from 812 Wharf Street. The friendly staff can answer most of your questions. They also book accommodations, tours and charters, restaurants, entertainment, and transportation, all at no extra cost. They sell local bus passes and map books with detailed area-by-area maps and stock an enormous selection of tourist brochures. Also collect the free *Accommodations* publication and the free local news and entertainment papers—the best way to find out what's happening in Victoria while you're in town. The center is open year-round 9 A.M.–5 P.M. daily.

Saanich Peninsula

Coming off the ferry from Vancouver, stop in at **Saanich Peninsula Visitor Info Centre,** three kilometers (1.9 miles) south of the terminal (9 A.M.–5 P.M. daily). It is operated by the local chamber of commerce (250/656-3616, www.spcoc.org).

BOOKSTORES AND MAIN LIBRARY

Bookstores

Don't be put off by the touristy location of **Munro's Bookstore** (1108 Government St., 250/382-2464 or 888/243-2464), in a magnificent neoclassical building that originally opened as the Royal Bank in 1909. It holds a comprehensive collection of fiction and non-fiction titles related to Victoria, the island, and Canada in general. Munro's may be the grandest bookstore in town, but it's not the largest. That distinction goes to **Chapters** (1212 Douglas St., 250/380-9009, open 8 A.M.–11 P.M. Mon.–Sat., 9 A.M.–11 P.M. Sunday). **Crown Publications** (521 Fort St., 250/386-4636) is a specialty bookstore with a great selection of western Canadiana and maps. In seaside Oak Bay, **Ivy's Bookshop** (2188 Oak Bay Ave., 250/598-2713) is a friendly little spot with a wide-ranging selection that includes local literature as well as current bestsellers.

For secondhand and rare West Coast and nautical titles, search out **Wells Books** (824 Fort St., 250/360-2929). Also, **Snowdon's Book Store** (619 Johnson St., 250/383-8131) holds a good selection of secondhand titles.

Main Library

Greater Victoria Public Library (735 Broughton St., at the corner of Courtney St., 250/382-7241, www.gvpl.ca) is open Mon.–Fri. 9 A.M.–6 P.M., Saturday 9 A.M.–1 P.M.

EMERGENCY SERVICES

In a medical emergency call 911 or contact **Victoria General Hospital** (1 Hospital Way, 250/727-4212). For non-urgent cases, a handy facility is **James Bay Medical Treatment Centre** (230 Menzies St., 250/388-9934). for dentistry contact the **Cresta Dental Centre** (3170 Tillicum Rd., 250/384-7711). **Shopper's Drug Mart** (1222 Douglas St., 250/381-4321) is open 7 A.M.–7 P.M. daily.

ACCESS FOR DISABLED TRAVELERS

Victoria has fewer amenities than Vancouver for disabled travelers, although things have improved greatly in the last few years. Many main route transit buses have wheelchair lifts while Handy-DART (250/727-7811) vans provide door-to-door wheelchair-accessible service beyond the bus system.

COMMUNICATIONS

Phone and Internet

The **area code** for Victoria is **250,** the same as all of British Columbia except Vancouver and the Lower Mainland. The cost for local calls at pay phones is CAN$.35 and from CAN$2.50 per minute for long distance calls.

Most of Victoria's downtown accommodations have in-room Internet access. Those that don't—like the hostel—have inexpensive Internet booths near the lobby. A good option for travelers on the run is the small café on the lower level of the Hotel Grand Pacific (463 Belleville St.) where public Internet access is free with a purchase. It's open 7 A.M.–7 P.M. daily.

Mail

The main **post office** (250/953-1352) is on the corner of Yates and Douglas Streets.

CURRENCY EXCHANGE

You'll find a currency exchange booth opposite the baggage carousels at Victoria International Airport, but to ensure the best rates head downtown to one of the major banks, such as the **Bank of Montreal** (1225 Douglas St., 250/405-2090). Private downtown exchange shops include **Custom House Currency Exchange** (818 Wharf St., 250/389-6007 or 800/345-0007) and **FX Connectors Currency Exchange** (1208 Wharf St., 250/380-7888).

PHOTOGRAPHY

Lens & Shutter (615 Fort St., 250/383-7443) is the best downtown photo shop, with a wide selection of film and digital accessories as well as a reliable developing service. One block away, the **One Hour Photo Express** (705 Fort St., 250/389-1984) is exactly that. On the road out of town, **Japan Camera** (Mayfair Mall, 3147 Douglas St., 250/382-4435) is no cheaper for film and processing, but is the only such shop open on Sunday. A reliable, centrally located repair shop is **Victoria Camera Service** (665 Queens Ave., 250/383-4311). If you're not a photographer, don't worry—the number of coffee-table books, postcards, and calendars sold along Government Street will astound you.

Transportation

BY AIR

A short hop by ferry from the San Juan Islands, getting to Victoria is easy, and once you've arrived, getting around the compact city is even easier.

Victoria International Airport

Vancouver Island's main airport is on the Saanich Peninsula, 20 kilometers (12.4 miles) north of Victoria's city center. The facility has undergone a complete revamp in recent years, with the new departure terminal completed in late 2004. Once you've collected your baggage from the carousels, it's impossible to miss the rental car outlets (Avis, Budget, Hertz, and National) across the room, where you'll also find a currency exchange and information booth. Outside is a taxi stand and ticket booth for the airporter. The modern terminal also houses a lounge and various eateries. Parking out front is CAN$2 per two hours.

HEADING NORTH ON VANCOUVER ISLAND

Vancouver Island, the largest isle in North America's Pacific, stretches 450 kilometers (280 miles) off the west coast of mainland British Columbia. Beyond the city of Victoria, there's much to explore. A magnificent chain of rugged snowcapped mountains, sprinkled with lakes and rivers and pierced by a number of deep inlets, effectively divides the island into two distinct sides: dense, rain-drenched forest and remote surf- and wind-battered shores on the west, and well-populated, sheltered, beach-fringed lowlands on the east. Combine this wilderness (with its excellent hiking, fishing, and camping) with hundreds of bed-and-breakfasts, tempting seafood restaurants, and a healthy smattering of indigenous art and culture and you've got another entire vacation just waiting for you.

Information Sources
Almost every island town has an information center, and while most are seasonal, they open daily through summer. Other sources of pre-trip information are the **Victoria Tourist Info Centre,** on the Inner Harbour (250/953-2033, www.tourismvictoria.com); **Tourism Vancouver Island** (250/754-3500, www.islands.bc.ca), and **Tourism British Columbia** (250/387-1642 or 800/435-5622, www.hellobc.com). *Moon Handbooks British Columbia* (Avalon Travel Publishing) by Andrew Hemstead also provides detailed coverage of Vancouver Island.

By Road
From downtown Victoria, take Douglas Street north for three km (1.9 miles) to Highway 1, which jogs westward through Victoria's residential suburbs before turning north and running up the east side of the island to Nanaimo (113 km/71 miles), Courtenay (220 km/137 miles), Campbell River (260 km/162 miles), and Port Hardy (495 km/309 miles).
   Island Coachlines (250/385-4411 or 800/318-0818, www.victoriatours.com) serves all of Vancouver Island, including Tofino, from the main bus depot centrally located in downtown Victoria at 710 Douglas St. (corner of Belleville Street). No bookings are taken, so just roll up, pay the fare, and jump aboard.

By Rail
VIA Rail (250/383-4324 or 800/561-8630, www.viarail.ca.) operates the *Malahat* passenger train on a schedule that departs Victoria for Courtenay Mon.–Sat. at 8:15 A.M. and Sunday at noon, and departs Courtenay for Victoria Mon.–Sat. at 1:15 P.M. and Sunday at 5:15 P.M. This route is so scenic that many make the train trip a one-day excursion, going as far as Nanaimo and spending a few hours in the city before returning; it's a cheap day out at under CAN$50 for the round-trip.

The **AKAL Airporter** (250/386-2525 or 877/386-2525, www.victoriaairporter.com) operates buses between the airport and major downtown hotels every 30 minutes; CAN$13 pp one way, CAN$20 roundtrip. The first departure from downtown to the airport is 4:30 A.M. A taxi costs approximately CAN$45 to downtown.

Airlines
Scheduled flights link the international airports of Vancouver and Victoria, but it's such a short flight (25 minutes from terminal to terminal) unless you are on a connecting flight, the alternatives are more practical. **Air Canada** (888/247-2262, www.aircanada.ca) and its connector airlines, as well as **WestJet** (800/538-5696, www.westjet.com), fly the route multiple times daily. Both airlines also fly to Victoria from most western Canadian cities. **Pacific Coastal** (604/273-8666 or 800/663-2872, www.pacificcoastal.com)

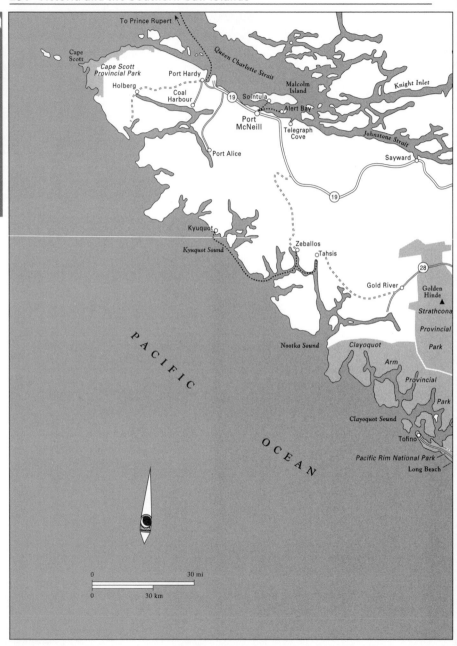

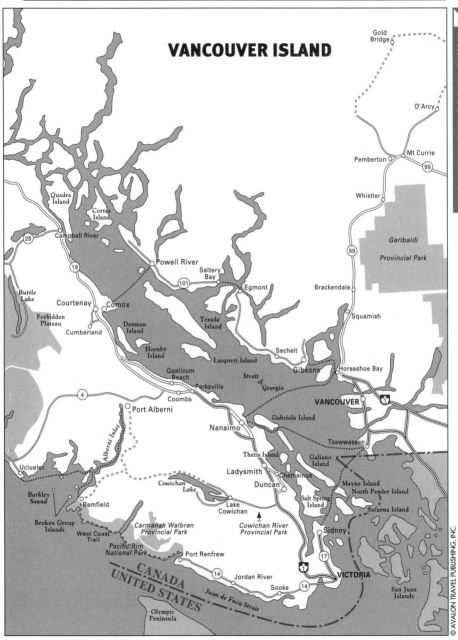

VANCOUVER ISLAND

and **Sonicblue Airways** (604/278-1608 or 800/ 228-6608, www.sonicblueair.com) fly into Victoria from the South Terminal at Vancouver International Airport.

Smaller airlines, including those with floatplanes, provide a handy direct link between Victoria and Vancouver, departing from the downtown Vancouver waterfront and landing on the Inner Harbour. These include **Harbour Air** (250/384-2215 or 800/665-0212, www.harbour-air.com) and **West Coast Air** (250/388-4521 or 800/347-2222, www.westcoastair.com). Both Victoria terminals are on Wharf Street.

From Seattle, **Kenmore Air** (425/486-1257 or 800/543-9595) offers scheduled floatplane flights between the north end of Lake Washington and Victoria's Inner Harbour.

BUS

From Vancouver

The main Victoria **bus depot** is behind the Empress Hotel at 710 Douglas Street. **Pacific Coach Lines** (604/662-7575 or 800/661-1725, www .pacificcoach.com) operates bus service between Vancouver's Pacific Central Station and downtown Victoria, via the Tsawwassen–Swartz Bay ferry. In summer, the coaches run hourly 6 A.M.–9 P.M.; CAN$32.25 one-way, CAN$62.50 round-trip, which includes the ferry fare. The trip takes three and a half hours. This same company also runs buses to the Victoria depot from downtown Vancouver hotels (CAN$36.25 one-way, CAN$70.50 round-trip) and from Vancouver International Airport (CAN$37.75 one-way, CAN$73.50 round-trip).

FERRY

From Seattle

Clipper Navigation (800/888-2535, www.clippervacations.com) offers a fleet of foot-passengers-only ferries connecting Seattle's Pier 69 with Victoria's Inner Harbour. Its turbojet catamaran, the *Victoria Clipper IV,* is North America's fastest passenger ferry, traveling at speeds of up to 45 knots (more than 80 kph). This speedy vessel makes the crossing in two

hours. The cost is adult US$81 one-way, US$133 round-trip. The company's other vessels make the trip in two and a half hours and cost adult US$70 one-way, US$114 round-trip. The service runs year-round. In summer, up to five sailings a day are offered, with some stopping off at Friday Harbor in the San Juan Islands through to Victoria. All vessels feature spacious seating arrangements, writing tables, complimentary tea and coffee, and light snacks. Discounts apply outside of the busy summer months and on tickets purchased 14 or more days in advance. Seniors also get a break, and children travel for half price.

Clipper Navigation also offers a plethora of reasonably priced accommodations and tour packages in Victoria (from US$165 including transportation from Seattle; high season). For schedules and tour information drop by one of its offices: Pier 69, Seattle, 206/448-5000, or at the Inner Harbour terminal on Belleville St., 250/382-8100.

From Anacortes and the San Juan Islands

Washington State Ferries (206/464-6400, 250/381-1551, or 888/808-7977, www.wsdot .wa.gov/ferries) runs a regular ferry schedule connecting Anacortes, the San Juan Islands, and the town of Sidney, on the Saanich Peninsula 32 kilometers (20 miles) north of Victoria. The one-way peak-season fare is US$13.80 for passengers and walk-ons, vehicle and driver US$46.75. Reservations must be made at least 24 hours in advance.

From Port Angeles

Black Ball Transport (250/386-2202 in Victoria, or 360/457-4491 in Port Angeles, www.cohoferry.com) operates the **MV Coho** across Juan de Fuca Strait between Port Angeles and Victoria's Inner Harbour. It makes four crossings daily in each direction from mid-May to mid-October, two crossings daily the rest of the year. Advance reservations are not accepted—phone a day or so before your planned departure for estimated waiting times. The one-way fare is adult US$7.75, child US$3.90, vehicle US$29.75.

The Port Angeles terminal is on Railroad Avenue, where nearby parking is US$10 per day.

The other option from Port Angeles is the passenger-only **Victoria Express** (250/361-9144 or 800/663-1589, www.victoriaexpress.com). This company operates 2–4 sailings daily in each direction between June and September; US$10 each way.

From Tsawwassen (Vancouver)

Ferries run regularly across the Strait of Georgia from Tsawwassen, 30 kilometers (19 miles) south of Vancouver, to the **Swartz Bay Ferry Terminal,** 32 kilometers (20 miles) north of Victoria. Through summer, ferries run hourly 7 A.M.– 10 P.M., the rest of the year slightly less frequently. The crossing takes 90 minutes. You can expect a wait in summer; limited vehicle reservations (604/444-2890 or 888/724-5223, www.bcferries.com) for CAN$15 per booking. Peak fares are adult CAN$10.25, child 5–11 CAN$5.25, vehicle CAN$35.75, motorcycle CAN$18. For information, contact **BC Ferries** (250/386-3431 or 888/223-3779, www.bcferries.com).

Try to plan your travel outside peak times, which include summer weekends, especially Friday-afternoon sailings from Tsawwassen and Sunday-afternoon sailings from Swartz Bay. Most travelers don't make reservations, but simply arrive and prepare themselves to wait for the next ferry if the first one fills. Both terminals have shops with food and magazines as well as summertime booths selling everything from crafts to mini donuts.

GETTING AROUND
Victoria Regional Transit System
Most of the inner-city attractions can be reached on foot. However, the local bus network is excellent, and it's easy to jump on and off and get everywhere you want to go. Pick up an *Explore Victoria* brochure at the information center for details of all the major sights, parks, beaches, and shopping areas, and the buses needed to reach them. Bus fare for travel within Zone 1, which covers most of the city, is adult CAN$2, senior or child CAN$1.25. Zone 2 covers outlying areas, such as the airport and Swartz Bay ferry terminal; adult CAN$3, senior or child CAN$2. Transfers are good for travel in one direction within 90 minutes of purchase. A DayPass, valid for one day's unlimited bus travel, costs adult CAN$6, senior or child CAN$4. For general bus information, call 250/385-2551 or click on www.transitbc.com.

Ferry
The most enjoyable way to get around the city is aboard a **Victoria Harbour Ferry** (250/708-0201). The company's distinctive 12-passenger ferries ply two routes departing from the Inner Harbour. One takes in harborside docks, including Fisherman's Wharf, Ocean Pointe Resort, and Westbay Marine Village, while the other heads up the Gorge Waterway; CAN$3 per sector, or make the round-trip as a tour for CAN$14–16.

Taxi
Taxis operate on a meter system, charging CAN$2.75 at the initial flag drop, plus around CAN$2 per kilometer. Call **Blue Bird Cabs** (250/382-4235 or 800/665-7055), **Empress Taxi** (250/381-2222), or **Victoria Taxi** (250/383-7111).

Car Rental
It's best to call around and compare prices for rental cars—some lesser-known agencies advertise cheaper daily rates than others, but their cars are often used, old, large, and less economical, and usually must be returned to Victoria. Renting by the week is the best deal, with unlimited kilometers thrown in as a bonus. If you don't want to return the car to Victoria, you'll probably have to pay a drop charge; the farther up the island you go, the higher the fee. For a used car in the low season, rates start around CAN$30 a day, plus CAN$.15 per kilometer, plus gas. As with accommodations and many attractions, prices are higher in peak tourist periods. One recommended local company is **Island Rent-A-Car** (250/384-4881, www.islandcar.ca). Local contacts for the majors are: **Avis** (250/386-8468), **Budget** (250/953-5300), **Discount** (250/310-2277), **Enterprise** (250/475-6900), **Hertz** (250/952-3765), **National** (250/386-1213), and **Thrifty** (250/383-3659).

Bikes and Such

Victoria doesn't have the great network of bicycle paths that Vancouver boasts, but bike-rental shops are nevertheless plentiful. Try **Sports Rent** (1950 Government St., 250/385-7368), **James Bay Bicycle Works** (131 Menzies St., 250/380-1664), or

Oak Bay Bicycle (1968 Oak Bay Ave., 250/598-4111). Expect to pay from around CAN$8 an hour, CAN$25 per day. As well as renting bikes, **Harbour Rentals** (directly opposite the information center at 811 Wharf St., 250/995-1661) rents strollers, scooters, and a variety of watercraft.

Southern Gulf Islands

Spread through the Strait of Georgia between mainland British Columbia and Vancouver Island, this group of islands are within Canadian territory but linked geologically to the San Juan Islands, immediately to the south. Five of the islands—Salt Spring, the Penders, Galiano, Mayne, and Saturna—are populated, and each is connected to the outside world by scheduled ferry service.

The mild, almost Mediterranean climate, beautiful scenery, driftwood-strewn beaches, quaint towns, and wide ranging choice of accommodations combine to make the islands very popular in summer, when laid-back locals share their home with flocks of visitors. Still, there's plenty of room to get away from the hustle, with mile after mile of remote coastline and easily reached peaks beckoning to be explored. After kayaking, biking, or hiking, the best way to end the day is at one of the many island restaurants, feasting on salmon and crab brought ashore that morning.

The Land

The islands have been partly cleared for agriculture, but where old-growth forests survive, you'll find stands of magnificent Douglas fir and western red cedar, with gnarled arbutus (Pacific madrone) dominating the shoreline. Closer to ground level, you'll see lots of daisies, as well as native roses, bluebells, and orchids flowering through summer. In late summer, gooseberries, huckleberries, and blackberries are ripe for the picking. The surrounding waterways host an incredibly diverse number of marine mammals, including sea lions, seals, sea otters, and orcas. If you spent a full year on the islands counting bird species, you'd come up with more than 300, including bald eagles, blue herons, cormorants,

hummingbirds, robins, wrens, finches, and swallows. Fall is the best time to watch for migrating shorebirds, who stop to rest and feed throughout the archipelago. Children will love exploring tidal pools, where colorful anemones and starfish are among the many critters that make a home. **Gulf Islands National Park** protects pockets of land on Mayne and Saturna Islands, the Penders, and 14 uninhabited islands.

Island Practicalities

Many visitors own island getaways or rent cottages by the week, but there are still plenty of options for shorter stays. Choices range from primitive tent sites to world-class lodges, with bed-and-breakfasts—there are hundreds—falling somewhere in the middle price range. Whatever your preference, make reservations for summer as far in advance as possible, especially for weekends. Be aware many bed-and-breakfasts close through winter and some don't take credit or debit cards.

You will find cafés and restaurants on each island, but not a single McDonalds or similar fast-food chain. Grocery and gas is available in most villages; banks and ATMs are less common.

Before you head for the islands, get the latest rundown from the Information Centre in downtown Victoria, from the Saanich Peninsula Info Centre on Highway 17 near the Swartz Bay Ferry Terminal, or from Tourism Vancouver Island (250/754-3500, www.islands.bc.ca). *Island Tides* is a free bimonthly publication; you'll find the most recent edition online at www.islandtides.com. The website www.gulfislands.net is loaded with tourist information, or pick up the free hard-copy version once you're en route by ferry.

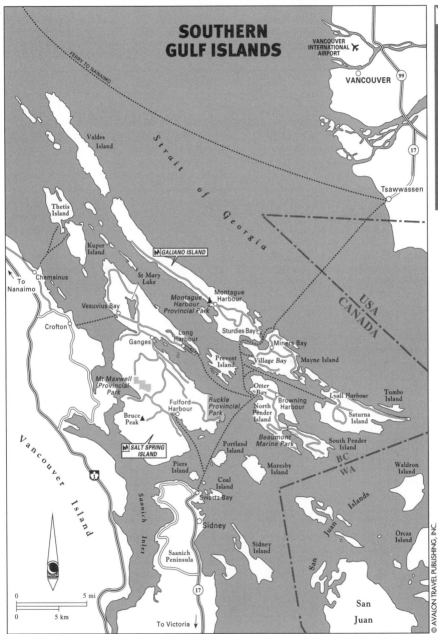

SOUTHERN
GULF ISLANDS

VANCOUVER
INTERNATIONAL
AIRPORT

VANCOUVER

99

FERRY TO NANAIMO

S t r a i t

o f

G e o r g i a

Tsawwassen

17

Valdes
Island

Thetis
Island

Kuper
Island

GALIANO ISLAND

Chemainus

To
Nanaimo

St Mary
Lake

Montague
Harbour

Montague
Harbour
Provincial Park

USA
CANADA

Vesuvius Bay

Crofton

Long
Harbour

Sturdies Bay

Miners Bay

Ganges

Prevost
Island

Village Bay

Mayne Island

Mt Maxwell
Provincial
Park

Otter
Bay

Lyall Harbour

Tumbo
Island

Fulford
Harbour

Ruckle
Provincial
Park

North
Pender
Island

Browning
Harbour

Bruce
Peak

Saturna
Island

SALT SPRING
ISLAND

Beaumont
Marine Park

South Pender
Island

V a n c o u v e r

Piers
Island

Portland
Island

Moresby
Island

BC
WA

Waldron
Island

1

I s l a n d

Coal
Island

Swartz Bay

S a a n i c h
I n l e t

Sidney

Sidney
Island

J u a n

Islands

Orcas
Island

MOON

Saanich
Peninsula

San

0   5 mi

0   5 km

17

To Victoria

San

Juan

© AVALON TRAVEL PUBLISHING, INC.

◪ SALT SPRING ISLAND

Largest of the Southern Gulf Islands, 180-square-kilometer (70-square-mile) Salt Spring (pop. 10,000) lies close to Vancouver Island, immediately north of Saanich Inlet. Ferries link the south and north ends of the island to Vancouver Island, and myriad roads converge on the service town of **Ganges.** The island is home to a large number of artisans, along with hobby farmers, retirees, and wealthy Vancouverites who spend their summers at private getaways.

Ganges

Ask any longtime local and they'll tell you the island's main town, Ganges, is over-commercialized. But it's still quaint, and well worth visiting—at the very least to stock up with supplies. Set around a protected bay, the original waterfront buildings have undergone a colorful transformation. Where once you would have found boat-builders, you can now browse through art galleries, shop for antiques, or dine on innovative cuisine. One of the most eye-catching shops is the boardwalk gallery featuring the whimsical painting of Jill Louise Campbell. On a smaller scale, **Mahon Hall** (114 Rainbow Rd., 250/537-0899, mid-May to mid-Sept. 10 A.M.–5 P.M. daily) is filled with arty booths, while the Saturday market in Centennial Park showcases the work of local artists. Head to **Salt Spring Books** (104 McPhillips Ave., 250/537-2812) to pick up some holiday reading or check your email on the public-access computers. Within walking distance of the waterfront, at the end of Seaspring Drive, is **Mouat Park,** a quiet reprieve from the bustle.

Exploring the Rest of the Island

Even if you've never kayaked, plan on joining a tour with Ganges-based **Sea Otter Kayaks** (250/537-5678 or 877/537-5678). Get a feel for paddling on the two-hour tour (CAN$35), enjoy the calm evening water on the Sunset Paddle (CAN$40), or spend a full-day (CAN$105) exploring the coastline, with a break for picnic lunch on a remote beach.

Landlubbers have plenty to see on Salt Spring.

From the Fulford Harbour ferry terminal, take Beaver Point Road east to 486-hectare (1,200-acre) **Ruckle Provincial Park.** The access road ends at the rocky headland of Beaver Point, from which trails lead north along the coastline, providing great views across to North Pender Island. The land now protected as a park was donated to the province by the Ruckle family; the Ruckles' 1876 farmhouse still stands.

Along the road north to Ganges, small **Mt. Maxwell Provincial Park** protects the slopes of its namesake mountain. A rough unsealed road off Musgrave Road leads to the 588-meter (1,930-foot) summit, from which views extend south across the island to Vancouver Island and east to the other Gulf Islands. South of Mt. Maxwell is 704-meter (2,300-foot) **Mount Bruce,** the island's highest peak.

Accommodations and Camping

The island's least expensive accommodation is **HI-Salt Spring Island** (640 Cusheon Lake Rd., 250/537-4149, www.hihostels.ca, mid-March to mid-Oct.), on the east side of the island. You can choose to stay in a regular dorm, but the most popular room is a tree house accessed via a ladder and hatch. The interior features a tree through the middle, a skylight over the bed, and wicker furniture. A caravan and a teepee are also spread around the four-hectare (10-acre) property. Rates start at CAN$17 for members of Hostelling International (CAN$21 for nonmembers).

Maple Ridge Cottages (301 Tripp Rd., 250/537-5977, www.mapleridgecottages.com, CAN$129–169 s or d) is on the banks of St. Mary Lake, a largish body of freshwater that holds a hungry population of bass and trout that can be caught right from the shoreline. For me, the allure of the wooden cottages is the location, but their rustic charm brings back families year after year. Relax on the deck while your catch of the day cooks on the barbecue for the full effect. Free use of canoes and kayaks is a popular bonus.

One of the island's premier accommodations is **Hundred Hills House** (104 Arnell Way, 250/537-1898, www.hundredhillshouse.com, CAN$200 s or d), a five-minute drive from Ganges. The styling is simple and elegant, with big windows to take in the water views. Most importantly for many, the two guest units have private entrances and en suites. Both also have a private deck, a fireplace, and high-tone extras, such as fine linens, a four-piece bathroom, and in-room entertainment centers. Breakfasts are elaborate.

Salt Springs Spa Resort (1460 North Beach Rd., 250/537-4111 or 800/665-0039, www.salty springs.com) commands lots of attention for its spa services, but the accommodations are also noteworthy. Each spacious unit features lots of polished wood topping out in a vaulted ceiling, a modern kitchen, a fireplace, and a two-person spa tub filled with mineral water. Guests have use of rowboats, mountain bikes, a game room, and a barbecue area. Summer rates are CAN$200 during the week and CAN$250 on weekends, discounted as low as CAN$120 in winter.

The campground in **Ruckle Provincial Park** conceals 78 sites in a forest of Douglas fir overlooking Swanson Channel. The camping area is a short walk from the parking lot, making this place unsuitable for RVs; CAN$14 per night. On the north side of the island on St. Mary Lake, **Lakeside Gardens Resort** (250/537-5773, April–Nov.) offers campsites with full hookups for CAN$25, rustic cabins that share bathrooms for CAN$65, and self-contained cottages for CAN$125.

Food

Head to Ganges and wander around the waterfront for the island's widest choice of dining options. In the heart of the action is the **M Tree House Café** (106 Purvis Ln., 250/537-5379, 8 A.M.–10 P.M. daily). The "tree" is a plum tree and the "house" is the kitchen. Most people dine outside in the shade of the tree, choosing freshly made dishes, such as salmon frittata (CAN$10) for breakfast, tuna melt on sourdough (CAN$8) at lunch, or Thai chicken curry (CAN$12) in the evening.

Around the corner from the Tree House is **La Cucina e Terrazza** (Mouat's Landing, 250/537-5747, 11 A.M.–9 P.M.), where the atmosphere is refined casual. The winsome menu ranges from Italian favorites like Gorgonzola linguine (CAN$14) to locally inspired dishes,

such as a duo of grilled salmon and halibut (CAN$21). Sit inside for the wonderful smells wafting from the kitchen or outside to soak up the harbor views.

Information

Salt Spring Island Visitor Info Centre (121 Lower Ganges Rd., 250/537-4223 or 866/216-2936, www.saltspringtoday.com) is in downtown Ganges, on the main road above the marina. It's open in summer 8 A.M.–6 P.M. daily, the rest of the year 8:30 A.M.–4:30 P.M. Monday–Friday.

Transportation

Salt Spring has two ferry terminals with year-round service to two points on Vancouver Island. If you're traveling up from Victoria, the Swartz Bay terminal is the most convenient departure point, with 10–12 departures daily for **Fulford Harbour,** a 20-minute drive south of Ganges. Sailings are even more frequent on the 20-minute run between Crofton, near the Vancouver Island town of Duncan, and **Vesuvius Bay,** at the island's north end. Interisland ferries depart from a third terminal, at **Long Harbour,** east of Ganges.

From the mainland, sailings depart the Tsawwassen terminal (south of downtown Vancouver) bound for Long Harbour. Direct sailings take 80 minutes, while those that make stops at other Gulf Islands take up to three hours—so check a timetable before boarding.

THE PENDERS

It's just a short hop by ferry from Salt Spring Island to **Otter Bay** on North Pender Island. Originally, North and South Pender Islands were joined, but around 100 years ago, a canal was dredged between the two as a shipping channel. Today, a rickety wooden bridge forms the link. Between them, the two islands are home to 2,000 people, most of whom live on North Pender. The island has dozens of little beaches to explore, with public roads providing ocean access at more than 20 points. One of the nicest spots is **Hamilton Beach** on Browning Harbour.

Accommodations and Camping

The least expensive way to enjoy an overnight stay on North Pender Island is to camp at **Prior Centennial Campground** (mid-May to mid-Oct.; CAN$14), a unit of Gulf Islands National Park. Sites are primitive, with no showers or hookups, but the treed location is excellent. The facility is located six km (3.7 miles) south of the ferry terminal.

The island's premier accommodation, located five km (3.1 miles) from the ferry terminal, is the **Oceanside Inn** (Armadale Rd., 250/629-6691, www.penderisland.com). Each room is elegantly furnished, and a wide balcony takes advantage of the waterfront location. Off-season rates start at CAN$149 s or d, rising to CAN$169–239 in summer. Rates include breakfast, use of a fitness room, and small luxuries, such as fluffy bathrobes.

Other Practicalities

The commercial hub of the Penders is the **Driftwood Centre,** a city-like shopping mall overlooking cleared pastureland south of the ferry terminal. In addition to gas, groceries, booze, and a bank are a number of eateries, including a super-busy bakery. For something a little more substantial, move along the mall to the **Pistou Grill** (250/629-3131, 11:30 A.M.–2:30 P.M. and 5:30–8:30 P.M. Tues.–Sat.) for surprisingly innovative cooking that includes seared halibut drizzled with a Chardonnay sauce (CAN$19). Also in the mall is **Talisman Books** (250/629-6944, 10 A.M.–5 P.M. Mon.–Sat., 11 A.M.–4 P.M. Sunday), stocking an excellent range of local literature and best sellers.

Pender Island Visitor Info Centre (250/629-6541, summer 9 A.M.–6 P.M. daily) is a small booth up the hill from the ferry terminal.

MAYNE ISLAND

Separated from Galiano Island by a narrow channel, Mayne Island is just 21 square kilometers (eight square miles) in area. It's year-round population of fewer than 1,000 triples in summer, but the island never really seems crowded. Ferries dock at village-less **Village Bay.** All commercial

facilities are at nearby **Miners Bay,** which got its name during the Cariboo gold rush, when miners used the island as a stopping point. From the ferry terminal, narrow roads meander to all corners of the island, including to **Georgina Point Lighthouse,** which was manned between 1885 and 1997. Island beaches are limited to those at **Oyster Bay,** but visitors can enjoy interesting shoreline walks or take the road to the low summit of Mount Park for panoramic views. For something a little different, wander through **Dinner Bay Park,** where a small Japanese garden takes pride of place.

The best island kayaking originates from the sandy beach in Bennett Bay, which is within Gulf Islands National Park. From its base in Miners Bay, **Mayne Kayaking** (250/539-5599) provides rentals and kayak drop-offs.

Accommodations

The least expensive island accommodation is **Springwater Lodge** (Village Bay, 250/539-5521, www.springwaterlodge.com), an old hotel overlooking Active Pass from the west side of Village Bay. Rooms are basic at best and bathrooms are shared, but at CAN$40 s or d you know what you're getting. Beside the hotel are four well-equipped cabins that go for CAN$95 per night. The inn also has a restaurant open daily for all three meals.

Overlooking Miners Bay, two km (1.2 miles) east of the ferry terminal, is **Tinkerers' Garden Retreat** (417 Sunset Pl., 250/539-2280, May–Oct., CAN$95–115 s or d). This delightful old house sits right on the bay, a great base for exploring the area on foot or bike (bike rentals available). Rooms are smallish and simply furnished, but guests have use of a communal lounge and the relaxing gardens. Rates include a full breakfast to fuel you up for a day of island exploration.

Set on four hectares (10 acres) overlooking a protected waterway, less than two km (1.2 miles) south of the ferry terminal, is **M Oceanwood Country Inn** (630 Dinner Bay Rd., 250/539-5074, www.oceanwood.com). Paths lead through the very private property, past herb and rose gardens and down to the water's edge. Within the lodge itself are four communal areas, including a well-stocked library, a comfortable lounge, and a restaurant. Each of the 12 rooms has its own character; some have a private balcony, others a deck or hot tub, and the largest features a split-level living area, luxurious bathroom, and private deck with hot tub. Rates start at CAN$179 s or d; rooms with ocean views range CAN$240–349. A cooked breakfast and tea and coffee throughout the day are included.

Camping at **Mayne Island Eco Camping** (359 Maple Dr., Miners Bay, 250/539-2667, www.mayneisle.com) is pleasant but primitive. Spread around the back of a short beach, some sites are right on the water, while others are dispersed through the forest. Facilities include outhouses a (hot) water-fed "tree" shower, and kayak rentals. Part of the same property is **Seal Beach B&B** (same contact information), where West Coast–themed guest rooms rent for CAN$115 s or d per night.

Food
No-frills, short order grills are the order of the day at the old **Springwater Lodge** (Village Bay, 250/539-5521). Head to the **Sunny Mayne Bakery Café** (Miners Bay, 250/539-2323, 7 A.M.–6 P.M. daily, until 7 P.M. on weekends) for freshly baked breads, sumptuous cakes and pastries, healthy sandwiches, and the island's best coffee concoctions.

The bright and breezy dining room at the **Oceanwood Country Inn** (630 Dinner Bay Rd., 250/539-5074) is primarily the domain of registered guests, but each evening at 6 P.M., the doors open to all for a four-course table d'hôte dinner (CAN$50 per person) that includes a choice of two entrées that focus on creative presentations of local produce and seafood.

Information and Books
The website www.mayneislandchamber.ca is loaded with useful information, including links to current weather conditions, accommodations, services, and, for those who fall in love with island living, real estate agents.

Stock up on reading material at **Miners Bay Books** (478 Village Bay Rd., 250/539-2667).

⋈ GALIANO ISLAND

Named for a Spanish explorer who sailed through the Strait of Georgia more than 200 years ago, this long, narrow island, 27 km (17 miles) from north to south but only a few km wide, has some delightful beaches and good kayaking. Most of the population (1,000) lives in the south, within a five-minute drive of the ferry terminal at **Sturdies Bay.**

Montague Harbour Provincial Park
Climbing out of Sturdies Bay, roads tempt exploration in all directions. Take Porlier Pass Road to reach Montague Harbour Provincial Park, which protects an 89-hectare (210-acre) chunk of coastal forest and a beach of bleached-white broken seashells. You can walk out along the beach and return via a forested trail in around 20 minutes. At the end of the beach are *middens,* manmade piles of empty shells that accumulated over centuries of indigenous feastings. The island is dotted with many less-obvious access points, many of which aren't even signed. The beach below Active Pass Road is typical; look for power pole numbered 1038 and make your way down the steep trail to a protected cove. Ask at the information center or your accommodation for a full listing of similar spots.

Other Recreation
The best way to explore local waterways is with **Galiano Island Kayaking,** based at the marina in Montague Harbour (250/539-2442). Three-hour guided tours, either early in the morning or at sunset, are CAN$45. Another tour takes in the local marine life on a six-hour paddle for CAN$75. Those with previous experience can rent a kayak; CAN$48 per day for a single or CAN$70 for a double.

Galiano Golf Club (Linklater Rd., 250/539-5533) is typical of the many courses on the Southern Gulf Islands, with nine holes, inexpensive greens fees (CAN$18), a relaxed atmosphere, and a clubhouse offering rentals and meals.

Accommodations and Camping
Many of the travelers you'll meet on the ferry

trip to Galiano will be staying for a week or more in an island cottage. If this style of vacation sounds ideal, check the website www.galianoisland.com for a choice of rentals, but do so well before planning your visit as the best ones fill fast. **Paradise Rock Ocean Front Cottage** (310 Ganner Dr., 250/539-3404, CAN$150) is typical in all respects—water views from a private setting, self-contained, and a deck with a propane barbecue—except that it can be rented for as little as two nights.

Set on Sturdies Bay waterfront is the **Bellhouse Inn** (29 Farmhouse Rd., 250/539-5667 or 800/970-7464, www.bellhouseinn.com, CAN$135–195), an 1890s farmhouse that has been taking in travelers since the 1920s. Each of the three guest rooms has water views and the most expensive features a hot tub, private balcony, and fireplace. Rates include a full breakfast and personal touches, such as tea or coffee delivered to your room before breakfast.

You'll see the magnificent gardens of the M **Galiano Inn** (134 Madrona Dr., 250/539-3388 or 877/530-3939, www.galianoinn.com), at the head of Sturdies Bay, before the ferry docks. The elegant guest rooms, infused with European charm, come in two sizes (Queen, CAN$249, and King, CAN$299) and all have views extending down the bay to Mayne Island. Other highlights include private balconies, super-comfortable beds, plush robes, luxury bathrooms with soaker tubs, and extras such as CD players and coffee-makers. The inn is also home to the **Madrona del Mar Spa,** the place to get pampered with a soothing hot stone massage or kick back in the seaside hot tub. Guests can also book a variety of tours aboard the inn's own motor cruiser, including wine-tasting on nearby Saturna Island.

The campground in **Montague Harbour Provincial Park,** 10 km (6.2 miles) from the ferry, is one of the best in the Southern Gulf Islands. Sites are set below a towering forest of old-growth cedar and fir trees and opens on to a white shingle beach that is aligned perfectly to watch the setting sun. As with all provincial park campgrounds, facilities are limited to picnic tables, pit toilets, and drinking water; CAN$14

per night and no reservations taken. The gates are open mid-April to mid-October.

Food

To immerse yourself in island life, plan on dining at the **Grand Central Emporium** (2470 Sturdies Bay Rd., 250/539-9885, 6:30 A.M.–3:30 P.M. Mon.–Fri., 7:30 A.M.–3:30 P.M. Sat.–Sun., and for dinner Tues.–Sun.), which is decorated with lumberjack artifacts and has seating ripped from old buses. Free-range eggs are the prime ingredient in the omelets, which are huge (ham and Swiss cheese for CAN$9). Sandwiches and burgers dominate the lunch menu. In the evening, the blackboard dinner menu (mains under CAN$20) reflects whatever is in season. There's often live music playing in the background. While you're waiting for a ferry—or even if you're not—line up at the **Max & Moritz** food wagon (in front of the parking lot at the ferry terminal, CAN$5), for a combination of German and Indonesian dishes, such as *nasi goring* (fried rice with various ingredients such as eggs and vegetables).

The stellar food is reason enough to dine at **Atrevida** (Galiano Inn, 134 Madrona Dr., 250/539-3388), but the unobstructed water views cost no extra. Although the upscale dining room has a touch of old-world elegance, the cooking is healthy and modern, with a seasonal menu that makes use of fresh island produce and local seafood. Professional service and an impressive wine list round out what many regard as the finest restaurant on the Southern Gulf Islands. In summer, a sunken patio buzzes with activity as locals and visitors from outlying islands enjoy lunchtime barbecues in a cultured garden setting.

Information and Books

Right at the ferry terminal is **Galiano Island Visitor Info Centre** (250/539-2233, www.galianoisland.com, July–Aug. 9 A.M.–5 P.M. daily). The Southern Gulf Islands have a surprising number of bookstores, and none are better than **Galiano Island Books** (76 Madrona Dr., 250/539-3340, daily 10 A.M.–5 P.M.), down the first left after exiting the terminal area. Stop by for works by island writers as well as Canadiana, children's titles, and some great cookbooks that use local ingredients.

SATURNA ISLAND

Most remote of the populated Southern Gulf Islands, Saturna protrudes into the heart of Georgia Strait and features a long, rugged northern coastline and over half its land area within Gulf Islands National Park. It offers a range of accommodations, but other services are limited (no banks or bank machines) and ferries only stop by a couple of times a day.

From the ferry dock at **Lyall Harbour,** the island's main road loops east then south along the coastline for 14 km (8.7 miles), ending at **East Point Regional Park.** Here you can go swimming or simply admire the sweeping views across the border to the San Juans. Before the park, **Winter Cove** is another picturesque diversion. On Canada Day (July 1), everyone gathers on this beach for a lamb barbecue.

Accommodations and Food

Most accommodations on Saturna Island are in private-home bed-and-breakfasts. A short walk from where the ferry docks is **Lyall Harbour B&B** (121 E. Point Rd., 250/539-5577 or 877/473-9343, CAN$85 s, CAN$95 d). Each of the three guest rooms is spacious and features modern furnishings, a fireplace, and a deck with ocean views. Breakfast is served in a sun-drenched solarium.

Overlooking Boot Cove and also within walking distance of the dock is **Saturna Lodge** (130 Payne Rd., 250/539-2254 or 888/539-8800, www.saturna-island.bc.ca, May–Oct.). Right on the water, this modern accommodation offers seven guest rooms, a hot tub, a lounge with fireplace, and extensive gardens. Rates range CAN$135–195 including breakfast. Within the lodge, a small restaurant has a big reputation for seafood, local game, and produce. The owners are involved in various projects around the island, including **Saturna Island Vineyards** (8 Quarry Trail, 250/539-5139, May–Oct. 11:30 A.M.–4:30 P.M. daily), which sources Pinot Noir, Merlot, and Chardonnay grapes from four island vineyards. Stop by the barn-shaped cellar door for tastings and a tour.

Off East Point Road, **Saturna's Café** (101 Narvaez Bay Rd., 250/539-2936) is open 9:30 A.M.–2 P.M. daily except Tuesday and Wednesday–Monday for dinner from 6 P.M. Expect simple home-style cooking, a casual ambience, and friendly service.

GETTING THERE AND AROUND

BC Ferries (250/386-3431 or 888/223-3779, www.bcferries.com) provides year-round service to the islands from both Vancouver Island and the city of Vancouver, plus transport among the Southern Gulf Islands. The main departure points are Swartz Bay, 32 kilometers (20 miles) north of Victoria, and Tsawwassen, on the south side of Vancouver. All ferries take vehicles (including RVs), motorcycles, bicycles, canoes, and kayaks. It's important to check the timetables (online or posted at each terminal) as some ferries are nonstop and others make up to three stops before reaching the more remote islands. Also try to avoid peak periods, such as Friday and Sunday afternoons. Aside from that, simply roll up and pay your fare.

Regardless of the final destination, the round-trip fare from Swartz Bay (Victoria) to any of the Southern Gulf Islands is a very reasonable adult CAN$6.50, child CAN$3.25, vehicle CAN$21. Interisland travel is charged on a one-way basis: adult CAN$3.50, child CAN$1.75, vehicle CAN$7.50. The fare system is flexible; for example, if you plan to travel to Galiano Island from Swartz Bay, with a stop on Salt Spring Island on the way out, you would pay the interisland fare departing Salt Spring, then use the return portion of the main ticket from Galiano, for a total of CAN$10/person.

From the mainland Tsawwassen terminal (south of downtown Vancouver), the fare is the same regardless of which island you travel to: one-way adult CAN$10.25, child CAN$5.25, vehicle CAN$38. This is the only route for which reservations are accepted; make your booking online at www.bcferries.com.

Know
the San Juan
Islands

The Land

ISLAND NAMES

A look at a map of northern Puget Sound will reveal a mélange of Spanish, British, and American names. None of the original Native American names remain in the San Juans, though surrounding areas kept a few indigenous terms, including Lummi Island, Samish Bay, and Skagit Island.

The Strait of Juan de Fuca is named for Apostolos Valerianos, a Greek who sailed for Spain under the alias of Juan de Fuca. The first European to sail the Northwest Coast of the United States and Canada, he entered Puget Sound in 1592, believing that he had found the fabled Northwest Passage. The Spaniard Francisco de Eliza and his assistant, Lopez Gonzales de Haro, explored these waters more thoroughly in 1791 and 1792, labeling the San Juan Islands, Haro Strait, Rosario Strait, and Orcas, Lopez, Eliza, Sucia, Patos, Matia, Guemes, and Fidalgo Islands.

Many regional landmarks—including Vancouver Island, Puget Sound, Georgia Strait, Cypress Island, Whidbey Island, Possession Sound, Mount Baker, and Mount Rainier—were named during English expeditions by Captain Cook in 1778 and Captain Vancouver in 1792.

Another major player in the naming game was Lieutenant Charles Wilkes of the U.S. Navy, who sailed through the San Juans on an 1841 scientific expedition. Wilkes applied the names of his naval heroes (along with several crew members) to everything in sight: Allan Island, Barnes Island, Blakely Island, Burrows Island, Clark Island, Decatur Island, Frost Island, Henry Island, James Island, Jones Island, Shaw Island, Sinclair Island, Spieden Island, Stuart Island, and Waldron Island. He also tried to rename the main islands of Orcas, San Juan, and Lopez, but his choices didn't stick.

THE SALISH SEA

In recent years, biologists have begun using the name Salish Sea for the waters surrounding the San Juan Islands. This great inland sea—named for the Coast Salish people who first made this their home—encompasses Puget Sound, the Strait of Juan de Fuca, and the Strait of Georgia off the west side of Vancouver Island. Enormous glaciers carved out the basin that became the Salish Sea more than 14,000 years ago.

The Salish Sea is a fertile place, with twice-daily tides that sweep massive amounts of water upwards over submerged ridges, thus bringing nutrients to the top layers and surface oxygen to lower depths upon tidal retreat. Rivers and streams supply additional nutrients to the mix, and the temperate climate supports a diverse ecological web. The result is an incredibly productive environment for all forms of marine life. Steve Yates's *Orcas, Eagles, and Kings* provides an in-depth introduction to the Salish Sea.

GEOLOGY

The San Juan Islands are composed of a complex and jumbled assemblage of rocks that were laid down in ancient oceanic trenches and then pushed up into mountains by tectonic forces. Over the last three million years, they were further shaped by a series of enormous glaciers that pushed southward from Canada and bulldozed everything in their path. The land that would later become the San Juans was buried several times beneath hundreds of feet of ice. When the last of the glaciers retreated around 12,000 years ago, they left behind evidence of their passing, including glacial erratics (large boulders that were carried atop the ice) and bedrock that shows the scratches and gouges of glaciers.

Other unusual rocks found on the islands include marine fossils on Sucia Island (in Fossil Bay, of course), impressive pillow basalts (created when lava flowed under the Pacific Ocean) along San Juan's west coast and Lopez's south side, and substantial limestone deposits on the north end of San Juan Island. This limestone was mined extensively in the early 1900s and used for the production of Portland cement. The old lime kilns are still visible at Roche Harbor Resort and Lime Kiln Point State Park. For a more detailed look at San Juan Islands geology, pick up *Roadside Geology of Washington* by David Alt and Donald Hyndman.

CLIMATE

Noting their location—in the middle of northern Puget Sound—one might assume that the San Juan Islands suffer from Washington's notoriously wet weather. Fortunately, such is not the case. Mountains on the Olympic Peninsula and Vancouver Island force clouds to drop much of their moisture before they reach the San Juans, creating a rain shadow effect. Summertime visitors are pleasantly surprised by the warm and sunny weather that predominates. Winters are typically overcast and rainy, though still drier than many other parts of Washington.

The San Juans do most of their tourist business between Memorial Day and Labor Day, when the weather is delightful. For locals, September and October are the best months of the year: The tourists are gone (and they left their cash behind), and the weather is still warm and relatively dry, with highs in the 60s and lows in the 40s or 50s.

Rain, Fog, and Wind

Rainfall amounts to around 29 inches per year on the San Juans, compared with 37 inches in Seattle. Precipitation varies across the islands, with the driest areas closer to Anacortes or southern Lopez and the wettest on the northwestern end of San Juan Island.

The sun shines an average of 247 days a year, much of that during the summer months; July and August each average only an inch of rain per month. May, June, and September are also relatively dry. November, December, and January comprise the rainiest season, with more than four inches of precipitation typically falling each month. Snow is uncommon in the San Juans—only around seven inches fall per year—and it rarely stays around for more than a few days. The one exception is the summit of Mount Constitution,

half a mile up, where snow occasionally gets two feet deep before a warm spell melts it again.

Fog can get thick around the islands at times, particularly in late summer. Fortunately, it is generally gone by early afternoon.

Winds are typically mild in the San Juans, but passes often funnel them, causing very different

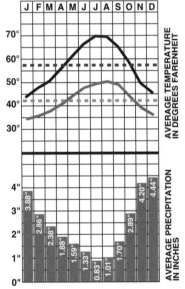

SAN JUAN ISLANDS CLIMATE

AVERAGE TEMPERATURE IN DEGREES FARENHEIT

AVERAGE PRECIPITATION IN INCHES

MAXIMUM TEMP.   AVERAGE MAXIMUM: 57.0°

MINIMUM TEMP.   AVERAGE MINIMUM: 42.4°

AVERAGE ANNUAL TOTAL PRECIPITATION: 29.00"

Maximum temperature is the average of all daily maximum temperatures recorded for the day of the year between the years 1971 and 2000.

Average temperature is the average of all daily average temperatures recorded for the day of the year between the years 1971 and 2000.

Minimum temperature is the average of all daily minimum temperatures recorded for the day of the year between the years 1971 and 2000.

Precipitation is the average of all daily total precipitation recorded for the day of the year between the years 1971 and 2000.

Source: Western Regional Climate Center, Reno, NV (website: www.wrcc.dri.edu)

conditions depending on your location around an island. Sailors take advantage of these winds, which often top 20 knots in open straits and channels. Small boaters—particularly sea kayakers—need to avoid such areas when the winds are blowing. Occasional winter storms can bring extreme events, such as the December 1990 nor'easter that flattened thousands of old-growth trees, particularly on Jones Island.

Temperatures

Temperatures on the islands are generally quite comfortable. Midsummer days are typically in the upper 60s and low 70s, and only rarely top 85°; the record high was 92° on July 17, 1941. Nighttime lows in the summer average 50°.

The record low for the San Juans was 8° on January 13, 1950, but most winters the thermometer doesn't even come close to zero. In January (the coldest month), daytime highs are typically in the low to mid-40s, with nighttime minimums a few degrees above freezing. The thermometer dips below freezing approximately 34 days a year.

Weather Updates

Get current weather and marine forecasts for the San Juan Islands—and anywhere else in America—from the National Weather Service's http://weather.noaa.gov. Another useful Web source for weather is through the *Journal of the San Juans* (www.sanjuanjournal.com). Boaters can also get the latest forecast on their VHF radio (channels 1, 2, and 8); it is broadcast continuously.

Water

Water—or the lack thereof—is a serious problem on the San Juan Islands, particularly during the all-too-frequent drought years. Relatively low annual precipitation, limited underground aquifers, and only a handful of year-round creeks and lakes make water a scarce commodity. As the population increases and development grows, the demands for water escalate. Old wells are drying up, and new ones are often contaminated by saltwater intrusion as the underground

aquifers are drained. Most bed-and-breakfasts and other lodging places use low-flow showerheads and other means to conserve water. Do your part by not wasting a drop. This means avoiding long showers, not leaving the water running while brushing your teeth or shaving, and not flushing the toilet as often.

PUBLIC LANDS

State Parks

A number of small—and one large—state parks (360/902-8844, www.parks.wa.gov) are scattered across the San Juans. **Moran State Park** on Orcas Island is the biggest and most famous of these, covering more than 5,200 acres of heavily forested terrain. It includes the islands' highest point, 2,409-foot Mount Constitution. A paved road leads to the summit, and the park offers camping, swimming, boating, fishing, and more than 30 miles of hiking trails. Smaller parks are **Spencer Spit State Park** on Lopez Island, a popular camping spot, **Lime Kiln Point State Park** on San Juan Island, a day-use-only park famous for views of killer whales from shore, and two small places on Orcas Island: **Obstruction Pass State Park** and **Point Doughty Marine State Park.**

Several smaller islands contain **marine state parks** that are open to hiking and camping and are accessible only by boat or floatplane. These include Blind, Clark, Doe, Jones, James, Matia, Patos, Posey, Stuart, Sucia, and Turn Islands. Small marine state parks are also located on Orcas and San Juan Islands.

National Wildlife Refuge

The San Juan Islands National Wildlife Refuge encompasses 84 islands and islets, most of which are off-limits to tourists, to protect birds and other animals. These islands provide vital nesting spots for bald eagles and seabirds, and the rocks are used as haul-out areas for harbor seals, California and Steller sea lions, and elephant seals.

Boaters (including sea kayakers) must stay at least 200 yards offshore from these islands. Landing is permitted only at two designated areas, on Turn and Matia Islands. The refuge is man-

PRESERVING THE SAN JUANS

To vacationers, the San Juans may seem like a recreational playground, but for island inhabitants, they provide sustenance. Puget Sound is becoming increasingly developed as the population spirals upward, leaving the islands as a place to rediscover the natural world. But the islands themselves are also under pressure as new homes encroach old farms or carve openings into remote shorelines, as public areas are closed off because the access trails cross private lands, and as increasing use impacts the natural areas. It's yet another case of wild places being loved to death. Several nonprofit organizations are working to protect the San Juans through land purchases and environmental action.

San Juan Preservation Trust

In existence for more than 25 years, the San Juan Preservation Trust (360/468-3509, www.sjpt.org) works with local landowners to protect special features of their lands for future generations through conservation easements and donations. Over the years the trust has protected more than 8,900 acres of land, including working farms, forests, picturesque shorelines, and wildlife-rich wetlands. Most of the property preserved by the trust remains in private hands, with public access by permission only. Membership costs $25 for individuals or $50 for families.

San Juan County Land Bank

Established by a 1990 ballot measure, the San Juan County Land Bank (360/378-4402, www.co.san-juan.wa.us/land_bank) is a public program funded by a one-percent real estate transfer tax. These taxes raise $2.5 million annually to acquire land or conservation easements. More than 2,700 acres have been protected in 13 natural areas, including such places as Hummel Lake and Upright Head Preserves on Lopez, Crescent Beach and Entrance Mountain Preserves on Orcas, and Westside and Limekiln Preserves on San Juan.

Friends of the San Juans

Based in Friday Harbor, Friends of the San Juans (360/378-2319, www.sanjuans.org) is a local environmental group that is deeply involved in protecting the islands. The Friends have succeeded in stopping such developments as a large supermarket at Orcas Village and continue to push for shoreline preservation throughout the San Juans. Annual membership is $35 for individuals or $50 for families.

The Nature Conservancy

An international organization, The Nature Conservancy (206/343-4344, www.tnc-washington.org) owns Deadman, Goose, Sentinel, and Yellow Islands, and has 480 acres on Waldron Island. Only Yellow Island is readily accessible to the public.

---

aged by the U.S. Fish & Wildlife Service (360/457-8451, http://pacific.fws.gov) and is based in Port Angeles; contact them for a small map of the islands. Marine navigation charts also show which islands are within the national wildlife refuge.

San Juan Island National Historical Park

The so-called Pig War is memorialized in the 1,750-acre San Juan Island National Historical Park (headquarters: 640 Mullis St., Friday Harbor, 360/378-2240, www.nps.gov/sajh). Established in 1966, the park is divided into two sections. American Camp occupies a beautiful grassy peninsula on the southeast end of the island, while English Camp is in a wooded, peaceful cove on the opposite side of San Juan. Both of these areas are worth a visit, not only for the handful of historical buildings, but also for excellent hiking trails and gorgeous beaches.

Other Public Lands

Seven **San Juan County parks** (360/378-8420, www.co.san-juan.wa.us/parks) are on the ferry-served islands: Agate Beach, Blackie Brady Memorial Beach, Odlin, and Otis Perkins county parks on Lopez Island, Ruben Tarte and

San Juan county parks on San Juan Island, and Shaw Island County Park on Shaw Island. Camping is available at Odlin, San Juan, and Shaw Island county parks; the others are for day-use only.

The **Washington Department of Natural Resources** (DNR: 360/856-3500, www.dnr .wa.gov) has considerable land on Cypress Island, with primitive campsites, hiking trails, and protected moorages. It also manages a campsite on Lummi Island.

The federal **Bureau of Land Management** (BLM: 509/665-2100, www.or.blm.gov) man-

ages several small natural areas on Lopez, Stuart, and Patos Islands. All have hiking trails and are for day-use only.

The **San Juan County Land Bank** (360/378-4402, www.co.san-juan.wa.us/land_bank) has acquired more than 2,700 acres in 13 natural areas scattered around the islands. These are open to the public for day-use only.

The Nature Conservancy (206/343-4344, www.tnc-washington.org) owns several small San Juan islands, plus 480 acres on Waldron Island, but only Yellow Island is readily accessible to the public.

Flora and Fauna

Plant and animal communities on the San Juans reflect local topographic and weather conditions. Forests dominate in many areas, but the islands also contain broad expanses of grassland, open meadows and fields, rich marine areas, marshes and lagoons, and a long and diverse shoreline that includes rocky cliffs, sheltered bays, and sandy beaches. There are even islets so dry that cacti grow. See *San Juan Islands Wildlife* by Evelyn Adams or *Wild Plants of the San Juan Islands* by Scott Atkinson and Fred Sharpe for an in-depth look at local natural history.

HABITATS
Forests
Dense coniferous forests (or ones regenerating after logging) cover large portions of the islands, and are typically dominated by Douglas fir, Western hemlock, and western red cedar. Common understory plants include salal, Oregon grape, red elderberry, thimbleberry, salmonberry, blackberry, wild roses, and various ferns. Dry, rocky sites commonly have picturesque groves of Pacific madrone, particularly along island shores. At higher elevations and on exposed ridges, shore pine often grows.

Forests are home to Columbian black-tailed deer, raccoons, beavers, mink, river otters, bats, shrews, and various introduced species of squir-

rels, along with such birds as ravens, woodpeckers, winter wrens, and owls. Good places to explore island forests include Moran State Park and Madrona Point on Orcas Island, English Camp and Jackle's Lagoon on San Juan Island, Odlin County Park on Lopez Island, Cedar Rock Biological Preserve on Shaw Island, and the boat-accessible marine state parks on Jones, Matia, and Sucia Islands.

Meadows
Meadows may be either natural grasslands, hilltops, and mountain slopes, or spaces created by the clearing of land for agriculture. Some of the best grasslands to explore include American Camp and the top of Mount Young on San Juan Island, Mount Constitution on Orcas Island, the wonderful floral displays on The Nature Conservancy's Yellow Island, and fallow agricultural land on all four of the main islands.

Animals commonly seen in island meadows include nonnative European rabbits, voles (meadow mice), shrews, alligator lizards, red foxes (a nonnative species on San Juan Island), and small birds, such as vesper sparrows, savannah sparrows, and American goldfinches. Overhead you might see birds of prey, such as bald and golden eagles or northern harriers. A few small islands (including Cactus, Gossip, and Cemetery Islands) contain areas called **Puget prairies,** with distinctive plants like the lance-leafed stone and even prickly pear cactus—the only species of cactus native to western Washington.

Wetlands

Swamps, lagoons, marshes, ponds, and other wetlands are vital areas for wildlife on the islands and are home to river otters, muskrats, beavers, raccoons, garter snakes, red-legged frogs, Pacific treefrogs, rough-skinned newts, red-winged blackbirds, great blue herons, Canada geese, belted kingfishers, and many species of ducks. Good places to find wetlands include Jackle's Lagoon and Egg Lake on San Juan Island, the Frank Richardson Wildlife Preserve on Orcas Island, and Spencer Spit Lagoon on Lopez Island.

Shorelines

San Juan County contains more than 375 miles of shoreline—the most of any county in the lower 48 states. This coast varies widely, from rocks to sand to mud, and supports an equally varied population of animals. Intertidal areas are particularly productive.

Beautiful **sandy beaches** are found on all of the larger islands, with some of the best at American Camp on San Juan Island, Obstruction Pass on Orcas Island, Spencer Spit State Park and Agate Beach County Park on Lopez Island, Shaw Island County Park on Shaw Island, Pelican Beach on Cypress Island, and Shallow Bay on Sucia Island.

Rocky shores are ubiquitous in the San Juans, and are welcoming areas for wildlife, including many species of birds. Good places to find them include San Juan County Park and Lime Kiln Point State Park on San Juan Island, Madrona Point and Point Doughty on Orcas Island, Shark Reef Park and Point Colville on Lopez Island, Cedar Rock Biological Preserve on Shaw Island, Eagle Cliff on Cypress Island, Doe Island Marine State Park, Turn Point on Stuart Island, and Ev Henry Finger on Sucia Island.

Marine Areas

The rich waters around the San Juan Islands abound with marine plant and animal life. The area is justly famous for killer whales, and a surprisingly large business has grown up around whale-watching. Other marine mammals spotted here include minke whales, harbor porpoises, Dall's porpoises, California sea lions, Steller sea lions, harbor seals, and elephant seals. Of course, these waters also contain many species of fish and other creatures. Divers are attracted to the vibrant undersea world of the San Juans, commercial whale-watching trips are a summertime staple, and fish are caught commercially and for sport.

One of the best ways to see killer whales—without impacting them in any way—is from the shore at Lime Kiln Point State Park on San Juan Island. Folks riding the Washington State Ferries are certain to see gulls and various seabirds along the way, and may also spot bald eagles and the occasional whale. San Juan Islands National Wildlife Refuge covers 84 islands and rocky points, providing protected breeding and resting areas for an incredible array of seabirds and mammals.

TREES

The most distinctive and photogenic tree species on the San Juan Islands is the **Pacific madrone,** commonly called madrona or arbutus. These trees grow on rocky sites, and are conspicuous as they angle out over the shoreline. Madrones are characterized by dark and leathery evergreen leaves and peeling reddish-orange bark that exposes a smooth under-skin. Pacific madrone grows from California to British Columbia.

Washington's state tree, the **Western hemlock,** is common in dense, shady forests throughout the archipelago. These trees can reach 500 years old, topping out at 200 feet. Look for the droopy crowns of Western hemlock to distinguish them from other trees at a distance.

Western red cedar has distinctive flat sprays and a stringy bark. The Coast Salish people prized this tree, using it for dugout canoes and splitting the wood for planks to build their houses. The sweet-smelling wood is resistant to decay. Western red cedar is a member of the cypress family, and is not a true cedar.

One of the most important trees on the San

Juans, **Douglas firs** can grow to six feet in diameter. They are commonly found with Western hemlock and western red cedar. Heavy ridges mark the bark of mature Douglas firs, and lower limbs fall off as the tree grows, making them a favorite of loggers who appreciate the knot-free wood.

Pacific yew has sharply pointed needles and grows in moist areas, particularly along streams. Yews are slow growing and never get very tall. The Coast Salish used the dense wood to carve paddles and bows. Today, the tree is best known as the source for a potent anti-cancer chemical, taxol.

Big-leaf maples are distinguished by—you got it—their big leaves, which can reach a foot in width. The trees can grow quite large (to 100 feet high), with spreading trunks. One of the largest is on the grounds of English Camp on San Juan Island. The yellow leaves of maples are particularly beautiful in the fall. Two other related (but smaller) species are also present on the islands, the **vine maple** and **Douglas maple.**

Shore pines are a subspecies of lodgepole pine, and are generally found on high, windswept bluffs, such as the summit of Mount Constitution on Orcas Island. Most are relatively stunted in height. The trees are well adapted to fire, with some cones that only release seeds when heat melts the sticky covering.

The **Rocky Mountain juniper** is commonly found in the Rockies, but also exists on the San Juans and nearby islands. The trees are stunted, rarely topping 20 feet in height. Cypress Island was misnamed by Captain George Vancouver when he sailed past it in 1792; the "cypress" he saw were actually Rocky Mountain junipers.

Other common trees on the San Juans include **grand firs,** recognizable by their long, flat needles with white undersides; **Sitka spruce,** which grows fast and tall and is common near the shore; and **red alder,** a common fast-growing plant in moist areas.

WILDLIFE
Wolf Hollow
Located on San Juan Island north of Friday Harbor, Wolf Hollow Wildlife Rehabilitation Center

Pacific madrone tree, Shaw Island

(360/378-5000, www.wolfhollowwildlife.org) is a nonprofit organization that works with injured, sick, or orphaned wild animals. Most of these animals were injured by human activities. Since its founding in 1983, Wolf Hollow has treated more than 200 species—from hummingbirds to seals—and has a songbird aviary, raccoon pen, and eagle flight cage. It offers educational programs at local schools and parks, but the facilities are not open to the general public. If you find an injured or orphaned animal on the San Juan Islands, call Wolf Hollow; the staff is available 24 hours a day.

Land Mammals
European rabbits were brought to the islands in the late 19th century as caged meat animals but were released when the breeders ran out of money. The rabbits are now common in grassy parts of San Juan and Lopez Islands, and also occur on other islands in the San Juans. In some

SLUGS

If western Washington had an official creature, it could easily be the common slug; the region is famous for them. The damp climate is just what slugs need to thrive: not too wet, because slugs aren't waterproof (they will absorb water through their outer membranes until their bodily fluids are too diluted to support them), and not too dry, because insufficient humidity makes them dry up and die. Optimum humidity for slugs is near 100 percent, which is why you'll see them crossing the sidewalk very early in the morning, at dusk, or on misty days.

During the dry parts of the day, slugs will seek refuge under the pool cover you casually tossed onto the lawn, or under the scrap lumber piled in the back of your lot.

Slugs look like snails that have lost their shells, or like little green or brown squirts of slime about 3–5 inches long. Though more than 300 species of slugs exist worldwide, the Northwest is home to little more than a dozen. The native **banana slug,** light green or yellowish with dark spots, has been rapidly outnumbered by the imported European **black slug,** which is now far more common in area gardens than the native variety. Slugs can curl up into a ball to protect themselves, or flatten and elongate themselves to squeeze into tight places. They move on one long foot by secreting mucus that gets firm where the foot must grab hold and stays slimy under the part that must slide. They see (probably just patterns of light and dark) with eyes at the ends of a pair of tentacles; they have a mouth and eat primarily plants and mushrooms.

Getting rid of slugs is no easy matter. Traditional home remedies include saltshakers and beer traps; both require a strong stomach. Most residents just try to avoid stepping on them.

© DON PITCHER

banana slug

places, such as the south end of San Juan Island at American Camp, there can be 500 rabbits per acre! Most of them remain underground during the day, emerging at dusk. Bald and golden eagles, red-tailed hawks, northern harriers, and red foxes all feed on them.

Columbian black-tailed deer are found almost everywhere on the San Juans, and may even be seen swimming between the islands. The deer are quite small, generally under 3 feet high and only rarely more than 200 pounds. Keep your eyes open for them in old fields and orchards or in brushy areas. The deer at Jones Island Marine State Park are famously abundant, tiny, and unafraid of people. During the summer, deer are commonly seen early in the morning or late in the day, when temperatures are cooler.

Other island mammals include raccoons, beavers, mink, river otters, vagrant shrews, white-footed (deer) mice, Townsend's voles, and several species of bats. Flying squirrels were recently discovered on San Juan Island and are presumably native. Introduced species include muskrats, Norway rats, and house mice, plus Townsend's chip-munk on Lopez Island and red foxes and European ferrets on San Juan Island. Three types of squirrels—Eastern gray squirrels, Eastern fox squirrels, and Douglas squirrels—have been introduced. Surprisingly, skunks, porcupines, and coyotes are not found on the San Juans. Elk were once found on them, but 19th-century market hunters killed off the last of them.

Reptiles and Amphibians

There are no poisonous snakes on the San Juans, but you might encounter three species of garter snakes (the double-striped common garter is most often seen). Other regional species include northern alligator lizards, Pacific treefrogs, red-legged frogs, northwestern toads, and rough-skinned newts, whereas bullfrogs and Western painted turtles were introduced.

Whales and Dolphins

The most famous local mammal—the **killer whale**—attracts more than half a million visitors to the San Juans each summer. (See the sidebar *Killer Whales* for details on these fascinating

killer whales near San Juan Island

© DON PITCHER

creatures.) An excellent source for information about these strikingly marked and social animals, as well as other marine mammals around the islands, is the Whale Museum's website at www.whalemuseum.com.

Minke whales are gray or brownish in color, with diagonal white bands on their pectoral fins. They are generally seen as solitary individuals, moving slowly and with a blow that is often inconspicuous. Minke are the most numerous of the world's baleen whales, and are frequently seen around the San Juans in the summer, but not at other times of the year. Minke whales feed by driving schools of small fish to the surface and then opening wide to engulf them. They also take advantage of clusters of fish that have been schooled together by other fish or birds; the minke pop to the surface through this ball of fish, sometimes scattering gulls and other birds when they emerge. Minke whales can reach 30 feet long, and the larger females may weigh up to 10 tons.

Gray whales are bigger than minkes and lack a dorsal fin. They have a mottled gray body and are often covered with patches of barnacles, especially on the head. They are generally seen in shallow coastal areas and migrate some 9,000 miles, from Alaska to Baja. In recent years, a few gray whales have stayed in the waters of northern Puget Sound through the summer, but they are rarely seen.

Humpback whales can reach up to 55 feet long, and are slate gray or black, with irregular knobs on the head and jaw and a short dorsal fin. Their blows are strong and obvious. Humpbacks are rarely seen around the San Juans, but are fairly common in more northern waters.

Other species of cetaceans sometimes seen around the San Juans include **false killer whales,** a relatively small whale that is mostly black; and **Pacific white-sided dolphins,** with a gray-black upper body accented by a white belly and grayish sides.

Porpoises

Visitors often think that the black-and-white sea creatures riding the bow waves of their tour boat are baby killer whales, but these playful characters are **Dall's porpoises.** They feed primarily on squid and small fish, and can reach lengths of six and a half feet and weights of up to 330 pounds.

The **harbor porpoise** is Puget Sound's smallest cetacean, growing to nearly six feet long and 150 pounds. Although similar in appearance to the Dall's porpoise, the much shyer harbor porpoise is rarely spotted in the wild. Accurate counts are impossible, but the population around the San Juan Islands has been estimated at fewer than 100.

Seals and Sea Lions

Harbor seals are the most abundant marine mammals in the San Juans. They can be seen at low tide sunning themselves on rocks in isolated areas, but they will quickly return to the water if approached by humans, particularly kayakers. Though they appear clumsy on land, these 100- to 200-pound seals (some males can reach 800 pounds!) are poetry in motion underwater; they flip, turn, and glide with little apparent effort, staying underwater for as long as 20 minutes. Harbor seals have a bad reputation with area salmon fishermen, although studies of the seals' stomach contents and fecal material indicate that they feed primarily on flounder, herring, pollock, cod, and rockfish, as well as some mollusks and crustaceans.

The **California sea lion** is a seasonal visitor to northern Puget Sound. These dark-brown sea lions breed off the coast of California and Mexico in the early summer, and then some adventurous males migrate as far north as British Columbia for the winter.

The lighter-colored **Steller sea lions** are often seen in the spring around the San Juan Islands, particularly Spieden Island. Males of the species are much larger than the females, growing to almost 10 feet in length and weighing over a ton, while the females are a dainty six feet long and 600 pounds.

Recent years have seen an increased population of **Northern elephant seal** in waters around the San Juans. Adult males have a large elephantine snout and the biggest may weigh upward of four tons. Females are much smaller. Both have a brownish-gray color and occasionally haul out on local beaches.

BIRDS

More than 200 species of birds live or travel through the San Juans, including large numbers of shorebirds in the spring and fall, nesting seabirds, great blue herons, trumpeter swans, Canada geese, wild turkeys (introduced in the 1970s), belted kingfishers, common ravens, rufous hummingbirds, and such predators as bald eagles, red-tailed hawks, sharp-shinned hawks, northern harriers, turkey vultures, and great horned owls. San Juan Islands National Historical Park and local bookstores sell a nicely designed *Wildlife of the San Juan Islands* checklist that includes all these birds, along with local mammals, reptiles, and amphibians. You can get it directly from Archipelago Press (360/378-5571).

The **National Audubon Society's** Washington state office (in Olympia, 360/786-8020, www .wa.audubon.org) has detailed information on birds and birding in the state. Call its rare bird alert line (425/454-2662) for unusual sightings in the San Juans and elsewhere. The **San Juan Islands Audubon Society** has monthly bird treks on one of the four main islands, and their website (www.sjiaudubon.org) lists recent sightings, upcoming bird walks, and other birding info.

Bald Eagles

The San Juan Islands are home to the largest year-round population of bald eagles outside Alaska. They are common sights soaring over the bays and channels or riding the thermals atop Mount Constitution on Orcas Island or Mount Findlayson and Mount Dallas on San Juan Island.

In the past, bald eagles were often blamed for the deaths of sheep and other domestic animals. Actually, eagles much prefer dead and dying fish to anything running around on hooves; their common fare, aside from dead salmon, is sick or injured waterfowl or rabbits that didn't make it across the road. An aggressive bird, the eagle will often purloin the catch of an osprey or other bird in favor of finding its own. The large nests of bald eagles, sometimes measuring more than eight feet wide and 12 feet high, are often found in old-growth spruce and fir snags (standing dead trees).

The adult bald eagle's distinctive white head and tail make it easy to spot. But it takes four years for it to acquire these markings, making the immature eagle difficult to identify, as it may show whitish markings anywhere on its body. In contrast, the somewhat similar golden eagle has distinct white patches on its tail and underwings.

Great Blue Herons

Another large bird seen throughout the San Juans is the Great Blue Heron, a long-legged bird that wades in shallow bays and marshes. Their diet consists of frogs, small fish, snakes, crabs, and other creatures. Look for them in places such as the Frank Richardson Wildlife Preserve on Orcas, English Camp on San Juan, or Weeks Wetland on Lopez; the long legs, slate-blue coloration, yellow bill, and ornate black plumes are distinctive.

History

North America has been inhabited for a very long time. Low ocean levels during the Pleistocene epoch (some 30,000–40,000 years ago) offered the nomadic peoples of northeastern Asia a walkable passage across to Alaska. One of the earliest records of humans in the Americas is a caribou bone with a serrated edge found in northern Yukon Territory. Almost certainly used as a tool, the bone has been placed at 27,000 years old by carbon dating. As the climate warmed and the great ice sheets receded toward the Rocky Mountains and Canadian Shield, a corridor opened down the middle of the Great Plains, allowing movement farther south. Recent scientific evidence suggests that ancient peoples also sailed or paddled along the coast from Asia to North America.

The Coast Salish

The place we now call the San Juan Islands has been occupied for some 5,000 years. When the first European explorers sailed around the San Juan Islands, they found them populated primarily by the Lummi and Samish tribes, though the Songhees and Saanich were present on parts of the western and northern islands. These closely related tribes are all considered Strait Coast Salish peoples. Lummi legends tell of a man named Swetan who landed on San Juan Island where he built a home, probably at Garrison Bay on San Juan Island. His descendants became the various family groups that settled the islands and surrounding shores. Nobody knows exactly when Swetan arrived, but he may represent the earliest influx of people to the area. The Salish culture underwent changes over the eons as people developed better ways to catch and preserve fish and shellfish.

Although the Coast Salish were a peaceable people, their Haida and Kwakiutl neighbors to the north were infamously aggressive, and the Salish found themselves under periodic threat from marauding parties who swept through the islands in 50-man war canoes. Salish men were often killed in these attacks, while the women and children were taken away as slaves. Once captured, a slave's only hope was to run away, since he or she could never marry a nonslave and was treated as property. To defend their territory against such raids, the Salish constructed rock stockades and armed themselves with whalebone clubs; these ancient fortifications are still visible on Lopez Island. Unfortunately, the northern tribes were some of the first to obtain firearms from Russian traders, making life even more difficult for the Salish. By the middle of the 19th century, the raiders were attacking not only the Salish, but also white settlers in the region.

The Cycle of Life

Strait Coast Salish life revolved around access to foods such as salmon, clams, and edible plants. The arrival of summer meant the return of salmon, and the Salish prepared by moving their families to temporary camps on the islands where they would be close to the migrating schools of fish. The salmon were caught in reefnets suspended from dugout canoes, and the fish were then preserved by air drying or smoking over a fire. Reefnets are still used today in the islands. Other important foods included clams, cockles, oysters, sea cucumbers, crabs, sea urchins, chitons, snails, barnacles, mussels, and various species of fish. Edible plants included wild strawberries, blackberries, gooseberries, huckleberries, purple great camas bulbs, horsetails, and tiger lilies. The Coast Salish used nets to catch black-tailed deer and ducks.

Men had the primary responsibility for fishing, hunting, house building, and carving canoes, while the women gathered, cooked, and preserved the food, and made clothing, wove mats, and coiled baskets. Coast Salish clothes were woven using processed cedar bark or roots, duck down, nettle fiber, wool, animal skins, and other materials. In the summer, they often went naked. After the busy summer season of hunting and gathering, the families returned to their winter village, which might be on the islands or the mainland. Fall was often a time for big potlatches. Guests were invited from throughout the region and the festivities always included games, canoe races, mock battles, intertribal marriages, and an elaborate potlatch ceremony in which the host gained prestige by giving away gifts.

Winter quarters—cedar plank houses and enormous longhouses used for potlatches—were built along protected beaches. A number of families lived inside each plank house. Sleeping platforms lined the outside walls, and mats hung from the rafters as partitions and to insulate from the cold. Families cooked over a central fire that also heated the house; smoke escaped through a hole in the roof. Western red cedar was important not just for the Salish homes but also in their carvings and dugout canoes, some of which reached 30 feet in length.

Death of a Culture

The Pacific Northwest tribes were introduced to the byproducts of the white man's culture, such as knives, guns, and the deadly smallpox virus (to which they were not immune), before ever laying eyes on a white explorer. The first disease outbreak in this era of death swept through in 1782, followed by additional plagues in the 1830s and early 1850s. Over this 75-year period, some 80–90 percent of the Coast Salish died from disease. They were not the only ones; the population of Native Americans in the entire Pacific Northwest may have numbered 1 or even 2 million before the diseases struck, but plummeted to 180,000 by the time Europeans arrived. Smallpox Bay on San Juan Island is named for an incident in the 1860s when many Salish died after two sick sailors were forced ashore from an unknown ship to keep them from contaminating other sailors.

It wasn't just disease that killed the Coast Salish. Alcohol took a deadly toll, and San Juan Island became known far and wide for its saloons, where drunkenness and violence were the norm at any time of the day or night. And direct conflicts with whites pushed the Salish from areas they had inhabited for thousands of years. This

combination of diseases, repeated raids by northern tribes, alcohol, and aggressive white settlers decimated the Coast Salish. By the 1840s, the San Juan Islands had no year-round residents; the survivors had moved to the Washington mainland or Victoria. The **Point Elliott Treaty** of 1855 established the Lummi Indian Reservation near Bellingham. The book *Lummi Elders Speak,* edited by Ann Nugent, has an insightful quote from one village elder, Herman Olsen. Describing Mitchell Bay on San Juan Island, he said:

> *A white fellow moved in there. They homesteaded the whole thing. They just plain homesteaded it wrong and everything. Then on the other side of the bay, what there was left, the Lummis moved across, just a stone's throw across the bay; they had two great big houses there. Then they had some more small houses, cabinlike, that they stayed in that got homesteaded so the Lummis just lost out there too. White people came and homesteaded the darn place and never even left their ground for the Lummis.*

For additional information on the original San Juan settlers, read Julie K. Stein's *Exploring Coast Salish Prehistory: The Archaeology of San Juan Island.* The book details excavations at a seasonal camp near American Camp and Salish winter quarters at English Camp. Both of these camps were used for thousands of years, and English Camp may have been in use up until just before the English soldiers showed up in 1859. There are literally hundreds of other archaeological sites on the islands. Also worth a read is *San Juan Island Indians,* a self-published work by Gary J. Morris that can be found in local libraries.

THE EUROPEANS ARRIVE
Spanish Explorers

In 1592, exactly a century after Columbus made his landfall in the Caribbean, a Greek explorer using the Spanish name **Juan de Fuca** sailed along Washington's coast and claimed to have discovered the fabled "Northwest Passage," an inland waterway crossing North America from the Pacific to the Atlantic. Later explorers did find a waterway close to where de Fuca indicated, but it led only into today's Puget Sound, not all the way to the Atlantic Ocean.

Spain, hoping to regain some of its diminishing power and wealth, sent out several expeditions in the late 1700s to explore the Northwest Coast. In 1774, Juan Perez explored as far north as the Queen Charlotte Islands off Vancouver Island and was the first European to describe the Pacific Northwest coastline and Olympic Mountains before being forced to turn back by sickness and storms.

In 1775, a larger Spanish expedition set out, led by Bruno de Heceta and Juan Francisco de la Bodega y Quadra. Heceta went ashore at Point Grenville, just north of Moclips on the Washington coast, and claimed the entire Northwest for Spain. Farther south, Bodega y Quadra sent seven men ashore in a small metal craft for wood and water; they were quickly killed and their boat torn apart in the whites' first encounter with coastal Native Americans. The two ships sailed away without further incident; Quadra named the island Isla de Dolores (Isle of Sorrows), today's Destruction Island off the Olympic Peninsula. Quadra continued his explorations as far north as present-day Sitka, Alaska, while Heceta sailed north to Nootka Sound. Heceta failed to note the Strait of Juan de Fuca, but he did come across "the mouth of some great river," presumably the Columbia, though the death or illness of much of his crew prevented further exploration and robbed Spain of an important claim.

It was not until 1791 that the first Europeans finally saw the San Juan Islands up close. In that year the Spanish explorer **Francisco Eliza** sent his schooner *Santa Saturnina* into what his pilot, Lopez Gonzales de Haro, described as "an indescribable archipelago of islands, keys, rocks, and big and little inlets." The Spaniards returned to the San Juans the next summer, this time better equipped to explore the islands in depth. But when they arrived, they found two other ships already present, the *Discovery* and *Chatham*, captained by their English competitors under George Vancouver. Despite the often-hostile relations between the Spanish and English, the two decided to work together as they explored the area. This cooperation may have been an augury of the later Pig War on San Juan Island in which two nations chose cooperation over conflict.

English Explorations

England was *the* force to be reckoned with in the battle for the Northwest. In 1776, Captain **James Cook** took two ships and 170 men on an expedition that brought him to the Hawaiian Islands, the Oregon coast, and Vancouver Island's Nootka Sound. Though he charted the coastline from Oregon to the Bering Sea, he made no mention of the Strait of Juan de Fuca. Hostile Hawaiians killed Cook in a 1779 dispute over a boat, and his crew returned to England.

Other English sailors continued in Cook's footsteps, and in 1787, Charles Barkley and his wife, Frances, explored and named the Strait of Juan de Fuca. Best known today, however, is the expedition led by **George Vancouver** in 1792. His goal was to explore the inland waters and make one last attempt at finding the Northwest Passage. The names of Vancouver's lieutenants and crewmembers are like a list of Washington place-names: Baker, Rainier, Whidbey, and Puget. (Many of the place-names were attached to curry political favor back home; almost anyone in a position of power had his name stuck on something.) The expedition carefully charted and thoroughly described all navigable waterways and named every prominent feature. Vancouver's survey crew reached the Strait of Juan de Fuca in May 1792, and one of his boats landed at Blind Bay on Shaw Island, where they found a Coast Salish settlement. Some of the Coast Salish people paddled canoes out to trade with the Englishmen, providing them with three freshly killed deer and a live fawn for venison.

American Explorations

An American, **Robert Gray,** sailed out of Boston to explore and trade along the Northwest Coast in 1792. Stopping first at Nootka Sound—the hot spot to trade on Vancouver Island—Gray worked his way south and spent three days anchored in today's Grays Harbor. Continuing south, Gray discovered the mouth of the Columbia River and traded there with the Chinook before heading home without finding Puget Sound and the San Juans. His explorations helped establish American claims to the Pacific Northwest.

The first American survey of the San Juan archipelago took place in 1841 under the leadership of Lieutenant **Charles Wilkes.** The surveyors were only in the islands for three days in July, but managed to see much of the country and to apply American names to virtually everything in sight. The predictable choices were American naval heroes from the War of 1812 or Tripoli, along with members of his expedition, including Stuart Island for his clerk, Fredrick D. Stuart, and Waldron Island for two of his crewmembers. Fortunately, some of his other name choices—Navy Archipelago instead of the San Juan Islands, Hulls Island instead of Orcas, Rodgers Island instead of San Juan Island, and Chauncys Island instead of Lopez—were later rejected by saner folks. Wilkes's charts of the islands did, however, later prove vital in the designation of the San Juans as American, rather than British property.

As head of both the Hudson's Bay Company and the governor of British Columbia, James Douglas was a forceful proponent of English sovereignty over the San Juans.

SETTLING THE ISLANDS

During the time between the early exploration and the permanent settlement of the Northwest, British and American trading posts emerged to take advantage of the area's abundant supply of beaver and sea otter pelts. Two English companies, the North West Company and Hudson's Bay Company, merged in 1821; American fur-trading outfits included many small, independent companies as well as John Astor's Pacific Fur Company and the Rocky Mountain Fur Company.

The most influential of them, the **Hudson's Bay Company,** built its temporary headquarters on the north side of the Columbia, 100 miles inland at Fort Vancouver. The settlers planted crops, raised livestock, and made the fort as self-sufficient as possible. At its peak, 500 people lived at or near the fort. When set-

tlers began arriving in droves and the beaver population diminished in the late 1840s, the Hudson's Bay Company was crowded out and moved its headquarters north to Fort Victoria on Vancouver Island.

Manifest Destiny

In the 1840s, the United States and England jointly occupied "Oregon Country" land north of the 42nd parallel. It included lands that today comprise Washington, Oregon, Idaho, and parts of Montana, Wyoming, and British Columbia. The westward movement gained momentum when a New York editor coined the phrase "Manifest Destiny" to symbolize the idea that all of the land west of the Rockies rightfully belonged to the United States. If you exclude trappers, prior to 1843, there were barely 40 white settlers west of the Rocky Mountains.

COURTESY OF SAN JUAN ISLAND NATIONAL HISTORIC PARK

Between 1840 and 1860, more than 50,000 American settlers moved west to Oregon Country to take advantage of the free land they could acquire through the Organic Act of 1843 and the Donation Land Law of 1850. Under the Organic Act, each adult white male could own a 640-acre section of land (one square mile) by simply marking its boundaries, filing a claim, and building a cabin on the land. The Donation Land Law put additional restrictions on land claims: 320 acres were awarded to each white or half-white male who was an American citizen and had arrived prior to 1851; another 320 acres could be claimed by his wife.

The promise of free land fueled the "Great Migration" of 1843, in which almost 900 settlers traveled to Oregon Country, six times the number of the previous year. More pioneers followed: 1,500 in 1844 and 3,000 in 1845. Most settlers came by way of the Oregon Trail from St. Joseph, Missouri; they followed the North Platte River, through southern Wyoming and southern Idaho into Oregon, then headed north to the Columbia River. Soon the route looked like a cleared road; traces of it can still be seen where the wagon tires dug ruts in stone and where wheels packed the ground so hard that grass still cannot grow.

Divvying Up the Northwest

Britain regarded the westward expansion with dismay, watching as the lands it claimed were increasingly populated by Americans. The Oregon Treaty of 1846 settled the dispute, giving possession of all lands south of the 49th parallel to the United States. Although the problem appeared resolved, the treaty failed to adequately describe the boundary through upper Puget Sound, causing both the United States and Britain to claim the San Juan Islands. Over time this issue came back to haunt both nations. Thirteen years after the treaty signing, an incident involving a potato-loving pig and an angry settler on San Juan Island nearly precipitated a war. The issue would not be finally resolved until 1872, when an arbitrator awarded the islands to the United States. (See sidebar, *The Pig War*, in the *San Juan Island* chapter for more information about this unusual story.)

Smuggling Takes Hold

Smuggling was an important part of life on the San Juans for many years, and some of the earliest businesses were illegal booze joints for soldiers, settlers, and Native Americans. Around 1880, large numbers of Chinese laborers began arriving on San Juan Island, working both in local potato fields and at the limestone operation along Roche Harbor. Smuggling of Chinese workers from Vancouver Island through the San Juans to Seattle became a big business. An even more lucrative one was (and still is) illegal drugs. The drug of choice at the time—primarily for Chinese workers in the United States—was opium. Legal in British Columbia, it was refined in factories there. Opium smuggling became an important source of income for many island folks, including the best-known smuggler, Larry Kelly.

During Prohibition, the islands were a way station for booze destined for Seattle speakeasies, and a new generation of profiteers emerged. Today, there are still occasional busts of people attempting to transport drugs through the islands, and a few folks have even been caught with drug-packed sea kayaks.

THE 20TH CENTURY

Once the Americans had successfully ejected the English from the San Juans, one of their first actions was a tax revolt. When Whatcom County imposed a tax, the locals managed to get the legislature to carve out a separate San Juan County for the 200 or so settlers on the islands. The initial seat of power was a ragtag and boozy settlement called Old Town that was located near American Camp on the south end of San Juan Island. Eventually, the more civilized town of Friday Harbor became the island's primary settlement, and it remains so to this day.

In the late 1800s and early 1900s, Roche Harbor on San Juan Island developed into one of the world's largest limestone mining operations under the leadership of "boss" John S. McMillan. Another industrialist, Robert Moran, had a more lasting impact, however. A shipbuilder and former Seattle mayor, Moran retired early on Orcas

Island, built a mansion (today's Rosario Resort), and donated thousands of acres of land for Moran State Park, one of the finest parks in Washington.

One surprising product of the islands from the 1890s through World War I was fruit, particularly apples, plums, and pears. Orcas Island was the primary fruit producer, but orchards spread across Lopez, Shaw, and San Juan as well. Insect infestations and competition from fruit growers in eastern Washington eventually doomed growers on the San Juan Islands, but many of these trees still produce today, more than a century after they were planted.

Cars and Ferries

Early in the 20th century, the San Juan Islands were home to a rough mix of farmers, fishers, miners, loggers, and smugglers. Tourism remained of minor importance on the San Juans until the middle of the century, when cars and ferries made the islands increasingly accessible to the masses.

Washington's ferry system had its origins in the early 1900s when a number of companies sailed Puget Sound waters in small steamers known as the "Mosquito Fleet." Competition and consolidation forced most of these companies under, and by 1935 only one remained, the Puget Sound Navigation Company, better known as the Black Ball Line.

That same year, the first auto ferry linked the islands with Anacortes and Sidney, British Columbia. As automobiles became an increasingly important part of the transportation mix in Puget Sound, Black Ball ferries acted as a link across the wide expanses of water. Prior to the ferries, steamers had sailed out of Seattle or Bellingham to deliver freight and passengers around the islands.

The state of Washington jumped into the ferry business in 1951 when it bought out Black Ball's ferries, terminals, and most other assets. The state

ferry system was originally intended to be a temporary measure until bridges could be built across Puget Sound, but the legislature rejected that idea in 1959. Since then, Washington State Ferries has become the largest ferry system in the nation (Alaska's is vastly longer, however), with 20 ports of call served by 25 vessels, the largest of which can carry 2,500 passengers and more than 200 vehicles. Today, Washington ferries transport more than 11 million vehicles and 26 million people annually around Puget Sound. The run from Anacortes to Lopez, Shaw, Orcas, and San Juan Islands and then on to Sidney, British Columbia, is not only extremely popular, but also the most scenic of all the cross-sound sailings.

DESTINATION ISLES

For the last 50 years or so, the San Juans have increasingly been a place of recreation and relaxation rather than industry. Small farms and pastures are still important, particularly on Lopez Island, and a number of commercial fishers call the islands home, but the real engines driving the economy are tourism and retirement. In the last decade or so, the islands have attracted national attention as a place to retire, and as a spot for affluent young professionals who work out of their homes. During the 1990s, San Juan County had the second fastest-growing population in Washington.

The population continues to grow and development pressure is increasing, along with water shortages, the loss of public access to island shorelines, and overpriced housing. Despite these troubles—which are minor compared with the vast wasteland of development spreading along the shores of Puget Sound—the San Juan Islands are an eminently livable place where the natural world still dominates. After all, even with a 40-percent increase in the 1990s, the total population on the islands is just 14,500 people.

Getting There

There are no bridges to the San Juan Islands, but ferries ply these waters, scheduled air service is available, and the islands are popular with boaters and kayakers who head out on their own. The main regional airports are Seattle's Sea-Tac International Airport and Vancouver International Airport. From either of these, you can rent a car and drive to Anacortes, where the Washington State Ferries depart for the islands. Shuttle buses also run from Sea-Tac directly to the Anacortes ferry dock. Both wheeled planes and floatplanes fly between Seattle and the San Juans.

WASHINGTON STATE FERRIES

If you can only take one ride aboard a Washington State Ferry (206/464-6400 for general info or 888/808-7977 in Washington and British Columbia, www.wsdot.wa.gov/ferries), the trip from Anacortes to the San Juans should be the one. The scenery is so beautiful that even amateur photographers can get spectacular sunset-over-the-islands shots. In the summer, ferries leave Anacortes at least a dozen times a day, 4:30 A.M.–12:15 A.M., stopping at the north end of Lopez Island, Shaw Island, Orcas Village on Orcas Island, and Friday Harbor on San Juan Island. It takes roughly two hours from Anacortes to Friday Harbor. Not every ferry run stops on each island, but nearly all of them pull into Friday Harbor.

Ferries between Anacortes and Sidney, British Columbia, run twice a day in the summer and once a day the rest of the year. Vehicle reservations are *required* for service between the San Juans and Sidney. The ferries have food and drinks onboard, with a duty-free shop on ferries heading to British Columbia.

Traveling Tips

The **Anacortes ferry terminal** is three miles west of town. Two restaurants are nearby, and the bulletin board notes current campsite availability at San Juan parks (meaning, often, that none are available). If you're taking your car across during the peak summer season, it's wise to arrive at least two hours early on Fridays and Saturdays, or an hour early on weekdays. On holiday weekends, you may find yourself in line for up to five hours! Heading east from the San Juans in the peak season, you should arrive an hour and a half or two hours in advance of your sailing. Find current wait times on the ferry system website: www.wsdot.wa.gov/ferries.

Avoid the crowds by traveling midweek, early in the morning, late in the evening (except Friday evenings), or better yet, by foot, kayak, or bike. Leave your car in the lot at the terminal ($20 for three days) and stroll aboard; there's always space for walk-on passengers. A **free park-and-ride lot** (no RVs or trailers) is located eight miles east of the terminal near the oil refinery at March Point. A free shuttle bus takes passengers to the ferry. These buses have bike racks, but they sometimes fill up. Credit cards can be used to purchase tickets in

ferry at Friday Harbor

© DON PITCHER

Anacortes and Sidney, but not at ferry terminals within the San Juan Islands.

The ferry system operates on a first-come, first-served basis, with reservations available only for the routes from Anacortes to Sidney, British Columbia, and from Orcas Island or San Juan Island to Sidney. No reservations for travel to the San Juans; just get in line and wait like everyone else. In Anacortes, tune your radio to **AM 1340** for broadcasts of current ferry status, including any backups or other problems.

If you are boarding a ferry and returning to the U.S. mainland from the islands, try to avoid sailings that started in Sidney, British Columbia; these all must clear customs in Anacortes, and the process can cause substantial delays.

Want a glimpse of travel aboard the ferries? Point your computer to www.ferrycam.net for current ferry conditions and to see photos of the trip from Anacortes to Friday Harbor. Speaking of computers, the Washington State Ferry system is gradually adding wireless Internet access to their ferries and it may be available in the San Juans by the time you read this.

Anacortes to the Islands

For travel to the San Juan Islands from Anacortes, the state ferry system charges higher rates Wednesday–Saturday and lower fares Sunday–Tuesday. Rates also change by season. Peak summer season Wednesday–Saturday fares from Anacortes to Friday Harbor (the last American stop) are $11.40 for passengers and walk-ons, or $43.75 for a car and driver. Bikes are $4 extra, and kayaks cost $19.20 more. Summertime fares to the other islands from Anacortes are $11.40 for passenger or $31.25 for car and driver to Lopez Island, and $11.40 for passenger or $37.50 for car and driver to Orcas or Shaw Islands.

Ferry travelers are only charged in the westbound direction. Eastbound travel within the San Juans—such as from Orcas to Lopez—or from the islands to Anacortes is free, with no tickets required. The only exception to this is for travelers leaving from Sidney, British Columbia. If you're planning to visit all the islands, save money by heading straight to Friday Harbor

and then working your way back through the others at no additional charge.

Interisland Ferries

Once you're on the San Juans, there is never a charge for passengers, walk-ons, or bikes to travel to another island in either direction. Also there's no charge for cars heading east within the islands, but the westbound charge is $15.75, whether it is just across the waterway from Shaw to Orcas, or all the way from Lopez to Friday Harbor. Rates are lower in the off-season.

Here's a tip that isn't widely publicized: If you're planning a short stop on one of the islands and then continuing westward to another island within 24 hours, request a **free vehicle transfer.** This is useful if you're on Lopez and heading to Friday Harbor (free stops at Shaw and Orcas), or going from Lopez to Orcas (free stop at Shaw). It saves you $15.75 for each stop, but you must ask for it on your departure island.

Anacortes to Sidney, British Columbia

Twice a day (once daily in winter), a Washington State Ferry connects Anacortes with Sidney, British Columbia; tickets cost $13.80 for passengers and walk-ons, or $46.75 for a car and driver. The charge is the same in the opposite direction (Sidney to Anacortes) or from Sidney to the islands, but if you stop on the islands, there are no additional charges to continue east all the way to Anacortes. Reservations are advised (but not mandatory) for ferry runs between Anacortes and Sidney.

The Anacortes-Sidney ferry stops at Orcas and San Juan Islands in both directions. If you get on at either of these islands, the passage westward to Sidney costs $5 for passengers, $23.75 for a car and driver, and $1 for bikes. Vehicle reservations are required to travel eastward from Orcas Island or Friday Harbor to Sidney, and must be made at least 24 hours in advance. Contact the ferry system (206/464-6400 or 888/808-7977, www.wsdot.wa.gov/ferries) for reservations.

When **crossing the border** between the United States and Canada, citizens of either country will need a photo identification (such as a drivers license) plus proof of citizenship, such as a birth certificate or passport (expired is okay). All baggage is subject to inspection.

PRIVATE FERRIES AND DAY CRUISES
From Seattle or Victoria
The passenger-only *Victoria Clipper* (206/448-5000 or 800/888-2535, www.victoriaclipper.com) runs high-speed catamaran day trips between Seattle and San Juan Island ($63 adults round-trip, $32 kids). Adults are $45 and kids under 12 are free if you book at least a day ahead. Cruises operate late May to early September, with daily service after mid-May. The company has a multitude of other travel options in the Northwest, including packages that add a night's lodging on San Juan Island or a sea-kayaking trip. *Victoria Clipper* also has direct year-round service between Seattle and Victoria for $120–133 round-trip.

Victoria Express (360/452-8088 or 800/633-1589, www.victoriaexpress.com) operates a 149-passenger ferry connecting Victoria and Friday Harbor, with daily service late May to early September. Round-trip fare is $52 (free for babies under age one), and there's no charge for bikes or kayaks. The boat also has daily runs between Victoria and Port Angeles. A popular loop-tour option for travelers out of Seattle is to take the *Victoria Clipper* from Seattle to Friday Harbor, then ride *Victoria Express* to Victoria, before returning to Seattle on the *Clipper*. Contact Victoria Clipper for details on this and other package options.

From Bellingham
The **San Juan Island Commuter** (360/734-8180 or 888/734-8180, www.islandcommuter.com) is a popular way to reach the islands. Its passenger-only boats depart from Bellingham on daily cruises to the San Juans mid-May to early September. Round-trip fares from Bellingham are $39 ($20 for ages 6–12) to Friday Harbor on San Juan Island. Bikes are an extra $5, and kayaks cost $20. A combination day trip to the islands and whale-watching voyage is $69 for adults or $39 for kids.

From Port Townsend
Puget Sound Express (360/385-5288, www.puget soundexpress.com) provides passenger-only service between Port Townsend and Friday Harbor. The boat leaves Port Townsend daily, May–October, and stays in Friday Harbor long enough for a quick three-hour visit, or you can overnight there and return to Port Townsend later. The charge is $55 round-trip ($38 for kids), and bikes and kayaks are $13 extra. Add $25 for a three-hour whale-watching trip out of Friday Harbor.

From Everett
The **Mosquito Fleet** (425/252-6800 or 800/325-6722, www.whalewatching.com) runs summertime boat tours from Everett to San Juan Island. These all-day trips ($79 for adults, $74 for seniors, or $40 for kids) take travelers through Deception Pass to Friday Harbor, with the chance to watch whales as the boat circumnavigates San Juan Island. Passengers get off in Friday Harbor for a brief one-hour stop before heading back to Everett. A much better option is to spend a night or more on the island. The cost is lower ($59 for adults, $54 for seniors, or $29 for kids) and you get the same tour. The Mosquito Fleet runs daily May to early October.

Water Taxis
Water taxis provide a quick and easy way to reach a specific place in the islands without dealing with ferry lines or vehicles.

Operating out of Skyline Marina in Anacortes, **Paraclete Charters** (360/293-5920 or 800/808-2999, www.paracletecharters.com) has been in business since 1992 and has a very experienced crew. They run three passenger boats—the largest is 58 feet long and can carry 64 passengers—to anyplace in the San Juans. This is the place to go for transportation to destinations off the route of the state ferry system, including the private islands. Rates depend upon the destination and number of passengers. As an example, Anacortes to Cypress Island costs $32 for one person each way, or $20 per person for five folks. In addition to passengers, Paraclete will haul anything from motorcycles and appliances to furniture and construction material. There's no charge for pets, and kids get discounted rates. Add $5 for bikes, or $10 for kayaks. The boats are designed for all weather conditions, and even provide 24-hour emergency transportation when planes aren't able to fly.

Based at Cap Sante Marina in Anacortes, **Island Express Charters** (360/299-2875 or 877/473-9777, www.islandexpresscharters.com) has a high-speed 32-passenger landing craft with plenty of deck space for kayaks, bikes, and gear. Rates depend upon the number of passengers. Skipper Rey Rubalcava provides transportation almost anywhere in the San Juans.

Based at Deer Harbor on Orcas Island, Marty Mead of **North Shore Charters** (360/376-4855, www.sanjuancruises.net) provides water-taxi service to Stuart, Sucia, Matia, Patos, and even to Anacortes or Bellingham. The boat can hold up to six passengers, plus kayaks and bikes.

MULTI-DAY CRUISES

Based on San Juan Island, **Fantasy Cruises** (360/378-1874 or 800/234-3861, www.sanjuan islandcruises.com) provides seven-day summertime cruises that begin in Seattle and take in the San Juan Islands, Victoria, Whidbey Island, Port Townsend, and other places. The 130-foot *Island Spirit* has 16 staterooms.

FLYING INTO WASHINGTON

Anyone flying into Washington will almost certainly be landing at **Sea-Tac Airport** (206/431-4444, www.portseattle.org), 12 miles south of Seattle. All major domestic, and many international, airlines operate out of Sea-Tac, and foreign travelers can change money in the main terminal. A **Visitor Information Booth** (open daily in the summer; brochures available anytime) is close to the baggage claim area.

The least expensive way to reach Seattle from the airport—just $2—is aboard one of **Metro Transit's** city buses, (206/553-3000 or 800/542-7876, http://transit.metrokc.gov). Buses 174 and

194 run between Sea-Tac and downtown Seattle. Taxis cost around $37 to downtown Seattle. Instead, save money by riding the **Gray Line Airport Express** (206/626-6088 or 800/426-7532, www.graylineofseattle.com), $11 one-way.

Car Rentals

All the major national car rental companies have desks near the baggage claim at Sea-Tac Airport. I've found the best rates with a web search at www.travelocity.com, www.expedia.com, or www.orbitz.com. AAA or Costco members should be sure to ask about any additional discounts. **Thrifty Car Rental** (800/847-4389, www.thrifty.com) and **Payless** (800/729-5377, www.paylesscarrental.com) often have some of the lowest rates and provide a starting point for price comparisons. For wheelchair-friendly van rentals, contact **Pacific Northwest Wheelchair Getaways** (206/367-3444 or 888/376-1500, www.wheelchairgetaways.com).

GETTING TO THE ISLANDS FROM SEATTLE

The San Juan Islands are 65 air miles northeast of Seattle, with access by air, boat, shuttle van and ferry, or car and ferry.

By Ferry

You will see a constant parade of Washington State Ferries departing from downtown Seattle, but none of these go to the San Juans. Instead, you'll need to get to Anacortes, where ferries head to the islands. There is, however, a private passenger-only ferry, the *Victoria Clipper* (see *Water Taxis*) that offers daily service to the islands from Seattle.

Shuttle Vans

Getting to the islands from Sea-Tac is easy. **Airporter Shuttle** (360/380-8800 or 866/235-5247, www.airporter.com), makes connections between Sea-Tac and the ferry terminal at Anacortes, along with Bellingham and points north all the way to Vancouver. The one-way cost is $31 ($16 for kids) to the ferry terminal. Vans run a dozen times or so a day and generally take three hours.

Island Airporter (360/378-7438, www.island airporter.com) provides direct van service daily from Sea-Tac to San Juan Island. The bus departs the airport and heads straight to the Anacortes ferry, where it drives on for San Juan Island, and then continues to Friday Harbor ($45) and Roche Harbor ($55). Prices include the ferry fare.

Trains and Buses

Amtrak trains serve Seattle from the King Street Station (3rd Ave. South and S. King St., 206/464-1930 or 800/872-7245, www.amtrak.com). The **Amtrak Cascades** train connects Seattle with Vancouver, stopping at Bellingham and Mount Vernon twice a day in each direction. Trains do not stop in Anacortes (where Washington State Ferries depart for the San Juan Islands), and the closest station is 18 miles away in Mount Vernon.

Catch-a-Train (800/457-3549, www.catch-a-train.com) is a travel agency that simplifies trips to the San Juans, offering a single ticket that includes train travel to Mt. Vernon from Seattle, a shuttle bus to Anacortes, and ferry transport to the islands.

Greyhound Lines (206/628-5508 or 800/231-2222, www.greyhound.com) has daily bus service throughout the lower 48 and to Vancouver, British Columbia, from its bus terminal at 9th and Stewart. It's the same story here as for Amtrak; Greyhound's closest stop is the town of Mount Vernon.

By Car

If you're driving from Seattle, it's 80 miles (90 miles from Sea-Tac) to Anacortes, where you catch the Washington State Ferry to the San Juans. The ride is very straightforward: follow I-5 north to Mount Vernon at Exit 230 and turn west onto U.S. 20, which goes straight into Anacortes. The ferry terminal is three miles west of downtown Anacortes via 12th Street.

Be sure to fill your tank in Anacortes before driving on the ferry. Because of the extra cost of shipping fuel (and because they can get away with it) gas stations on the islands charge at least 30 percent more than on the mainland.

FLYING TO THE SAN JUANS

The quickest way to reach the islands is by air, but there are no direct flights from Sea-Tac Airport. You'll need to take a free shuttle to Boeing Field (a few miles closer to Seattle) for San Juan Airlines or to Seattle's Lake Union for Kenmore Air.

Kenmore Air

The San Juans are served by a legendary floatplane company, Kenmore Air (425/486-1257 or 800/543-9595, www.kenmoreair.com). In business since 1946, it is now the world's largest full-service seaplane operation, with 26 planes and a summertime staff of more than 200. Kenmore is best known for its De Havilland Beavers (a favorite workhorse of Alaskan Bush pilots), but also flies the larger turbine Otters and Cessna Caravans. Its yellow-and-white floatplanes are a familiar sight on Lake Union in Seattle and nearby Lake Washington in Kenmore.

Kenmore Air has daily scheduled flights from Lake Union and Lake Washington to Friday Harbor and Roche Harbor on San Juan Island, to Lopez Islander Resort on Lopez Island, and to Rosario Resort, Deer Harbor, and West Sound on Orcas Island. They also fly daily to Oak Harbor on Whidbey Island and to various places along British Columbia's Inside Passage, including Victoria. A free shuttle provides transport to Lake Union from Sea-Tac. Pack light for your trip since a 24-pound baggage weight limit is in effect, and excess baggage costs $1/pound. Kenmore also offers flightseeing trips and charter service to other destinations in the San Juans—including Sucia and Jones Islands—but you'll need to pay for a round-trip flight from Seattle.

San Juan Airlines

Based at the Anacortes airport, San Juan Airlines (360/293-4691 or 800/874-4434, www.sanjuan airlines.com) has scheduled daily wheeled-plane service to the San Juans. Planes depart Seattle's Boeing Field, Anacortes, and Bellingham, and will stop at most island runways, including San Juan, Orcas, Lopez, and Blakely Islands on a scheduled basis, along with Center, Crane, Decatur, Eliza, Sinclair, Stuart, and Waldron Islands on a charter basis. Flightseeing and air charters are available to other destinations, including Victoria. If you're flying into Sea-Tac, the company provides a free shuttle to Boeing Field.

Charter Flights

Charter flights to the San Juans can be cheaper than scheduled flights if you have four or more passengers. **Rugby Aviation** (360/376-7139, www.rugbyaviation.com), based on Orcas Island, and **Island Air** (360/378-2376 or 888/378-2376, www.sanjuan-islandair.com), on San Juan Island, provide charter flights throughout the region, including to Boeing Field in Seattle.

Rose Air (503/675-7673, www.roseair.com) offers charter service (maximum three people) from Portland, Oregon, to the San Juan Islands.

FLYING INTO BRITISH COLUMBIA

The primary hub for flights into Western Canada is through the city of Vancouver, though there are also quite a few flights into nearby Victoria on Vancouver Island. There are no airport shuttles between **Vancouver International Airport** and Anacortes, but you can catch **Quick Shuttle Service** (604/244-3744 or 800/665-2122, www.quickcoach.com) to Bellingham and then take the San Juan Island Commuter passenger ferry to the islands. Car rentals at the Vancouver airport are another option if you want to drive south across the border to Anacortes and then catch the Washington State Ferry to the islands.

If you are flying into **Victoria International Airport,** take a taxi to the town of Sidney, where the Washington State Ferry disembarks for the San Juans every day.

Getting Around

Information on local water taxis, charter flights, and flightseeing for each island is discussed in the *San Juan Island, Orcas Island,* and *Lopez Island* chapters. Interisland ferry travel is detailed in *Interisland Ferries* above.

CAR AND MOPED RENTALS

Avoid the lengthy summertime waits by parking at the Anacortes ferry terminal by walking onboard the ferry and renting a car once you reach the San Juans. **M&W Auto Rentals** (360/378-2886 or 800/323-6037, www.sanjuanauto.com) has rental cars at Orcas Village on Orcas Island and Friday Harbor on San Juan Island. **San Juan Airlines** (360/293-4691 or 800/874-4434, www.sanjuanairlines.com) rents cars at airports in Eastsound on Orcas Island and Friday Harbor on San Juan Island. Rates start around $50 for a compact or $70 for an SUV, but fewer vehicles are available on Orcas and the variety is limited. Rental vehicles are allowed off the islands to the Washington mainland and Canada.

If you're flying to Sea-Tac and then heading to the islands for a week or more, you're probably better off renting a car at the airport since rates are lower than on the islands.

Susie's Mopeds (360/378-5244 or 800/532-0087, www.susiesmopeds.com) rents mopeds and three-wheel scootcars from offices at the Orcas ferry landing and Friday Harbor.

BUSES AND TAXIS

San Juan Transit & Tours (360/378-8887 or 800/887-8387, www.sanjuantransit.com) operates hourly shuttle buses around San Juan Island in the summer, providing a reasonable way to reach the most-visited points. The buses can also carry bikes.

Orcas Island Shuttle (360/376-3414 or 800/516-9010, www.orcasislandshuttle.com) provides scheduled service from the Orcas ferry landing to most places on the island. Buses run four times a day in the summer, and can carry bikes.

Taxis are available on San Juan, Orcas, and Lopez Islands.

Tips for Travelers

CROSSING THE BORDER

Ferry passengers and small boats crossing between British Columbia and the San Juans will be checked by either the United States Customs Service or Canada Customs. The **U.S. Customs & Border Protection** (800/562-5943, www.cbp.gov) has stations at Roche Harbor (mid-May through September, 360/378-2703) and Friday Harbor (year-round, 360/378-2080) on San Juan Island. Folks heading to Vancouver Island from the San Juans will need to clear **Canada Border Services Agency** at Sidney (204/983-3500 or 800/461-9799, www.cra-arc.gc.ca).

Crossing between the United States and Canada is not as simple as it was in the days before bomb-sniffing dogs, surveillance cameras, and terrorism concerns. Citizens of either country need a photo identification (such as a drivers license) plus proof of citizenship, such as a birth certificate or passport (expired is okay). Your social security card, voter registration card, or MasterCard—even a platinum one—doesn't count. Children and youths traveling with their parents also need a birth certificate, passport, or photo identification card. If only one parent is with the child, the absent parent will need to provide a signed permission note in advance. All other foreign visitors must have a valid passport and may need a visa or visitor permit depending on their country of residence.

Entry by Private Aircraft or Boat

Anyone entering Canada by private plane or boat must contact the **Canada Border Services Agency** in advance for a list of official ports of entry and their hours of operation.

Returning to the United States

On reentering the United States, if you've been in Canada more than 48 hours, you can bring back up to US$400 worth of household and personal items, excluding alcohol and tobacco, duty-free. If you've been in Canada fewer than 48 hours, you may bring in only up to US$200 worth of such items duty-free.

If you're planning to make any large purchases in British Columbia, pick up a brochure describing what you can bring back without being charged extra duties. Americans are entitled to refunds on the GST tax paid in British Columbia, so save your receipts.

HEALTH AND SAFETY

The closest hospitals are in Anacortes or Victoria, but San Juan, Orcas, and Lopez Islands all have medical clinics with at least one physician available 24 hours a day. All three islands also have dentists, massage therapists, and a range of alternative medical practitioners (visit www.islandcalm.com for many of these).

For medical emergencies and fires, call 911; EMTs and paramedics are available, and a helicopter or fixed-wing plane can transport patients to larger hospitals in Seattle or elsewhere. If you're using a cellular phone, dial 360/378-4141 for a medical, fire, or police emergency in San Juan County. That number will connect you, 24 hours a day, with a dispatcher in the islands. If you dial 911 on a cell phone you might reach an emergency dispatcher anywhere from Victoria to Seattle.

Safety in the Outdoors

There are no bears, mountain lions, or poisonous snakes on the San Juan Islands, and the greatest threat to campers is probably the drive up I-5 from Seattle. Mosquitoes are not particularly bad, but yellow jackets can be a problem in the summer, particularly for those with allergies. **West Nile virus** cases have occurred in Washington, so it's wise to use mosquito repellants. Head to www.doh.wa.gov for more on this potentially fatal disease.

Another potential threat is **hantavirus,** which is spread by deer mice. The disease it causes can be fatal, and at least one infection has been reported from the San Juans. Prevention is the best strategy, and it simply means minimizing your contact with rodents. Never handle deer mice, stay away from their nests, and sleep inside a tent when camping—not on the open ground. For additional hantavirus information and safety precautions, see the Centers for Disease Control and Prevention's website, www.cdc.gov.

Hypothermia

Anyone who has spent much time in the outdoors will discover the dangers of exposure to cold, wet, and windy conditions. Even at temperatures well above freezing, hypothermia—the reduction of the body's inner core temperature—can prove fatal. Hypothermia is a problem for people in small boats and sea kayaks who are exposed to the weather and can quickly become chilled if not properly dressed.

In the early stages, hypothermia causes uncontrollable shivering, followed by a loss of coordination, slurred speech, and then a rapid descent into unconsciousness and death. Always travel prepared for sudden changes in the weather. Wear clothing that insulates well and that holds its heat when wet. Wool and polypro are far bet-

ter than cotton jeans, and clothes should be worn in layers to better trap heat and help you adjust to conditions. Always carry a hat, since your head loses more heat than any other part of the body. Bring a waterproof shell to cut the wind. Put on rain gear *before* it starts raining; head back or set up camp when the weather looks threatening; eat candy bars, keep active, or snuggle with a friend in a down bag to generate warmth.

If someone in your party begins to show signs of hypothermia, don't take any chances, even if the person denies needing help. Get the victim out of the wind, strip off his clothes, and put him in a dry sleeping bag on an insulating pad. Skin-to-skin contact is the best way to warm a hypothermic person, and that means you'll also need to strip and climb in the sleeping bag. If you weren't friends before, this should heat up the relationship! Do not give the victim alcohol or hot drinks, and do not try to warm the person too quickly, because it could lead to heart failure. Once the victim has recovered, get medical help as soon as possible. Of course, you're far better off keeping close tabs on everyone in the group and seeking shelter *before* exhaustion and hypothermia set in.

Information and Services

TRAVEL INFORMATION

Each of the three main islands has a chamber of commerce office stocked with local brochures. For maps and other information before you arrive, contact the San Juan Islands Visitors Bureau (360/378-9551 or 888/468-3701, www.guidetosanjuans.com) to request their official *San Juan Islands Visitors Guide.*

Two fat free publications are found onboard the ferries and in racks around Friday Harbor and Anacortes: *The San Juan Islands Springtide,* published by Sound Publishing, (www.islandssounder.com), and *San Juanderer,* published by the *Anacortes American* (www.gosanjuans.com). Both offer helpful details on the islands and are full of ads from local businesses. They generally come out in May for the busy

summer season. Also check out the free *Islands Almanac,* with relocation info and tons of facts about the San Juans. It's published by *The Journal of the San Juans* (www.sanjuanjournal.com). **MacGregor Publishing** (www.plaidnet.com) produces free visitors guides covering Anacortes, Whidbey Island, and La Conner.

Websites

Virtually all San Juan lodging places and many other local businesses maintain websites. A number of general sites are also worth investigating in addition to the Visitors Bureau site. The **San Juan Islander,** (www.sanjuanislander.com) is a Web-only newspaper with community news, events, weather, classified ads, the local police blotter, links to regional newspapers, and useful visitor information. It's updated daily, and is a fine way to keep abreast of local events before (or after) your visit to the islands. Another good source for local news is **San Juan Update** (www.san-juan.net).

At **Island Cam** (www.islandcam.com), you'll find live webcam images from Roche Harbor and Friday Harbor on San Juan Island, Rosario Resort and Orcas Village on Orcas Island, Fisherman Bay on Lopez Island, and the Anacortes ferry landing. It's a good way to check the ferry lines and weather, or to see what special deals are offered by local bed-and-breakfasts and air taxis.

The *Anacortes American's* San Juan website, www.gosanjuans.com, is another helpful place with historical info, links to lodging options, and details on wildlife, weather, cycling, hiking, whale-watching, and much more. Also worth a look are **San Juan Web,** www.sanjuanweb.com, and **Kanaka,** www.kanaka.com. The latter includes tide charts and the marine forecast.

The author's website (www.donpitcher.com) has a complete listing of websites found in this book. His website provides an easy way to access hundreds of businesses, information sources, and attractions.

MONEY

Canadian and other non-U.S. currency can be changed at banks on San Juan, Orcas, and Lopez Islands. **Travelers' checks** are probably the safest way to carry money, but buy them from a well-known U.S. company, such as American Express, Bank of America, or Visa. They are accepted without charge in most stores and businesses. It's not a good idea to travel with travelers' checks in non-U.S. currency.

Most travelers do fine using just credit cards and automated teller machine (ATM) cards. The major **credit cards**—especially Visa and MasterCard—are accepted virtually everywhere, even in grocery stores. **Automated teller machines** are located at Friday Harbor on San Juan Island, Eastsound on Orcas Island, and Lopez Village on Lopez Island, but not on Shaw Island. These ATMs tack on a charge (typically $1.50) in ad-

dition to your own bank's fees, making this an expensive way to get cash, especially for small amounts. You can avoid this rip-off surcharge by making a purchase at a grocery store that take ATMs and asking for extra cash back.

COMMUNICATIONS AND MEDIA
Newspapers

Two surprisingly good weekly newspapers provide useful print and online info for the San Juans. In business since 1906, *The Journal of the San Juans* (360/378-4191, www.sanjuanjournal.com) has its editorial staff in Friday Harbor on San Juan Island. *The Islands Sounder* (360/376-4500, www.islandssounder.com) is headquartered at Eastsound on Orcas Island. Both papers come out on Wednesdays.

Based on Lopez Island, *The Islands' Weekly* (360/468-4242 or 800/654-6142, www.islandsweekly.net) is an advertisement-filled paper distributed to all local residents for free. It is also sold in a few places around the islands, primarily on Lopez. You won't find much in the way of hard news coverage, but it does have community events, articles on health, arts, and Dave Barry's column. Sound Publishing, based on Bainbridge Island, owns all three of these papers.

Phone Calls

The area code for northern Puget Sound, including the San Juans, is 360. All phone calls among the various San Juan Islands are local calls. Cellular service is reasonably good on the main islands, but may be nonexistent in hilly areas or where other islands block the signal. There is considerable local opposition to adding more cell phone towers, particularly on Lopez Island. While on the islands, set your cell phone's "emergency" button to dial 360/378-4141, not 911.

Internet Access

A number of places provide online access if you want to check email or surf the Web while traveling in the islands. Libraries on San Juan, Orcas, and Lopez Islands all have computers that you can use for free, as do those in Anacortes, Bellingham, and other Washington cities. Computer rentals (with Web access) are available in Friday Harbor on San Juan Island and Eastsound on Orcas Island. Pelindaba Lavender Café in Friday Harbor has free wireless Internet access, as does Penguin Coffee in Anacortes.

If you're traveling with a laptop computer and need Internet access for a week or more, get a temporary account from **The Computer Place** (360/378-8488, www.compplace.com) or **Orcas Online** (360/376-3222, www.orcasonline.com) for around $24/month.

Post Offices

Post offices can be found on Orcas Island at Eastsound, Deer Harbor, Olga, and Orcas. On San Juan, they are located at Friday Harbor and Roche Harbor. Lopez Island has its post office in Lopez Village, and the Shaw Island post office is right next to the ferry dock. Most of these are open 8 A.M.–5 P.M. Mon.–Fri., though some may also open for a few hours on Saturdays. When closed, their outer doors usually remain open, so you can always go in to buy stamps from the machines. Many grocery store checkout counters also sell books of stamps with no markup.

WEDDINGS

Grand scenery, sunny weather, picturesque settings, luxurious bed-and-breakfasts, and excellent caterers combine to make the San Juans an idyllic place for weddings and honeymoons. The best source for details on island wedding services—from makeup artists to wedding planners—is the **San Juan Islands Visitors Bureau** (360/378-9551 or 888/468-3701, www.guideto sanjuans.com/weddings.html). They have a printed wedding directory, but the same info is on their website. Marriage licenses are issued by the **San Juan County Auditor's** office (360/378-2161, www.co.san-juan.wa.us/auditor).

For flowers, contact the following florists: **Orcas Island Flower Company** (360/376-3800 or 877/983-6300, www.islnadweddingflow-

ers.com) on Orcas **Robin's Nest** (360/378-6562, www.robinsnestsanjuan.com) on San Juan Island, **San Juan Florist** (360/378-2477 or 800/582-9978, www.sanjuanflorist.net) on San Juan Island, and **Sticks & Stems Floral Shop** (360/468-4377) on Lopez Island.

Christina's Carriage Company (360/378-2872, www.interisland.net/drafthorse) has special-occasion transportation if you want to arrive at your wedding in old-fashioned style.

Popular Wedding Spots

Anyone planning a wedding should start as early as possible since some of the most popular island sites are booked a year in advance. The two largest resorts in the San Juans, **Rosario Resort** (360/376-2222 or 800/562-8820, www.rosari-oresort.com) on Orcas Island and **Roche Harbor Resort** (360/378-2155 or 800/451-8910, www .rocheharbor.com) on San Juan Island, are both exceptionally popular with wedding parties and are happy to help with all the arrangements. Roche Harbor is particularly beautiful, with a wonderful flower garden and a chapel that doubles as the only privately owned Catholic church in America; the wedding site fee is $500. At Rosario Resort, the wedding ceremony site fee is $1,000 for a one-hour service on a point of land affording a 360-degree bay view. At both of these resorts you'll need to add in the other associated costs (food and drinks, entertainment, decorations, makeup artists, musicians, ad infinitum) for the reception. Not to mention lodging, transportation, the photographer, flowers, cake, and the myriad of other expenditures that appear when wedding bells chime, along with credit (or marriage) counseling afterwards.

Another notable wedding spot is **Victorian Valley Chapel** (360/376-5157 or 866/424-2735, www.victorianvalleychapel.com), a New England–style miniature church in a hidden valley on Orcas Island. Also well worth a look are the sumptuous gardens and orchards at **Green Dolphin Farm** (360/376-4904, www.christinas.com) in West Sound on Orcas Island. Owner (and chef) Christina Orchid allows a few weddings on this picturesque and historic farm each year.

On San Juan Island, be sure to check out the fairy-tale setting **Wood Duck Ponds** (360/378-2356, www.woodduckponds.com). There are two large ponds, one of which is crossed by an arching footbridge, while the other is home to two white swans, a romantic gazebo dock, and a cedar arbor. Another distinctive San Juan wedding spot is the historic schoolhouse at **San Juan Vineyards** (360/378-9463 or 888/983-9463, www.sanjuanvineyards.com).

Public places popular for weddings include **San Juan Island National Historical Park** (English Camp, American Camp, and South Beach), and **San Juan County Park.**

Accommodations

LODGING CHOICES

The lodging scene on the San Juan Islands includes a mix of small hotels and inns, luxurious bed-and-breakfasts, resorts, and vacation rentals. Budget accommodations are scarce, and they are even more difficult to find when families start planning their summer vacations and school lets out. Most places on the islands have just a few rooms, so space is at a premium. It also costs a premium; only a handful of places have rooms for less than $100 d in the peak summer season. Hostel-type accommodations are available at Doe Bay Resort & Retreat on Orcas Island and Wayfarers Rest on San Juan Island.

Throughout this book I list prices for lodging places as one person (single or s) or two people (double or d). Add a total of 9.7 percent (7.7 percent sales tax plus 2 percent lodging tax) to all lodging rates quoted in this book, including bed-and-breakfasts.

The High Season Shuffle

The San Juans are immensely popular in the summer, particularly during the peak season of July and August. If you plan a visit during these times, there may well be no room at the inn, and not a lot of mangers available either. Save yourself a headache by making reservations far in advance. At the older and more established bed-and-breakfasts and resorts, this means calling at least four months ahead for a midsummer weekend reservation! This is particularly true if you want a place for less than $120 a night in August. Do *not* arrive in Friday Harbor on a Saturday afternoon in July and expect to find a place; you won't. Anyone looking for space on Memorial Day, the 4th of July, or Labor Day should make reservations up to a year in advance.

Many resorts, inns, and cottages also offer weekly rates and require a minimum summertime stay of at least two nights (sometimes a week). Also note that most island bed-and-breakfasts cater almost exclusively to couples and do not allow kids. Families are often better off with a vacation rental by the week or a campsite at one of the island parks.

In the winter you'll find fewer fellow travelers, lower lodging rates (sometimes less than half the summer prices), and less of a problem getting a room, but the weather won't be quite as inviting, the scenery won't be as green, and some businesses will be closed. The lowest rates are typically Sunday–Thursday from October–April. Winter holidays (especially Christmas to New Year's) are likely to be booked well in advance.

Accessible Rooms

Some hotels, resorts, and bed-and-breakfasts in the San Juans provide ADA rooms with wheelchair-accessible facilities. These include Lakedale Resort, Friday's Historic Inn, Roche Harbor Resort, The Friday Harbor Inn, and Friday Harbor Suites on San Juan Island; Outlook Inn, Rosario Resort, and Turtleback Farm Inn on Orcas Island; and Lopez Farm Cottages and Edenwild Inn B&B on Lopez Island.

Vacation Rentals

Several real estate companies on the islands offer weekly and monthly home rentals; see the individual island chapters for specifics. In addition,

BUYING PARADISE

Many San Juan visitors dream of moving to the islands and living out their fantasies of a simpler life where they would sit on the deck along their private cove, sip champagne, and watch the sailboats, eagles, and killer whales play. Okay, that works for Bill Gates and other Microsoft billionaires, but is a bit of a stretch for mere mortals. As with other resort areas, housing prices on the San Juans are high, and property values are the highest in Washington. You might find a fixer-upper for less than $200,000, but the median price for San Juan homes is more than $400,000, with waterfront mansions often topping $1 million. Feeling flush with cash? There are still a few private islands for sale if the bank is willing to loan $6 million or so.

Many of the homes are occupied only seasonally or belong to retirees. (Because of all these retired folks, the median age of islanders is 10 years over the statewide average.) Don't come to the islands with the expectation of getting rich since half of the local jobs are in the services sector. The islands are, however, a great place if your money flows in from outside sources or a trust fund from Aunt Judy; dividends and investments comprise more than half the income for the average islander.

Anyone considering a move to the islands should take into account not just the economics of the venture, but also the environmental problems associated with increased growth and development on the islands. Water is in short supply, and will only become a greater problem as more people move to the San Juans. If you are planning a move to the islands, try to make it one that doesn't involve building a new place on undeveloped land.

Selling land and houses is a big business in the San Juans today. If you're in the market, or just want to indulge your island dreams, a number of real estate companies will be happy to assist you. State ferry brochure racks are packed with glossy publications from island brokers, and you can cruise through property descriptions on their websites.

vacation rentals are often listed in the Seattle newspapers or the three local weekly papers: *The Journal of the San Juans* (www.sanjuanjournal.com), *The Islands' Sounder* (www.islandssounder.com), and *The Islands' Weekly* (www.islandsweekly.net).

Another option is through one of the online vacation rental brokers, such as **Vacation Rentals by Owner** (www.vrbo.com), **CyberRentals** (www.cyberrentals.com), **Vacation Homes** (www.vacationhomes.com), or **Owner Direct** (www.ownerdirect.com).

Home Swaps

Visitors to the San Juans may also want to investigate a house exchange. A number of online companies list homeowners on the islands who are interested in a trade if you have an upscale home. If you live in Hawaii, Costa Rica, or Aspen, your home might be a hot property. If you live in North Dakota, good luck. Companies

worth investigating include **Home Exchange** (310/798-3864 or 800/877-8723, www.homeexchange.com), **Home Link** (813/975-9825 or 800/638-3841, www.swapnow.com), **Intervac** (800/756-4663, www.intervacus.com), and **Holi-Swaps** (602/604-1537, www.holi-swaps.com).

CAMPGROUNDS

Public campsites are most abundant at beautiful **Moran State Park** on Orcas Island, but even these fill up almost every day in July and August. San Juan Island has a handful of spots at **San Juan County Park,** and additional public camping can be found at **Odlin County Park** and **Spencer Spit State Park** on Lopez Island, along with **Shaw Island County Park.** County and state park campsites can be reserved ahead of time (strongly advised in the summer). Walk-in campsites (no reservations) are at **Obstruction Pass**

San Juan Island (and all Islands)
Coldwell Banker (360/378-2101 or 800/451-9054, www.sanjuanislands.com)
Friday Harbor Realty (360/378-2151 or 800/258-3112, www.sanjuans.com)
Re/Max San Juan Island (360/378-5858 or 877/757-3629, www.sanjuanrealestate.com)
Windermere Real Estate San Juan Island (360/378-3600 or 800/262-3596, www.windermeresji.com)

Lopez Island
Island House Realtors (360/468-3366 or 800/781-2882, www.islandhouse.com)
Lopez Island Realty (360/468-2291 or 866/632-1100, www.lopezislandrealty.com)
Lopez Village Properties (360/468-5055 or 888/772-9735, www.lopezproperties.com)
Windermere Real Estate Lopez (360/468-3344 or 866/468-3344, www.wrelopez.com)

Orcas Island
Cherie Lindholm Real Estate (360/376-2204, www.lindholm-realestate.com)
Coldwell Banker (360/376-2114 or 800/552-7072, www.cb-orcasisland.com)
Gudgell Properties (360/376-2172, www.gudgellproperties.com)
Orcas Island Realty (360/376-2145, www.orcasislandrealty.com)
John L. Scott Real Estate (360/376-2155 or 800/553-5786, www.orcas-is.com)
Re/Max Island Properties (360/376-6202 or 800/551-1677, www.realestateonorcasisland.com)
Windermere Real Estate Orcas Island (360/376-8000 or 800/842-5770, www.orcasisland.com)

State Park on Orcas Island, while **Griffin Bay Marine State Park** on San Juan Island and **Point Doughty Marine State Park** on Orcas Island are accessible only by kayak. In addition to these, many of the more remote marine state parks have primitive campsites accessible by boat or kayak.

San Juan, Orcas, and Lopez Islands all have private campgrounds, offering a mix of standard tent sites and RV spaces with water and electrical hookups.

Camping Trailers
Trailers to Go (360/376-3033 or 888/317-6516, www.trailerstogo.com) is a unique service that rents vacation trailers and delivers them any-where on the four main islands in the San Juans and even to Whidbey Island and the mainland. These are a good deal for folks who don't want to drag along a camper. Trailers to Go does the transport; you just show up. The 19-foot trailers have a double bed and rent for $60 per night ($325 per week), while 25-footers with a queen bed cost $75 per night ($400 per week). All units can sleep four. No extra charge for Orcas (where TTG is based), but you'll pay an additional ferry charge to have your trailer delivered to San Juan, Lopez, or Shaw Islands. All units include bath with a tub, fridge with freezer, stove, sink, CD player, bedding, linen, dishes, pots, and pans. Call ahead to book these popular units.

Food and Drink

Food prices on the islands are somewhat higher than in Anacortes or Victoria, so you may want to stock up on groceries before climbing onboard the ferry. There are no 24-hour stores in the San Juans, and some dinner restaurants close as early as 9 P.M., so call ahead.

RESTAURANTS

Given the location it should come as no surprise that seafood gets center-stage treatment at many local restaurants. Fresh salmon and halibut are always favorites, along with fresh oysters from Westcott Bay on San Juan Island or Judd Cove on Orcas Island. Competition is stiff among island restaurants, and there are some real Northwest cuisine standouts. Reservations are wise at the nicer restaurants, especially in peak season. All three main islands also have excellent unpretentious eateries with nicely prepared meals. Fish and chips are a delicious fast-food option. And speaking of fast food, you won't find McDonald's, Burger King, Taco Bell, or any of the other grease factories on the islands, though you can always slake your urgings in Anacortes or Victoria.

A helpful website with reviews of several dozen restaurants on the San Juans is www.sanjuanislands.kulshan.com. The reviews tend to be a bit gushing at times, but are worth a read. *San Juan Islands Dining & Lodging Guide* is a free publication that includes menus from many local restaurants. You'll find it on the ferries and in regional visitor centers.

FARM FRESH

Farming was once a substantial business on the islands, and peas, fruit, hay, and dairy products were all important at one time or another. Many of the old apple, pear, and prune orchards dotted around the islands still produce fruits more than a century after they were planted.

Small-scale agriculture is once again growing (yuk, yuk) in popularity, particularly on Lopez and San Juan Islands, where dozens of farms produce such specialty products as kiwi fruit, goat milk and cheeses, organic wines, apple cider, and even oysters and clams. For a complete list, get *Farm Products Guides* for San Juan and Lopez Islands from local visitors centers or the Cooperative Extension (360/378-4414, http://sanjuan.wsu.edu).

Saturday **farmers markets** are a fun summertime event where you can buy local produce, flowers, crafts, clothing, and art. These take place not just on San Juan, Orcas, and Lopez Islands, but also in Bellingham, Anacortes, and Whidbey Island.

ALCOHOL

Local grocery stores all sell beer and wine, and you can buy the hard stuff from state liquor stores at Eastsound and Orcas Village on Orcas Island, Lopez Village on Lopez Island, and Friday Harbor on San Juan Island.

Recreation

The San Juans abound with outdoor pleasures: cycling, sea kayaking, camping, hiking, bird-watching, scuba diving, boating, sailing, whale-watching, skateboarding, and fishing, to name a few.

BICYCLING

The San Juans are very popular cycling destinations, offering up mild weather, a wide diversity of terrain, gorgeous scenery, excellent facilities, and little traffic. If you have a family in tow or aren't in great shape, head to slow-paced Lopez with its bucolic countryside, good camping (or inns), and friendly locals. Shaw is small but fun to explore, with quiet roads that are perfect for families; no lodging, but there is a campground. Orcas has the most rugged rides—including a tough haul to the top of 2,409-foot Mount Constitution—and the most challenging roads, but the diversity and beauty make it unique. San Juan offers varied terrain, the most services (especially at Friday Harbor), and wide shoulders, but also the heaviest traffic.

You won't find any separate bike paths on the islands, and some roads can be narrow and winding with minimal shoulders. Use some common sense even if you are on vacation. Local bike shops carry maps that denote routes with problems (such as heavy traffic or narrow and winding roads), and they offer travel tips. The **San Juan Island Trails Committee** website (www.sanjuanislandtrails.org) also has details on San Juan Island bike routes.

Bikes on the Ferries

You can bring your own bike on the ferry for an extra $4 round-trip (a lot cheaper than hauling your car, and you won't have to wait). Ferry loading procedures vary, so be sure to follow the instructions of terminal personnel. Always walk your bike on and off the ferry. Space is always available for bikes.

Bike Rentals

Bike rentals are available on the three major is-lands by the hour, day, or week. Most shops rent touring and mountain bikes for around $35/day or $75 for three days, including bike helmets. Specialized equipment, such as tandems, racing bikes, child bikes, panniers, child carriers, and bike trailers are also generally available, but reserve ahead to be sure.

Bike Tours

Several companies offer multi-day cycling tours of the San Juans, with food, lodging, and a support vehicle included in the rate. Bike rentals are also available, and you can choose your own pace on these relatively leisurely tours. All of these differ in routing and amenities, so call for their catalogs or surf the Web to see which one works for you.

Based in Olympia, **Bicycle Adventures** (360/786-7989 or 800/443-6060, www.bicycleadventures.com) leads a variety of cycling tours around the San Juans, starting at $1,000 for a five-day trip that includes biking, some hiking and kayaking, and camping. An easier version that includes lodging at island inns starts at $1,700 for five days. They also have family biking treks on the islands.

Berkeley, CA-based **Backroads** (510/527-1555 or 800/462-2848, www.backroads.com) has six-day cycling tours of the San Juans many times a year. For around $1,300, you camp out at night; for around $2,300, lodging is included at local inns and bed-and-breakfasts. Kayaking is extra.

Denver-based **Timberline Adventures** (303/368-4418 or 800/417-2453, www.timbertours.com) leads eight-day bike adventures that include time in Olympic National Park, Whidbey Island, and the San Juans. The cost is $2,200, with lodging at inns and a day of sea kayaking.

Based in Wisconsin, **Trek Travel** (866/604-8735, www.trektravel.com) is another company with six-day San Juan bike treks for $2,300, lodging included.

The Seattle YMCA's **Camp Orkila** (360/376-2678 or 206/382-5009, www.seattleymca.org)

offers an excellent 11-day cycling program for kids that covers the San Juan Islands, along with Canada's Vancouver and Gulf Islands.

Safety on the Road

A number of common-sense precautions are wise for anyone heading out on a bike in the San Juans; visit www.co.san-juan.wa.us/publicworks for safety tips.

- Always wear a helmet, even for short trips.
- Be especially cautious in the vicinity of ferry docks, particularly when a ferry has just disgorged its load of vehicles. Get off the road to let the traffic pass safely.
- Watch out for long lines of traffic heading up the road when a ferry has just docked.
- Always keep to the right and ride in single file.
- Ride straight ahead and avoid weaving into traffic.
- Keep your groups small, with three or four riders together spaced widely apart. Larger groups should divide up to make it easier and safer for cars to pass.
- Pull well off the road whenever you stop, particularly when the visibility is poor, at hilltops or on corners.
- Stay off roads that are posted as private property.
- Avoid riding at night, and be cautious when roads are slick from recent rain.
- Wear reflectors and use strobes to show your presence when light conditions are poor.

HIKING

Hiking trails in the San Juans are somewhat limited, and there are no overnight backpacking trips anywhere on the islands. The longest and best trails are within Moran State Park on Orcas Island. Other pleasant day hikes can be explored within San Juan Island National Historical Park and at smaller state and county parks and other public lands on San Juan, Orcas, Lopez, Shaw, and Cypress Islands. Many of the marine state parks have trails, including delightful paths to old lighthouses or remote beaches.

Ken Wilcox's *Hiking the San Juan Islands* is an authoritative pocket-size source for anyone

planning a hike on the islands. It covers not just the main islands in the archipelago, but also marine state parks, private islands, and trails on Whidbey, Camano, and Fidalgo Islands.

HORSEBACK RIDES

The rolling farm country in rural parts of the San Juans are perfect for horses and riding. Several outfits offer trail rides on the islands, including places on San Juan Island (Saddle Up Trailriding and Houseshu Ranch) and Orcas Island (Blue Moon Ranch and Walking Horse Country Farm). In addition to rides, the ranches also provide riding lessons and horse boarding. Some have arenas, and one (Horseshu) even has pony rides for kids.

SEA KAYAKING

The relatively protected waters, diverse landscapes, rich wildlife (including killer whales), and myriad bays and coves make the San Juans a marvelous place to explore by sea kayak. This is one of the finest ways to see the islands, as more and more folks are discovering each year. A number of companies offer guided trips, and several will also rent kayaks to experienced paddlers. No kayaking experience is necessary on any of the guided tours, but it certainly helps to be in good physical condition. All necessary instructions and paddling gear are provided, and you'll typically use a stable two-person kayak.

Guided Trips

Recommended kayaking companies are on San Juan, Orcas, and Lopez Islands, as well as Anacortes. Any of these will do a good job on a day trip, but for longer paddles, you may want to look around to find a company that best meets your needs. One of the most professional is **Shearwater Adventures** (360/376-4699, www .shearwaterkayaks.com), based on Orcas Island. In addition to day trips, they teach kayaking classes, set up custom tours, and have a shop that sells paddling gear and kayaks.

Several San Juan Island–based kayak compa-

© DON PITCHER

sea kayakers at Roche Harbor, San Juan Island

nies offer multi-day trips, including **Outdoor Odysseys** (360/378-3533 or 800/647-4621, www.outdoorodysseys.com), **Sea Quest Expeditions** (360/378-5767 or 888/589-4253, www.sea-quest-kayak.com), and **San Juan Kayak Expeditions** (360/378-4436, www.sanjuankayak.com). **Discovery Sea Kayaks** (360/378-2559, www.discoveryseakayaks.com) has a kayak shop in Friday Harbor.

Island Outfitters (360/299-2300 or 866/445-7506, www.seakayakshop.com) in Anacortes is a big kayak store that features the latest boats and gear.

REI Adventures (800/622-2236, www.rei.com) has six-day sea-kayak trips in the San Juans, though its guides typically come from one of the local companies.

On Your Own

From a ferry, the waters around the San Juan Islands often appear tranquil, and sea kayaking seems to simply involve getting in and paddling. Beginners may be fine on a calm day in a protected cove, but conditions can quickly turn treacherous in the more exposed channels. Particularly deadly are situations where strong tidal currents are pulling one way while winds are pushing in the opposite direction, creating large waves. Even experienced paddlers are best off starting out by taking a trip through a San Juan Islands–based sea-kayak company where they can learn details of the local conditions before heading out on their own.

The Canadian Hydrographic Service (www.chs-shc.dfo-mpo.gc.ca) produces a *Tide and Current Tables* book that is very useful for kayakers; find it in local marinas or bookstores. Randel Washburne's detailed *Kayaking Puget Sound, the San Juans, and Gulf Islands* is packed with information on destinations, tide rips, current and wind problems, difficulty ratings, and launching points, and includes coverage for quite a few San Juan Islands paddling trips. Kayakers heading out on their own should probably read this book first.

Minimizing Impact

Sea kayakers sometimes develop an unwarranted degree of self-righteousness. After all, they're the ones paddling, while other boaters are tooling around wasting fossil fuels and polluting the air. The reality is that kayakers can be particularly damaging to the environment even while attempting to have a low impact. Many sailors and some motorboaters "camp" in their boats, while San Juan Islands kayakers always depend on the fragile islands for a campsite. This can mean lots of trampled plants and can impact upon the animals that live there as well. A park ranger told me of once seeing 72 kayak campers on Posey Island Marine State Park (near Roche Harbor). The island covers a total of one acre, so the campers' "wilderness experience" was more like a crowded tenement with just one outhouse for everyone.

Kayakers also can have surprising impacts on wildlife, particularly seals and sea lions hauled out on the rocks. To a snoozing seal, a paddler and kayak may look like a cruising killer whale scoping them out for a meal. Don't get too close to marine mammals, particularly at San Juan Islands National Wildlife Refuge islands, where all boats are legally required to stay 200 yards offshore. The Whale Museum's Soundwatch program (360/378-4710 or 800/946-7227, www .whalemuseum.com) recommends a number of other precautions for kayakers heading out to watch killer whales.

Cascadia Marine Trail

The Cascadia Marine Trail covers water-accessible campsites throughout Puget Sound, including more than a dozen in the San Juan Islands. These campsites ($10/night) are only open to those in sea kayaks and other small and beachable human- or wind-powered crafts. All permit money goes to marine trail maintenance and expansion. Designated Cascadia Marine Trail campsites are not just for one tent, and you may have quite a few neighbors during the peak season. Limits, however, are placed on the number of campers at the most popular marine state parks in the San Juans.

The following marine state parks, county parks, and DNR lands in the San Juans contain designated Cascadia Marine Trail campsites: Blind Island, Cypress Head (Cypress Island), Griffin Bay (San Juan Island), James Island, Jones Island, Lummi Island, Obstruction Pass, Odlin County Park (Lopez Island), Pelican Beach (Cypress Island), Point Doughty (Orcas Island), Posey Island, Saddlebag Island, San Juan County

whale-watching boat near San Juan Island

© DON PITCHER

Park (San Juan Island), Spencer Spit (Lopez Island), Strawberry Island, and Stuart Island. On Whidbey Island, Cascadia campsites are located at Deception Pass State Park, Joseph Whidbey State Park, Fort Ebey State Park, and Oak Harbor City Park.

Water Taxis

Several companies provide transportation to the more remote islands in the San Juans. All of them will transport your kayak (generally $10 extra each way), and prices vary depending upon the destination and number of people. Anacortes-based **Paraclete Charters** (360/293-5920 or 800/808-2999, www.paracletecharters.com) has been in business since 1992 and operates three boats. Also operating out of Anacortes is **Island Express Charters** (360/299-2875 or 877/473-9777, www.islandexpresscharters.com) with a high-speed landing craft. From Orcas Island, hop aboard **North Shore Charters,** (360/376-4855, www.sanjuancruises.net) with a shallow-draft landing craft for service to Sucia, Patos, Matia, and other state marine parks popular with kayakers.

SKATEBOARDING

Skateboard enthusiasts flock to the impressive **Orcas Island Skateboard Park** (www.skateorcas.org), recognized as one of the best skate parks in the Northwest. No bikes allowed, and helmets are required. Skateboard rentals are available from a nearby shop. On San Juan Island, the skateboard park (very popular with bikers) is at the San Juan County Fairgrounds, and on Lopez it's in Lopez Village.

WHALE-WATCHING

The waters around the San Juans are famous for whales, particularly the exciting killer whales, or orcas, that pursue migrating salmon. Other marine mammals commonly seen around the islands include minke whales, harbor porpoises, Dall's porpoises, harbor seals, California and Steller sea lions, and even elephant seals.

The best time to see orcas is mid-June to mid-July, but they are periodically visible anytime from mid-May to mid-September. Three resident pods, or families, of orcas are frequently spotted. They have been extensively studied for more than 30 years, and individuals are identifiable from distinctive body markings.

Watching whales is a favorite activity around the San Juans, and dozens of commercial whale-watching boats operate in the summer months. Daily tours depart from San Juan and Orcas Islands, but whale-watching trips are also available out of Anacortes, Bellingham, Port Townsend, Everett, Seattle, and Victoria. See individual chapters for details on local operators. In the peak season, be sure to make advance reservations for these popular trips. During the winter, when the whales are elsewhere, some of these companies switch to wildlife-viewing cruises.

The excellent **Whale Museum** in Friday Harbor maintains a **Whale Hotline** for sightings and stranding information (800/562-8832, www.whalemuseum.com). If you're heading out in your own kayak or other vessel, be sure to stay at least 100 yards from whales (it's the law) and 200 yards from seal and sea lion haul-out areas since the animals are easily spooked. Contact the Whale Museum for a brochure with detailed whale-watching guidelines for boaters. To lessen the likelihood of impacting the whales while watching them, the museum encourages visitors to watch from the shore; a great spot is **Lime Kiln Point State Park** on the west side of San Juan Island.

BOATING

The San Juan Islands are one of the top three sailing destinations in the nation, and are equally popular with power yachts. Boat charters are available at San Juan, Orcas, and Lopez Islands in the San Juans and from marinas throughout the area, particularly in Anacortes and Bellingham. Two types of charters are offered. For **bareboat charters,** the company provides the boat and you do everything else, from captaining to swabbing the decks. You'll be required to show navigational and on-the-water skills in advance or the charter company won't let you take the boat. (Some companies also offer learn-to-cruise classes for landlubbers.) **Skippered charters** are for those who either lack the knowledge to head out on their own or want someone else doing the work. These cost considerably more, of course, and typically include an experienced local skipper and three meals a day. Much to the relief of those who appreciate peace and quiet, **jet skis** and similar craft are prohibited anywhere in San Juan County waters.

Charter Companies

Anacortes is home to one of the largest concentrations of bareboat charters in North America, with more than 350 power yachts and sailboats available. If you don't have boating skills, these companies can also provide a qualified skipper and a cook for absolute luxury. The largest Anacortes charter companies are **ABC Yacht Charters** (360/293-9533 or 800/426-2313, www.abc yachtcharters.com), **Anacortes Yacht Charters** (360/293-4555 or 800/233-3004, www.ayc .com), **Charters Northwest** (360/378-7196 or 800/258-3119, www.chartersnw.com), and **Ship Harbor Yacht Charters** (360/299-9193 or 877/772-6582, www.shipharboryachts.com).

Bellingham is another major center for boaters heading to the islands. The following companies offer powerboat or sailing charters from there: **Bellhaven Charters** (360/733-6636 or 800/542-8812, www.bellhaven.net), **Bellingham Yacht Sales and Charters** (360/671-0990 or 800/671-4244, www.bellinghamyachts.com), **Northwest Explorations** (360/676-1248 or 800/826-1430, www.nwexplorations.com), **Par Yacht Charters** (360/752-5754, www.parcharters.com), **Sail the San Juans** (360/671-5852 or 800/729-3207, www.sailthesanjuans.com), **San Juan Sailing** (360/671-4300 or 800/677-7245, www.sanjuansailing.com), and **San Juan Yachting** (360/671-8089 or 800/670-8089, www.sanjuanyachting.com).

Based on San Juan Island, **Charters Northwest** (360/378-7196 or 800/258-3119, www .chartersnorthwest.com) has 35 or so powerboats and sailboats available at Friday Harbor. This is the only bareboat charter service in the islands.

The classic '65 wooden motor yacht, *Arequipa,* is available for island charters.

On Orcas Island, sailboat charters are available at **Deer Harbor Marina** (360/376-3037, www .deerharbormarina.com) and **Rosario Resort Marina** (360/376-2222 or 800/562-8820, www .rosarioresort.com).

On Your Own

Boaters heading out on their own will want to pick up one of the cruising guides to the islands. Recommended is the oddly named *Gunkholing the San Juans* by Jo Bailey and Carl Nyberg. By the way, "gunkhole" is slang for a protected anchorage. Check out the **Northwest Boating** website (www.nwboating.com) for pithy descriptions of many islands. The *San Juans Navigator* (www.sanjuansnavigator.com) is an informative boaters' guide with maps, port info, and lists of local services. Also look over the *Waggoner Cruising Guide* (www.waggonerguide.com) for coverage from Puget Sound all the way to Prince Rupert, British Columbia, and visit the **San Juan Sailing** website (www.sanjuansailing.com) for a very helpful cruising guide to the islands.

Boaters need to avoid most of the 84 islands within the **San Juan Islands National Wildlife Refuge.** To preserve vital wildlife habitats, you are not allowed closer than 200 yards from these; the only exceptions are portions of Turn and Matia Islands. These refuges are marked on nautical charts.

FISHING

Fishing for salmon (mainly kings, silvers, and sockeye) is best in August and September, with other fish—including blackmouth bass, bottomfish, halibut, and lingcod—available at other times of the year. Charter-fishing operators generally provide fishing gear and bait, but you'll need to have a current saltwater fishing license. Fishing trips on Haro Strait can often provide a simultaneous chance to see killer whales.

The **Washington Department of Fish and Wildlife** (360/902-2700, www.wdfw.wa.gov) is in charge of fishing, hunting, and clamming on the islands. Pick up the fat *Fishing in Washington* pamphlet at sporting goods or other stores that sell fishing licenses. Freshwater fishing licenses cost $22 for Washington residents or $44 for nonresidents. Combination licenses for both freshwater and saltwater fishing, plus shellfish (including clams), are $40 for Washington residents or $81 for nonresidents. A two-day combination license for nonresidents is $7. Be sure to get (and fill out) a catch record card for salmon, sturgeon, and steelhead from the vendor who sells your license.

Clamming

Clams and other mollusks were a major part of the diet of the Coast Salish people who first lived on the San Juans, and they are still dug today along many island beaches. For information on clamming, including regulations and safety issues, contact the Washington Department of Fish and Wildlife (360/902-2700, www.wdfw.wa.gov).

Some years, the overabundant growth of microorganisms causes clams to build up dangerous levels of toxins, including domoic acid, a chemical that can cause seizures, cardiac arrhythmia, coma, and even death. Before digging, it's always a good idea to check the Department of Health's **Shellfish Biotoxin Hotline** (360/796-3215 or 800/562-5632, www.doh.wa.gov/ehp/sf) for the latest on the edibility of clams.

SWIMMING

The three main islands all have popular lakes where swimming is allowed. On Orcas, Cascade Lake within Moran State Park is the main destination. On Lopez, it's Hummel Lake. On San Juan, swim at privately owned lakes at Lakedale Resort for a fee. Both Orcas and San Juan Islands have swimming pools at resorts, health clubs, and summer camps that are open to the public.

DIVING

Locals say the San Juans offer the finest coldwater diving anywhere, with something for all levels of ability. Beneath the surface, the waters are chilly (48–52°F year-round), with currents that feed an abundance of marine plants and animals, from plankton to killer whales. Jacques Cousteau considered the San Juans one of his favorite places to dive in the world.

The ocean floor around the archipelago is a garden of colors, with sponges, hydroids, corals, jellyfish, crabs, sea stars, sea cucumbers, kelp, and many species of fish, including sculpin, rockfish, scorpion fish, greenling, surfperch, prickleback, eel, ronquil, goby, clingfish, midshipman, and flounder. Many of the world's largest marine species are here, including the giant Pacific octopus, the two largest scallops, the world's tallest anemone (reaching 3 feet), and the largest sea slug, chiton, barnacle, and sea urchin. These waters are also home to dolphins, whales, seals, and other marine mammals.

All told, you'll find more than 500 dive sites here, covering a diversity that will please all levels, from those who learned at a Mexican resort to tech divers using rebreathers. In addition to wall dives, reefs, and pinnacles, there are dozens of wrecks to explore—including a 366-foot destroyer that was intentionally sunk off the Southern Gulf Islands. Local currents are important

Know the San Juan Islands

in your dive planning, since they can reach seven knots when the tides are in full flux. There are, however, a number of beginning shore dives and some very good dives close to the islands. The best diving is often in the winter, when visibility increases due to less phytoplankton in the water.

For additional information, see Betty Pratt-Johnson's *99 Dives from the San Juan Islands in Washington to the Gulf Islands* or Edward Weber's *Diving and Snorkeling Guide to the Pacific Northwest. Northwest Dive News* (www.nwdivenews.com) is a free monthly publication available from ferry brochure racks and regional visitor centers.

Heading Out

Island Dive and Water Sports (2A Spring Street Landing in Friday Harbor, 360/378-2772 or 800/303-8386, www.divesanjuan.com) is *the* dive company on the San Juans. Its operation includes a full-service dive shop in Friday Harbor on San Juan Island and a smaller shop at Rosario Resort on Orcas Island. Island Dive has two dive boats, and offers charters, dive masters, training (including advanced training with rebreathers and other hi-tech equipment), rental equipment, snorkeling gear, and scuba tank fillings. Two-tank boat dives cost $75 if you provide the gear, or $125 if they provide everything (including wetsuit). The owners put together dive packages for all budgets, starting at just $100/day, including lodging.

Over on the mainland, **Anacortes Diving and Supply** (2502 Commercial Ave., 360/293-2070, www.anacortesdiving.com) is another full-service shop that runs a variety of dive trips to the San Juans and surrounding areas.

One of the oldest dive shops in the nation, Bellingham's **Washington Divers** (903 North State St. in Bellingham, 360/676-8029) guides day trips to the San Juans and the Strait of Georgia.

Safety

The diving around the San Juans is superb, but it can also be treacherous, with cold water, powerful currents, and a host of other hazards. Stay within your limits, and never take chances. If you lack experience in cold water and currents, get local training and go with a knowledgeable operator who can safely get you into these spectacular waters.

At least five divers have died in the San Juans over the last decade or so. In 1998, a physician and highly experienced diver drowned while shooting underwater videos in a strong current near San Juan Island. At the time, he was utilizing a rebreather apparatus. In 2001, an experienced young diver drowned at a popular spot off Orcas Island while diving with her mother. Her body was found in 90 feet of water with a full tank of air and working equipment, but the regulator was not in her mouth. The cause of her death remains a mystery.

Arts and Entertainment

If you've come to the San Juans in search of nightlife, you are probably in for a disappointment. The islands are all about getting away from the hustle and noise of city life, with most travelers opting for an evening stroll along the shore over a steamy night on the dance floor. There are, however, a few bars and restaurants on San Juan, Orcas, and Lopez that offer live music, particularly on summer weekends. San Juan and Orcas also have movie theaters.

Many artists call the San Juans home, displaying their works at local galleries, particularly around

Orcas Island and in the town of Friday Harbor. The Lambiel Museum on Orcas displays hundreds of pieces from the finest island artists. Orcas, Lopez, and San Juan Islands all have modern community theaters that host performing arts, musical programs, and other productions year-round.

For details on **San Juan Islands' Artist Community,** visit www.sanjuanartistcommunity.com, where you'll find links to local artists and information on local arts organizations, upcoming art classes, studio tours, workshops, art openings, galleries, and more.

EVENTS

Some of the biggest island celebrations take place over the **4th of July** weekend, when parades, fireworks, barbecues, street dances, and other events draw locals and tourists to Friday Harbor, Roche Harbor, Lopez Village, and Eastsound. **Memorial Day** in late May is another time for play, with a parade, artist studio open houses, an Art and Nature Festival on San Juan Island, and the Bite of Orcas restaurant sampling at Eastsound. The **Celebrity Golf Classic** on San Juan in early June is the county's biggest annual fundraising event. San Juan Island National Historical Park puts on an impressive **Encampment** at English Camp in August with British and American "soldiers" and others in 19th-century period costume.

The islands burst with musical performances all summer, including major chamber music festivals on Orcas and San Juan Islands, weekly brown-bag concerts in Eastsound, musical weekends at the Lopez Center, and weekly concerts on the lawn in Friday Harbor.

Don't miss the premier playtime of the year, the **San Juan County Fair** on the third week of August in Friday Harbor. Other popular events include the **Summer Arts Fair** in July on San Juan, **Orcas Island Fly-In** in August, Tour de Lopez bike ride in April, Best of the San Juans fair at Roche Harbor over Labor Day weekend, and the **Playwrights Festival** in September at Friday Harbor. San Juan, Orcas, and Lopez all have holiday arts-and-crafts fairs a couple of weeks before Christmas.

Boaters take part in the **Round San Juan Island** yacht race in May, **Whidbey Island Race Week** in mid-July, and the **Shaw Island Classic** yacht race the second weekend of August.

Suggested Reading

DESCRIPTION AND TRAVEL

Bower, Holly, and Sarah Eppenbach. *With Love and Butter: An Island Cookbook and Memoir.* Lopez, WA: Hummel Lake Press, 2002. This is a beautiful blend of great recipes and Lopez Island history, with arty block prints. Author Holly Bower owns the respected Holly B's Bakery.

Halliday, Jan, editor. *Best Places Destinations: San Juan & Gulf Islands.* Seattle: Sasquatch Books, www.sasquatchbooks.com, 2000. Part of the respected Best Places series, this one uncovers the finest lodging, restaurants, and outdoor fun on the islands.

Harrison, Lorrie. *Kindred Spirits: Stories, Passions, and Portraits from the Heart of Community.* Anacortes, WA: Island Time Press, 2001. This book's sharp design and attractive black-and-white photos immediately grab your attention, and the stories of the eccentrics who populate the island keep your interest. Nowhere in the book is this mysterious place identified, but here's a hint: the island starts with "L" and ends with "Z."

Hempstead, Andrew. *Moon Handbooks Vancouver, Including Victoria.* Emeryville, CA: Avalon Travel Publishing, www.moon.com, 2005. A great source for up-to-date coverage of Vancouver, Victoria, and the Gulf Islands.

Meyer, Barbara. *Sketching in the San Juans. . . and a Bit Beyond.* Eastsound, WA: Paper Jam Publishing, www.rockisland.com/~paperjam, 1996. This attractive book is filled with hundreds of colorful and expressive watercolor sketches, created during Barbara Meyer's quarter-century on the islands.

Mueller, Marge, and Ted Mueller. *The San Juan Islands: Afoot & Afloat.* Seattle: The Mountaineers, www.mountaineersbooks.org, 2004. A relatively complete guide to natural areas within the San Juan archipelago, including the smaller islands.

Mueller, Marge, and Ted Mueller. *The Essential San Juan Islands Guide.* Medina, WA: JASI Publishers, 2001. Focuses on lodging, restaurants, shopping, and tours. Unfortunately, the book reads at times like a P.R. handout from the various businesses.

Pitcher, Don. *Moon Handbooks Washington.* Emeryville, CA: Avalon Travel Publishing, www.moon.com, 2002. At more than 800 pages, this is the heftiest and most complete guide to Washington.

Veal, Janice, and Dawn Ashbach. *San Juan Classics Cookbook.* Anacortes: Northwest Island Associates, 1987. A delightful introduction to cooking, San Juan Islands style. Recipes are from local chefs and the authors' own collections.

Veal, Janice, and Dawn Ashbach. *San Juan Classics Cookbook II.* Anacortes: Northwest Island Associates, 1998. The second in a set of nicely illustrated books by local authors. The emphasis is on natural ingredients from the Northwest.

Wilcox, Ken. *Hiking the San Juan Islands.* Bellingham, WA: Northwest Wild Books, www.nwwildbooks.com, 2001. A fine pocket-sized guide with dozens of hiking trails on the San Juans and surrounding areas, including Whidbey Island.

ON (AND IN) THE WATER

Bailey, Jo, and Carl Nyberg. *Gunkholing the San Juans.* Seattle: San Juan Enterprises, 2000. A chatty boater's bible with 300 fact-filled pages about cruising the islands. Worthwhile for sailors, motorboaters, and kayakers, and also of interest if you're just looking for details on hidden parts of the islands. Not only does it cover all the San Juans, but also surrounding areas, including Guemes, Cypress, and Lummi Islands, along with Deception Pass, Bellingham, Anacortes, and La Conner.

Canadian Hydrographic Service. *Canadian Tide and Current Tables Volume 5: Juan de Fuca Strait and the Strait of Georgia.* Canadian Hydrographic Service, www.chs-shc.dfo-mpo.gc.ca. This detailed Canadian government publication is available at local marinas and bookstores. It provides vital information that is especially useful for those traveling in small boats and sea kayaks around the San Juans.

Douglass, Don, and Reanne Hemingway-Douglass. *Exploring the San Juan and Gulf Islands: Cruising Paradise of the Pacific Northwest.* Anacortes, WA: Fine Edge Productions, www.fineedge.com, 2003. Part of a series of respected cruising guides by the authors, this one details anchorages and attractions in the islands, with suggested itineraries, GPS way stations, and distance tables.

Hale, Bob. *Waggoner Cruising Guide.* Bellevue, WA: Weatherly Press, www.waggonerguide.com, 2005. An authoritative guide for boaters, this book covers the waters from Puget Sound to Prince Rupert, British Columbia, including the San Juans. It contains text on anchorages, piloting, and what to expect at each port, along with a bit of history.

Pratt-Johnson, Betty. *99 Dives from the San Juan Islands in Washington to the Gulf Islands.* Surrey, British Columbia: Heritage House Publishing Co., www.heritagehouse.ca, 1997. The most up-to-date guide to island diving.

Vassilopoulos, Peter. *Anchorages and Marine Parks.* Vancouver: Seagraphic Publications, www.marineguides.com, 1999. A useful guide for boaters along the British Columbia coast, this book also includes limited coverage of the San Juans.

Washburne, Randel. *Kayaking Puget Sound, the San Juans, and the Gulf Islands.* Seattle: The Mountaineers, www.mountaineersbooks.org, 2002. Filled with details on destinations, routes, ratings, and launching information, this guide explores the nooks and crannies of this fascinating waterway, including nine paddling trips in the San Juans.

Weber, Edward. *Diving and Snorkeling Guide to the Pacific Northwest: Includes Puget Sound, San Juan Islands, and Vancouver Island.* Houston: Gulf Publishing Co., 1993. A useful (but dated) guide for scuba divers heading to the San Juans.

LITERATURE

Blanchet, M. Wylie. *The Curve of Time.* Sidney, British Columbia: Gray's Publishing, 1968. This lovingly written book is the classic memoir of a newly widowed woman and her five children who explored the waters off Vancouver Island in the 1920s and '30s. It's a wonderful book to read while boating in the San Juans and points northward.

Burn, June. *Living High.* Friday Harbor, WA: Griffin Bay Bookstore, 1969. A delightful autobiographical story about June and Farrar Burn, who homesteaded on tiny Sentinel Island in 1919. The island is now managed as a natural area by The Nature Conservancy.

Burn, June; edited by Theresa Morrow and Nancy Prindle. *100 Days in San Juans.* Friday Harbor, WA: Long House Printcrafters & Publishers, 1983. In 1946, June and Farrar Burn purchased an old sail-rigged rowboat from the Coast Guard and spent 100 days sailing through the San Juans. Their stories appeared that year in the *Seattle Post-Intelligencer,* and were later collected to form this book. Out of print, but available in used bookstores in the area.

Glidden, Helene. *Light on the Island.* Woodinville, WA: San Juan Publishing, 2001. Originally published in 1951, when it was a regional best-seller, this volume tells the adventures of a Patos Island lighthouse keeper and his family. A good read, but not necessarily the gospel truth.

Gutterson, David. *Snow Falling on Cedars,* Vintage Books, www.randomhouse.com, 1995. This slow-paced but evocative novel is set in the San Juan Islands, and portions of the movie of the same name were filmed on the islands. The love story/murder trial tale is a fine read, bringing to the fore the nation's mixed emotions about Japanese-Americans living in a white town after World War II. The movie is even sleepier than the book.

Stewart, Hilary. *On Island Time.* Seattle: University of Washington Press, www.washington.edu/uwpress, 1998. Stories and drawings about life on Quadra Island. It's a bit precious in places, but this is an important book about the rhythms of the natural world. Quadra Island is north of the Gulf Islands near Campbell River. Filled with pen-and-ink drawings by the author.

HISTORY

Morris, Gary J. *San Juan Island Indians.* A Xeroxed publication from 1980 available in island libraries, this work is filled with details about the lives of the islands' original settlers.

Peacock, Christopher M. *Rosario Yesterdays: A Pictorial History.* Eastsound, WA: Rosario Productions, 1985. Available from Rosario Resort and local bookstores, this book provides a fascinating history of Robert Moran and the mansion he built.

Richardson, David. *Pig War Islands.* Eastsound, WA: Orcas Publishing Co., 1990. Written in a way that vividly brings the past to life, this book provides a detailed overview of island history with an emphasis on the Pig War and various scandalous events. His treatment of Native Americans is dated (the book was first published in 1971) and bordering on racist at times, but the book remains a fascinating read.

Stein, Julie K. *Exploring Coast Salish Prehistory: The Archaeology of San Juan Island.* Seattle: University of Washington Press, www.washington.edu/uwpress, 2000. Written by a curator of archaeology at UW's Burke Museum, this small book provides an introduction to the Native Americans based on evidence from two important sites within San Juan Island National Historical Park.

Vouri, Michael. *The Pig War.* Friday Harbor, WA: Griffin Bay Bookstore, 1999. The definitive book on the Pig War by a longtime ranger from San Juan Island National Historical Park.

NATURAL HISTORY

Adams, Evelyn. *San Juan Islands Wildlife: A Handbook for Exploring Nature.* Seattle: The Mountaineers, www.mountaineersbooks.org, 1995. This isn't what you might expect. Although it does contain details about wild animals on the islands, it is primarily a series of Adams's nature essays. The writing is strong but a bit pompous.

Alt, David D., and Donald W. Hyndman. *Roadside Geology of Washington.* Missoula, MT: Mountain Press Publishing Co., www.mtnpress.com, 1984. A fine book for anyone with an interest in geology, with easy-to-understand descriptions of how volcanoes, glaciers, floods, and other processes shaped the state's topography over the eons.

Atkinson, Scott, Fred A. Sharpe, and David Macaree. *Wild Plants of the San Juan Islands.*

Seattle: The Mountaineers, www.mountaineersbooks.org, 1993. The definitive guide to island plants, with descriptions of more than 190 species, arranged by the habitat in which they are found.

Baron, Nancy, and John Acorn. *Birds of the Pacific Northwest Coast.* Renton, WA: Lone Pine Publishing, www.lonepinepublishing.com, 1997. Nicely illustrated, this is the best all-around guide to identifying birds found on the San Juans.

Ford, John K. B., Graeme M. Ellis, and Kenneth C. Balcomb. *Killer Whales.* Vancouver: University of British Columbia Press, www.ubcpress.ca, 2000. Written by scientific experts, this is the finest book on the natural history and genealogy of orcas in Washington and British Columbia. Includes a photographic genealogy for field identification of individual whales. Nicely illustrated, too.

Lewis, Mark G., and Fred A. Sharpe. *Birding in the San Juan Islands.* Seattle: The Mountaineers, www.mountaineersbooks.org, 1987. Detailed information on the islands' birds and where to find them. This is not, however, a field identification guide.

Yates, Steve. *Orcas, Eagles, and Kings.* Seattle: Sasquatch Books, www.sasquatchbooks.com, 1994. This beautifully written and photographed book takes readers on a tour through the Salish Sea, the inland waterway that includes Washington's Puget Sound and British Columbia's Georgia Strait.

Internet Resources

Washington State Parks and Recreation Commission
www.parks.wa.gov

This site has details on San Juan state parks, along with many others across the state. You can make online campground reservations here for Moran State Park and Spencer Spit State Park.

Washington Department of Fish and Wildlife
www.wdfw.wa.gov

Head to this official website for details on fishing licenses and seasons. You can even buy your license online.

Washington State Ferries
www.wsdot.wa.gov/ferries

The state ferry system's very helpful website, with details on schedules, fares, system delays, and much more.

San Juan Island National Historical Park
www.nps.gov/sajh

This small national park offers a fine blend of history and scenery; check here for details.

San Juan County Parks
www.co.san-juan.wa.us/parks

Check here to get details on county parks and to make campsite reservations.

San Juan Islands National Wildlife Refuge
http://pacific.fws.gov

The refuge is scattered across 84 islands, islets, and rocky reefs in the San Juans. Learn more at this website.

San Juan Marine Parks
www.sjmp.org

A useful online source for the regional marine state parks.

U.S. Customs & Border Protection
www.cbp.gov

Customs stations are located on San Juan Island at both Roche Harbor and Friday Harbor.

Canada Border Services Agency
www.cra-arc.gc.ca

Travelers heading into Canada from the San Juans will need to clear customs at Sidney, British Columbia.

San Juan Islands Visitors Bureau
www.guidetosanjuans.com

This website has many links to local businesses, and is a good starting point for Web surfers. The Visitor Information Service also produces an excellent printed booklet, *San Juan Islands Visitors Guide.*

San Juan Island Chamber of Commerce
www.sanjuanisland.org

Start here for specific San Juan Island information.

Orcas Island Chamber of Commerce
www.orcasisland.org

The official Orcas Island business website.

Lopez Chamber of Commerce
www.lopezisland.com

A useful starting point for Lopez Island information.

Tourism Victoria
www.tourismvictoria.com

Tourism Victoria's website has all the details on British Columbia's beautiful capital city.

Don Pitcher
www.donpitcher.com

Don Pitcher's website provides links to most of the websites found in this book. You can quickly connect to hundreds of lodging places, whale-watching companies, sea-kayaking businesses, information services, regional sights, and much more.

Tourism Association of Vancouver Island
www.islands.bc.ca

An excellent base for Vancouver Island details.

The Gulf Islander
www.gulfislands.net

A good place for the latest news from Canada's Gulf Islands, with many island links.

British Columbia Ferries
www.bcferries.com

These popular ferries link Canada's mainland with Vancouver Island and the Gulf Islands.

The Ferry Traveller
www.ferrytravel.com

This private website has details on ferries in the San Juan and Southern Gulf Islands, as well as other public and private ferries from Puget Sound to Alaska.

Index

Whale-Watching

Acknowledgments

I am indebted to many people for this second edition of *Moon Handbooks San Juan Islands,* particularly the islanders who took the time to offer tips on local history, sights, kayak companies, great restaurants, the coolest hikes, and little-known island parks.

Rich Osborne of the Whale Museum and David Castor of Washington State Parks provided expert commentary for areas where my own knowledge was particularly deficient. Also deserving of accolades are the following people: Peter Allen from Kangaroo House B&B, Ed Broome from Anaco Bay Inn, Tana Chung from Secret Garden B&B, Priscilla Heidecker from Oak Harbor Chamber of Commerce, Christine Jenkins from Bellingham/Whatcom County Convention & Visitors Bureau, Loretta Martin from Langley Chamber of Commerce, Debbie Pigman from Friday Harbor Chamber of Commerce, Phyllis Potter from Islehaven Books, Diane Priebe from the Bureau of Land Management, Beth Prins and Michael S. Broome from Anacortes Chamber of Commerce, Karen Speck from Cherie Lindholm Real Estate, and Judy Whiting from Moran State Park.

A big tip of the hat goes to Andrew Hempstead for providing text and illustrations for the Victoria and the Southern Gulf Islands chapter.

The many employees of Avalon Travel Publishing—including editor Erin Raber—deserve a big thank you for sending this book through the production process and onward to bookstores.

And last—but certainly not least—a very special thank you goes to my wonderful wife Karen Shemet, and our children Aziza and Rio, for sticking with me on yet another book project.

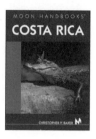

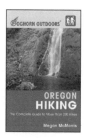

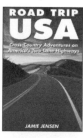

U.S. ~ Metric Conversion

1 inch = 2.54 centimeters (cm)
1 foot = .304 meters (m)
1 yard = 0.914 meters
1 mile = 1.6093 kilometers (km)
1 km = .6214 miles
1 fathom = 1.8288 m
1 chain = 20.1168 m
1 furlong = 201.168 m
1 acre = .4047 hectares
1 sq km = 100 hectares
1 sq mile = 2.59 square km
1 ounce = 28.35 grams
1 pound = .4536 kilograms
1 short ton = .90718 metric ton
1 short ton = 2000 pounds
1 long ton = 1.016 metric tons
1 long ton = 2240 pounds
1 metric ton = 1000 kilograms
1 quart = .94635 liters
1 US gallon = 3.7854 liters
1 Imperial gallon = 4.5459 liters
1 nautical mile = 1.852 km

To compute Celsius temperatures, subtract 32 from Fahrenheit and divide by 1.8. To go the other way, multiply Celsius by 1.8 and add 32.

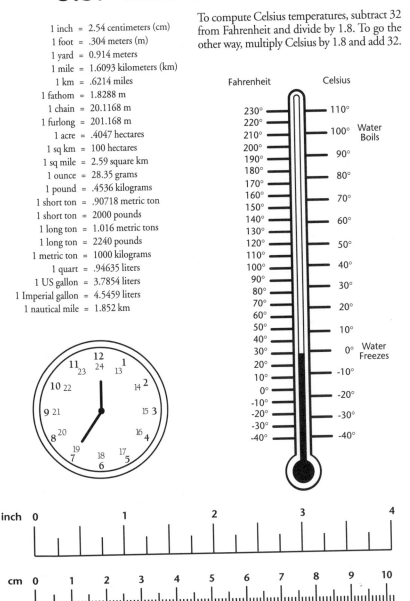

Keeping Current

Although we strive to produce the most up-to-date guidebook humanly possible, change is unavoidable. Between the time this book goes to print and the moment you read it, a handful of the businesses noted in these pages will undoubtedly change prices, move, or even close their doors forever. Other worthy attractions will open for the first time. If you have a favorite gem you'd like to see included in the next edition, or see anything that needs updating, clarification, or correction, please drop us a line. Send your comments via email to atpfeedback@avalonpub.com, or use the address below.

Moon Handbooks San Juan Islands
Avalon Travel Publishing
1400 65th Street, Suite 250
Emeryville, CA 94608, USA
www.moon.com

Editor: Erin Raber
Series Manager: Kevin McLain
Acquisitions Manager: Rebecca K. Browning
Copy Editor: Kim Marks
Graphics Coordinator: Justin Marler
Production Coordinator: Darren Alessi
Cover Designer: Kari Gim
Interior Designer: Amber Pirker
Map Editor: Kevin Anglin
Cartographers: Kat Kalamaras, Sheryle Veverka
Proofreader: Erika Howsare
Indexer: Rachel Kuhn

ISBN: 1-56691-872-3
ISSN: 1539-2295

Printing History
1st Edition—November 2002
2nd Edition—June 2005
5 4 3 2 1

Text © 2005 by Don Pitcher.
Maps © 2005 by Avalon Travel Publishing, Inc.
All rights reserved.

Avalon Travel Publishing
An Imprint of
Avalon Publishing Group, Inc.

AVALON
publishing group incorporated

Some photos and illustrations are used by permission and are the property of the original copyright owners. Portions of this book have previously appeared in *Moon Handbooks Vancouver & Victoria,* © 2005 by Andrew Hempstead.

Front cover photo: © 2005 Don Pitcher

Printed in the USA by Malloy, Inc.